THE POLITICS
OF INDECISION

Written under the auspices of the Center for International and Strategic Affairs, University of California, Los Angeles.

A list of other center publications appears at the end of this book.

THE POLITICS
OF INDECISION

Origins and Implications
of American Involvement
with the Palestine Problem

Dan Tschirgi

PRAEGER

PRAEGER SPECIAL STUDIES • PRAEGER SCIENTIFIC

Library of Congress Cataloging in Publication Data

Tschirgi, Daniel.
   The politics of indecision.

   "Written under the auspices of the Center for
International and Strategic Affairs, University of
California, Los Angeles."
   Bibliography: p.
   Includes index.
   1. United States—Foreign relations—Palestine.
2. Palestine—Foreign relations—United States.
3. Zionism—United States. 4. Jewish-Arab relations
—1917-1949. I. Title
E183.8.I7T73   1983   327.7305694   82-15115
ISBN 0-03-062361-8

Grateful acknowledgement is made to Faber and Faber, Ltd. and to
Harcourt Brace Jovanovich, Inc. for use, at the end of this volume,
of a portion of "The Love Song of J. Alfred Prufrock" in *Collected
Poems 1909-1962* by T.S. Eliot; copyright © 1936 by Harcourt Brace
Jovanovich, Inc., copyright © 1963, 1964 by T.S. Eliot. Reprinted by
permission of the publishers.

Published in 1983 by Praeger Publishers
CBS Educational and Professional Publishing
a Division of CBS Inc.
© 1983, Praeger Publishers
All rights reserved
456789 052 98765432
Printed in the United States of America

For Necla

FOREWORD by Lord Caradon

I write this early in July 1982 as day by day and hour by hour we get reports of more dreadful events and even greater dangers from Lebanon and all the Middle East. It would be tempting, therefore, to concentrate on present rapidly changing developments: the violence, the suffering, and the receding hopes of peace.

So much is at stake, yet it is quite impossible to predict what the situation will be even a week from now. Nearly everyone—commentators as well as combatants—has been wrong in past judgments and expectations. So I resist the temptation to repeat my own intensely strong views or to advocate my own proposals for an ultimate peaceful settlement.

Nevertheless, even in these days of catastrophe and crisis I turn most willingly to read Dan Tschirgi's brilliant book. For the story he tells so well gives the most thorough and searching account of U.S. policy in the Middle East during the decade leading up to the creation of the State of Israel. After that period events moved even faster and dangers grew even greater, and in the book's concluding sections Professor Tschirgi provides some shrewd comment on subsequent events. It is impossible, however, to judge U.S. policies under Presidents Reagan and Carter without going back to see how the United States formulated policy (or failed to do so) under Presidents Roosevelt and Truman. Professor Tschirgi has done us all a fine service by presenting us with a book that tells the story so fully and so faithfully and so attractively. I found it fascinating.

I have myself been much involved in the Middle East for a good deal of my working life, first as the most junior member of the administration of Palestine in the 1930s, then in Transjordan (including the advance early in World War II to Damascus and Beirut), and subsequently as a minister in the United Nations. In 1938 I was transferred from Nablus in Palestine to London and in 1943 I went off from Amman to Cyprus, Jamaica, and Nigeria. So there were big gaps in my personal experiences of Middle East affairs.

I could not have wished for a more complete and a more convincing account of all the dramatic events when I was away in other territories. The research is impressive, the story vividly told, and on questions that excite so much partisan controversy and so much misrepresentation the comment has been perceptive and balanced.

I have the greatest respect not only for Professor Tschirgi's knowledge and understanding of the Middle East but also for his achievement as a

---

Lord Caradon was British Minister of State and Representative of the United Kingdom at the United Nations from 1964 to 1970, having previously served in Palestine, Transjordan, Libya, Cyprus, and Nigeria. He is the acknowledged author of UN Security Council Resolution 242 that has to date set the parameters of the search for a Middle East peace.

scholar. I hope that one day he will be able to write another volume entitled THE POLITICS OF DECISION to tell the story of the 1980s, with the United States at long last adopting a positive and constructive policy in the United Nations in cooperation with Europe and the Soviet Union and everyone else. The agreed aim then will be to bring freedom to the Palestinians and security to Israel, one necessarily dependent on the other, to achieve a comprehensive settlement—with Jerusalem not a barrier but a gateway to a lasting peace.

PREFACE

A sizable body of literature devoted to Israel's creation has developed over the past 34 years. However, relatively few studies have focused on American policy toward Palestine in the crucial decade that led to the establishment of the Jewish state. Of these, most earlier works were produced by partisans seeking to justify or criticize Israel's existence. For a long while even the more objective efforts to understand the dynamics of U.S. policy toward pre-1948 Palestine were severely hampered by lack of primary evidence. Inevitably there resulted only a desultory debate over broad interpretative answers to questions such as these: Were Presidents Roosevelt and Truman morally committed to help resolve the Palestine issue, or were they essentially cynical political actors? Was American Zionism the primary influence in the formulation of U.S. Palestine policy prior to 1948? Was the American government divided between inveterately opposed factions typified by a "pro-Zionist" Congress and an "anti-Zionist" Department of State? Was the American public generally sympathetic to Zionist goals, or was Zionist propaganda cleverly manipulated to create this impression? Was American policy under Roosevelt and Truman actually a successful effort to avoid London's attempts to bring the United States to the rescue of imperial British interests in the Middle East?

Only within the past few years has the availability of key primary sources permitted scholars to move away from essentially speculative interpretations toward tightly focused and highly documented accounts of the specific steps that comprised Washington's approach to Palestine. Books by John Snetsinger (1974), Kenneth Ray Bain (1979), and Evan M. Wilson (1979) stand as valuable scholarly contributions to our understanding of American policy toward Palestine.

The present effort tries to follow the trend established by these writers, yet differs in terms of both scope and purpose. First, this study focuses far more strongly on the complex welter of attitudes that underlay the developing U.S. role in Palestine. Second, it concerns itself equally with the Roosevelt and Truman administrations during the seminal decade that preceded Israel's birth. By doing so, the following pages inevitably dwell on aspects of continuity and distinctiveness in American policy that are beyond more limited examinations. Finally, and most importantly, the purpose of this work is not only to describe and analyze American policy but also to relate it progressively to the course of events within Palestine.

While preparing this book I accumulated various heavy intellectual debts for which mere acknowledgement is small repayment. For the time and resources originally permitting me to undertake the task, I thank the University of Toronto and the International Studies Programme of the University of Toronto. The Center for International and Strategic Affairs at the University of California, Los Angeles (CISA) provided a stimulating and enjoyable environment for preparing the manuscript's final draft. I am particularly grateful to CISA's Roman Kolkowicz, Michael Intriligator, William Potter, Donna Beltz, and Gerri Page. The index at the end of the book appeared swiftly and painlessly as a result of the congenial wizardry of Raúl Crespo Rivera and Ofelia Cervantes Villagomez of the Computer Center (CECUA) at the University of the Americas, Puebla, Mexico, and the yeoman efforts of Alejandro Mendez Rock of the Department of International Relations at the same university.

The research demanded by the project could not have been accomplished without help from the staffs of a great many institutions, among which must be mentioned the Butler Library at Columbia University, the Library of Congress, the Robert Muldrow Cooper Library at Clemson University, the Georgetown University Library, the Madison State Historical Library in Madison, Wisconsin, the New York City Public Library, the National Archives of the United States, the Franklin Delano Roosevelt Library in Hyde Park, New York, the Harry S Truman Library in Independence, Missouri, and the Zionist Archives in New York City.

The list of individuals who contributed time and expertise is far too extensive to mention fully. However, special appreciation is expressed to George Barakat, Rabbi Elmer Berger, Benjamin Freedman, Dr. Nahum Goldmann, the Hon. Loy W. Henderson, Dr. Philip K. Hitti, Dr. Alfred Lilienthal, and Mrs. Faris S. Malouf. Sincere gratitude is expressed to my editors at Praeger, Ron Chambers and Patty Sullivan, without whose patience and hard work this volume would not exist.

Several brave souls read earlier versions of the manuscript in its entirety and strove mightily to keep me from errors of fact or interpretation. If I have failed in these respects, it is certainly through no fault of Drs. Bennett Kovrig, James Barros, William C. Berman, and Mr. Evan M. Wilson. I am immensely grateful to each of these fine scholars.

Many colleagues and friends facilitated my work. Sometimes their aid was subtle, not necessarily obvious even to themselves, yet always significant. I am happy to thank Ron and Gloria Duncan, Paul Jabber, Yereth K. Knowles, Norman McLeod, John and Carol Patsalides, Bennett Ramberg, and John Roman.

My parents have been as unstinting as ever in their support. The same is true of the rest of my family, including that part of it which I fortunately acquired through marriage.

Above all, I thank Necla, my wife and colleague, who in her typically amazing way served simultaneously as my most inexhaustible and exacting critic as well as my most consistent and vital source of encouragement.

CONTENTS

PART III:
THE TRUMAN ADMINISTRATION
AND PALESTINE

INTRODUCTION

To argue for a clear distinction between "pre" and "post" 1948 Arab-Jewish tensions in the Middle East is not to deny the intimate bond between the problems of each period. Certainly, today's Middle East conflict grew out of the political struggle that festered throughout the history of the Palestine mandate. Yet to claim an identity between the tensions of each period is to obscure an understanding of either.

The proclamation issued by Israel's founding fathers in May 1948 did not itself mark the boundary between the "Palestine problem" and its immediate successor (which in the interest of clarity might best be termed the "Arab-Israeli problem"). No such clear-cut event joins the two issues. Actually, the nexus is more accurately seen as having been organically forged during the complete collapse of central authority that attended the end of British rule in Palestine, a process that may conveniently be dated from the passage of the United Nations General Assembly's resolution of November 29, 1947 recommending the country's partition into Arab and Jewish states. The vacuum created by Britain's eclipse was immediately filled by a raging and bloody confrontation between Arabs and Jews that did not subside until the conclusion of an armistice in early 1949.

During this period of "trial by chaos" the question that had rocked the mandate since its beginning—whether or not there would be a Jewish state in Palestine—was resolved. After 1948 the political issues that continued to surround Palestine could not be formulated in terms implying that the creation and consolidation of that state were problematical. Even the most intractable opponents of Jewish statehood could now only challenge its continuity.

The same tumultuous events that settled the question of whether Jewish sovereignty would arise within Palestine's borders also deeply colored the new Arab-Jewish controversy over whether, or under what terms, Israel would continue to exist. Among the enduring elements that the confused end of the mandate bequeathed to the Arab-Israeli problem were the following:

1. The heightened passions that inevitably engulfed Jews and Arabs both inside and outside of Palestine as a result of intercommunal bloodletting, and particularly in consequence of atrocities perpetrated by both sides against noncombatants.

2. The direct military confrontation between the forces of the newly proclaimed state of Israel and those of several Arab states, and the psychological repercussions of the initial armed conflict on all parties involved.

3. The passions and problems arising from the fact that some 750,000 Palestinian Arab refugees found themselves unable to return to their homes within areas controlled by the new Jewish state.

4. The confusion surrounding the nature and location of the boundaries separating Israel from the Arab territories on its periphery.

This work is mainly a study of American policy toward Palestine in the years 1939–48. Yet it proceeds against the backdrop of the seminal confrontation that developed in Palestine at the close of this period. The purpose at hand is not only to present the dynamics that led to American involvement in Palestine and to describe the course of that involvement, but also to suggest how and why the involvement of the United States contributed to the final breakdown of order and authority in that country.

This last objective implies an assumption that the anarchic situation that occurred in 1948 Palestine—a situation that immediately benefited neither the Arab nor Jew who experienced it first-hand—was not inevitable. However, it does not involve any claim that the Palestine problem would have ended differently had the United States pursued another course between 1939 and 1948. What is asserted is simply that under different circumstances there might have been a chance for an alternative ending. Far too many participants influenced events in Palestine for any one party to be "blamed" for the final chaotic denouement. Nonetheless, responsibility, even when shared, cannot be disclaimed. This effort will try to clarify the rightful portion that may be allotted to the United States.

It is easy enough to characterize Washington's approach to the Palestine problem as vacillating and indecisive. Yet it cannot be labeled erratic. Throughout most of the period considered here, American "indecision" entailed closely planned and tightly executed tactics designed to evade the core of the Palestine question: whether Arab or Jew, or whether in some way both, would dominate politically in that country.

In retrospect it is clear that this calculated indecision involved a degree of callousness as well as of irresponsibility on the part of policy makers. To the—not inconsiderable—extent that they lacked concern for demonstrable consequences of their actions within Palestine, they were callous. In the final analysis, they were irresponsible because their actions during the decade under review tended to further a terminal confrontation between Arab and Jew; a possibility that—with the exception of one brief period—was consistently perceived by policy makers themselves as detrimental to American interests.

The exception to that assessment came near the end of 1947, when Washington opted to espouse partition at the United Nations. As will be seen, the nature and the form of American support of partition was consciously devised in light of a virtual certainty that it would lead to an anarchic bloodbath in Palestine. Underlying this development was a temporary conviction that American interests would be less harmed by an intercommunal explosion than by efforts to achieve a more orderly settlement.

The abrupt reversal of the U.S. propartitionist stand a few months later did not occur because of any change of heart over the intrinsic significance of an Arab-Jewish war. Instead, it was based on a reappraisal of the implications of that war for American interests.

What emerges very clearly from a review of American involvement with the Palestine problem between 1939 and 1948 is that Palestine-related decisions were rarely taken with reference to the issues at stake within Palestine itself. The fundamental reason for this was that American decision makers found little of interest in the question of whether Arab or Jew predominated in Palestine, or under what conditions some arrangement between the two might be possible. On the other hand, certain ramifications of the Arab-Zionist controversy were of great concern to these same men. These ramifications, secondary effects of the primordial contest over the ultimate political disposition of Palestine, formed a peculiarly American abstraction that in the halls of Washington constituted the "Palestine problem." It was, in fact, an abstraction composed of elements quite foreign to the points at issue within Palestine.

Given the many inputs affecting foreign policy decisions in the United States, it is necessary to conceive of the American outlook on Palestine as a composite entity distilled from various perspectives that influenced the conduct of foreign relations. Following a historical introduction, Part I of this work attempts to identify and analyze politically relevant attitudes linked to the American approach to Palestine. Focusing on government institutions as well as the broader public, Part I perforce avoids a strictly chronological narrative.

Parts II and III deal with the Roosevelt and Truman administrations. Undertaken within a chronological framework, these sections try to identify the forces that led to an American role in the Palestine issue, to trace the development of, and modifications in, Washington's view of the "Palestine problem," and to assess the impact of American policy on Palestine.

The concluding chapter tries to draw lessons from the past that not only help explain U.S. policy toward the Arab–Israeli problem since 1948, but also illuminate the implications of recent events—Israel's 1982 invasion of Lebanon and the ensuing slaughter by others of unarmed Palestinian civilians—for choices Washington must make in the future.

I: FORMULATION OF A PROBLEM: PALESTINE IN AN AMERICAN CONTEXT

I. BACKGROUND: THE UNITED STATES AND PALESTINE

On October 13, 1917, President Woodrow Wilson penned the following note to his trusted aide, Colonel Edward M. House:

> I find in my pocket the memorandum you gave me about the Zionist Movement. I am afraid I did not say to you that I concurred in the formula suggested from the other side. I do, and would be obliged if you let them know it.[1]

The memorandum referred to by the president had been handed to him a week earlier by House. It relayed a message from the British government setting forth the latest, though not final, draft of a proposed announcement to the effect that Great Britain was sympathetic to Zionist hopes for a Jewish national home in Palestine. On November 2, 1917, that announcement was made in the form of a letter from British Foreign Secretary Arthur James Balfour to Lord Rothschild:

> His Majesty's Government view with favor the establishment in Palestine of a national home for the Jewish people, and will use their best endeavors to facilitate the achievement of this object, it being clearly understood that nothing shall be done which may prejudice the civil and religious rights of existing non-Jewish communities in Palestine, or the rights and political status enjoyed by Jews in any other country.[2]

This carefully prepared text, known as the Balfour Declaration, set the stage for more than 30 years of conflict among Arabs, Jews, and British troops in Palestine. There is no evidence that Wilson saw the final version of the statement before it was communicated to Lord Rothschild. What is clear is that the preoccupied wartime president, casually finding House's week-old memorandum in his coat pocket and jotting down his acceptance of the

1

course then contemplated in London, did not consider the affair of particular concern to the United States.

Wilson's attitude typified the American approach to Palestine for the next two and a half decades.[3] While sympathy for the Zionist Movement was occasionally expressed by policy makers, Palestine was seen as a British responsibility and care was taken to avoid any official commitment to the creation of a Jewish national home in that country.[4]

THE U.S. AND
PALESTINE TO 1939

Following the award of the Palestine mandate to Great Britain in 1920, Congress passed a joint resolution endorsing the Balfour Declaration. The sponsor of the resolution in the House of Representatives was at pains to point out that passage of the measure would involve no commitment to an "entangling alliance or to any obligation to use military or naval force or the expenditure of any money." The legislation was described as "merely an expression of sympathy and favorable attitude in establishing in Palestine a refuge for the persecuted Jews of the world."[5]

Since it was not a member of the League of Nations, the United States secured "most favored nation" status in Palestine by concluding a convention with Great Britain in 1924. Under this agreement the United States recognized the legality of the British administration in Palestine and in return was guaranteed equal treatment with members of the League of Nations in matters pertaining to that country.[6] In later years, once Zionists began to fear that Britain would default on the obligation imposed by the mandate to "secure the establishment of a Jewish national home," American supporters of Zionism argued that the Anglo-American Convention empowered Washington to veto administrative measures in Palestine that it considered violations of the original League of Nations directive. This contention was never accepted by the British or American governments.[7] A public memorandum issued by the Department of State in 1938 sought to clarify Washington's view that it had no right to prevent changes in the terms of the Palestine mandate. Shortly afterward, President Roosevelt made the same point in a letter to the mayor of Hartford, Connecticut.[8]

American aloofness from Palestine during the interwar period was a product of a generally low level of involvement with the Middle East as a whole. Historically, sustained American contact with the region began with the determination of intrepid New England protestant missionaries to carry the Gospel to the Islamic world in the early decades of the nineteenth century.[9] Although never abandoning hope of bringing Arab Moslems into the Christian fold, the pioneer missionaries soon discovered that direct means were unlikely to win many converts. They increasingly turned their energies to education and medicine, in expectation that such examples of disinterested service would demonstrate the merits of Christianity in practice. Philanthropy became the dominant pattern of American missionary activity in the Middle East.

After World War I, Washington helped open the way for the development of private American commercial interests in the Middle East. Although economic relations with the countries of that region long remained only minimally important, policy makers were anxious that Americans not suffer economic discrimination. The conventions between the mandatory powers in the Middle East and the United States were designed to ensure this.

A particularly worthwhile result of Washington's preoccupation with commercial rights was American participation in the hunt for Middle East oil. In 1928 American concerns joined the British-French-Dutch oil consortium, the Iraq Petroleum Company. In 1930 American diplomacy helped gain permission for a Canadian subsidiary of Standard Oil of California to search for oil in Bahrein. The same formula obtained four years later in Kuwait.[10]

Somewhat ironically, what later proved to be the single greatest American investment in Arab oil was obtained in 1933 without official aid from Washington when Saudi Arabia granted a 360,000-square-mile concession to the Standard Oil Company of California. This was the birth of the famous Arabian-American Oil Company (ARAMCO).[11]

Despite the successful introduction of an American presence into the Middle East oil industry, Washington continued to show little desire to enhance its political influence in the area. A contributing reason for this was that overall American trade with the region remained modest in the years before World War II. Moreover, the first years during which Americans worked their oil concessions produced no startling finds. Petroleum deposits in commercial quantities were not found in Bahrein until 1932, or in Kuwait until 1938. Exploration in Saudi Arabia was started in 1934 but proved discouraging until the Dammam oil field was tapped in 1938. Finally, the isolationist ethos that colored U.S. foreign relations after World War I also militated against the assumption of a more active role in the Middle East by the American government.[12]

Only months before the outbreak of World War II, policy makers were still reluctant to launch a more energetic policy toward the Arab world, even for the express and limited purpose of protecting the budding commercial interests of the United States. Early in 1939, executives of oil companies operating in Saudi Arabia began seriously urging the State Department to establish diplomatic ties with the desert kingdom. In support of this appeal, the oilmen argued that lack of official support rebounded to the benefit of their competitors.[13] Several months later, having had no success earlier, the same executives informed the State Department that Japanese oil companies, strongly backed by the Japanese and Italian governments, were energetically seeking permission to operate in Saudi Arabia.[14] Even this news initially failed to impress Washington. Not until 1940 did the American minister in Cairo present his credentials to the Saudi government. The State Department did not station a resident official in Saudi Arabia until 1942.

Notwithstanding the government's preference for noninvolvement in Middle Eastern affairs, circumstances soon conspired to give the United States an important role in the political life of the region. One such factor was the radical alteration in relations between the Zionist movement and the British government that occurred in the spring of 1939. Feeling themselves forsaken by London, Zionist leaders looked to the large and potentially influential American Jewish community to bring the United States into an active partnership with their cause.

Another set of forces helping to propel the United States into a position of influence in the Middle East was unleashed in September 1939 by the outbreak of World War II. The war years witnessed a revolutionary change in the nature of American interest in the Middle East. In an immediate sense, Washington's traditional concern with established philanthropic, cultural, religious, and academic enterprises was quickly superseded by military considerations as vast tracts of the area became potential or actual battlegrounds between Allied and Axis forces. Almost simultaneously, American policy makers began attributing more value to Middle Eastern oil, in which they recognized an important military asset.

The end of the war did not reinstate the old cultural interests as the primary focus of American policy in the Middle East. American nonintervention had died at Pearl Harbor. However, in the Middle East it was not immediately replaced by any comprehensive framework for the formulation of foreign policy. Still, certain concrete objectives were seen as constituting definite interests in the Arab world. Chief among these were the security of American access to Middle Eastern oil and the preservation of cordial relations with the Arab Middle East.

While these regional interests were generally accepted as valid by American policy makers even before the end of World War II, their importance relative to other aspects of U.S. foreign policy was an object of confusion throughout the period falling within the scope of this study. It was, however, painfully evident that the Arab world's extensive concern with Palestine would require Washington to make some effort to define its position on the tangled Arab-Zionist controversy. This was not a revelation that came only with the development of long-term American objectives in the Middle East. The same lesson had been learned during the early years of World War II, when American policy toward the area had essentially aimed at short-term goals formulated on the basis of military necessity.

In short, 1939 stands as a watershed in the American approach to the Palestine problem. On the one hand, the termination of the Anglo-Zionist alliance in Palestine led directly to the creation in the United States of a large, vocal, and influential pressure group dedicated to enlisting Washington as champion of the Zionist cause. On the other hand, the accelerated development of American interests in the Middle East occasioned by World War II faced policy makers with the need to satisfy Arab curiosity about U.S. objectives toward Palestine. Although both sets of factors obviously carried diametrically opposed implications insofar as the policy choices they urged upon the American government, they each helped foreclose noninvolvement in the Palestine controversy as a real option for the United States.

THE PALESTINE
PROBLEM IN 1939

Despite the complexity it attained over the years, the Palestine problem has always had at its core the conflict between Arabs and Zionists for political domination in Palestine. The intricate nature that this seminal controversy assumed by 1948 was in large measure due to the continued inability of either side to prevail without external support. This led both protagonists, at various times and with varying degrees of energy and success, to seek the involvement of third parties in the essentially bilateral conflict.

The birth of Zionism as a secular political movement is credited to the Hungarian-born journalist, Theodore Herzl. Convinced that anti-Semitism was an inevitable concomitant of Jewish minority status in Gentile society, Herzl argued that only a Jewish state would allow Jews to lead normal lives. Although he was prepared to consider various locations for the establishment of such a state, the majority of those in the movement he created adamantly maintained that only in Palestine could Jewish political life be revived. In 1897 the First Zionist Congress met in Basle. It defined Zionism's objective as being "to secure for the Jewish people a publicly recognized, legally secured homeland in Palestine."[15]

By the spring of 1916 British officials were giving serious attention to arguments advanced in London by Dr. Chaim Weizmann, a Russian-born chemist who was to be the principal spokesman of the Zionist movement for the next 30 years. A naturalized British subject and committed anglophile, Weizmann divided his time during the war between bending science to Britain's military advantage and promoting the idea that London should sponsor Zionist goals in Palestine as part of its postwar Middle East policy.[16] Through the aid of influential friends acquired during more than ten years of residence in England, Weizmann—along with other Zionists having connections with government circles—initiated the negotiations that culminated in the Balfour Declaration.

The Ottoman Empire's adhesion to the Central Powers permitted the nations of the Entente to plan the realization of their ambitions in the Middle East. Anglo-French discussions in 1915 and 1916 produced the secret Sykes-

Picot Treaty, under the terms of which Turkish holdings in the Arab world were to fall at the end of the war under a British-French condominium divided partly into areas ruled directly by each country, partly into zones that each would indirectly control, and partly into jointly administered areas.[17] Palestine, toward which both London and Paris held ambitions, was to come under some unspecified form of joint administration.

Palestine figured very much in the minds of British statesmen as they plotted the dismemberment of the Middle East. The unalterable reality of geography opened the possibility that a future unfriendly power in that area could, as the Turks were then doing, seriously threaten the Suez Canal. Moreover, in the postwar period it would be to London's benefit to have Palestine stand as a buffer between the French in Syria and the British in Egypt.

These long-term issues were skillfully played upon by Zionist spokesmen. At the same time, British policy makers also took into account more immediate considerations, particularly the propaganda value that a pro-Zionist declaration might have in winning the support of American Jewry for the entry of the United States into the war.[18]

These factors, combined with some degree of humanitarian inclination to help persecuted Jews obtain a territory of their own, helped produce the Balfour Declaration. However, the fact that the statement reeked of conscious and carefully formulated ambiguity was evidence of the British government's actual indecision over its final policy toward Palestine. The declaration expressed His Majesty's government's favorable attitude toward the creation in Palestine of a "national home" for the Jewish people. But what constituted a "national home"? It also committed Britain to support the "civil and religious rights of existing non-Jewish communities in Palestine." But what were those rights, and how did they relate to the limits of a Jewish national home? As J. M. N. Jeffries points out, "these unfathomable phrases were employed just because they were unfathomable and could be interpreted to pleasure."[19]

Considered in retrospect, the Balfour Declaration's strongest single implication was not directly linked to the issue of Palestine's eventual political disposition. The phrase "national home" was, after all, a means of keeping precisely that question open. Rather, the document's paramount implication was that the national home required some degree of Jewish immigration into Palestine. Yet even this central point remained cloudy. Years later, shortly before the close of British rule in Palestine, another British Foreign Secretary, Ernest Bevin, would agonize aloud over Lord Balfour's imprecision, pointing out that "nobody indicated . . . when the national home would be established." For Bevin, the Palestine problem revolved around the "great puzzle" of how much Jewish immigration was needed to establish a national home: "Was it millions of Jews; was it a majority; was it a Jewish state; or what was it?"[20]

Bevin's pained search for meaning came too late to avoid three decades of strife. As approved by the League of Nations in 1922, the mandate acknowledged a special relationship between world Jewry and Palestine, and it expressly required that "an appropriate Jewish Agency" be recognized as a public body with the task of advising and cooperating with "the Administration of Palestine in such economic, social and other matters as may affect the establishment of the Jewish national home."[21] Initially, the World Zionist Organization, recognized by the mandatory as the responsible agency for this purpose, provided the channel for Jews outside Palestine to share in building the national home. However, the Zionist Organization could lay no claim to being truly representative of world Jewry. In 1929 an expanded Jewish Agency for Palestine was created in order to allow Jews who rejected Zionism's political content to collaborate in furthering Jewish life in Palestine. Despite the inclusion of non-Zionists, the Zionist Organization's control over the formulation and execution of policies affecting the national home was not appreciably reduced.[22]

Under the direction of Chaim Weizmann, Zionists followed a "gradualist" policy toward Palestine. This approach was characterized by its concentration on the practical tasks of building up the strength of the country's Jewish community without voicing ultimate political demands.[23] By 1939 Zionism had profoundly altered the character of Palestine. Although that country had received some Zionist immigrants prior to World War I, by 1920 the Jewish community numbered only slightly over 60,000; that is, 10.1 percent of Palestine's population.[24] In 1939, however, Palestine held over 445,000 Jews—about 30 percent of the population. During the same period, Jewish land holdings doubled (although by 1939 Jews still held title to only 5.7 percent of the area of Palestine), New Jerusalem and Tel-Aviv grew into Jewish urban centers, and some 120 million pounds sterling had entered the country as Jewish capital.[25]

The Jewish community of Palestine, the Yishuv, developed into a cohesive and well-coordinated body. Structured along democratic lines, it was directed by what amounted to a communal quasi government that levied taxes, ran the Jewish educational system, and maintained a semisecret and illegal militia, the Haganah.[26] Although submission to the discipline of the Yishuv was technically voluntary, the overwhelming majority of the Jewish community was enthusiastically loyal to the communal institutions. Exceptions were found among members of extreme rightist and leftist groups and among ultraorthodox Jews. The most important of the dissident groups was the right-wing Revisionist faction.

The organized Yishuv provided scope for a multiplicity of political parties that competed vigorously for office within the communal political system. These differences were mirrored in the composition of the Jewish Agency. Although no single party dominated the Yishuv, a working coalition of labor parties—ranging ideologically from Marxist to moderately socialist—established itself as the chief political force in the Jewish community by the mid-1930s. The acknowledged leader of this group was David Ben Gurion.

By the start of World War II, then, Zionism had successfully led to the establishment in Palestine of a dynamic, coordinated, and largely self-contained Jewish minority. More important than the tangible manifestations of this success—the agricultural settlements, the buildings of Tel-Aviv, or the relatively modest beginnings of local Jewish industry—was the growth of Jewish national consciousness within Palestine. Modern Zionism, originally the product of an oppressive European milieu, had survived its transplantation to the Middle East; and for the Jewish colonizers and their offspring, Zionism was no longer rooted primarily in a reaction to a hostile environment but rather in a driving attraction to the reality of Palestine's Jewish community and to its potential for further development.

The growth of the Yishuv was not accomplished without cost to Palestine's tranquility. The native Arab community, with moral and at times material help from other parts of the Arab world, offered rising levels of resistance to Jewish colonization after the Balfour Declaration. By the start of World War II, the mandatory had been forced to weather a series of mass protests, riots and, ultimately, even a full-scale rebellion.

Arab resentment over Palestine's fate at the end of World War I was linked to the belief that European imperialism had duped the Arab world. Under the Ottoman administrative system, Palestine formed an integral part of Syria, and it was largely upon the dream of an independent Syria that Arab nationalism, a phenomenon that developed in the final quarter of the nineteenth century, had come to focus at the time of World War I.[27] When Britain became embroiled in conflict with the Ottoman Empire, London quickly endeavored to turn anti-Turkish feeling among the Arabs to its own advantage. As early as 1914 British officials were urging the sherif of Mecca, Hussein Ibn Ali, to launch a revolt against the Ottoman regime in the Arab world.[28]

Instrumental in convincing Hussein to take this step were assurances he received from Sir Henry McMahon, the British high commissioner in Egypt. In later years, Arab spokesmen found it significant that the basic elements of the McMahon-Hussein understanding were agreed upon more than two years before the Balfour Declaration was issued.

In October 1915 McMahon was in possession of Hussein's demand for a British commitment to support Arab independence in Syria, Lebanon, Iraq, Palestine, and (with the exception of Aden) the Arabian Peninsula. In answer, McMahon pledged his government's recognition of Arab independence in the areas cited by Hussein excepting the following three territories: the Cilician districts of Mersin and Alexandretta, Lebanon and the part of Syria west of a line between Aleppo and Damascus, and southern Iraq from

Baghdad to Basra. Anthony Nutting has observed that on the basis of the communications between Hussein and McMahon, the Arabs were "fully entitled" to regard Palestine among the territories whose independence had been accepted by Britain.[29]

Arab awareness of the inconstancy of British diplomacy began in 1917. In that year the revolutionary Soviet regime in Russia published a copy of the Sykes-Picot Treaty found in the files of the Czarist government. It was also in 1917 that the Balfour Declaration was issued. London employed a variety of devices to calm the fears these events raised among the Arabs. News of the Sykes-Picot agreement was described by British officials as a malicious distortion, renewed promises were made to the effect that postwar arrangements in the Middle East would entail the consent of the governed, and a special emissary was dispatched to Hussein to explain away the Balfour Declaration as merely implying that "a Jewish settlement in Palestine would only be allowed insofar as would be consistent with the political and economic freedom of the Arab population."[30]

The full extent of British duplicity would become obvious to the Arabs immediately upon the end of the war. Nowhere was this more true than in Palestine, with respect to which Lord Balfour privately admitted that "the Powers have made no statement of fact which is not admittedly wrong, and no declaration of policy which, at least in the letter, they have not always intended to violate."[31]

Arab nationalists quickly rallied in an effort to prevent the dissection of the Middle East by the British and French. In July 1919 an elected General Syrian Congress assembled in Damascus and passed resolutions that, *inter alia*, denounced the idea that the Arab inhabitants of Syria were less fitted than other nations to govern themselves, protested against their prospective relegation to a status "requiring the tutelage of a mandatory power," demanded immediate independence for the state of Syria, and rejected Zionist claims to "that part of southern Syria known as Palestine."[32]

Even before the mandate was confirmed by the League of Nations, Palestinian Arabs demonstrated their opposition to the Jewish national home. In April 1920, riots broke out in Jerusalem, causing some loss of life and giving further impetus in the Arab community to spiraling tensions, which at year's end brought forth calls for a Palestinian Arab congress in Haifa.[33] The congress, composed of Arab Christians and Moslems, convened in December 1920. In addition to establishing a Palestinian Arab Executive, the assembly voiced several demands, the first three of which were: the abolition of the principle of a Jewish national home in Palestine; the creation of a national government responsible to an elected Parliament voted upon by "the Palestinian people who existed in Palestine before the War"; and the cessation of Jewish immigration "until such time as a National Government is formed."[34]

In the spring of 1921, renewed fighting broke out between Arabs and Jews, this time originating in Jaffa and then spreading to other parts of the country. When the rioting ended, there were nearly 200 Jewish, and over 100 Arab, casualties.[35] A British investigative team found the fundamental cause of the disturbance to be "a feeling among the Arabs of . . . hostility to the Jews, due to political and economic causes . . . and their conception of Zionist policy as derived from Jewish exponents."[36]

The violence of 1921 was the last major confrontation in Palestine for eight years. In the interval, the Arab community kept up a steady stream of political activity to demonstrate its refusal to acknowledge the validity of either the Jewish national home concept or the mandate that promoted it. Through contacts with the British government and the Council of the League of Nations, Palestinian Arabs continued to demand self-government.[37] However, despite this degree of unity, they failed to develop an enduring organizational base for nationalist agitation. Before the end of the decade, the executive structure created at the Haifa Congress was moribund, and in the early 1930s it passed into oblivion without formal dissolution.[38]

The essential malaise of Arab political activity in Palestine was that it rested on the semifeudal relationships underlying Arab society. Ideology played virtually no role in the formulation of political programs, and the key to political organization continued to be the personalized allegiance that traditional leaders could command. Political leadership tended to be the function of established aristocratic families, and, accordingly, was complicated by equally well-established frictions among those clans. The downfall of the machinery set up by the Haifa Congress was largely the result of traditional hostility between two of these families, the Husseinis and the Nashashibis.[39]

However, Palestinian Arab opposition to Zionist colonization was not a product of machinations by the "effendi" class. Political consciousness in the country's largely peasant society was directly affected by the growth of the Jewish community. In 1929 a Royal Commission investigating Arab-Zionist clashes denied the contention that "the fella [peasant] takes no personal interest in politics."

> Villagers and peasants alike are taking a very real and personal interest in the effect of the policy of establishing a [Jewish] national home and in the question of the development of self-governing institutions in Palestine.[40]

Among the characteristics of the national home that most forcefully touched Palestinian Arabs was the exclusion of Arab labor from Jewish enterprises. This practice had been promoted since the beginning of the mandate by the strong Labor faction within the Zionist Movement, largely on grounds that the Jewish colonial effort should not exploit native workers.[41] However, Zionists also frankly admitted that boycotting Arab workers served the interests of the national home.[42] In this connection it should be noted that until 1939 the sole criterion by which the mandatory administration regulated Jewish immigration was the "economic absorptive capacity" of Palestine.[43] While several categories of Jews enjoyed unlimited entry, immigration schedules for Jewish workers were set semiannually by the mandatory administration after negotiations with the Jewish Agency determined the Yishuv's labor requirements. Not unreasonably, this reinforced the Zionists' view that it was in their interest to preserve a closed Jewish economy.

In August 1929 anti-Zionist feeling burst forth in a five-day orgy of violence that brought death to 133 Jews and 87 Arabs, leaving many more wounded on each side.[44] Although the immediate cause of the bloodshed was a controversy over the rights of Arabs and Jews at a portion of the wall surrounding the Haram esh-Sharif (the Wailing Wall), it was evident to British administrators that underlying the ostensibly religious conflict were the deeper political troubles that plagued the country.[45]

Soon after the 1929 riots, the British government dispatched Sir John Hope Simpson to investigate problems related to economic development, immigration, and land settlement. Hope Simpson's report was a comprehensive study of the prevailing economic and political situation in Palestine. It was highly critical of certain policies followed by Zionists and the mandatory administration, and its conclusions left no doubt of its author's conviction that justice could be accorded to all of the country's inhabitants only by a radical alteration of British policy.

Hope Simpson was especially critical of the Zionist boycott of Arab labor, seeing it as a fundamental source of political tension. Commenting on the relationship between Zionist labor practices and Zionist land purchases, he argued:

> The present [practice], precluding employment of Arabs in the Zionist colonies is undesirable, from the point of view of both justice and of the good government of the country. . . . It is impossible to view with equanimity the extension of an enclave in Palestine from which all Arabs are excluded. The Arab population already regards the transfer of lands to Zionist hands with dismay and alarm. These cannot be dismissed as baseless in the light of the Zionist policy which is described above.[46]

In the fall of 1930, a White Paper prepared by the colonial secretary, Lord Passfield, revealed London's response to the Hope Simpson report. In effect, the Passfield White Paper accepted the validity of Hope Simpson's analysis and promised remedial action. Specifically, it indicated the mandatory's intention to curtail Jewish immigration and land purchases in Palestine. Organized Zionist pressure, coupled with attacks on the Passfield

White Paper by members of both major parliamentary parties, soon caused the British government to "explain away most of those features objectionable to Zionists."[47]

Arab disillusionment with the mandate deepened during the next few years. Hitler's rise in Germany led to a dramatic increase in the number of Jews immigrating into Palestine after 1933. While in 1931 only 4,075 immigrants, or about 16 percent of the total Jewish migration in the world that year, landed in Palestine, in 1935 some 62,000 Jews, 79 percent of that year's migration, took up residence in the country.[48] By 1936 the Jewish population had risen to over 400,000—an increase of 166,000 since 1933. This influx exacerbated tensions within the Arab community, and these in turn resulted in demands for the principal Palestinian spokesmen to lay aside personal rivalries in favor of a united front for effective political action.

In 1936 there were six Palestinian Arab political parties, although the factions led by the Husseinis, whose actual head was Haj Mohammed Amin al-Husseini, the mufti of Jersusalem, and the Nashashibis continued to dominate the Arab community's political life. In April, popular pressure caused the various parties to form a coalition under an executive body known as the Arab Higher Committee, whose president was the mufti of Jerusalem.

Initially, at least, the Higher Committee adopted policies dictated by the mood of the Palestinian Arab masses. By the spring of 1936 the Arab community was a virtual powder keg. Prior to the establishment of the Higher Committee, local "National Committees" sprouted throughout the towns and villages of Palestine, and one such group in Nablus had issued a call for a general economic strike against the mandate. The Higher Committee assumed leadership of this strike and announced that its objective was to end Jewish immigration and land purchases and, ultimately, to bring about the establishment of a national Palestinian government responsible to a representative assembly. This position was later endorsed at a general meeting of delegates from all National Committees in Palestine.[49]

It was not long before the strike was marked by widespread violence. In time, the fighting reached the proportions of an actual rebellion against the mandatory regime.[50] The uprising continued intermittently until the end of 1938.

A common misconception—both at the time and later—was that the rebellion had been engineered by leading elements of the so-called effendi class. In fact, quite the opposite was true. The moving spirits of the revolt came from the working and agricultural strata of Palestinian Arab society. In the minds of the fighters who gathered in the hills, Zionist expansion had been made possible largely through the willingness of members of the upper classes to sell vast tracts of land to Jewish settlers.[51] In this sense, the violence that broke out in 1936 reflected the failure of established Arab political leaders to gain concessions from the mandatory authorities that would have allayed the growing irritation of the peasantry.[52]

The rebellion ultimately proved disastrous to the Arabs. The strike and the virtual state of war that lingered for nearly three years played havoc with the Arab economy. In September 1937 the mandatory took severe measures against the political arm of the Arab community: the Higher Committee and all local National Committees were declared illegal; several members of the former body were arrested and exiled to the Seychelles Islands; and several other Higher Committee members who were already out of the country were not permitted to return. In this last group were the mufti of Jerusalem, who had escaped to Lebanon, and his cousin and chief assistant, Jamal al-Husseini.

The revolt was also costly in terms of human life. Between 1937 and 1939, no less than 112 Arabs were executed by the mandatory administration.[53] Many more, of course, were killed while fighting British troops. An added element of mayhem was contributed to the chaotic situation when the outlawed Higher Committee was reconstituted in Damascus by the escaped mufti and his colleagues. The Higher Committee now became an instrument of the Husseinis. From asylum beyond the borders of Palestine, Haj Amin exhibited a ruthless political ambition that he vented by having his henchmen eliminate, through intimidation and murder, his personal enemies within the Palestinian Arab community.[54] Although a definitive statement of Arab casualties during the turbulent years between 1936 and 1939 is not available, it is probable that around 5,000 were killed and several thousand more were injured.[55]

The demoralization of the Arab community at the end of the rebellion may be understood from the words of George Wadsworth, the American consul general at Jerusalem. Returning to Palestine after a four-month absence in the latter half of 1939, Wadsworth found among politically minded Arabs "an undercurrent of helplessness amounting almost to resignation. They are without effective leadership, largely impoverished."[56]

Britain's reaction to the revolt was not limited to the considerable military effort made to restore order. In November 1936 a Royal Commission of Inquiry was sent to Palestine under the direction of Earl Peel. The Peel Commission's report concluded that the terms of the mandate allowed no redress for Arab grievances about Jewish immigration, Jewish land acquisition, and the mandatory's failure to develop self-governing institutions. On the other hand, the report also contended that the fulfillment of British obligations to the Jewish people could be achieved only through a policy of "repression against an unwilling Arab population [which] would run counter to the very spirit of the mandates system and accepted British principles."[57] Peel suggested dividing the country between Arabs and Jews, and advanced a plan that would have given the Jewish community a state comprising 20 percent of the total area of Palestine. On the day the Peel report was made public, the British government announced it had decided the mandate was unworkable and therefore concurred with the partition proposal.

The reaction of the two communities in Palestine was mixed. All Palestinian Arab factions immediately denounced the very idea of partition.[58] The Zionist reaction was less clear. Although considerable sentiment existed against surrendering Jewish claims to any part of Palestine, the increasingly dire need of a refuge for European Jews, coupled with the fact that the British appeared willing for the first time to offer sovereignty to the Yishuv, gave a certain attraction to the concept of partition.[59] Moreover, Zionist leaders such as David Ben Gurion were quick to point out that acceptance of partition need not be construed as acquiescence to the perpetual limitation of the Jewish state to only a small area of Palestine.[60] The controversy between maximalist and pragmatically inclined Zionists was laid aside in the summer of 1937 when the Twentieth Zionist Congress empowered its Executive to ascertain precisely the borders of the Jewish state envisaged by the British government. The real issue of principle, whether or not partition was acceptable to Zionism, was left undecided.

Events beyond either Zionist or Arab control soon rendered Peel's recommendations academic. In April 1938 a British technical commission began a study that eventually led London to conclude that the partition scheme was administratively, politically, and financially unworkable.[61] At the same time, London revealed that its new approach to Palestine would aim at producing an agreed settlement between Arabs and Zionists. For this purpose, the government would invite representatives of the two sides to a conference in London. Significantly, the Arabs would not be limited to spokesmen for the Palestinians, but would also include representatives of the governments of Egypt, Iraq, Saudi Arabia, and Yemen.

The London Conference opened in February 1939, and it was clear that the deteriorating international political situation was behind the British government's eagerness to stabilize conditions in Palestine. German and Italian propaganda had long been able to capitalize on anti-British feeling generated by the Palestine problem throughout the Arab world. Limited aid had also been given by the Fascist states to Arab rebels during the revolt. In the event of war in Europe, it would be strategically vital to Britain that the Arab East remain quiescent. The paradox was that at the very time that the force of Palestinian Arab nationalism had been dissipated in futile rebellion, the international situation raised the political bargaining power of the Arabs to hitherto unreached heights.

The conference in London was a desultory affair. The Jewish Agency delegation arrived fearful of British intentions but determined not to accept any fundamental changes in the mandate's administration.[62] A last-minute, and temporary, reconciliation between the Nashashibis and Husseinis permitted both factions to be represented on the Palestinian Arab delegation. Meanwhile, Britain released those members of the Higher Committee who had been exiled to the Seychelles Islands and announced they would be permitted to attend the London talks as part of the Arab delegation. However, the British government remained firm in its refusal to welcome the fugitive mufti of Jerusalem to the conference.

It was evident from the outset that little hope of a settlement existed. The Jewish Agency insisted that the mandate be retained in its original form and that immigration be increased to accommodate the growing numbers of Jews desiring to flee Europe.[63] The Palestinian Arabs, directed by Jamal al-Husseini, countered with demands for the immediate stoppage of Jewish immigration and land purchases and for the establishment of Palestine as an independent state.[64] British hopes for a compromise quickly collapsed. On March 17 the London Conference was officially terminated.

Impelled by the deteriorating international political scene, the British government acted unilaterally. Britain's new policy toward the mandate was proclaimed in a White Paper issued on May 17, 1939. London declared itself ready to grant independence to Palestine after ten years—if at the end of that period relations between Arabs and Jews permitted the removal of foreign authority. In the interim, Jewish land purchases were to be freely allowed only in one part of the country, totally prohibited in another, and restricted in a third area. The White Paper linked Jewish immigration to political conditions in Palestine and ruled that immigration was to be permitted without Arab acquiescence for only five more years, during which a maximum of 75,000 Jews would be granted entry certificates.[65]

The immediate reactions of Arabs and Zionists were not surprising. The latter considered the new policy to be a breach of the obligations imposed by the mandate and a violation of the Balfour Declaration. Arab reaction was mixed. The Arab governments, as well as Arab leaders inside Palestine, appeared to feel that the decision was favorable to their cause. On the other hand, the mufti and the Higher Committee denounced the White Paper, arguing that it made Palestine's independence problematical since it offered Zionists an opportunity to engage in obstructionist tactics.

However, neither Arabs nor Zionists believed the White Paper was the final word on Palestine's political future. In Britain, a significant body of opinion, which extended into both major political parties, saw the government's new approach as a dishonorable repudiation of firm commitments. The Chamberlain government won a vote of confidence over the White Paper only by a clearly unimpressive majority. Among those voting in opposition was the future prime minister, Winston Churchill.

Further doubts over the White Paper's propriety were raised by the League of Nations Mandates Commission, which in July 1939 rendered an advisory opinion to the effect that the new policy was not in accord with the terms of the mandate. Finally, the imminence of war led both Arabs and Zionists to conclude that the next few years were likely to witness a restructuring of the international environment in ways that would have serious implications for Palestine's future. The Zionists, at least, soon left no doubt of their belief that the United States would assume a leading role in the approaching final act of the Palestine drama.

2. THE 1939 WHITE PAPER AND THE AMERICAN GOVERNMENT

On the eve of the London Conference, Zionists launched a campaign to obtain official American support against any alteration of British policy that might harm their position in Palestine. Coordinated from abroad by the leadership of the Zionist Movement, this effort sought to enlist the help of President Franklin Roosevelt.

It was not only the logic of the American political system, in which the key role in foreign policy execution is occupied by the presidency, that led Zionists to concentrate on winning over the White House. Circumstances more peculiar to the moment also shaped the nature of their campaign. Chief among these was the urgency of the London negotiations. Britain's haste to shore up its strategic position in the Middle East left Zionists no time to rely primarily upon public opinion and congressional support to propel the American government into action. If American intervention was to come in time to prevent a harmful shift in British policy, Zionist arguments had to be taken straight to the president.

Moreover, Zionists drew encouragement from Roosevelt's reputation as a friend of the Jewish people.[1] Indeed, the president had publicly expressed concern over the persecution of German Jewry on many occasions. His interest in the problem led him to call for the international conference on political refugees, which met in 1938 at the French lakeside town of Evian-les-Bains. The failure of the Evian Conference to solve the problem of finding resettlement areas for refugees did not reduce American Jewry's esteem for Roosevelt.[2]

Finally, Zionists were encouraged to carry their case to the White House by the knowledge that various individuals sympathetic to their cause enjoyed easy access to the president.

Despite the priority given to enlisting Roosevelt's support, Zionists did not neglect efforts to mobilize friendly opinion in other branches of government or among the general public. Both Congress and the State Department were urged to speak out against the impending shift of British policy in Palestine. At the same time, Zionists promoted popular interest in their views through a variety of well-publicized events.

In the end, of course, the campaign failed. Notwithstanding the Roosevelt administration's reluctance to admit it, Zionist pleas for American intercession were for all practical purposes rejected. The White Paper was issued on May 17.

An examination of Washington's reaction to the White Paper issue is a valuable introduction to the subsequent course of American involvement with Palestine. On the one hand, the conclusions drawn by the Zionist leadership from its initial failure to obtain American support led directly to the tactics adopted later to work toward the same end. On the other hand, the attitudes displayed by the White House, Congress, and the Department of State during the White Paper controversy were in many ways embryonically characteristic of those that dominated their approaches to the Palestine problem in later years.

THE ROOSEVELT ADMINISTRATION'S
RESPONSE TO THE WHITE PAPER

By 1939, public opinion in the United States—to the extent that it expressed itself on matters related to Palestine—was generally sympathetic to Zionism. In keeping with this, American periodical coverage during the years of the Arab rebellion tended to endorse Zionist contentions.[3] Pro-Zionist articles frequently expounded upon the legal and historic rights of the Jews to Palestine, as well as on the immediate need for a refuge capable of receiving large numbers of persecuted European Jews.

It was not surprising, therefore, that news of Britain's intention to call a conference for the purpose of establishing its future policy toward the mandate provoked alarm in the United States. Although the lead in raising the issue was taken by American Jews, many non-Jews were induced to condemn the idea of restricting the development of Jewish Palestine.

The first major reaction against the approaching alteration of British policy came shortly before the opening of the London Conference at a United Palestine Appeal (UPA) meeting in Washington, D.C. Heavy stress was given during the UPA conference to the need of upholding Jewish rights in Palestine. The assembled delegates, numbering more than 1,500 Jewish spokesmen from all parts of the United States, called upon the mandatory to double the previous year's quota for Jewish immigration. Political observers described the meeting as designed to impress the British government with the readiness of American Jews to combat all limitations on the national home in Palestine.[4]

The UPA conference was given added importance by the two key speakers who addressed the delegates: David Ben Gurion and Robert H. Jackson, then solicitor general of the United States. Ben Gurion warned that the negotiations in London would be crucial, and he endeavored to link the Arabs to European Fascism—and particularly to Hitler, whom he termed "the big Mufti who sits in Berlin." Jackson praised Zionist colonization efforts and argued that only Palestine could receive a large influx of European Jews.[5] Although he spoke in a private capacity, Jackson's reputation as a rapidly rising member of the Roosevelt administration—within a year he would become attorney general, and by 1942 would be appointed to the Supreme Court—helped give importance to his remarks.

By the end of February 1939 the London Conference had very nearly run its course. With the conference deadlocked, British negotiators offered proposals that closely approximated the points eventually embodied in the White Paper. This produced a burst of public indignation by Zionists and their supporters in the United States. The mood of the times was captured by Dr. Solomon Goldman, president of the Zionist Organization of America, who accused London of "sinking into a bog of violence." The American Jewish Congress charged the British government with betraying the Jewish people. The patriarch of American Zionism, recently retired Supreme Court Justice Louis D. Brandeis, called for resolute resistance to the new British policy.[6] In early March, Zionist spokesmen announced that 20 senators and congressmen, 10 state governors, and various mayors and city councils across the nation had joined in requesting Roosevelt to prevent Britain from "abrogating" its responsibilities in Palestine. Supporting stands were promptly taken by groups of clergymen, labor leaders, and other dignitaries.[7]

It was against this background of public agitation that Zionists pressed their campaign for Roosevelt's intercession. Although the leading Zionist figure in the United States, Rabbi Stephen S. Wise, enjoyed an acquaintanceship with Roosevelt dating back to 1914, the approaches made to the president at this juncture were channeled through pro-Zionists whose positions in government afforded access to the White House.

Several such persons existed within the upper echelons of the administration. While not all of them were actively involved in the effort to convince Roosevelt to try his hand at preventing the White Paper, their presence was counted as an asset by the Zionists. It is probably best to mention something of these people at this point, since each of them tried at one time or another to influence the president on behalf of Zionism.

A man who enjoyed both a close relationship with Roosevelt and links with the leaders of the Zionist Movement was Secretary of the Treasury Henry Morgenthau, Jr. The president's long-time friend was not himself a Zionist; however, he was deeply worried over the need to establish havens capable of receiving Jews fleeing Europe.[8] After the outbreak of World War

II, Morgenthau's humanitarian inclinations made him progressively more sympathetic to Zionism. During the war he occasionally served as an intermediary between Roosevelt and the Zionist leadership. After resigning from the government in 1947, he became chairman of the United Jewish Appeal.[9]

The most outspoken supporter of Zionism within Roosevelt's cabinet was Secretary of the Interior Harold L. Ickes. Ickes, who drew pleasure from the sobriquet "Old Curmudgeon," had long been an active advocate of "a viable Jewish homeland in Palestine."[10] Less than six weeks before the start of the London Conference, he delivered a speech to the Cleveland Zionist Society expressing hope that the United States would extend "moral and material support" to help harried European Jews settle in Palestine.[11] Noted for strong opinions, the interior secretary lived up to this reputation when it came to Zionism. In answer to an explanation of the Arab view on Palestine sent to him by the Arab-American leader George M. Barakat, Ickes characterized the Arab position as "narrow, paralyzing nationalism" and suggested it would be better if Arabs "reclaimed their own desert areas, instead of wasting their energies bewailing the fact that the Zionists are doing so."[12] Although it is not known whether, or to what extent, Ickes discussed the London Conference of 1939 with Roosevelt, the president was undoubtedly aware of the secretary's uncompromising pro-Zionism.

Perhaps the man Roosevelt admired most among his pro-Zionist intimates was Felix Frankfurter. Having first met as young attorneys prior to World War I, Roosevelt and Frankfurter developed a mutual esteem that marked their relationship until Roosevelt's death in 1945. After Roosevelt's first election to the presidency in 1932, Frankfurter unofficially assumed the role of trusted White House advisor.[13]

As a leading figure in the American Zionist Movement during World War I, Frankfurter represented the Zionist Organization of America at the Paris Peace Conference in 1919. Although an internal difference of opinion that gripped the Zionist Organization in the early 1920s caused Frankfurter to sever his official connection with that body, his faith in Zionism did not abate. He remained on intimate terms with prominent Zionist leaders and occasionally assumed Zionist assignments.[14]

With his relationship to Roosevelt on a first-name basis, it was natural that Frankfurter would discuss Zionism with the president. Roosevelt admitted to being thoroughly impressed by his friend's intellectual capacity, and it seems likely that he enjoyed receiving Frankfurter's comments on Palestine.

Frankfurter's appointment to the Supreme Court in January 1939 lessened neither his interest in Zionism nor his intimacy with Roosevelt. His preoccupation with the possibility that Britain might reduce its commitment to Zionism is evident from a letter he sent to President Roosevelt near the end of November 1938. On that occasion Frankfurter argued that the Chamberlain government's duty was to utilize Palestine as the "obvious first line of relief" for the persecuted Jews of Germany.[15] In the following months, his fears over British intentions confirmed by the London Conference, Frankfurter remained in close contact with Chaim Weizmann and David Ben Gurion. Soon after the release of the White Paper, he visited Roosevelt to convey the disappointment felt by these Zionist leaders. It is not known whether Frankfurther also acted as an intermediary between Zionists and the White House during the three-month interval between the opening of the London Conference and the issuance of the White Paper. Given the informality and frequency of his contact with the president, it would have been natural for him to do so.[16]

Frankfurter's close relations with the president and leading figures of the Zionist Movement enabled him to play a role that, with the exception of that fulfilled by his own protégé, Benjamin V. Cohen, was unmatched in its "constant influence in the highest reaches of the Roosevelt Administration in pleading the cause of Zionism."[17]

Like Frankfurter, Cohen had long been a proponent of Zionism. In 1919 he also attended the Paris Peace Conference, serving as legal counsel to the American Zionist delegation. When the 1939 London Conference opened, Cohen was in a position to bring the Zionist point of view before the president. Writing to David Ben Gurion in the spring of 1939, the president of the Zionist Organization of America, Solomon Goldman, described Cohen as "our friend who is closest to Roosevelt." However, Goldman doubted whether Cohen was "capable of making vigorous demands" on the president. In Goldman's view, the only person meeting this necessary requirement was Louis D. Brandeis.[18]

When the Arab-British-Zionist talks opened in London in early 1939, Louis Brandeis was 82 years old and serving his 23rd year as a Supreme Court Justice. His years on the bench gave him a degree of prestige that commanded attention not only in the nation's capital but throughout the country as well. Having been actively involved in the Zionist Movement as early as 1913, Brandeis was the recognized leader of American Zionism by the beginning of World War I, a role he continued to fill for some years after his appointment to the Supreme Court in 1916. In 1921, following a disagreement with Chaim Weizmann over the proper method of colonizing Palestine, Brandeis withdrew from the leadership of Zionism in the United States. However, he preserved an interest in Zionist affairs and occasionally participated in some of the major steps that marked the growth of the movement in North America.

The London Conference brought Brandeis once more to the front ranks of American Zionism. Upon resigning from the Supreme Court in mid-February 1939, he turned to the task of preventing a change of British policy in Palestine. Keeping closely in touch with Weizmann and Ben Gurion, Brandeis spearheaded the campaign to induce Roosevelt's intervention against the White Paper.

On March 15 the Arab and Jewish delegations to the London Conference received Britain's plan for Palestine. The proposal looked to the eventual establishment of an independent state in which both communities would share authority, although in the absence of Arab agreement to the contrary, Jews would be relegated to permanent minority status. However, independence was to come only after an interval of at least ten years. Even then, the British plan provided for an open-ended continuation of the mandate should Arabs and Jews be unable to agree on a final political arrangement. More importantly, until a political settlement was attained, Jewish immigration and land purchases would be severely restricted.[19]

Zionists reacted to this expected British demarche by abandoning the conference and renewing their appeals for American intervention. Brandeis was immediately urged to lay the matter before the White House. Writing to Roosevelt on March 16, the aged jurist outlined the British scheme and, after pointing out that London would soon publicly announce its new policy, asked the president to intercede.[20] A few days later, Brandeis received the following reply:

> All I have been able to do so far has been to postpone any British announcement until next week. I am trying to put it off still further. Apparently the British are very much worried by German and Italian incursions into the whole Mohammedan area.[21]

In light of what had transpired between Washington and London, Roosevelt's note was clearly designed to exaggerate his own efforts on behalf of Zionists. Actually, the only initiative taken by the American government in response to the Zionist request occurred on March 19, when Roosevelt had Undersecretary of State Sumner Welles ask the American ambassador in London, Joseph P. Kennedy, to suggest "informally" that in view of the critical situation developing in Europe, "a short delay" in publicizing the Palestine plan might be advantageous.[22] Following interviews with the British foreign and colonial secretaries, Kennedy reported London's willingness to postpone announcing its new Palestine policy.[23] The implication in Roosevelt's note to Brandeis that the president had sought more than a brief delay of the British announcement was patently misleading. Since there is no record of subsequent American approaches to the British over this matter, it appears the same was true of the president's statement about "trying to put it off still further."

To what, then, can be attributed the fact that two months lapsed before the British government released the White Paper revealing its new policy toward the mandate? One factor was precisely the deteriorating international political climate in Europe referred to by Welles in his cable to Kennedy.[24] On March 15, the very day the British officially broached their final proposals at the London Conference, German troops occupied Bohemia and Moravia. Within three weeks, Italy invaded Albania.

Another, and more immediately relevant, factor was very likely the turn taken in British-Arab relations at the end of the discussions in London. Although the London Conference officially ended on March 17, with the Arabs also rejecting Britain's Palestine plan, it was followed by a continuing dialogue between the British government and the Arab states. In April, representatives of the Palestinian Arabs, the Arab states, and the Moslems of India met in Cairo where they hammered out an unofficial set of counterproposals regarding Palestine for discussion with the British.[25] This Arab initiative, despite its eventual failure, appeared to raise the possibility of an Arab-British agreement on Palestine's political future.[26]

Nonetheless, Roosevelt seized the opportunity to reinforce the Zionists' impression that he was exerting himself on their behalf. In early April, David Ben Gurion, who had returned to Palestine from the abortive London Conference, received a letter from Solomon Goldman recounting a meeting with Roosevelt that had left American Zionist leaders "brimming with optimism." According to Goldman, the president explained to his Zionist visitors that the British government was justifying its intended shift on Palestine by claiming that German and Italian propaganda was penetrating the entire Arab and Moslem world. Roosevelt added that he "understood the British were exaggerating, although there was a slight element of truth in what they said." What most encouraged the Zionists was Roosevelt's claim that he was in "daily contact" with Ambassador Kennedy and had instructed him "to demand that the British Government plan should not be published." Finally, the president promised he would continue to "press for" a postponement of the British announcement. Understandably enough, Goldman and his colleagues left the White House feeling they had "found a far better friend than expected."[27]

Zionists quickly attempted to follow up their apparent initial success. Apprised of the continued Arab-British talks and of the intra-Moslem discussions in Cairo, Zionist leaders became fearful that a bilateral agreement over Palestine might be reached by Britain and the Arabs. In mid-April these fears were discussed in a cable sent by Jewish Agency leaders in London to the headquarters of the American Zionist Organization. The message urged that efforts be undertaken "to secure once more White House assistance to avert [a] hasty and premature decision."[28] Brandeis again served as the intermediary through which this appeal was transmitted to the president. Forwarding a copy of the Jewish Agency cable to Roosevelt, he included a personal note imploring the president to exercise his "wise counsel" to prevent unfavorable action by the British government.[29] Apparently, Roosevelt did not reply to the message.

Almost simultaneously with Brandeis' latest approach, Zionist leaders were laying final touches on a political strategy by which they hoped to deter the British from making fundamental changes in the administration of the mandate. In the words of David Ben Gurion, the new approach was based on a decision to offer armed opposition to any restrictions in Palestine "and so compel the Government to use force against us, for then Britain could no longer rely on bayonets alone."[30] Derivatives of this core decision included plans for ensuring "greater Jewish power and capacity" in Palestine by increasing Jewish populations in key points throughout the country, establishing "civilian industries of military value," continuing immigration and settlement regardless of any limits the mandatory might try to impose, and nonparticipation by the Yishuv in all institutions designed to pave the way for Palestinian independence under conditions unacceptable to Zionists.

This strategy of confrontation was essentially political. Haganah, the armed force of the Yishuv, could not hope to wrest Palestine from Britain through open combat. Moreover, in the spring of 1939 the Haganah suffered to such an extent from lack of leadership, training, and equipment that it was considered by Zionist leaders to be virtually useless.[31]

On the other hand, Zionists knew that a threat to force Britain into armed repression of Palestinian Jewry might be politically advantageous. If credible, it would increase any doubts held by the Chamberlain government over its new approach to the mandate. Zionists could hope that the British government would balk at embarking on a policy likely to cause it the embarrassment, both at home and abroad, and particularly in the eyes of the United States, of using troops to suppress Jewish settlers. Then, too, the same strategic considerations that had led the British to think in terms of the White Paper might be made to work in favor of the Zionists. With the Arab community now demoralized and devoid of leadership after nearly three years of bloody fighting, Zionists hoped to convince London that stability in Palestine could best be obtained by not arousing the wrath of the country's Jewish population. Weizmann launched the confrontation policy by warning London that its plan for Palestine could be implemented only by "using force against the Jews."[32]

The specter of Jewish resistance was also used to encourage Roosevelt to take up the Zionist cause. Following his warning to the British prime minister, Weizmann sent a more vigorous cable to Brandeis asking him to discuss the issue with Roosevelt.[33] Strangely, Roosevelt's files contain no mention of such an effort by Brandeis. In view of the justice's faithful cooperation with the Zionist leadership during this period, it is possible that Brandeis conveyed the message orally. In any case, it is certain that the president was informed of the possibility of armed clashes between the British and Jewish settlers in Palestine.[34]

The month of April passed with no indication of further effort by the White House to influence the Chamberlain government. Zionists were dismayed by reliable information indicating that only days remained before London would announce restrictions on the Jewish national home.[35] On May 4, Brandeis once more served as the Zionists' avenue to the White House, writing a final and hurried personal request to Roosevelt for renewed action to gain postponement of the threatened announcement.[36] A few days later, Chaim Weizmann cabled an emotional appeal for presidential action in order to avert "catastrophe" in Palestine.[37]

Despite these pleas, Roosevelt did not reopen the issue with Britain. On May 17 the White Paper was issued in London. Although the Jewish Agency executive released a statement implying that Palestinian Jewry would take up arms to defeat the White Paper policy, the threat lacked credibility. The nature of the brewing European crisis left Jews little choice but to support Britain in its struggle against Germany.

THE PERSPECTIVE OF CONGRESS ON PALESTINE

Contrasting the U.S. Congress with what he argues was a fundamentally anti-Zionist State Department, Frank E. Manuel notes that "the Department of State and Congress, of course, never thought alike on Palestinian affairs under any administration because they moved in different orbits."[38] J. C. Hurewitz's comment on congressional attitudes toward Palestine defines the orbit that bounded the congressional perspective: "Congress was sensitized to American public opinion."[39]

The pro-Zionist tenor of articulate public opinion in the United States was reflected by congressional reaction to the British White Paper. Just before the collapse of the London Conference, the Palestine issue was brought before the Senate by Arizona's Henry Ashurst, who in an earlier telegram to Secretary of State Cordell Hull had urged the president and the State Department to impress upon Great Britain that "catastrophe" would result were the Balfour Declaration violated.[40]

A far stronger expression of senatorial interest in Palestine occurred when a joint statement representing the views of 28 senators was inserted into the *Congressional Record*. As the considered opinion of nearly one-third of the Senate, the statement merits some attention. It first called upon the British government to abandon any intention of liquidating the mandate in Palestine "based upon the Balfour Declaration," and then, ignoring the fact that the Jewish community in Palestine constituted only one-third of the country's population, deplored the possibility that a change in British policy might result in "a new state dominated by a narrow [non-Jewish] majority."[41] The statement gave prominence to both the Balfour Declaration and the 1924 Anglo-American Convention on Palestine as binding commitments precluding the British government from reducing its support for the Zionist colonization of Palestine. There was no indication that the 28 senators perceived any ambiguity in the terms of the Balfour Declaration or that they were cognizant of President Roosevelt's 1938 statement to the effect that the

Anglo-American Convention did not empower the United States to prevent alterations in the Palestine mandate.

Publication of the White Paper on May 17 brought forth similarly dogmatic statements, all of which were pro-Zionist, in both the House and Senate. Senator William King of Utah argued that the Balfour Declaration and the Anglo-American Convention rendered the White Paper illegal. He also discussed Arab hostility to Zionism. Informing his listeners that he had previously visited Palestine "for the purpose of investigating economic, political and other conditions," King stated that his "rather careful examination" showed that Zionism "materially advanced the cause of the Arabs." Noting that the "claim is made by some that the Arabs in Palestine have opposed Jewish immigration," he countered by asserting that "the Arabs in Palestine have greatly benefitted by the advent of the Jews and . . . thousands of them have found employment with the Jews." He acknowledged, however, "that a limited number of Arabs belonging to terrorist organizations have, by assassination and intimidation, endeavored to prevent the development of Jewish enterprises," but assured his audience that "these terrorist gangs were not *bona fide* residents of Palestine."[42]

In the House, Representatives Everett Dirksen and Ralph Church voiced indignation over the White Paper in terms admitting neither the ambiguity of the Balfour Declaration nor the existence of a delicate political problem in Palestine.[43] Representative Bender drew applause when he labeled the White Paper "a surrender to [Arab] force and violence," and called upon the American government "to demand" that London rescind its new policy.[44] Before the end of May, 15 members of the House Committee on Foreign Affairs jointly denounced the White Paper as a violation of the Balfour Declaration and urged the State Department to inform the British that the implementation of the White Paper policy would be considered a breach of the 1924 Anglo-American Convention.[45]

The *Congressional Record* reveals that all statements made in Congress against the White Paper between January 1 and May 25, 1939, shared the following characteristics:

1. The implication that the Balfour Declaration was an unambiguous and easily understandable British commitment to support Zionist aims in Palestine.

2. Expressions of support for continued Jewish immigration into Palestine because of the need of a haven for persecuted Jews.

3. The implication that the British government could not legally impose restrictions on Jewish immigration into Palestine or on Jewish land purchases in that country without the explicit consent of the United States.

4. The implication that the phrase "Jewish national home" signified an easily identifiable condition in Palestine.

5. An implicit discounting of Arab opposition to Zionism, either by explaining it away (as did Senator King) as baseless, minimal and perverse, or by not mentioning it at all.

It is interesting to note that none of the remarks made in Congress against the White Paper in the first half of 1939 included any reference to possible American participation in the administration of the Palestine mandate as a means of ensuring the success of Zionism. Nor did any refer to the possibility of providing a haven in the United States for Jewish refugees should they be blocked from entering Palestine because of the White Paper. Congressional sympathy for Zionism stopped short of a willingness to assume active responsibility in Palestine; congressional humanitarianism did not include a willingness to open American borders to the persecuted.

Nonetheless, Zionists were gratified by the response of Congress. However they also saw a need for further work among members of that body. David Ben Gurion later recalled the lesson.

[We had] many devoted friends in Congress. It was a pity though that most of them were uninformed and knew nothing about Palestine, or about the promises of the British and the achievements of the Jews.[46]

Reporting to Ben Gurion in April 1939, Solomon Goldman revealed even more clearly the casual, but enthusiastic, acceptance of Zionist claims that characterized Congress:

Most of the Senators have given us declarations which are astoundingly sympathetic to the National Home. It can be said that in every sector of Washington we find sympathy for our cause. But we must instruct them all in Zionism, for it is a closed book to them.[47]

Throughout the years 1939–48, the dominant congressional attitude toward Palestine was not essentially derived from either the substance or the course of the Arab-Zionist struggle. While the overwhelming majority of the members of both houses habitually exhibited a marked lack of concern over the precise nature of Palestine's political future, the same lawmakers tended to utilize popularly acceptable phrases such as the "Jewish national home" and "a free and democratic Jewish Commonwealth" when speaking on behalf of Zionism. The measure of their actual disinterest in the political disposition of Palestine is found partly in their evident lack of curiosity over what such concepts implied for a system of government in Palestine. It is also partly found in an almost total absence of inquiry into the sources of Arab opposition to Zionism.

In short, a characteristic feature of the congressional approach was that it was not based upon consideration of the issues at stake within Palestine itself. Nor was it based to any great extent upon consideration of international repercussions occasioned by the Arab-Zionist quarrel. Instead, the reference point for congressional action tended to be domestic public opinion. As the American Zionist Movement developed into a well-organized and efficient political pressure group after 1939, Congress became visibly more responsive to Zionist arguments.

However, it was not solely the pressure of organized pro-Zionist public opinion that produced congressional enthusiasm for Palestine's establishment as a Jewish national home. Congress also responded to another, less positive, sort of public opinion: the widespread reluctance to permit increased immigration into the United States.[48] For example, in 1938–39 less than 9 percent of Americans polled by Elmo Roper agreed with the idea of opening the doors of the United States to greater numbers of refugees than were admitted under restrictive quotas established by Congress in 1924.[49] In the ensuing years, statements on Palestine by American legislators abounded with references to that country as the "only" spot in the world capable of receiving large numbers of Jewish immigrants. On occasion, congressmen referred in even more specific terms to the difficulties of considering immigration into the United States as a means of helping alleviate the plight of Jewish refugees. In 1944 Senator Owen Brewster cited these difficulties as a compelling reason for supporting Zionism:

> From the standpoint of those who feel strongly that the United States has reached the point of saturation and that any further immigration must be very severely restricted there should be the heartiest support for the idea of a Jewish National Home in Palestine as a haven for persecuted peoples from other countries.[50]

Michigan Congressman George Sadowski justified his support of Zionism at the height of World War II in words that were perhaps more tactful, but that conveyed the same message:

> When this war is concluded the hundreds of thousands of Jews, perhaps millions, will seek new homes in a world which will be inhospitable to immigration. There will be no other opportunities for mass immigration anywhere else in the world. They will have no place to go, except Palestine. Trickles of immigration may be permitted to this country or that, but waves of immigration will be fiercely resisted. Of course, we all hope and pray that it may be otherwise, and that the nations of the world will open their doors to refugees; but these things did not happen after the last war, and speaking realistically, they may not happen after this war.[51]

In 1944, Representative Clare Boothe Luce considered the possibility of relieving the plight of Jewish refugees by expanding opportunities for immigration into the United States rather than opening Palestine to unrestricted Jewish immigration. Her conclusion was: "This would require a revision of our own immigration laws, which I do not need to tell you is a political impossibility at this time."[52]

More eloquent than the comments, or the silence, of members of Congress on the subject of refugee immigration into the United States was the treatment they eventually accorded to calls for a postwar emergency liberalization of immigration laws. Not until 1948, one month after the creation of Israel, was such legislation passed. Even then, the highly limited measure openly discriminated against Jewish and Catholic refugees.

THE PERSPECTIVE OF THE
DEPARTMENT OF STATE ON PALESTINE

Manuel's metaphorical distinction between the State Department and Congress is correct. The two did move in different "orbits." While Congress tended to view the Palestine problem in terms of its domestic significance, the State Department considered the issue in light of its international implications.

Shortly before the start of the 1939 London Conference, the prevailing State Department outlook on Palestine was captured by the chief of the Division of Near Eastern Affairs, Wallace Murray, in a memorandum to Secretary Hull and Undersecretary Welles:

> It is altogether desirable that the United States Government refrain from injecting itself in any way into the London discussions and wait until a solution has been reached, or, failing such a solution, until the British Government announces its own plan of procedure.[53]

Aware of the likelihood of Zionist appeals for official American support during the Conference, Murray urged that the United States "refrain from pressing the British." In support of this advice he cited "scores" of reports from diplomats and consular officers warning of an unfavorable Arab reaction should the United States appear to uphold Zionism. Similar information, he pointed out, had also been received from American educators and oilmen in the Middle East. However, the main argument adduced by Murray on behalf of the "hands off" policy he advocated was Palestine's strategic importance in the event of war in Europe:

> From a strategic point of view, Palestine is absolutely essential to the safety of the British Empire. . . . It is apparent that the British cannot arrive at a

decision [on the future of Palestine] which would make lasting enemies of the Arab states bordering Palestine.

This reasoning was accepted by higher officers of the department. When Roosevelt partially acceded to Zionist requests by having Ambassador Kennedy informally suggest to the British government a delay in publication of the White Paper, the State Department was not pleased. Two weeks before Roosevelt rendered that limited service to the Zionists, Kennedy cabled the department to ask whether he was to make any specific representations to the British on the Palestine question. Perhaps aware that Roosevelt might opt for intervention, Secretary Hull sent the ambassador a guarded reply that fell short of giving real direction. His answer, however, clearly indicated his own preference:

> I may say in strict confidence that I feel we should be cautious about being drawn by the British into any of their preliminary proposals in advance of any final plan which they may decide upon for a solution.[54]

Zionist attempts to obtain Roosevelt's help were opposed by Undersecretary of State Welles on grounds that the deteriorating political situation in Europe made it inexpedient for the United States to challenge the British government. Personally sympathetic to Zionist aspirations, Welles no doubt arrived at this conclusion reluctantly.[55]

It was not only the international situation in the spring of 1939 that caused Secretary of State Hull to frown on Zionist requests for support. Until his resignation in the fall of 1944, Hull maintained a rigid and narrow outlook on the legitimate scope of U.S. interest in Palestine:

> Our relations to Palestine rested on the American-British Mandate Treaty of December 3, 1924, whereby the United States had recognized Britain's mandate. . . . This provided for nondiscriminatory treatment in matters of commerce; nonimpairment of vested American property rights; permission for Americans to establish and maintain educational, philanthropic, and religious institutions in Palestine; safeguards with respect to the judiciary; and, in general, equality of treatment with all other foreign nationals. We had no right to prevent the modification of the mandate, but we could refuse to recognize the validity of any modification as it affected American interests.[56]

Notwithstanding Hull's legalistic frame of reference, advice given to the president by the State Department after 1939 on matters pertaining to Palestine tended to be based on international political considerations rather than on restrictive interpretations of American rights and obligations under the 1924 agreement with Britain. This was only to be expected. Long before Hull left office, events showed that neither the State Department nor the White House could avoid the Palestine issue by citing the Anglo-American Convention. As the Zionist Movement consolidated its strength in the United States, and as the American government began to perceive important economic and strategic interests in the Arab world, Washington came under increasing pressure to define its attitude toward Palestine's future. It became progressively difficult for Washington to avoid the Palestine question by parroting the conception of American interests that had been formulated 20 years earlier.

However, it is notable that between 1939 and 1948 the State Department's concern with Palestine was not directly over the question of whether Arabs or Jews would eventually rule that country. Rather, the department was preoccupied with possible harmful effects that the basic Arab-Zionist political struggle might have on American interests lying outside Palestine. Thus, in the spring of 1939, the main problem raised by Palestine for the State Department was that the Arab-Zionist controversy might benefit the Axis powers by undermining Britain's security in the Middle East. In later years the department focused on the effects of the Palestine issue on U.S. relations with the countries of the Arab Middle East as well as with non-Middle Eastern states, American oil interests in the Middle East, and the overall strategic position of the United States in world politics.

In consequence, the various steps the department urged in relation to Palestine were rarely designed, or advocated, primarily as means of affecting the fundamental contest between Arabs and Zionists. In part, this reflected the legacy of the traditional premise that Palestine was a British responsibility. However, it was also due to the lack of direction given by the White House. In the absence of definite indication from the president as to what sort of political solution in Palestine was required by American interests, the State Department was incapable of suggesting a purposeful course of action.

This problem did not escape notice by State Department officials, particularly those in the Division of Near Eastern Affairs (after 1944, the Office of Near Eastern and African Affairs). Yet the White House was generally unmoved by the occasional warnings those men gave over the dangers of reacting to Palestine without a set of objectives or principles by which policy might be guided.

There was widespread recognition among the department's Near East officers that the United States would benefit if Arabs and Jews could resolve their rivalry through some orderly political settlement. In 1939 Wallace Murray found this reason to praise the British government's new turn of policy toward Palestine:

> It is in the highest degree significant that the hitherto insoluble problem of the British in reconciling the purposes of the Mandate to secure the establishment of a Jewish National Home and to develop self-governing institu-

tions is now shifted to Jewish and Arab shoulders. This has been brought about by conditioning the regulation of Jewish immigration after four year [sic] upon Arab consent and the establishment of an independent Palestine upon Jewish consent.[57]

At a later date, when for a short time Roosevelt appeared interested in the subject, members of the Near Eastern division were able to devote more attention to possible arrangements upon which a Jewish-Arab compromise might be based. Although the Division found this subject worthy of sustained consideration, its enthusiasm was never matched by the White House or at the upper levels of the State Department.

Relations between Zionists and the State Department remained tense throughout the period 1939–48. Initially, at least, this was partly due to the Zionists' desire to enlist the United States as an active ally, an ambition at odds with the established State Department view of legitimate American concern with Palestine. Another factor contributing to poor relations was the Zionists' use of organized public support on behalf of their requests to the American government. The State Department tended to deplore this practice because it injected domestic political calculations into the sphere of foreign policy formulation, a realm that department officials preferred to see dominated by the quiet contemplation of diplomatic realities. Shortly after the 1939 White Paper was issued, Assistant Secretary of State Adolf A. Berle complained to Roosevelt that "the active Zionists are high-pressuring the Congressmen asking us to make representations to Great Britain."[58]

In the summer of 1944, as national elections drew near, Hull asked both Republican and Democratic party leaders to "refrain from making statements on Palestine during the campaign that might tend to arouse the Arabs or upset the precarious balance of forces in Palestine itself."[59] In late 1947, Undersecretary of State Robert Lovett complained to Secretary of Defense James V. Forrestal that he "had never in life been subjected to as much pressure" as that exerted upon him by American Zionists during the UN General Assembly's consideration of the Palestine problem.[60]

Friction between Zionists and the State Department, however, did not arise simply because the Zionist Movement in the United States was a mass-based political pressure group dedicated to influencing American foreign policy. Having the responsibility of evaluating Zionist requests for support in light of their implications for the international position of the United States, department officials were necessarily involved in the value-laden task of recommending the priorities to be followed in the conduct of foreign policy. Both during and after World War II, the department granted higher priority to relations with allies, enemies and potential enemies, and the oil producing countries of the Middle East, each of which it concluded would be harmed by American sponsorship of Zionist political ambitions. In general, then, the State Department opposed the extension of official American support for Jewish statehood in Palestine on the grounds that such a step would be harmful to national interests. This was the root of the strained relations between Zionists and department officials.

On the other hand, it is not true that the department simply denied the existence of Jewish interests in Palestine. Significantly, the few attempts made in the department to devise a constitutional program that Washington might advance as a solution to the Palestine problem were predicated on a specific rejection of any arrangement whereby the Jewish community of Palestine would be politically dominated by the Arab majority. Indeed, department officials hoped to strike upon a formula that would guarantee a large measure of political autonomy to the Jewish community in any eventual settlement.

Zionists tended to ascribe their difficulties with the State Department to lower officials, particularly to those dealing with Near Eastern affairs. Chaim Weizmann noted that the Zionists' "difficulties were not connected with the first rank statesmen. . . . It was always behind the scenes, and on the lower levels, that we encountered an obvious, devious and secretive opposition which set at naught the public declarations of American statesmen."[61]

This view persisted throughout the Zionists' campaign for a Jewish state. Other Zionist commentators elaborated on Weizmann's observations by implying, or charging outright, that the Near East Division was so dedicated to the destruction of Zionist hopes that it ignored, and even sabotaged, specific White House directives that it considered pro-Zionist.[62] In the eyes of many Zionists and their supporters, members of the Near East Division were largely guided by pro-Arab or pro-British biases, or simply by anti-Semitic inclinations.[63]

It is impossible, of course, to determine the extent to which such prejudices may have motivated each of the individuals associated with Near Eastern affairs between 1939 and 1948. However, the analyses submitted by the division to higher levels of the department consistently evaluated the question of American support for Zionism in terms of repercussions that might affect the international interests of the United States as contemporaneously defined by higher levels of the government. Although it may be assumed that their extensive professional involvement with the Arab world left members of the division with some degree of sympathy for the aspirations of the people of that area, emotionalism appears to have played little role in the division's advice on the Palestine issue. In support of its repeated admonitions against American sponsorship of Zionist political aims in Palestine, the division counted heavily upon reports from American diplomatic agents in the Middle East. These consistently warned that a pro-Zionist course would undermine American interests in the region.

Charges that the division actively intrigued against policies set by the White House also appear to be unfounded. State Department files covering the ten-year period prior to the establishment of Israel fail to lend credence to that contention. However, it is true that in the relatively close-knit organizational environment that characterized the department during the war years, the Near East Division enjoyed a high degree of influence that, with the support of the secretary of state, may have at times extended into the White House.[64] Perhaps this caused those who headed the division prior to Israel's creation to be cast prominently in the Zionist demonology. Both Wallace Murray, who effectively controlled the Division of Near Eastern Affairs between 1929 and 1945, and Loy Henderson, who supervised its work after 1945, were the objects of such intense wrath that Zionists and their supporters repeatedly demanded sanctions against them.[65]

Henderson assumed his post after having served during the war as American minister to Iraq, although he was actually a specialist in East European politics. Despite the heavy criticism leveled at him by Zionists during his involvement with the Palestine problem, more balanced analyses of that period have attempted to rehabilitate Henderson's image. A subordinate in the Division of Near Eastern Affairs has described Henderson as "completely objective and fair in his attitude toward the Palestine question and sincerely interested in finding a solution."[66]

Murray was considered by Zionists to be even more hostile than Henderson. This belief gained currency as a result of Murray's demeanor during encounters with Zionist spokesmen. Convinced that most American Jews were not pro-Zionist, Murray's manner toward Zionists "sometimes suggested that he regarded them as intruders on an otherwise placid, or relatively placid, Near Eastern scene."[67] Yet convincing evidence indicates that he approached the Palestine problem in the hope that some solution might be found that would entail a minimum of disruption to the Middle East as a whole. Contrary to the impression held by most Zionists, Murray was not inveterately opposed to the prospect of a Jewish state in Palestine.[68] Under Murray, as under Henderson, those who daily conducted the department's policies toward the Middle East voiced little concern over whether Arab or Jew would ultimately rule Palestine—so long as the process of resolving that issue did not adversely affect recognized American interests outside Palestine.

THE PERSPECTIVE OF THE
PRESIDENCY ON PALESTINE

Standing at the summit of the American foreign policy-making process, Franklin Roosevelt became the focal point for the conflicting views, advice, and pressures from which the American government's reaction to the White Paper was distilled. As president, it was Roosevelt's responsibility to determine a course of action while listening to the contradictory suggestions that emanated, on the one hand, from Congress and many of his closest advisors, and, on the other, from the Department of State. In many ways the president's approach to the limited question of the White Paper presaged that which the White House would follow during the next decade.

The White Paper controversy placed Roosevelt in a decidedly uncomfortable position. Aware of the strategic calculations underlying Britain's desire to revise its Palestine policy, the president nonetheless appears to have been personally receptive to arguments advanced by his pro-Zionist intimates. Yet he did not agree with congressional calls for strenuous pressure upon the British. Nor did he accept the State Department's view that strict detachment was in order.

Roosevelt's actions in regard to the White Paper were not fully in accord with any of the advice he received. Even the tentative overtures he made to the British government through Ambassador Kennedy were contrary to the desires of the State Department. Had their real nature been known, they would have been even more displeasing to those favoring American intercession on behalf of the Zionists. The care taken by Roosevelt to give Zionists an exaggerated impression of his efforts on their behalf may be assumed to have been prompted to some extent by a desire to appear in tune with a well-publicized and popular cause. Yet the president does not appear to have been engaging in a completely cynical display of dissimulation in his relations with American Zionists. The truth of the matter seems to be that in the spring of 1939 he had not decided how to react to the White Paper.

For example, one week before the new British policy was announced in London, Roosevelt's uncertainty caused him to write to Hull and Welles: "I still believe that any announcement about Palestine at this time by the British Government is a mistake and I think we should tell them that."[69] However, the State Department's concern with Britain's strategic security in the Middle East was sufficient to make him drop any plans to urge Britain once more to refrain from publishing the White Paper.

On the other hand, the president was not fully convinced by the department's arguments. In early May, Undersecretary Welles suggested telling Zionist leaders that Washington would not intercede with the British government. He also urged that the reasons for the decision be made explicit. Welles suggested that Roosevelt include the following in a note to Brandeis:

> The situation of the British Government at this moment is so critical . . . it would be unwise . . . at this juncture to press upon that government a request which in their judgement undoubtedly would involve an issue affecting questions of national defense.[70]

Only a day before raising the possibility of a new approach to London, Roosevelt flatly rejected Welles' advice. The president answered Brandeis' anxious final inquiries about American intervention against the White Paper by simply expressing his desire "again to assure you that everything possible is being done."[71] While in fact nothing was being done, Roosevelt was still debating the issue in his own mind.

Eight days later, with Washington adhering to its studied silence on Palestine, the White Paper was released. On the same day Roosevelt unburdened himself to Hull in a lengthy memorandum. Describing his own reaction as one of "dismay," he argued that the Chamberlain government was not "wholly correct" in maintaining that the framers of the Palestine mandate "could not have intended that Palestine should be converted into a Jewish state against the will of the Arab population of the country":

> My recollection is that this way of putting it is deceptive for the reason that while the Palestine Mandate undoubtedly did not intend to take away the right of citizenship and of taking part in the Government on the part of the Arab population, it nevertheless did intend to convert Palestine into a Jewish Home which might very possibly become preponderantly Jewish within a comparatively short time. Certainly that was the impression given to the whole world at the time of the Mandate. . . . Frankly I do not see how the British Government reads into the original Mandate . . . any policy that would limit Jewish immigration. . . .
>
> My snap judgement is that the British plan for administration [as embodied in the White Paper] can well be the basis of an administration to be set up and to carry on during the next five years; that during the next five years the 75,000 additional Jews should be allowed to go to Palestine to settle; and at the end of five years the whole problem could be resurveyed and at that time either continued on a temporary basis for another five years or permanently settled if that is then possible. I believe that the Arabs could be brought to accept this because it seems clear that 75,000 additional immigrants can be successfully settled on the land and because also Arab immigration into Palestine since 1920 has vastly exceeded the total Jewish immigration during this whole period.[72]

The president's comment on Arab immigration into Palestine was, of course, erroneous.[73] However, the real significance of the memorandum lay not in what it showed to be Roosevelt's deficient factual grasp of the Palestine controversy, but in what it revealed as the sources of his ambivalence toward the White Paper. It is obvious that in 1939 the president was personally convinced that a "correct" administration of the Palestine mandate would lead eventually to a Jewish state. The conflict between this belief and Roosevelt's awareness of the immediate importance of British strategic requirements gave rise to the uncomfortable indecision he exhibited toward the White Paper. In the end, Roosevelt resolved the dilemma in favor of immediate necessity. Still, as his message to Hull made clear, the president considered the White Paper to be an interim measure that was to be laid aside in favor of a permanent solution once circumstances permitted.

Roosevelt's response to the White Paper demonstrated his instinctive understanding that any policy purposefully directed toward the Palestine problem had to proceed from a conception of the sort of political future to be sought for Palestine. In reacting to the White Paper, he consciously opted for a policy of expediency, but he did so in the belief that this was adequate only as a temporary measure.

In the years leading to his death in 1945, the president continued to respond to the Palestine problem primarily on the basis of immediate pressures. Because of this, no policy dealing directly with the substance of Arab-Zionist tensions was developed during his administration. However, once the exigencies of the war against the Axis abated, Roosevelt gave ample evidence of recognizing that the fundamental problem facing him in Palestine was to clarify the American view of that country's optimum political disposition. His sudden demise makes it impossible to know what he might have decided. It is interesting that by the closing months of the war he seemed to have modified the views he expressed on the day the White Paper was issued.

Roosevelt's successor also responded to the Palestine problem mainly on the basis of immediate considerations; but there is little to indicate that Harry Truman realized that a purposeful policy had to be linked to a conception of Palestine's future.

Thus, between 1939 and 1948 the involvement of the United States in Palestine proceeded without clear direction. While Congress advocated policy on the basis of one set of values and the State Department answered with contrary recommendations based on an opposing set of values, it remained for the White House to define national priorities. Roosevelt perceived this and consciously deferred an answer. Truman either failed to recognize, or was incapable of answering, the question.

3. ZIONIST MOBILIZATION IN THE UNITED STATES

The 1939 White Paper destroyed the foundation of Zionist cooperation with the British government. With London now committed to a restrictive policy toward the Jewish national home, Zionists could no longer hope to build a Jewish majority in Palestine through gradual immigration.

In this altered context, the center of Zionist attention shifted to the United States. Zionist leaders calculated that Washington's support would offer the best chance of having the White Paper withdrawn, or, failing that, of attaining their ends in Palestine despite British recalcitrance. They also correctly believed that the United States would emerge as the dominant international power in the postwar world.[1]

However, Zionists were forced to question the strategy they had pursued in attempting to bring the U.S. government to prevent publication of the White Paper. Direct appeals to the president, even though advanced through influential intermediaries, had produced little more than token responses. Were Zionists to succeed in the more difficult task of enlisting Washington's aid in overturning the White Paper, they would clearly have to build a strong base of support beyond the confines of the Oval Office. Moshe Shertok, head of the Jewish Agency's political department, succinctly defined the issue when he pointed out that before the White Paper was issued, Zionists had relied "on somebody's personal acquaintance with Roosevelt or some other political figure." In Shertok's view, the problem with American Zionists was that they "never. . . got as far as the application of strong public pressure . . . by using means which count in modern politics."[2] In the wake of the White Paper, Zionists decided to secure official support by obtaining firm commitments from key elements of the American political system, including both houses of Congress and the major political parties. But first it would be necessary to strengthen their own organization in the United States and to enhance the support they received from the American public.

38

A major factor in these considerations was the American Jewish population. By 1939 nearly 5 million Jews lived in the United States. Enjoying a
relatively high degree of affluence and education, this group could be expected to act forcefully on behalf of a cause to which it was committed.[3]
Then, too, the sensitivity of national officials to Jewish public opinion was
assured by the concentration of American Jewry in politically significant
states.[4]

The spirit of self-examination that swept Zionist ranks as a result of the
White Paper showed that full use of this potential political force had not
been made. The Zionist Organization of America (ZOA) pointed out the following:

> There are 4,500,000 American Jews. Only a small number are affiliated
> with the Zionist Movement. Only a few hundred thousand give their sup-
> port to the Palestine Fund. Only a handful appreciate the significance of
> Zionism, are raised in self-confidence and faith through Zionist ideals.
> Only a handful are able to see how closely knit together all of Jewish effort
> is with the building of the Homeland. This American field it is our duty to
> win for Zionism. The fate of the Homeland depends upon the measure of
> support—moral, and financial—given by the Jews of America in the next
> few years.[5]

The dissatisfaction of the ZOA was shared by the leaders of the Jewish
Agency for Palestine. On a visit to the United States in early 1940, Chaim
Weizmann encountered a distinctly "uncomfortable" situation.[6] American
Jews, including committed Zionists, were not alive to the crisis facing world
Jewry and the Zionist Movement. Weizmann found the spirit of isolationism
so strong that "America was, so to speak, violently neutral."[7] At Zionist
meetings he discovered it necessary to speak "with the utmost caution, seeking to call the attention of my fellow Jews to the doom hanging over European Jewry and yet avoiding anything that might be interpreted as
[warmongering] propaganda."[8]

David Ben Gurion has recounted a discussion in the spring of 1940 with
Moshe Shertok and Eliahu Golomb. Ben Gurion, who was about to visit the
United States, was given a stark assessment of the Zionist Movement in
North America. Basing himself on the assumption that Washington would
have "a decisive influence at the end of the war," Shertok described the prob-
lem in these terms:

> There are millions of active and well-organized Jews in America, and their
> position in life enables them to be most dynamic and influential. They live
> in the nerve centers of the country, and hold important positions in poli-
> tics, trade, journalism, the theater, and the radio. They could influence
> public opinion, but their strength is not felt, since it is not harnessed and
> directed at the right target. . . .

> There are many elements within the American [Jewish] community that demand cooperation and guidance. The various bodies can be united in one broad framework, and their activity directed to the good of our work in Palestine. Only if such an active Jewish body is created, which knows what it wants, and directs its efforts toward Palestine—only then will we be able to test whether the American Government can be induced to support us.[9]

Golomb, then the head of Haganah, doubted whether American Jewry was willing to fight for Zionism. However, he also felt that grounds for optimism existed:

> This does not mean that American Jewry is devoid of Zionist feelings. On the contrary, Zionist feelings are much stronger among them than it would appear from the condition of the Zionist Organization of America. A force can be crystallized from among American Jews for political action and practical aid for our cause. But so far it does not actually exist—it is only a potential force. To bring it into being much work needs to be done.

The "major question," he said, was whether "the Jews of America will *want* to throw their political weight into the balance, whether they will have the courage to link the interests of World Jewry and of Zionism with their political weight in America."[10]

Ben Gurion agreed with these analyses, although he was confident that Zionism could count on the support of American Jews. He maintained that the numerical weakness of avowedly Zionist groups should not be overemphasized, and that consideration be given instead to the possibility of arousing the "latent energies" of unorganized American Jewry and gaining the support of important non-Zionist American Jewish organizations.[11]

Zionists were to discover that the task was time consuming. Not until late 1943 could the Zionist leadership claim to be backed by the bulk of American Jewry. In the meantime, Zionists not only won support from the American Jewish community but also from a significant section of non-Jewish opinion. In the former case, it was shown that Ben Gurion, by placing his hopes largely in the officially non-Zionist elements within the Jewish community, had a deep understanding of the nature of Zionism and non-Zionism, and of the relationship between them, in an American context.

ZIONISM AND NON-ZIONISM
IN THE UNITED STATES

Any discussion of modern Zionism must take into account the impossibility of providing an all-embracing definition of the movement that has commonly gone by that name. As conceived by Theodor Herzl, Zionism was the postulation of a political solution to the problem of anti-Semitism: a Jewish state. Although Palestine loomed large in Herzl's thoughts, it was secondary to the establishment of a Jewish state. Thus he also gave serious attention to other territories, such as Uganda, Cyprus, and the Sinai Peninsula, in which a Jewish polity might arise. But if Herzl eventually did not pursue these ideas as he did that of Palestine, it was precisely because his own strictly political outlook had to find common ground with the Jewish masses, particularly with those in the oppressive atmosphere of Eastern Europe. Only Palestine could provide this. Zionism, therefore, was quickly and firmly linked to Palestine. However, in terms of its adherents and the objectives they hoped to realize, Zionism was a pluralistic movement.

Solomon Schecter, president of the Jewish Theological Seminary, once spoke of Zionism in these words:

an ideal and as such indefinable. . . . [Zionism] is . . . subject to various interpretations and susceptive to different aspects. It may appear to one as the rebirth of national Jewish consciousness, to another as a religious revival, whilst to a third it may present itself as a path leading to the goal of Jewish culture; and to a fourth it may take the form of the last and only solution to the Jewish problem.[12]

While the Zionist Movement embraced a multitude of social and political philosophies, its unifying emphasis was on the objective of gaining for the Jewish people "those attributes which characterize a modern nation."[13] To Herzl and subsequent Zionist leaders, this meant nothing less than sovereignty, an end toward which they consistently worked.[14] The ultimate triumph of the movement was largely a result of the willingness of Herzl and his successors to exercise patience and to refrain from dogmatic insistence on their final objective. In no case was this ability of more value than in obtaining support for the Zionist Movement in the United States.

The initial reception accorded to Zionism by American Jewry at the turn of the century was inauspicious. More established elements of the American Jewish community, consisting mainly of Jews of German extraction whose forebears arrived in the United States in the mid-1800s, rejected Zionism as a nationalistic threat to their own political and social emancipation and to their incorporation into American democracy.[15] Newly arrived Jews from Eastern Europe were too busy establishing themselves in their adopted country to provide much support. In 1914 less than 15,000 persons formed the membership of the entire American Zionist Movement.[16] In 1930, despite a certain degree of acceptability given to the movement by the Balfour Declaration, the combined membership of American Zionist organizations still totalled only slightly over 80,000. Since there were overlapping memberships among these organizations, the number of individuals represented by this figure was even less.[17]

Philanthropic interest in Palestinian Jewry increased during World War I. Following the creation of the Palestine mandate, Zionists sought to capitalize on the proven generosity of American Jews. Chaim Weizmann proposed to enlarge the Jewish Agency for Palestine in order to include non-Zionists on an equal basis with Zionists. Weizmann showed his eagerness to cooperate with the American Jewish community by offering its representatives 40 percent of the non-Zionist seats on the Agency Council.[18] Eventually, American non-Zionist leaders were convinced that participation in the Jewish Agency would enable them to work on behalf of Palestine's Jews without assuming any commitment to Zionism's political program. In 1929 the Jewish Agency was enlarged along the lines suggested by Weizmann.

The political requirements of Zionists' relations with American non-Zionists jelled nicely with the demands of their relations with Great Britain and the Arabs to produce the policy of "gradualism," the effort to build up Palestine's Jewish community without voicing the ultimate aim of political control. In the decade before the promulgation of the White Paper, Zionists deliberately downplayed the final objective of Jewish colonization in Palestine.

In 1929 Louis Marshall, president of the American Jewish Committee and the man most responsible for leading non-Zionists into the Jewish Agency, gave his reasons for supporting collaboration with Zionists over Palestine. Marshall's own organization, essentially the organ of the older element in the American Jewish community drawn from German stock, had long been firmly opposed to the idea of a Jewish state. Said Marshall:

> I am not a Zionist. I am, however, concerned with the rehabilitation of Palestine, and I regard it as the duty of every Jew to aid in that cause. Political Zionism is a thing of the past. There is nobody in the [World] Zionist Organization who has the slightest idea of doing anything more than to build up the Holy Land and to give those who desire a home there the opportunity they cherish.[19]

The non-Zionist approach, although accepting and welcoming the mandate's provision for Jewish immigration and the establishment of a national home for the Jewish people, assumed that Palestine's political future would not be the state advocated by Herzl. The well-known American Zionist leader, Emanuel Neumann, subsequently described this vague outlook:

> the National Home, interpreted as a "spiritual center," seemed a nobler and loftier conception, and one that offered practical advantages. A "spiritual center" required little space, no majority and no political sovereignty.[20]

This concept offered no way of determining the relationship between the Jewish national home and Palestine's political development. Despite non-Zionists' pretensions to the contrary, the logic of their support of the undefined national home, and of the interpretative argument that the mandate required Britain to promote Jewish immigration into Palestine without regard for the wishes of the country's Arab population, placed them very near to the full Zionist program. Moreover, whatever reservations non-Zionists retained with regard to statehood, their involvement in the immediate task of upbuilding Palestine had the significant effect of muting any serious anti-Zionist expression in the United States between 1929 and the outbreak of World War II.[21]

Viewed against the backdrop of the rising communal passions that scarred Palestine in the 1920s and 1930s, non-Zionists' failure to consider the political implications of the national home is hard to understand. Yet when the Arab rebellion of 1936 brought forth a British proposal to partition Palestine into Arab and Jewish states, non-Zionists were sincerely dismayed—though hard pressed to explain why. The American Jewish Committee (AJC), for example, reacted to the British offer by announcing its opposition to Jewish statehood in any part of Palestine on the basis of "a host of emotional, economic, social, cultural, and political reasons." The AJC then tried to explain its ten-year tenure on the Jewish Agency:

> If you ask why [non-Zionists] entered the Jewish Agency, they answer that when they entered the Agency they did not expect that within their lifetime the Jewish state would be a problem for consideration . . . now that a Jewish state is actually proposed . . . they suddenly find themselves forced to face a problem they did not envisage.[22]

The rapid demise of the 1937 partition proposal allowed the non-Zionist position to remain quietly nebulous. However, it soon became evident that non-Zionists had not abandoned their support of the Jewish national home or of the notion that the mandatory had no right to limit Jewish immigration into Palestine on any grounds but economic capacity. Impelled by the need for a refuge for European Jewry, American non-Zionists denounced the 1939 White Paper as bitterly as did Zionists.[23]

The type of Zionism that developed in the United States during the interwar period, and the nature of its relationship to non-Zionism, helped create the milieu in which Zionists endeavored to organize the American Jewish community for political action during World War II. The expansion of the Jewish Agency in 1929 demonstrated that the distinction between American Zionists and non-Zionists was limited to an intellectual plane that involved few practical differences. Although by 1940 the membership of American Zionist organizations had grown considerably, only small numbers of American Jews had emigrated to Palestine.[24] American Zionists were clearly not prepared to accept the elements of Zionist theory that implied gloomy futures fo. all Jews in predominantly Gentile societies.

The outbreak of World War II, and subsequent revelations of Hitler's campaign to exterminate European Jewry, intensified the desire of American Jews to help their coreligionists. Ideological distinctions over the question of Jewish statehood were "swept out of court" by the specter of genocide. In the United States, as elsewhere, this produced a rising demand for "Jewish Unity for Jewish Action."[25]

Before the war's end, Zionists transformed the common sentiments that linked them with American non-Zionists into organizational ties that created a pro-Zionist political pressure group of significant promise. Although only some 200,000 American Jews were officially enrolled as Zionists by 1943, the political power available to the Zionist leadership was considerably greater than this figure might indicate.

ZIONIST ORGANIZING: THE AMERICAN JEWISH COMMUNITY

Meeting in late August 1939, the Twenty-first World Zionist Congress focused its attention on the United States. The conclave established an Emergency Committee for Zionist Affairs, which was to be based in the United States and charged with mobilizing American Jews behind the Zionist banner. In the spring of 1940, Nahum Goldmann, chairman of the World Zionist Congress and a member of the Jewish Agency Executive, arrived in the United States to direct the committee's operations.[26] Although Goldmann had long accepted Weizmann's "gradualist" policies, he was now inclined toward the views of David Ben Gurion, who far more than Weizmann had been convinced by the White Paper that a new era of "fighting Zionism" had dawned.[27] Dissatisfaction with Weizmann's preference for calm negotiation with the British government was already evident among his coleaders in the Jewish Agency and the Palestinian Yishuv. It was feared that Weizmann's approach would neither sway Britain away from the White Paper nor propel American Jews into energetic political activity. Eliahu Golomb expressed these feelings when he offered the following interpretation of Weizmann's philosophy:

> Justice is bound to emerge victorious, and so things can't be too terrible;
> for the time being we must register our protest [against the White Paper]
> and that is the only political action that can now be taken.[28]

Golomb saw no hope in this outlook. His experiences in the United States convinced him that the American Jewish public, and perhaps non-Jews as well, would "be won over either by *successful* Zionism or by *militant* Zionism."[29]

Goldmann shared this view when he assumed leadership of the Zionist Emergency Committee. His first task was to win over existing American Zionist organizations to the idea of a more militant strategy.[30] However, this could not be done immediately. Relations among the constituent groups on the committee were hampered by factional and personal frictions and by poor leadership.[31] The Emergency Committee initially amounted to no more than "an interparty body for receiving reports and for deciding on matters of common interest."[32] Only after many months did the committee develop an organizational capacity that permitted it to turn seriously to the job of influencing American public opinion.

American Zionism was, then, a somewhat disjointed but growing and robust movement in 1942, when the major Zionist groupings in the United States first moved toward truer coordination by affirming in ringing tones their unity in the fundamental Zionist demand: a Jewish state in an undivided Palestine. The forum for the declaration was New York's Biltmore Hotel, where between May 6 and 11 an Extraordinary Zionist Conference was held.

The attendance of David Ben Gurion, Chaim Weizmann, and Nahum Goldmann lent the conference the character of a World Zionist Congress. The climax of the meeting came when the delegates, moved by calls for a return to Herzlian Zionism, passed a series of resolutions that gained fame as the "Biltmore Program." The eighth paragraph of the program, after urging that the Jewish Agency be vested with control of immigration into Palestine, demanded the establishment of that country as a "Jewish Commonwealth."

Ironically, Chaim Weizmann's presence underscored the ascendancy in Zionist ranks of those who favored more combative tactics. In his address, the elderly Zionist leader proclaimed himself as desirous of a Jewish state as any of his listeners, but he went on to argue that passage of a resolution demanding Palestine's independence on Zionist terms would be premature.[33] The rejection of this counsel showed that the bulk of American Zionists favored the more militant approach advocated by Ben Gurion.

In fact, the Biltmore Program was based on a memorandum prepared some months earlier by Ben Gurion with the aid of Felix Frankfurter and Benjamin Cohen.[34] The resolutions adopted at the Biltmore Hotel in 1942 stamped American Zionism at last with the mark of an "enthusiastic, dynamic nationalism."[35] In later years American Zionists and their supporters would retain their distinction as the most uncompromising advocates of Jewish statehood.

Having rallied behind the Biltmore Program, Zionists focused more directly on obtaining effective support from American non-Zionists. Throughout 1941 and 1942, Zionists endeavored to reach a common position with non-Zionists. Particular emphasis was given to negotiations with leaders of the influential American Jewish Committee. These contacts eventually led to an agreement by the non-Zionists to support Jewish nationalist aims in Palestine—provided that Zionists renounced all practices and beliefs stemming from the idea of Jewish "universal nationalism": the concept that Jews in every country were part of the same scattered race and had equal need of a Jewish state.[36] However, a reaction by AJC members who considered this position excessively conciliatory forced an end to the negotiations.

Failure to reach an accord with the American Jewish Committee caused Zionists to revise their plans for enlisting the aid of American Jews. The new strategy sought to avoid the opposition of established non-Zionist leaders by appealing to grassroots Jewish sentiment. Weizmann and Goldmann, together with such Zionist leaders as Stephen Wise and Louis Lipsky, conceived the notion of convening a democratically elected conference to speak on behalf of all American Jews.[37]

The Jewish community elections preparatory to the conference—in which the American Jewish Committee refused to participate after alleging the existence of irregularities—resulted in an overwhelming Zionist victory. Of 379 locally chosen delegates, 240 were members of the Zionist Organization of America or other Zionist groups. When the conference opened in late August 1943, a system of bloc representation permitted formal Zionist organizations and their allies to control four-fifths of the votes.[38]

It was hardly surprising that the conference overwhelmingly endorsed the Biltmore Program. The militant attitude of the delegates was fanned by the oratory of Rabbi Abba Hillel Silver, who consistently favored aggressive tactics. The determined mood of the conference was also shown by the adoption of the strong stand on Palestine despite warnings from dissidents that Washington would disapprove of any immediate attempt to raise maximal Zionist demands.[39] Whatever Washington's misgivings may have been, Zionists could credibly claim in the wake of the conference that their plan for Palestine was actively supported by the great majority of American Jews.

The Emergency Committee for Zionist Affairs was reorganized shortly after the American Jewish Conference ended. At Chaim Weizmann's request, Abba Hillel Silver and Stephen Wise became cochairmen of the newly structured body, whose name was changed to the American Zionist Emergency Council (AZEC). The group now included not only representatives from the four major American Zionist organizations (Zionist Organization of America, Hadassah, Mizrachi, and Paole Zion) but also observers from smaller ones. AZEC promptly expanded its ties to the American Jewish community. More than 400 local "Zionist Emergency Committees" were established to carry the Zionist message into every major community. AZEC's emphasis on publicity was evident: Of the 14 professionally staffed committees set up as part of its general reorganization, eight were devoted to public relations.[40] Other significant changes included an enlarged budget (reaching to over $500,000), and the opening of an AZEC branch in Washington.

By the end of 1943, Zionists completed the preparatory work undertaken in the United States at the outset of the war. Having attracted the majority of American Jews to the support of Jewish statehood, Zionists prepared to influence the American public and American government in favor of their political program. Once able to devote full attention to this task, Zionists benefited from an organized and vocal group of non-Jewish supporters that had been created early in 1941.

ZIONIST ORGANIZING:
THE NON-JEWISH COMMUNITY

Since the days of Herzl, the proponents of a Jewish state never underestimated the value of non-Jewish support. Under the direct supervision of the Zionist Emergency Committee's Emanuel Neumann, steps were taken in 1941 to expand, and to organize as an effective political tool, the existing reservoir of American non-Jewish sympathizers. At the end of April of that year, Neumann's efforts produced the American Palestine Committee (APC), an organization of prominent pro-Zionist Gentiles.[41] A few months later Neumann helped organize another group known as the Christian Council on Palestine. The latter organization especially attracted numerous protestant clergymen.[42] In 1948 the two groups merged into a new body known as the American Christian Palestine Committee.

In terms of influence and membership, the American Palestine Committee was the more important of Neumann's projects. The APC's origins and activities provide an example of the techniques used by Zionists to muster politically useful support.

The man chosen by the Zionist leadership to head the new committee was Senator Robert F. Wagner, a New York Democrat with a reputation for liberalism and a sympathetic interest in Jewish problems. Although Wagner represented the state with the largest concentration of Jewish voters in the country, his pro-Zionism did not stem primarily from the demands of his constituents. Instead, it was a sincere manifestation of his personal values.

Nonetheless, Wagner was sensitive to the political importance of Zionist sentiment. In late 1938, for example, he sought an interview with Roosevelt in order to convey a Zionist request for presidential support. Whether by way of avoiding Roosevelt's anger should his intercession be considered an annoyance, or whether he was expressing his real feelings at the time, Wagner gave the impression that his initiative was little more than a necessary political move. A memorandum prepared by a White House secretary when the senator telephoned to make the appointment shows that Wagner offered the following explanation:

> I don't know what the President can do [about the Palestine problem] but, politically, it is pretty important to me.

What we would like is an app[ointment] . . . in H[yde] P[ark]. . . .

I don't know what can be done . . . but politically—with this tremendous Jewish population—it is important that I do that much. . . .

I know that [the President] won't like this but we all have to do things to help ourselves and I really am concerned about the terrible time [the Jews] are having.[43]

Wagner was first asked to organize the American Palestine Committee by Rabbi Wise in late January 1941. After conferring with Emanuel Neumann, he acceded to the request.[44] The senator moved quickly. In less than a week he persuaded 26 members of the Senate, including the majority and minority leaders, to join.[45] From the constant stream of correspondence between the Zionist Emergency Committee in New York and Wagner's Washington office, it is evident that Emanuel Neumann was the moving force behind these efforts. Ever alert, Neumann even sent instructions to the senator's secretary on such details as possible intermediaries who might convince Vice-President Henry Wallace to become honorary APC chairman.[46]

Although Wagner failed to enlist the vice-president, he did bring many prominent non-Jewish Americans from all walks of life into the pro-Zionist Committee. When the APC was formally constituted on April 30, 1941, its roster listed a host of illustrious personalities, among whom were Secretary of the Interior Ickes, the newly appointed Attorney General Robert Jackson, 68 senators, 200 congressmen, and several state governors.[47] Many of these individuals attended the APC's inaugural banquet in Washington, at which Chaim Weizmann delivered the main address.[48]

Following its much-publicized inception, the APC developed rapidly. Emissaries were dispatched across the country to organize local chapters. Eventually, more than 75 groups were created. After 1943 the APC benefited from funds set aside by AZEC for work among non-Jews.[49] This expansion was accompanied by an increase in the tempo of the committee's activities. Within one year, Neumann could state that the APC had "become a force to be reckoned with," and had "kept the cause of the Jewish Homeland before the American public and in the forum of international discussion." Among the accomplishments that Neumann listed to support his appraisal were: the doubling of the committee's membership to "800 distinguished and representative citizens from all parts of the country," the establishment of several local APC chapters, public addresses on behalf of Zionism by "scores of members of the committee," and the dissemination of pamphlets, memoranda, press reprints, and other material "in tens of thousands of copies."[50]

Neumann's reference to the committee's role in keeping the pro-Zionist viewpoint in the "forum of international discussion" alluded to the fact that pro-Zionist statements made by some of the internationally known APC members were sometimes reported in both the American and foreign press.

However, by 1945 the APC was consciously promoting Zionism internationally by establishing links with other national "Palestine Committees."[51] These contacts led to an International Christian Conference for Palestine, held in Washington near the end of 1945. The Conference established a World Palestine Committee (WPC), which was to coordinate the activities of the various national Palestine Committees, plan for greater expression of Christian pro-Zionism, publicize the plight of European Jews, and generally promote support for a Jewish state in Palestine.[52] Although the new body possessed an impressive and cosmopolitan Executive Committee, upon which Wagner served as vice-chairman, its headquarters remained in Washington. The managing officer of the American Palestine Committee, Howard LeSourd, assumed the same function in the World Palestine Committee.

Actually, the WPC was directed by the ranking Zionist leaders in the United States. A glimpse into the internal workings of the organization is afforded by the minutes of one of the first meetings of its Executive Committee.[53] Of the seven WPC officers theoretically in charge, only the two who served as staff at the Washington headquarters attended. Also present, however, were the following Zionist leaders, all officers of the Jewish Agency: Eliezer Kaplan[54], Gottlieb Hammer[55], Mayer Weisgal[56], Eliahu Epstein[57], and Moshe "Toff" (Tov).[58]

The interest shown by Zionist leaders in extending the APC's activities to an international level was merely an aspect of their involvement in all facets of the committee's life. During its first two-and-a-half years of operation, the APC's headquarters were in the New York offices of the Zionist Emergency Committee. Wagner, as chairman of the Palestine Committee, occasionally had information concerning the group's activities sent to him in Washington.[59] Official APC correspondence was often drafted in the Zionist offices and sent to Wagner for his signature.[60] Occasionally telegrams were composed in New York and sent over the senator's signature, Wagner or his secretary being advised after the fact.[61] Mail addressed to Wagner in his capacity as head of the APC was opened in New York and kept in the Zionist offices, copies being forwarded to Wagner. This procedure was followed even when communications addressed to the senator originated in the White House or the State Department.[62]

Major APC functions, such as the widely publicized Annual Dinners, were planned in detail by the Zionist Emergency Committee or its constituent members.[63] The physical separation between the APC and the Emergency Committee that occurred when the latter moved to another New York address did not lessen the Zionists' guiding role in Wagner's committee.[64]

Such was Wagner's identification with the Zionist position on Palestine that on at least one occasion, and quite possibly on another as well, he allowed an article to be prepared by AZEC officials for publication under his name.[65] Despite his position on the Senate Foreign Relations Committee, the senator made little effort to understand the dimensions of the smoldering confrontation between Arabs and Jews in Palestine. This point is brought out forcefully by a comment scrawled across a letter Wagner received from a group of Arab-Americans attempting to promote the Arab side of the Palestine conflict. Unable to find and file three pamphlets that had been enclosed with the letter, a frustrated secretary added a notation that, in style worthy of Lewis Carroll, captured the spirit that prevailed in Wagner's office when it came to Palestine: "Not Here. (Don't tell me somebody read them!)"[66]

It is impossible to judge the precise influence of the American Palestine Committee. As a public relations tool, it helped sensitize Americans to the tragic situation confronting European Jews and to Zionist aspirations for the establishment of a Jewish state. By attracting large numbers of senators, congressmen, and state and local officials to its ranks, the committee helped foster the impression among the unknowing both at home and abroad that American foreign policy was committed to the support of Zionist political ambitions in Palestine. The same impression was furthered by various endorsements, no matter how innocuous their wording, secured by the APC at various times from high public officials, including the president.

Despite Wagner's early assurance to Roosevelt that the APC had "the simple and sole objective of expressing the sympathy and good-will of the American people for the movement to re-establish the Jewish National Home in Palestine," the American Palestine Committee was organized primarily to generate pro-Zionist public opinion.[67] Although other vehicles for the expression of American Christian support of Zionism also existed prior to 1948, Wagner's committee remained the preeminent symbol of pro-Zionist sentiment among the non-Jewish American public.

PALESTINE IN
THE AMERICAN FORUM

By the end of 1943 the consolidation of American Jewry behind the Zionist program, together with the rapid development of the American Palestine Committee, enabled Zionist leaders to call forth massive and well-coordinated manifestations of support on a national scale. The principal methods of articulating favorable public feeling were rallies and mail campaigns directed at government leaders.

The centralized leadership of the American Zionist Emergency Council after 1943 allowed Zionists to make full use of these instruments through careful orchestration. From AZEC offices in New York, local Zionist Emergency Committees throughout the country received the following instructions in the proper use of public demonstrations:

They must be a united nationwide effort, carefully planned and organized, utilized at some decisive moment. . . . It is not difficult to imagine the cumulative effect of a hundred or more mass meetings held simultaneously on one day throughout the United States in all major communities and extensively reported in the press. It cannot for a moment be doubted that such a demonstration would have a highly significant meaning in Washington.[68]

The instructions were quickly put into effect. On the twenty-sixth anniversary of the Balfour Declaration (November 1943), 15,000 persons were turned away from an overflowing Zionist meeting in Carnegie Hall, while tens of thousands more attended pro-Zionist rallies in over 100 communities across the nation. One of the largest rallies in the United States was held in 1945 when more than 200,000 persons gathered in New York's Madison Square Garden.[69]

Mail campaigns were equally well organized. Rank-and-file sympathizers were provided with prepared messages to be sent to Washington officials.[70] The files of prominent political figures of the period offer ample evidence that Zionist leaders were capable of bringing down veritable torrents of mail upon the nation's capital.[71]

In 1951 a study of pro-Zionist mail sent to the White House was undertaken by Andie Knutson at the request of Truman's aide, Philleo T. Nash. Although the study was restricted to items that arrived between 1946 and 1951, Knutson's findings reflect trends established much earlier. Knutson's breakdown of incoming mail on the basis of "State of Origin," for example, establishes that Jewish individuals and organizations were responsible for the greater part of the messages. His investigation also revealed that mail campaigns reflected the strategic approach followed by Zionists in their overtures to the American government: that of making limited, but in terms of the future of Palestine progressively more significant, requests for specific actions by Washington.

The demands or requests from the interest groups were usually focused toward achieving some specific and immediate objective: the immediate immigration of Jews into Palestine, specific conditions in Palestine, the arms embargo [of 1947–48], Jewish representation in the United Nations, the recognition of Israel. . . .

The long-range goal—the establishing of [a] national Jewish Homeland—was usually not the direct subject of the telegram, although it was often mentioned along with the request for action. Specific reference to the long-range goal increased as this goal was approached.

Each specific decision or action [by the Government] in accord with a demand constituted a positive, almost irreversible step toward satisfying the long-range goal. Each administrative delay led to protests. Positive statements or actions were followed by waves of approval and appreciation, but usually these messages of thanks also urged action on the next step toward the goal.[72]

The dissemination of Zionist views through the mass media attained impressive proportions. The American Yiddish press, long supportive of Zionism, was subscribed to by 425,000 families in 1945.[73] By the same year, Zionist organizations were sponsoring 27 English-language publications. These national and local publications regularly reached more than 600,000 families in 1945. To this figure must also be added some 250,000 subscribers to such normally pro-Zionist periodicals as the *Reconstructionist*, the *Jewish Spectator*, the *B'nai B'rith Monthly, Congress Weekly*, and *Opinion*.[74]

The non-Jewish American press was cultivated by Zionists through personal contacts, press conferences, and press releases. In 1945 the Zionist Organization of America (ZOA) reported that 25 percent of 4,000 news columns reprinting ZOA news releases were found in the non-Jewish press.[75] With the sole exception of the New York *Times*, no general American newspaper was accused by the Zionist leadership of indulging in anti-Zionist bias prior to Israel's creation.[76]

The Zionist Movement also directly produced and distributed propaganda material aimed at the general public. In 1944 the ZOA, only one major Zionist group in the United States, distributed over 1 million pamphlets and leaflets to libraries and community leaders. The Zionist Emergency Council was fully or partially responsible for publishing several books, among which were Reuben Fink's *America and Palestine*, Carl Friedrich's *American Policy Towards Palestine*,[77] and Frank Gervasi's *To Whom Palestine*.[78]

Zionism's message was also spread by radio. Throughout the war and postwar years, Zionist and pro-Zionist speakers frequently discussed the need for a Jewish national home in Palestine. Perhaps the largest radio success was "Palestine Speaks," a series of dramatic presentations about Jewish life in Palestine sponsored by the ZOA for nine months in 1943–44. The program, which featured nationally known entertainers, was carried weekly by stations in all but two states.[79]

No comprehensive content analysis of Zionist propaganda in the United States prior to Israel's establishment has been made. However, Inis Claude's examination of addresses by Zionist leaders indicates ten consistent themes running through their presentations:

1. Zionism is a mark of Jewish honor, and the sensitive Jew will help Palestine.

2. Jewish successes in Palestine provide an inspiration for all men, and they bolster Jewish self-respect.

3. The Jews form one people. What happens to Jews in one land has consequences for Jewish status in other countries. American Jews must help European Jewish refugees.

4. Zionism offers an opportunity for socially useful and pleasant activity.

5. Since Zionism aims at Jewish self-determination, it is a positive way of solving the Jewish problem. Zionism is better than philanthropy. Jews have to rely upon themselves and not upon charity. Palestine is the only country in the world where Jews are wanted.

6. Zionism will provide for the perpetuation of Judaism and for the survival of the Jewish people. Palestine will invigorate Jewish life. This will ultimately benefit the entire world.

7. Zionism undermines anti-Semitism by ending Jewish homelessness. Jews can feel more secure because of the sense of peoplehood fostered by Zionism.

8. The Jewish state will arise inevitably. The determination of Palestinian Jewry, Biblical prophecy and pressing humanitarian considerations all lead to Jewish statehood in Palestine.

9. Support for Jewish Palestine is an example of pro-Americanism since Palestine is a bastion against Nazism and the sense of Jewish community forms the stronghold of democracy in the Middle East.

10. The Zionist program is just. Jews are entitled to form a state in Palestine because of the suffering they have undergone throughout history.[80]

Claude's analysis accurately reflects a basic feature of Zionist propaganda prior to 1948: despite the struggle between Arabs and Zionists in Palestine, Zionist spokesmen were generally able to concentrate on the relevance of the national home to Jewish life and to Jewish-Christian relations. Yet, Zionist partisans could not always ignore Arab hostility. A review of relevant literature establishes that when dealing with the opposition of Palestine's Arab majority, Zionists commonly developed one or a combination of the following themes:

1. The Zionist program for Palestine is sanctioned by the international community in formal endorsements of the Balfour Declaration and in the League of Nations Mandate for Palestine. Arab opposition, therefore, flies in the face of the international community.[81]

2. Deeply-rooted Arab opposition does not really exist. Jewish colonization of Palestine has benefited the Arab masses of the country. The Arab peasantry fully realizes and appreciates this. Manifestations of hostility toward Zionism in Palestine are actually due to nefarious schemes hatched by the rich Arab "Effendi" class whose economic and social interests are threatened by the liberal, democratic concepts introduced into Palestine by Zionists.[82]

3. Arab opposition exists, but it cannot be justified. The Jews have never actually relinquished ownership of Palestine. Forced from the country

nearly 2,000 years ago, they retained living ties with the land through remnants of the original community and through pilgrimages by the faithful. The Arabs are only one of a series of invaders of the national homeland, among which can also be counted Egyptians, Romans, Crusaders, and Turks.[83]

4. Arab opposition is the product of Islamic fanaticism. The Arabs are a backward people and the uneducated masses neither take any initiative in political matters nor have strong political feelings. The Islamic leaders of Palestine simply cannot tolerate the presence of another religious group.[84]

5. Arab opposition is fomented by leaders who are Fascists. The Jews of Palestine have fought valiantly beside the Allies in World War II, while the sympathies of the Arabs lay with the Axis. Therefore, Arab opposition can have no weight in the resolution of the Palestine problem.[85]

6. Arab opposition stems from pathological nationalism. The Jews, having suffered immeasurably for two millenia, and particularly in the twentieth century, must have a homeland. Jews ask only that Palestine be theirs. The Arabs, who have vast stretches of land at their disposal, do not really need Palestine.[86]

7. From an Arab perspective, opposition to Zionism is justified. Palestine is the focus of a controversy between two rights. However, the world at large, as a third party, must weigh the two on the basis of equity. In this case the claim of the Jews will be seen to outweigh that of the Arabs.[87]

Despite the fact that between 1939 and 1948 American Zionism was fundamentally directed toward the political goal of obtaining Washington's support for the movement's ambitions in Palestine, the arguments propounded by its spokesmen were never subjected to sustained and widespread public challenge. Consequently, many of the basic political and moral questions raised by the Zionist-Arab confrontation were never the objects of close public scrutiny.

Both opponents and supporters of political Zionism have noted the uncritical acceptance of Zionism that characterized the American mass media in the 1940s.[88] No simple explanation for this can be given. Instances of organized Zionist pressure in reaction to unfavorable press commentary are recorded, but it can hardly be assumed that such tactics would cause the mass media not only to abstain from criticism but also to lend support.

The answer seems to lie in such broader issues as a genuine sympathy for the Jewish people in light of Hitler's anti-Semitic atrocities, and a widespread lack of knowledge of, or interest in, the Arab world and the Palestinian Arabs. The intuitive explanation of one-sided American press commentary offered by Richard Crossman prior to the creation of Israel seems apt. Basing his judgment on the assumption that public opinion tends to accept facts that suit its mood, Crossman concluded that the attitude of the American press was a result of "the intimate relations between the newspaper and its readers. In America there was no strong public demand for the Arab point of view."[89]

To the extent that opinion studies may be considered valid indications of public opinion, it is interesting to observe that in the period between the latter part of World War II and the establishment of Israel, polls indicated the existence of a mixture of humanitarian sympathy for the Jewish people and a large degree of apathy toward the political situation in Palestine. In 1944, opinion studies showed that only one-third of the American public felt it "knew what the Palestine problem was about or felt any connection with it," while nearly three-fourths of the public had "little or no interest" in news of American policy toward Palestine.[90]

At the end of 1945, by which time Washington was more directly involved with the Palestine affair, some 55 percent of the population claimed "to have followed" discussions about letting Jews settle in Palestine. A slightly smaller percentage indicated an awareness of disorders in that country. However, much of this "awareness" consisted merely of "a general notion that a problem existed, not a familiarity with its current specifics." Thus, while 50 percent of Americans in the spring of 1946 "knew of a proposal to admit 100,000 Jewish refugees to Palestine," only 25 percent had heard or read about the report of the Anglo-American Committee of Inquiry, in which that proposal formed an integral part of an intended non-Zionist political settlement in Palestine. However, of those familiar with the proposed admission of 100,000 refugees, 75 percent supported the idea.[91]

This pattern, formed on the one hand by substantial apathy toward the Palestine issue, and on the other, by large-scale support of Zionism among the more conscious segment of the population was a consistent feature of public opinion. Between 1947 and 1949 an average of nearly 56 percent of the public was shown by polls to have no fixed position or opinion on the Palestine question. Of those having firm views, supporters of the Jewish cause were double those of the Arab side.[92]

An insight into the collective American outlook on Palestine is afforded by a State Department survey of public opinion sent to presidential aide Clark Clifford in the last half of 1948. Based on unpublished results of polls conducted in February and June 1948—a period marked by the Palestine problem's bloody climax—the State Department's Division of Public Studies found that "relatively few Americans (24 percent) profess a 'great deal' of interest in the Palestine question; and as many as 39 percent express no opinion as to U.S. policy." Commenting on this, the report concluded that

The fact that 2 out of every 5 Americans gave no opinion as to U.S. policy doubtless reflects not only the complexity and strangeness of the Palestine problem but also the relatively low interest which the general public has taken in the question.[93]

Even more Americans expressed neutrality in their sympathies than the rather high numbers who claimed no interest in U.S. policy toward Palestine. In February 1948, polls indicated that 49 percent of the public favored neither the Arabs nor the Jews. In June, one month after the birth of Israel, this figure rose to 54 percent. At the same time, Americans who sympathized with the Zionist cause consistently outnumbered those upholding the Arab view. In February 1948, some 35 percent of the public supported the Zionists while only 16 percent sympathized with the Arabs. In June these figures had altered respectively to 34 and 12 percent.[94]

The basis of the support given to Zionism was largely emotional and apparently conditioned by the suffering of European Jewry during the Holocaust and the immediate postwar era. Investigations conducted in 1948 found that a majority of pro-Zionists (55 percent) based their feelings upon either the persecution Jews had suffered or the Jews' need of a homeland.[95]

The fate of European Jews under Hitler not only affected those who were already inclined to support Zionism or those who knew little of Zionism and the Middle East; it also touched persons who without being anti-Semitic were more likely to view Zionism as impinging upon Arab rights and American national interests. Virginia Gildersleeve, dean of Columbia University's Barnard College for Women, noted this in a passage that attempts to describe the prevalent American attitude in the early postwar years:

> Surprisingly few Americans knew anything about the background of this tragic situation [in Palestine]. The spotlight of publicity had been focused so brightly by the Zionists on their plan for Palestine that to many of our citizens the rest of the Middle East was shrouded in darkness. Of the few who had any real knowledge of the circumstances, almost no one was willing to speak out publicly against the Zionists. The politicians feared the Jewish vote; others feared the charge of anti-Semitism, and nearly all had a kind of "guilt complex" in their emotions toward the Jews because of the terrible tragedies inflicted on them by Hitler.[96]

Nonetheless, the eventual success of the Zionist Movement in coloring the American approach to Palestine cannot be attributed to an entire absence of overt opposition. Throughout most of the decade 1939–48, organized efforts were made to contest the growth of Zionist influence over the American public and government. The failure of anti-Zionist groups to attract popular support provided grounds for increasing militancy on the part of Zionists and was therefore an indirect factor helping shape the course of American involvement with the Palestine problem.

4. ORGANIZED OPPOSITION TO ZIONISM IN THE UNITED STATES

An examination of the Palestine problem in an American context would be incomplete without some reference to the development of organized efforts to oppose Zionism in the United States between 1939 and 1948. Quite obviously, the story of American anti-Zionists is one of shattered hopes, frustrated enterprises, and ultimate political defeat. The initial expectations held by anti-Zionist leaders were soon deflated by the apathy or outright hostility that greeted their efforts.

It is easy to dismiss anti-Zionists as inconsequential to the development of American policy. Indisputably, they had virtually no influence on decisions made in Washington between 1939 and 1948. Yet this raises questions that cannot be ignored in trying to understand American involvement with the Palestine problem.

The fate of American anti-Zionism takes on importance as a result of the nature of Zionism in the United States, and particularly in light of the latter's development after 1939. For it was after that date that Zionists and their supporters were welded into a virile political pressure group that was avowedly and effectively dedicated to influencing U.S. foreign policy. During the ten years examined here, Zionist demands frequently clashed with traditional and developing conceptions of American interests held in Washington. However, it is striking that no significant domestic political opposition to Zionism unfolded within the United States. Why was this so? Why did groups that did attempt to challenge the rising influence of American Zionism so utterly fail to have an impact?

Answers to these questions do not simply chronicle defeats suffered by American anti-Zionist organizations prior to 1948. The groups themselves, though generally ignored or excoriated, were integral parts of American society. Their futile efforts indirectly reveal many elements that helped form the context in which the United States reacted to the Palestine problem.

Moreover, albeit of admittedly secondary interest, the development of anti-Zionist groups in the United States is itself worthy of attention. Why did particular groups arise? Upon what did they base their anti-Zionism? How, and to what end, did they endeavor to propagate their views? Clarifying these points reveals aspects of the Arab-Zionist struggle for control of Palestine that were personally significant to parts of the American public. In the philosophic, or normative, outlooks of anti-Zionist groups, as well as in their organizational structures and activities, are also found keys to their failure to influence the American approach to Palestine.

Historically, opposition to Zionism existed in the United States since the days of Herzl. In the early twentieth century it was primarily voiced by Jews who were well-integrated into American society and who feared that Jewish nationalism might undermine their position in Gentile eyes. Orthodox Jews, prevented by religious belief from approving any Jewish "return" to Palestine until the Divinity intervened to occasion it, also strongly opposed Zionism.[1] Finally, anti-Semites—those whose inclinations automatically caused them to oppose virtually everything Jewish—were also quick to argue against Zionism. As early as 1921, for example, the anti-Semitic *Dearborn Independent* assailed Zionists' desire for Palestine and ominously warned against permitting Jews to obtain control of that historically strategic land.[2]

However, this chapter will consider only those organizations established in direct reaction to American Zionist agitation after 1939. Each of the groups discussed below opposed the Zionist concept of a Jewish state in Palestine as well as the growing impact of Zionism upon American foreign policy. The following pages attempt to identify more closely the grounds upon which each based its anti-Zionism, how each sought to challenge Zionism, and why the opposition each extended did not have more than a marginal effect upon discussions of both Zionism and Palestine in the United States prior to Israel's establishment.

THE FAILURE OF
ANTI-ZIONISM: 1942–48

The largest and best known anti-Zionist organization in the United States was the American Council for Judaism. It was also distinguished as the anti-Zionist group that had most difficulty in clarifying its aims and deciding upon the means to reach them. In many respects, these problems were products of the grounds of the council's opposition to Zionism.

Tracing its origins to a conference of Reform Jewish rabbis in 1942, the American Council for Judaism (ACJ) argued that Zionist ideology promoted the insularity of American Jews. Denying the existence of national-racial ties among Jews, the ACJ affirmed that Jews were distinguished from non-Jews only by religious conviction. Thus, the ACJ opposed the idea of a

Jewish state in Palestine on grounds that the ideological basis of such a polity would inevitably lead to the alienation of Jews residing in predominantly Gentile societies.

Initially funded by a small group of laymen, the ACJ began to organize in the spring of 1943. Lessing J. Rosenwald, chairman of the board of Sears, Roebuck, became president of the group. Rabbi Elmer Berger was the organization's director and leading theoretician.

The ACJ was launched in a flurry of activity. Within 18 months the new organization embraced 5,300 persons spread across 340 communities. Fully organized ACJ chapters were operating in nine cities. In more than 30 other localities, clusters of council members functioned as temporary "working groups."[3]

Despite their energetic efforts, the ACJ's leaders suffered from an initial failure to clarify the organization's objectives. The basic problem was the council's inability to establish priorities between two major goals that, by 1943, had become mutually exclusive. On the one hand, the organization was determined to defeat the possibility of a Jewish state in Palestine. On the other, it hoped to promote among American Jews a "Positive Program" of "integration" into American society.[4] In effect, this gave the ACJ a discordant ambition to struggle politically against the growth of Zionist influence in the United States while simultaneously attracting Jewish adherents to its "integrationist" philosophy.

Not recognizing that American Zionism appealed to a complex welter of emotions, and had indeed drawn its strength from a reservoir of Jewish ethnic (or communal) consciousness, the council persisted in identifying pro-Zionism as an aberration springing from a darkly pessimistic *Weltanschauung* or grounded in misguided philanthropy. This mistaken impression caused ACJ leaders to aim at creating a Jewish movement that would successfully compete with Zionism for the support of American Jewry. The ACJ's founders initially felt that they would quickly attract sufficient followers to meet, and to best, Zionist political influence in Washington.[5]

The means through which the ACJ sought these objectives developed on two levels. On one, the political, the council utilized a variety of channels— including private interviews with policy makers, congressional forums, and publications—to attack the notion that American Jews were united behind Zionism. The second level consisted of an "educational campaign" directed at American Jewry. Here the ACJ challenged the Zionist concept of a Jewish nation and advanced philosophic and historic arguments to support its contention that "integration" was more in keeping than Zionism with the political position and responsibilities of Jews in Western democratic states.

Both approaches soon encountered difficulties. The "educational campaign" foundered on the inability of the ACJ—despite repeated attempts— to devise a clear "Positive Program" that would make the theory of "integration" applicable to Jewish life. Notwithstanding reams of polemical debate between ACJ spokesmen and Zionists over the "reality" of Jewish identity, the council was never able to draw a sharp distinction between integration and simple assimilation.

On the political level, the ACJ fared little better. Largely, of course, this was a result of its failure to attract a significant membership. In Washington, where "the Jewish vote" was gaining steady importance in matters pertaining to Palestine, the ACJ was unable to compete with the Zionist Movement.

Yet the ACJ's inability to trigger debate over the political implications of the Zionist program stemmed also from its own ambivalence. Determined to oppose Jewish statehood, while remaining equally determined not to alienate the very audience it desired to convert to its "integrationist" outlook, the ACJ lapsed into a confused pattern of temporizing on the Palestine question. Nowhere was this more evident than in its handling of the centrally important issues of Jewish immigration into pre-1948 Palestine and that country's ultimate political status.

The ACJ's approach to immigration was dictated by various factors. In principle, it opposed the 1939 British White Paper's restrictions on immigration and land settlement because of the political distinctions they created between Jews and non-Jews. Moreover, the ACJ could not afford to appear callous or indifferent toward either the Jewish community in Palestine or the need of a refuge for European Jews. However, the council could hardly ignore the importance that Zionists traditionally attached to immigration as a means toward Jewish statehood. The upshot was that the ACJ at times argued that "every Jew who wants to go to Palestine should be allowed to go there within the limitations of the country to support a population," although on other occasions it urged that immigration be determined by Palestine's "economic absorptive capacity and political stability." Then again, it occasionally advanced only Palestine's "absorptive capacity" as the ideal yardstick without specifying whether, or how, economic or political factors should be considered.[6] None of these reflected a definitive ACJ position. Each formula was simply symptomatic of the embarrassment caused to the organization by "a particularly difficult question."[7]

The problem of Palestine's eventual political structure was no easier. Unwilling to espouse the Arab view that Palestine should be an Arab state, and equally unwilling to confront the prospect that any compromise between Arabs and Zionists would almost certainly have entailed the creation of "Jewish" political rights in Palestine—a possibility unwelcome to the ACJ because of its implications of a "Jewish" political status—the council generally retreated into nebulous platitudes when discussing the country's future.[8]

Obviously the ACJ misjudged its chosen constituency. Impelled by the same factors that prompted their support of Zionism, American Jews overwhelmingly rejected the ACJ. Prior to 1948 the peak membership gathered by the council did not exceed some 15,000, a figure falling under 2 percent of the combined rosters of the four major American Zionist organizations.[9]

Although on at least two occasions Berger and his colleagues flirted with the idea of broadening the organization to include Gentiles, the council's Jewish character remained unchanged. Solicitations for membership and offers of financial support from non-Jews were routinely rejected, often with a politely phrased note to the effect that Zionism posed problems "which Jews must solve by themselves."[10]

As was true of so many facets of the council, its relations with Gentiles were often inconsistent. The ACJ did try to attract the interest of non-Jews; yet in view of its tendency to treat the related issues of Zionism, the Arab-Zionist conflict, and American policy toward Palestine as particularly Jewish concerns, it is not surprising that Gentiles frequently reacted to these overtures by firmly refusing to get involved in a "Jewish" difference of opinion.[11]

There was unquestionably an element of contradiction in the ACJ's approach: inasmuch as Berger and his coworkers saw Zionism as incompatible with the liberal, democratic values that made Jews and Gentiles indistinguishable in all save religion in the United States, consistency required that they unreservedly seek and accept active support from all Americans. The policy adopted by the ACJ arose from an inherent conflict in its intellectual underpinnings. While denouncing Jewish nationalists for believing that anti-Semitism was the inevitable concomitant of Jewish minority status, Berger and other ACJ leaders seemed to share the Zionists' unease over the Jewish situation in Gentile society. It is difficult to avoid concluding that the ACJ refrained from involving non-Jews in its fight against Zionism largely because of misgivings over the possibility that in a broadened context anti-Zionism would degenerate into anti-Semitism.

Thus, although the ACJ criticized Zionists and anti-Semites alike for sharing the premise that Jews constituted a people apart "upon one basis or another," it appeared less than sure of its claim that Jews shared only a common faith. For, if in no other respect than its implicit acknowledgment of the Jewish community's potential for subjection to irrational hatred as a group, the council undermined its contention that religion alone bound Jews to one another.

Unlike the American Council for Judaism, other pre-1948 anti-Zionist groups did not have difficulty in setting their objectives. Nonetheless, for a variety of reasons, they ultimately came to have even less visibility in the American forum than did the ACJ.

In this category must be placed the Institute of Arab American Affairs. Inspired by Princeton University's Philip K. Hitti, the institute sprang from its founder's belief that the United States was being lured to the support of an injustice in Palestine. By 1944 Hitti urged the formation of an Arab-

American organization that would counter Zionist claims and try to dispel the general ignorance of Middle Eastern affairs that characterized the American public. The institute was formally established in November 1944 at the conclusion of a two-day conference attended by 150 delegates from various Arab-American groups. Faris S. Malouf, a Boston attorney, became the organization's president. Hitti took up duties as "Supervisor of Activities."[12]

Despite the seemingly impressive circumstances of its birth, the Institute of Arab American Affairs rested on an exceedingly shallow organizational foundation. Although by 1940 there were over 350,000 American citizens of Arab extraction, it was difficult—and indeed technically incorrect—to speak of a single Arab-American community. A combination of historical and sociological factors gave most Arab-Americans little interest in the problem of Palestine.[13]

Hitti, Malouf, and other institute leaders were aware of the constraints that would be imposed by the nature of the group upon which they depended for support. Still, they hoped to develop the institute's capacity to contradict Zionist arguments and to propound the view that basic democratic values required that Palestine's Arab majority be allowed to determine the country's future.

The institute relied on various means to advance its outlook. Chief among these was a monthly *Bulletin*, mailed without charge to as wide a readership as possible. The publication was small, usually numbering not more than seven or eight pages. However, it provided a medium of expression for the institute's support of the Palestinian Arabs and for its generalized sympathetic view of the Arab world.

Institute staff members also kept busy by replying to apparently biased press coverage of Palestine events, mailing pro-Arab literature to Washington officials and influential private individuals, and speaking at public discussions of Palestine and the Arab Middle East.

These activities were restricted by financial realities. Soon after the institute's creation, Hitti and Malouf canvassed potential contributors and discovered stringent limitations on available resources. Particular difficulties were experienced in raising funds from wealthy Arab-Americans in the New York area, many of whom were involved in the garment industry and feared to antagonize important Jewish clients. During its first year, the institute worked with a budget of less than $15,000, an amount that remained fairly constant throughout the organization's existence.[14]

The institute's limited capabilities engendered frustration and resignation in the organization's leadership. Years later Hitti recalled his experience:

> Our basic idea was to have somebody, a spokesman to represent the opposite point of view for the Americans. We started with the idea, at least in my mind, that the Zionists were flooding all America with their propa-

ganda. It was time we had something. And I know it was adventurous, it was risky, it was quite heroic—but we couldn't do anything else. . . . We knew that we wouldn't count but we had to do the best we could. . . .[15]

Perhaps the most that can be said of the institute's impact is that the organization briefly provided a consistent and relatively accessible presentation of the Arab view of Palestine for those sufficiently interested to be curious.

Two other anti-Zionist groups must be considered. The more important, formed only two months before Israel's establishment, was virtually stillborn. Yet it was notable as the first organization formed by persons having no ethnic ties to the Middle East for the specific purpose of urging Washington to oppose Zionist plans for Palestine.

Following the UN General Assembly's resolution of November 1947 calling for the partition of Palestine, Virginia C. Gildersleeve, dean of Columbia University's Barnard College for Women, concluded that anti-Zionists should do more to promote their views. Together with a small coterie of like-minded individuals, some of whom had served with her as advisors to the Institute of Arab American Affairs, she began to muster support for a new anti-Zionist organization.[16]

The objective of the group that eventually gathered around Gildersleeve was to cause a reversal of Washington's commitment to partition and thereby remove what it saw as a long-term danger to American military, political, and economic interests in the Middle East. The group also hoped to convince the government to oppose any final solution to the Palestine question until a peaceful compromise between Arabs and Jews could be arranged. It was decided to create a committee composed of a select membership that would ensure the organization a respectful hearing by both government officials and the public.

This core group was organized by early March 1948. Known as the Committee for Peace and Justice in Palestine, it was an elite body composed mainly of educators and clergymen. Gildersleeve was elected chairman; Henry Sloane Coffin, president of Union Theological Seminary, became vice-chairman; Garland E. Hopkins, associate foreign secretary of the Methodist Church, emerged as secretary; and Kermit Roosevelt, grandson of President Theodore Roosevelt, accepted the salaried post of director. The organization also included a National Council of 100 prominent personalities, most of whom were also educators, clergymen, journalists, or authors.[17]

As anticipated, this impressive roster provided the committee with ready coverage in the national press and open doors in Washington. During its short lifetime, the committee energetically pursued its anti-Zionist campaign through both channels. The group's initial public statement strongly opposed Jewish statehood and declared that the Palestine controversy could still be solved on the basis of an Arab-Jewish compromise. It also called upon the United States and other countries to help solve the plight of post-war displaced Jews and urged that the Palestine issue be removed from American domestic politics.

While the committee's leaders made these same points in conferences with high-ranking Washington officials (among whom was Secretary of State George Marshall), they gave more emphasis on such occasions to the dangers they perceived in American support of partition: specifically, the possibility that American support of Zionist ambitions would lead to Soviet penetration of the Middle East.[18]

Despite its relatively rapid mobilization, the Gildersleeve Committee was formed too late to have an appreciable influence on American policy—which by the spring of 1948 was in any case floundering in an ineffectual effort to keep pace with the onrush of events in Palestine. At the time of Israel's establishment, the committee had grown by only 50 members and Gildersleeve was already turning her attention to the Arab refugee problem.[19]

The final anti-Zionist organization to be reviewed here was known as the League for Peace with Justice in Palestine. Antedating the Gildersleeve Committee, this so-called league was hardly more than a vehicle for the views of a wealthy and somewhat eccentric Jewish anti-Zionist from New York named Benjamin Freedman. Freedman first became aware of the Palestine problem in 1936. By the end of World War II he developed a deep personal antipathy toward Zionism. His feelings, he explains, grew from the conviction that the Zionist Movement was endeavoring to perpetrate a severe injustice against the Arabs of Palestine.[20] Initially, Freedman supported existing anti-Zionist groups. However, he soon became disillusioned with both the American Council for Judaism and the Institute of Arab American Affairs.

Freedman conceived the idea of creating a massive anti-Zionist pressure group open to all Americans. He planned to do this through an advertising campaign that would protest the injustice of Zionist aspirations and offer membership in his league for the nominal price of one dollar.[21] Confident that the scheme would quickly yield at least $1 million for operating expenses and further expansion, he began placing advertisements in the American press in early 1946. Each announcement was signed on behalf of the League for Peace with Justice in Palestine by Freedman as "Representative of Americans of Jewish Faith," H. I. Katibah as "Representative of Americans of Arab Ancestry," and R. M. Schoendorf as "Representative of Americans of Christian Faith."[22]

Freedman soon discovered that the campaign was ineffective. Moreover, Zionists promptly undermined the league's credibility by pointing out that Schoendorf was actually Freedman's mother-in-law and that Freedman himself had formally abandoned Judaism some years earlier and was, therefore, hardly "representative of Americans of Jewish faith."[23]

Unbowed by these setbacks, Freedman continued sponsoring anti-Zionist advertisements throughout 1946 and 1947. Subsequently, he claimed to have spent more than $100,000 during this period on advertisements alone.[24] Despite the prodigious funds and energy expended in support of his anti-Zionist inclinations, Freedman never managed to convert the league into more than a one-man organization. Other anti-Zionist groups were wary of his style and motivation and sought to dissociate themselves from him.[25] The public remained apathetic to his appeals. Following the establishment of Israel, Freedman continued to engage in anti-Zionist activity, but there exists quite a bit of evidence that after 1948 he increasingly aligned himself with anti-Semitic individuals and groups.[26] By 1973 he claimed to have spent $3 million on his personal crusade against Zionism.[27]

OVERVIEW: THE SEARCH FOR A CONSTITUENCY

Between 1939 and 1948, American anti-Zionists never seriously challenged Zionist influence in the United States. There was, in fact, no real anti-Zionist "movement" during the decade preceding Israel's establishment. Rather, the growth of Zionism as a factor in American policy toward Palestine gave rise to discrete reactions. Thus the two leading anti-Zionist organizations, the American Council for Judaism and the Institute of Arab American Affairs, arose from fundamentally different concerns. Preoccupied with the future status of Jews in the United States, the former sought to overcome the dominant position captured by Zionists within the American Jewish community. To do this it was necessary that the council not appear to be simply supporting Arab claims over those advanced by Jews. In its treatment of the basic Arab-Zionist political controversy, the ACJ unsuccessfully tried to find a middle ground from which it could simultaneously avoid conflict with American Jewry's desire to secure Jewish settlement rights in Palestine while denouncing the Zionists' political demand for sovereignty. On the other hand, the Institute of Arab American Affairs rejected the very notion that any "rights" toward Palestine could exist without the consent of the country's indigenous population. It attempted to counter Zionist arguments by simply insisting that democratic principles should not be sacrificed to Jewish nationalism, and by trying to dispel the general lack of knowledge in the United States about conditions in the Arab world.

The foci of the two organizations were, therefore, distinct. Concerned with the problem of Jewish integration into Gentile society, and worried over the possible retardation or destruction of that process by Zionism, the ACJ dealt with Palestine only as a secondary issue; and even then in ways calculated to minimize offense to an American Jewry already emotionally committed to the Jewish community in Palestine. For its part, the institute concentrated on the political controversy between Arabs and Jews, trying to relate it to the prevailing democratic political values in the United States. Although the two groups were aware of one another, they did not attempt to cooperate or coordinate their activities. This in itself was indicative of the basic difference between them.

Significantly, both organizations were "ethnic groups" in the sense that they sought support and active membership primarily from recognized minority groups. The ACJ, of course, hoped to reduce Zionist strength by attracting American Jews to its banner. The institute, while more often directing its propaganda toward a broader public, still depended upon Arab-Americans for manpower and financial backing. To a great extent the limited effectiveness of both organizations stemmed from their failure to obtain adequate support from their chosen constituencies. American Jews by and large rejected the ACJ with vehemence. American-Arabs remained overwhelmingly apathetic to the pro-Palestinian message of the Institute of Arab American Affairs.

Although the ACJ and the institute also attempted, in varying degrees, to attract the attention and support of the larger American public, their efforts met with little success. The reasons for this may never be fully fathomable. However, one contributing reason does suggest itself. This is found in the ethnic character of both organizations. In the case of the American Council for Judaism, concrete proof exists that Gentiles confronted with its anti-Zionist position often reacted by firmly disclaiming any interest in an "intra-Jewish" difference of opinion.[28] It may well be that the activities of the Institute of Arab American Affairs were seen by many Americans as only manifestations of an interethnic controversy.

Whatever the case, the fact remains that throughout the period leading up to the establishment of Israel, the bulk of American citizens did not perceive the problem in Palestine as a cause for concern.[29] In the face of this apathy it is doubtful whether the anti-Zionists could have successfully created a public counterweight to the Zionist Movement in the United States.

It was precisely this task that Benjamin Freedman set for himself. Ironically, in view of his rejection by established anti-Zionist groups, it was only Freedman who, through his advertisements, explicitly raised the possibility of a united front against Zionism formed by individuals of all faiths and backgrounds.

The Gildersleeve Committee marked the first organized effort of Americans having no ethnic interest in the Arab-Zionist quarrel to call for the United States to oppose Zionist political aims. However, the group was formed too late to determine whether its prestigious membership would have succeeded in kindling the interest of the American public and in generating support for the committee's policy recommendations to Washington.

The most visible asset of the Zionist campaign to sway American policy makers was the active support they received from the American Jewish community. Acting upon this bedrock, Zionist lobbyists were able to influence the government to take steps that eventually helped produce a Jewish state in Palestine. On the other hand, American anti-Zionists were unable to find, or to create, a committed constituency. While the American Council for Judaism unsuccessfully attempted to replace the Zionist Movement as the acknowledged spokesman for American Jewry, the Institute of Arab American Affairs disseminated pro-Arab propaganda without generating politically significant activity. Freedman remained an isolated and unproductive voice of opposition. The Gildersleeve group did not emerge in time to influence events in the United States or in Palestine.

In short, anti-Zionists never managed to generate a widespread debate within the United States. While Zionists were able to count upon the enthusiastic and sustained support of the bulk of the Jewish community in the United States, as well as that of the prestigious, non-Jewish American Palestine Committee, the majority of Americans remained uninterested in Palestine's political future.

II: THE ROOSEVELT ADMINISTRATION AND PALESTINE

5. Downplaying Palestine: The Roosevelt Administration, 1939–43

Cordell Hull, who recalled a "flood" of protests pouring into the State Department when the 1939 White Paper was issued, noted that Zionist activity in the United States tapered off considerably upon the outbreak of World War II.[1] Two reasons underlay this lull. First, the primary task facing American Zionism in 1939 was internal reorganization rather than public agitation. Second, it was clear that the Middle East might quickly become a theater of military operations. Most Jews in Palestine saw no choice but to support Britain against the spread of German power. American Zionists therefore had to temper their ire over London's Palestine policy with the realization that the immediate situation demanded British primacy in the Middle East.

Zionist activities in the early war years focused largely on projects for the defense of the Middle East. Shortly after hostilities began, Zionists called for a Jewish army, raised from Palestine's Jewish population, to fight alongside Allied forces. The British government, mindful of Arab opinion and anxious to avoid having to confront restive native populations, was cool to the idea. Not until the fall of 1944 was a Jewish Brigade formed in partial, and belated, fulfillment of the Zionists' wish.

In the interval, Jews enthusiastically joined Palestinian units of the British Army. Although the mandatory originally hoped to balance Arab and Jewish enlistments, only small numbers of Arabs volunteered. By the end of the war, 27,000 Palestinian Jews had enrollled for service as opposed to 12,500 Arabs.[2]

These figures underscored the lengthy frustration of Arab national feeling. Embittered by British and French policies after World War I, Arabs generally had little emotional commitment to the Allied cause. As noted by George Wadsworth, American consul general in Jerusalem, Palestinian Arabs believed they were better off under British, rather than German, domination but nonetheless felt they suffered only "the less objectionable of two imperialisms."[3] Similar views prevailed throughout the Arab Middle East.

Through the introduction of agents and unceasing propaganda—much of it devoted to linking the Allies with Zionism—the Axis attempted to foment unrest in the Middle East. In 1941 these efforts were partly responsible for a brief clash between Britain and Iraq that resulted in the overthrow of Rashid Ali Al-Galani.

With the development of North Africa into a battleground and Axis troops advancing toward the oil fields of the Caucasus, Allied commanders uneasily contemplated the prospect of a pincer movement against the Middle East. The threat dissipated only after the destruction of Rommel's force at el-Alamein in November 1942 and the final annihilation of Von Paulus' army at Stalingrad shortly thereafter. In the meantime, the Allies considered it vitally important to avoid anything that would exacerbate Arab resentment against the Western democracies.

However, as American Zionism became better organized after 1939, it called increasing attention to the demand that Palestine be converted into a Jewish state. The Roosevelt administration devised a variety of means to cope with this situation.

WASHINGTON'S REACTION TO
THE PALESTINE PROBLEM, 1939–43

The crisis created by the war, and the relative disorganization of American Zionists, helped keep the Palestine problem from becoming an issue in the presidential election of 1940. Unlike what occurred four years later, neither the Democratic nor Republican platform included a "Palestine plank." Nor was Palestine even discussed at the national conventions.

Once the Roosevelt administration was reinstated, however, its respite from the Palestine problem drew to a close. The creation of the American Palestine Committee in the spring of 1941 was the first major public indication of renewed Zionist activity in the United States. As the organizational structure of American Zionism consolidated, these signs multiplied and culminated with the Biltmore Program of 1942 and the American Jewish Conference in 1943.

During the early war years the White House and the State Department engaged in a concerted attempt to limit discussion of Palestine to levels that would minimize the risk of Arab ferment. However, American policy makers had to act with care lest their actions produce a contrary effect. No legal grounds existed for Washington to force a cessation of, or a reduction in, Zionist activities. Any brazen effort to silence Zionist spokesmen ran the danger of arousing a vociferous reaction against the administration and, at the same time, making the Palestine problem the focus of an unwelcome public controversy.

Washington dealt with this dilemma by relying upon informal representations to dissuade Zionists from pressing their demands. Simultaneously, the administration tried to preserve Zionist goodwill through various flowery, but noncommittal expressions of sympathy, calculated hints to Zionist leaders that their cause would receive favorable official consideration once the pressures of war were removed, and occasional instances of outright subterfuge.

It was a static approach that sought no more than to contain public interest in Palestine. Its manifestations accordingly tended to appear as discrete responses to immediate situations. Nonetheless, taken as a whole, the actions to which it gave rise reveal the existence of a limited, but coherent, framework that was recognized and faithfully followed by the chief executive and his foreign policy advisors.

A good example of the administration's policy was its reaction to the formation of the American Palestine Committee under Senator Robert Wagner in 1941. The APC caused concern in official Washington circles over possible repercussions in the Arab world. The Turkish ambassador in Washington, Mehmet Ertegün, warned the State Department that since "people abroad were quite aware of the importance and influence of United States Senators," the APC's membership might create problems for the Allies.[4]

The British Embassy was also prompt to voice misgivings. Neville Butler, counsellor of the embassy, spoke with Wallace Murray about the possibility that the APC would be featured in Axis propaganda. He urged the department to explain this consideration to any committee members who might sympathize with London's concern.[5]

While State Department officials were also uneasy, they were not quite sure what could be done. Reporting on his conversation with Butler, Murray offered this opinion:

> It is impossible to overemphasize the difficulties which can be caused the British throughout the Arab-speaking world by propaganda issued by the Axis Powers to the effect that Great Britain and the United States are supporting the Jewish National Home in Palestine to the detriment of the Arab peoples.[6]

However, Murray did not suggest what steps might be taken to minimize publicity surrounding the APC's establishment. For his part, Assistant Secretary of State Adolf Berle informed Senator Wagner's office of the British Embassy's views. Having done this, however, he felt the best course was "to play the matter down a little." In keeping with his own advice, the assistant secretary suggested that the White House refuse a request made earlier by

Wagner for a presidential message of good wishes to be read at the APC's inaugural dinner.[7]

Although the president rejected Berle's advice, this was not a sign of disagreement between Roosevelt and his State Department advisors over the desirability of reducing public attention given to Zionism and the Palestine issue. Instead, the president avoided offering a definite snub to the committee—something that would have focused more attention on the administration's Palestine policy.

Pro-Zionist organizations composed of more ordinary citizens than those belonging to the APC fared less well when they sought presidential salutations.[8] Such applications were routinely forwarded to the State Department. With White House approval, the department, particularly in the years when the Middle East was directly threatened by Axis forces, regularly returned negative replies.[9]

There is no doubt that Roosevelt set the guidelines that up to 1943 caused the American government to discourage the airing of the Palestine controversy in the United States. The president's attitude was evident when he met Chaim Weizmann in early 1940. The Zionist leader found the interview distinctly unproductive and later recalled that although Roosevelt had been friendly and chatty, their discussion remained "theoretical."[10]

Occasionally the president used his personal influence to reduce Zionist agitation. In the spring and summer of 1941 he refused separate requests from Justice Brandeis and Rabbi Stephen Wise to intervene in support of the formation of an exclusively Jewish military force in Palestine. While the president explained his action to Brandeis by simply referring to the situation in the Middle East, his letter to Wise was more detailed:

> In their Near Eastern campaign, the British must of necessity have the support not only of the Jews in Palestine but also of a far larger number of Arabs in Palestine, Transjordania, Saudi Arabia, and in the northern Arab states.[11]

When Justice Frankfurter tried to obtain an interview for David Ben Gurion, Roosevelt had his private secretary, Grace Tulley, send the following reply:

> The President asks me to tell you that he is very sorry he cannot see Mr. David Ben Gurion. He also asks me to tell you, that quite frankly, in the present situation in Egypt, Palestine, Syria and Arabia, he feels that the less said by everybody of all creeds, the better.[12]

At times, Roosevelt coupled efforts to lessen Zionist activity with statements indicating a readiness to support Zionist goals in Palestine at the end of the war. In late 1942, for example, he accidentally learned that Henry J. Morgenthau, Jr. was planning a private meeting at which Palestine would be discussed. Cautioning the secretary of the treasury to "go easy" on that issue, Roosevelt declared that he had "pretty well made up [his] mind as to what [he was] going to do [on Palestine]" and went on to outline a pro-Zionist solution that could be implemented after the war.[13]

Nearly a year later a similar event occurred when the president, having just refused to meet with representatives of a group of 500 pro-Zionist rabbis, turned to his advisor and speech-writer, Samuel Rosenman, and spoke favorably about the possibility of eventually "settling the Palestine question by letting Jews in to the limit that country will support them—with a barbed wire around the Holy Land."[14] Whether these utterances expressed Roosevelt's convictions or were instead designed to lull Zionists' anxiety in hope of keeping the Palestine problem dormant remains an open question. However, whatever his intentions may have been when he made these early pro-Zionist comments, the president's later actions were not in accord with them.

Those close to Roosevelt occasionally witnessed exhibitions of anger and frustration over his inability to prevent Zionists from trying to further their cause. In January 1942, Leo Crowley, who subsequently directed the Office of Economic Warfare, suddenly found himself listening to a private lecture by the president on the subject of relations between the White House and the Jewish and Catholic minorities in the United States. To Crowley's amazement, Roosevelt exclaimed: "This is a protestant country, and the Catholics and Jews are here on sufferance," and he concluded by stating that "it is up to both [Jews and Catholics] to go along with anything that I want at this time." Morgenthau, to whom Crowley related the incident, had undergone a similar experience with the president sometime earlier.[15]

Another outburst of presidential ire, and one that is perhaps revealing of Roosevelt's ability to disguise his true feelings, occurred in the summer of 1942 following a visit to the White House by Chaim Weizmann. The Zionist leader asked Roosevelt to persuade the British government to allow the return to Palestine of Colonel Orde Wingate, a British officer who had become popular with Palestinian Jews during the Arab rebellion of 1936.[16] Weizmann hoped Wingate might command a Jewish army of 40,000 men. When he subsequently discussed the interview with Henry Morgenthau, Weizmann conveyed the impression that Roosevelt had responded favorably.[17]

It was therefore an extremely surprised secretary of the treasury who several days later saw the president display intense anger over the encounter with Weizmann. Pounding his desk for emphasis, Roosevelt said he had informed the Zionist leader that "this was positively no time to bring up the matter," that supplies were unavailable for equipping a Jewish army, and that what also had to be considered was the question "as to whether the

Arabs have an uprising."[18] As far as the Wingate matter was concerned, the president had indeed contacted the British to explore possibilities of the colonel's return to Palestine, but he had not done so in connection with any idea of raising a large Jewish force. The only thing in his mind, the president said, was that Palestinian Jews might play a useful role in small commando groups and Wingate might perhaps be the officer to lead them.[19]

The State Department's role in curbing public interest in Palestine was not limited to being a buffer between the president and Zionists. Whenever an opportunity arose the department took steps to forestall possibilities that the Palestine issue might surface in public forums. Nor were efforts along these lines directed solely at pro-Zionist activities.

In 1942, for example, the department dissuaded William Yale, then teaching at the University of New Hampshire, from publishing a scholarly article detailing a joint British-Zionist attempt to prevent Henry J. Morgenthau, Sr. from carrying out a secret mission entrusted to him by President Wilson in 1917.[20] Department officials felt that Yale's article would revive old controversies and allow Axis propaganda ample opportunity to embarrass the Allies in the Middle East.[21]

In 1943 the department also discouraged Myron Taylor, then the president's personal representative to the pope, from publicly arguing that many Jews would have to rebuild their lives in Europe after the war since there was "naturally a limit to absorptive capacity of existing places of refuge, such as Palestine, and others."[22] Again, the department reasoned that such remarks might spark a controversy that would provide fuel for Axis propaganda efforts to generate unrest in the Middle East.[23]

It was more difficult for department officials to urge Zionists to drop their increasingly visible public activities; nonetheless, the effort was made. In the spring of 1941, when Rommel's forces in Libya were seriously menacing the British in Egypt and the American Palestine Committee was preparing its gala dinner in Washington, Assistant Secretary of State Berle suggested that Zionist leaders be told frankly that their insistence on a Jewish state in Palestine was encouraging a politically explosive situation in the Middle East. Berle proposed to speak with Chaim Weizmann and urge him to seek an understanding with the Arabs on the basis of a modified Zionist program. Berle calculated that if approached openly Weizmann would be receptive:

[He] ought to be able to see the main desideratum, namely that if the Mediterranean is closed, the extermination of the Zionists in Palestine is only a question of time. If he does see this, it might be possible to get him to take a more reasonable attitude than has been taken heretofore, namely that the British ought to put enough force into Arabia [sic] to guarantee the Zionists political domination.[24]

In mid-April Berle met with Weizmann's personal representative, Emanuel Neumann. The assistant secretary later reported that after outlining the seriousness of the Axis threat to the Middle East, and raising the prospect that British forces might have to be removed from Palestine for duty elsewhere, he expressed himself to Neumann in the following vein:

> It would be part of statesmanship for the group Dr. Weizmann represented to consider what they might do in that situation. They would then be face to face with the Arabs, without any screen of protecting force. It would seem that some sort of understanding with the Arabs might at that time become a crucial necessity. I did not presume to suggest whether, or how, it could be done—but merely expressed the personal hope that they would consider the matter and possibly consult a little with Mr. Wallace Murray, in the event that they had any tangible ideas.[25]

It was perfectly clear to his listener that the settlement Berle urged would have required Zionists to abandon their goal of Jewish statehood in Palestine and to accept limitations on Jewish immigration into that country. Moreover, according to Neumann, Berle abandoned discreet terminology and bluntly spoke his mind. A memorandum prepared by Neumann described the conversation from the Zionist leader's perspective:

> By dint of questioning I drew out what he had in mind; there should be prompt negotiations with Arab leaders; we should be prepared to renounce our political claims to Palestine; a large part of the Yishuv might be evacuated to Kenya and to Saudi Arabia under the protection of King Ibn Saud. In return, and by way of compensating for our renunciation, we might get a kind of "Vatican City" in Palestine after the war, and a real territory for building a Jewish nation elsewhere.[26]

Apparently these remarks convinced Zionist leaders that the assistant secretary was simply engaging in a crude attempt to intimidate them. Joseph Schechtman argues that Berle's "amazing suggestions," among which Schechtman includes Berle's reference to a possible Jewish evacuation of Palestine, may have originated from "some British or Arab source," and that in any case "it is . . . evident that conversations of this kind were going on behind the scenes and that various strings were being pulled in diplomatic correspondence."[27]

Actually, there is no evidence to support either the suggestion that Berle's views were inspired by some foreign source or the implication that they were part of a joint strategy with other governments. Moreover, it is very likely that Berle did not refer to a possible evacuation of Palestinian Jewry as part of a Zionist-Arab settlement, but rather as a contingency that might be acted upon in the event of an Axis breakthrough in Egypt.[28]

The man most sympathetic to Zionist aspirations in the upper ranks of the State Department was Undersecretary Sumner Welles.[29] Aware of this, Zionists maintained close contact with Welles until his resignation in 1943. Yet, despite his personal approval of Zionism, Welles worked in his own way to reduce public activity on behalf of Jewish statehood. The undersecretary used his relations with Zionist leaders for this purpose in early August 1941 when Stephen Wise and Emanuel Neumann approached him with a far-reaching request that "the American Government . . . elicit from the British Government assurances that nothing would be said or done affecting the future of Palestine without prior consultation with the United States," and that in the event of diplomatic exchanges between the two governments regarding Palestine, "the United States . . . consult with the Zionist leadership before taking any definite position."[30]

Since the first part of the appeal was tantamount to asking the United States to assume active partnership with Great Britain in the disposition of Palestine, it raised an issue well beyond the purview of an undersecretary of state. Welles, however, did not point this out. Instead, he agreed to both portions of the request. Shortly after his interview with Welles, Rabbi Wise forwarded to the undersecretary a memorandum in which the Zionist request was specified, and which concluded by expressing appreciation to Welles "for so kindly offering to act promptly in this matter."[31]

By the end of September, Wise was reminding Welles that Zionists had "as yet no information regarding any action in this matter."[32] At this point Wallace Murray asked for a clarification of what had been told to the Zionist leaders. Although Welles denied any commitments had been made, it is notable that at no time (at least between August and October) did he attempt to make the same point to any of the Zionist spokesmen with whom he was in contact.[33] If Zionists erred in their impression that Welles was committed to seek an assurance from the British government along the lines they desired, or to try to motivate the Roosevelt administration to seek one, the undersecretary's failure to clarify the point amounted to a passive act of duplicity. From his answer to Murray, it is clear that Welles saw nothing reprehensible in such tactics:

> For reasons of policy as well as for reasons of expediency, I consider it in the highest degree important that everything be done by this Government to prevent Jewish groups within the United States from opposing the British war effort, or from adding in any way to the obstacles already confronted by the British Government in the Near East. For that reason I shall continue to keep in close touch with Dr. Wise and his associates with the hope that misunderstandings between the Zionist movement in this country and the British Government can at least be minimized, if not altogether avoided.[34]

Secretary of State Hull had relatively little direct contact with Zionists. However, he too followed the administration's policy of avoiding confrontation with American Zionists while simultaneously downplaying their political demands. In 1942, for example, Hull recognized the twenty-fifth anniversary of the Balfour Declaration with a public statement that condemned Hitler's anti-Semitic policies but that also cast the solution to the Jewish problem in a universal context:

> The Jews . . . have long sought a refuge. I believe that we must have an even wider objective; we must have a world in which Jews, like every other race, are free to abide in peace and honor.[35]

Thoroughly dissatisfied with this comment, Rabbi Wise immediately sent a message to Hull complaining that the statement was being interpreted as an example of hostility toward Zionism. So that such impressions might be laid to rest, Wise suggested that a department official attend a planned Balfour Day celebration at Carnegie Hall and deliver "a brief message of encouragement."[36] Since the invitation failed to arrive at the department until after the Carnegie Hall celebration, Hull was spared the necessity of reacting to it.

Thus, until the battles of el-Alamein and Stalingrad eliminated the immediate military threat to the Middle East, both the White House and the Department of State worked to minimize Zionist agitation in the United States. At the most obvious level, this policy was manifested in the reactions of the president and his State Department advisors to various Zionist initiatives, or to developments that seemed likely to further public interest in the Palestine problem and in American policy toward that issue.

However, it was not long before the administration began to consider the possibility of supplementing its established policy of reaction with a more positive initiative designed to place the Palestine problem officially into abeyance for the duration of the war.

THE ROOSEVELT ADMINISTRATION SEEKS A MORATORIUM ON PALESTINE

As American Zionism became better organized after 1939, Washington found it more difficult to limit discussion of the Palestine question. Soon after the Biltmore Conference the rising tempo of domestic Zionist activity caused government officials to consider direct steps to bring about a moratorium on the Palestine issue within the United States. In late May 1942 a high-level meeting of State Department officers was held in Hull's office to discuss the "harmful effects of Zionist activity on the war effort."[37] Hull and his subordinates decided the problem of Zionist agitation could best be resolved through an official policy statement that would nullify Zionist hopes of gaining American support for Jewish statehood in Palestine.

On Hull's instructions, Wallace Murray drafted the statement for submission to the president. Murray's draft contained three points, two of which laid down guiding principles for American policy toward Palestine while the third was obviously intended to stem Zionist attempts to obtain Washington's backing for the idea of immediately establishing a Jewish fighting force in Palestine.

The first principle suggested by Murray was that American policy toward Palestine be based explicitly on the Atlantic Charter's promise that the Allies did not wish to see "territorial changes that do not accord with the freely expressed wishes of the people concerned," and that the Democratic powers would maintain respect for "the right of all peoples to choose the form of Government under which they live." Second, Murray suggested that U.S. policy be clearly and explicitly based on the belief that it was "highly desirable" that an agreed political solution be reached between the Arab and Jewish communities in Palestine.[38]

In regard to the creation of an indigenous Palestine force, Murray's draft first stressed that Palestine was a British responsibility but then added that the United States had no objection to the formation of separate Arab and Jewish military units "if equipment were available and it is deemed necessary."[39]

Murray also prepared a supporting letter for Hull to send to the president. This argued that issuance of the statement was necessary to ensure the security of the Allies' military position in the Middle East and to counteract Axis propaganda that was raising fears among the Arabs over Anglo-American intentions toward Palestine. It also argued that a definite refusal to support Jewish statehood in Palestine might encourage progress toward an Arab-Zionist compromise:

> So long as the Zionists feel they can obtain outside support which will enable them to impose their own solution, they will not be disposed to treat with the Arabs on equal terms. A settlement in Palestine resulting from the use, or threat, of force would of course be completely opposed to the principles for which we fought the last war and are fighting the present one.[40]

However, the president had a different view. On July 7 he wrote to Hull:

> The more I think of it the more I feel we should say nothing about the Near East or Palestine or the Arabs at this time. If we pat either group on the back, we automatically stir up trouble.[41]

Murray and his colleagues continued to promote the idea of a policy statement. After several futile attempts, strong support was given to their position by Lieutenant Colonel Harold B. Hoskins. In 1943 Hoskins spent over three months touring the Middle East and North Africa on behalf of the Office of Strategic Studies. His report, which arrived at the State Department in late April, warned that serious unrest pervaded the Arab world. It suggested that Jewish leaders in the United States be told frankly that continued calls for a Jewish state in Palestine threatened the Allies' position in the Middle East.[42]

Cordell Hull was sufficiently impressed to decide that Washington could no longer remain silent. In early May he sent a copy of the Hoskins Report to the White House, along with a suggested United Nations statement:

> The United Nations have taken note of the public discussions and activities of a political nature relating to Palestine and consider that it would be helpful to the war effort if these were to cease. Accordingly, the United Nations declare . . . that no decision altering the basic situation in Palestine should be considered until after the conclusion of the war. When the matter is considered, both Arabs and Jews should be fully consulted and their agreement sought, in the event that they are unable to reach agreement between themselves prior to the end of hostilities.[43]

This time Roosevelt agreed completely with Hull's suggestion. The State Department was authorized to proceed with its plans. A few days later the president received a report from General Patrick J. Hurley, his personal representative in the Middle East, that could have only made it seem more urgent to stem Zionist activity in the United States.

Hurley reported that Palestine's political future formed the major topic of public interest in the Middle East. Although the general refrained from passing explicit judgment on the claims of Arabs and Jews, the tone of the report indicated that he was not impressed favorably by Zionism. He cautioned Roosevelt that Britain and the United States would almost certainly share eventual responsibility for the ultimate decision on Jewish statehood as well as "for the consequences of such a decision."[44] Roosevelt, who considered Hurley a highly dependable observer, was undoubtedly affected by these views.[45]

Meanwhile, the State Department had approached the British government over the proposed UN statement. Not surprisingly, the British were delighted with the idea. However, during the course of the Anglo-American talks it was decided, with Roosevelt's approval, that the declaration be issued solely in the name of the United States and Great Britain.[46] It was planned to release a slightly revised version of the statement drafted in early May simultaneously in London and Washington on July 27. This schedule was subse-quently altered by 24 hours to enable Foreign Minister Anthony Eden to make the announcement in Parliament. By July 24, then, all was in readiness for the Anglo-American declaration to be issued at noon, July 28.[47]

The statement was never made. The circumstances surrounding this de-velopment are worthy of close examination, for they reveal a vacillating pat-tern of response to conflicting domestic and international considerations that was to become a basic feature of Washington's approach to the Palestine problem. It is interesting that in this instance "domestic considerations" did not result so much from the exercise of Zionist "pressure" as from the Roosevelt administration's assessment of Zionism's potential domestic polit-ical effectiveness. In itself, this was a tribute to the skill with which American Zionism had been molded into an interest group since 1939.

Forty-eight hours before the Anglo-American declaration was to be is-sued, American diplomats were informed of a "brief postponement."[48] In fact, Roosevelt and Hull had suddenly concluded that they could not accept even minimal public responsibility for the statement. They wanted the an-nouncement to be made unquestionably in the name of the "war effort."

On July 26 Hull dispatched Wallace Murray and Paul Alling to secure a written request from the War Department that steps be taken to curtail do-mestic pro-Zionist actions. Robert P. Patterson, serving as acting secretary of war in the absence of Henry Stimson, reviewed the impending declaration and promptly agreed to do as asked. A suitable letter to Hull was drafted and approved by Chief of Staff George Marshall. Since all this was done in the presence of State Department men, Hull was dismayed to find that the letter he received from Patterson the next day differed from the original draft. All references linking political activity in the United States to unrest in the Mid-dle East had been deleted. However, Patterson's message strongly implied serious concern over any source of tension in Palestine:

> Disorder in Palestine would affect adversely the situation in the whole area and possibly even the entire course of the war. . . . It is clearly in the mili-tary interest that for the duration of hostilities the situation in Palestine remain quiet. The military requirements in this area must be accorded precedence over adjustment of any political question.[49]

On the face of it, this seemed to provide reasonable military grounds for the administration to ask for a moratorium on discussion of Palestine. Yet Hull insisted that the War Department be more explicit in identifying Zionist agitation as a danger to Allied military interests.

When action was delayed on this renewed request, Hull began to suspect that Stimson—who had by then returned to Washington—would balk. This led the secretary of state to conceive another plan to force the Zionists into silence. On July 30 Hull suggested to Roosevelt that it might be preferable to end unwanted discussion of Palestine by exercising strong, but discreet, pressure on Zionist leaders. Patterson's letter, although deemed inadequate for a public confrontation with Zionists, seemed an ideal weapon for more covert steps:

> I desire to raise the question whether it would not be well to present [the Patterson letter] to a suitable assemblage of Jews representing especially discordant and vociferous elements. At such time they could be told that unless they are willing to desist from further agitation, this Government will be obliged to make public the letter . . . and also to publish the proposed statement of the two Governments requesting that further agitation cease.

The analysis Hull provided in support of this scheme leaves no doubt that the administration's eleventh-hour trepidation over the Anglo-American statement stemmed from its fear of Zionist reaction:

> Such a Jewish gathering might decide to call off the unfortunate agitation being carried on, especially in this country. If they should refuse, however, this Government would be in the strongest possible position from the standpoint of attack and criticism of the proposed action of the two Governments.[50]

Roosevelt immediately authorized Hull to proceed with the plan.[51] Although Zionists remained ignorant of this latest turn of events, they were by now aware of the proposed Anglo-American statement. On August 3 Rabbi Wise wrote to Hull asking that Zionists be consulted before the formulation of "any statement which may affect the future of Palestine, or the assertion of Jewish claims with respect thereto."[52] A few days later, Congressman Emanuel Celler, Democratic Representative from New York, publicly implied that secret machinations by American oil companies operating in the Middle East were largely responsible for the State Department's anti-Zionist attitude.[53] Celler also took up the issue in a letter to President Roosevelt. The letter, which Celler immediately made public, charged the existence in the State Department of "a cabal . . . to discredit the work of Jews in Palestine" and demanded that Roosevelt take action against the involved officials. According to Celler, those who had "contributed their bit to the betrayal of Palestine" were General Patrick Hurley, Colonel Hoskins, and Wallace Murray.[54] Actually, the congressman's ire was voiced too late to influence the Anglo-American statement on Palestine.

That project had already been killed by Secretary of War Stimson's refusal to comply with Hull's request for a letter. Stimson's reaction proved so adverse, in fact, that it also destroyed the alternative plan agreed upon between Hull and Roosevelt. Not only did the secretary of war refuse to participate in the administration's offensive against the Zionists, but he also "withdrew" Patterson's earlier letter.[55]

Hull was forced to abandon the idea of a statement. On August 7 the British government was informed that Washington had reversed its earlier decision to join in a declaration urging restraint on discussion and activities relating to Palestine.[56]

In early 1944 the notion of an Anglo-American declaration was briefly revived.[57] However, it did not gain the momentum attained by the earlier effort and it was quickly dropped.

The efforts to produce an official statement on Palestine in the spring and summer of 1943 were the culmination of nearly four years during which Washington was determined to avoid any substantive consideration of the Arab-Zionist conflict. In the months and years that followed, the American government found it increasingly harder to remain aloof from that controversy. Although it waged a long, and eventually unsuccessful, struggle to evade a commitment on Palestine's political disposition, it became progressively obvious after 1943 that in one way or another a recognizable American "Palestine policy" would emerge. The issue that loomed over Washington was whether that policy would develop as the result of disjointed reactions to the pressures that surrounded the Palestine conflict, or, on the contrary, as part of a comprehensive and calculated effort to determine the best interests of the United States.

6.   SEARCHING FOR
A SOLUTION: 1943

The Roosevelt administration's desire for a moratorium on the Palestine controversy in 1943 was rooted in the realization that changing circumstances were swiftly eroding the efficacy of tactics that had so far allowed it to avoid taking any position on the Arab-Zionist conflict. The year was a period of transition for the American approach to Palestine.

Both the administration's plans for an Anglo-American statement and the short-lived Hull-Roosevelt plot to coerce Zionists into inaction stemmed from Washington's eagerness to hit upon new ways of coping with the Palestine issue. On the other hand, these options were considered only because they seemed to offer avenues for continuing the government's policy of avoiding any definition of its aims in terms of Palestine's political future.

Following the burial of the Anglo-American statement, the administration's search for a new approach expanded beyond mere attempts to devise imaginative new dilatory methods. For a short while at least, the administration appeared to heed General Hurley's warning that the United States would have to share responsibility for the ultimate outcome of the Arab-Zionist struggle. By June 1943, Washington was trying to settle upon a position toward the rival Arab and Jewish claims. By the end of the year it was attempting to construct a political formula that could be promoted as a long-range solution for Palestine.

Changes in international and domestic realities had undermined the methods that allowed policy makers to avoid a direct confrontation with the disturbing question of Palestine prior to 1943. The most important domestic factor was the increased militancy and rapidly expanding organizational strength of American Zionism. Under the impetus of the Biltmore Program, Zionists became progressively less willing to respond to moral suasion based on the priority of the war effort, or to superficially sympathetic statements occasionally issued by high-ranking officials.

It was not simply the commitment and organizational skill of Zionist leaders that led to this situation. The increased vigor of pro–Zionist agitation could not be divorced from the global impact of war-related developments, principal among which were two: public recognition after 1942 of the enormity of Hitler's genocidal onslaught against European Jewry, and the Allied armies' shift to the offensive after the Axis defeats at el-Alamein and Stalingrad. As it became more evident that the defense of the Middle East was no longer a pressing concern, it proved more difficult for the Roosevelt administration to plead "military necessity" as an excuse for temporizing on Palestine.[1]

Broadened international considerations also made it more difficult for Washington to evade the Palestine problem. The early years of World War II witnessed the rapid development of long-term American interests in the Middle East. At first reluctantly, and then with perhaps unseemly eagerness, the American government grew determined to protect these interests. Oil was the cornerstone of Washington's increased attention to the affairs of the Middle East. As policy makers started placing more value on that area of the world, they perceived a greater need to mollify Arab fears over American intentions toward Palestine.

At the beginning of the war, the Roosevelt administration clung to the traditional assumptions that America's Middle East interests were of minor consequence and that the region was essentially a sphere of British influence. Saudi Arabia, despite the operations of ARAMCO, was not considered an exception to this rule. In mid-1941, for example, Roosevelt was urged by representatives of American oil companies to alleviate the wartime dislocation of the Saudi economy that was leading Ibn Saud to greater dependence upon the British government. Although recognizing the desirability of preserving the stability of the Saudi regime, Roosevelt hoped London could continue to "take care" of the king since he felt Saudi Arabia was "a little far afield for us."[2]

Within two years this attitude changed drastically. A watershed was reached in early 1943 with Roosevelt's declaration that Saudi Arabia was "vital" to the defense of the United States and therefore entitled to aid under the terms of Lend-Lease.[3] Underlying the president's action was the concern of civilian and military officials over the depletion of oil reserves in the United States. Although American oil exports declined after the outbreak of the war, domestic consumption rose by more than 20 percent between 1939 and 1941.[4] In following years the continuing drain on domestic reserves generated consternation in official circles.[5] Secretary of the Interior Ickes, who after 1942 also became petroleum administrator for war, was particularly worried about the long-range aspects of the problem.[6] Ickes developed strong views on the necessity of American-controlled foreign supplies. These were generally supported by military leaders, who in mid-1943 called for steps to ensure the availability of foreign oil.[7]

Roosevelt's response was to create the Petroleum Reserve Corporation (PRC), a government establishment whose board of directors was formed by the secretaries of state, war, and interior. Given a wide mandate to acquire control of oil reserves abroad, the PRC immediately launched a futile effort to purchase the ARAMCO operation in Saudi Arabia. When this failed, the PRC turned to the idea of an American pipeline from the Persian Gulf to a terminus on the eastern Mediterranean. In early 1944, agreement in principle over that project was reached with ARAMCO. However, strong opposition quickly developed within the greater part of the American oil industry, where it was feared that a government-owned pipeline would result in an influx of cheap Arabian oil into the United States.[8]

Nonetheless, the PRC's brief foray into the oil business showed the depth of Washington's desire for secure foreign petroleum. This enduring consideration was destined to play a constant role in the American approach to Palestine.

While oil sensitized American leaders to the importance of Ibn Saud's goodwill, it soon became evident that the Saudi king was intensely interested in the Palestine question. In April 1943 the monarch sent a verbal message to Roosevelt explaining that he had so far remained silent on Palestine only because of a desire not to create difficulties for the Allies' war effort. However, he requested private assurances that the United States would take no action on Palestine without first allowing him to make his position known.[9] A few days later he reiterated these points in a written communication, and added the warning that "if—God forbid!—the Jews were to be granted their desire, Palestine would remain forever a hotbed of troubles and difficulties."[10]

In answer, Roosevelt sent Ibn Saud a definite pledge that "no decision altering the basic situation of Palestine should be reached without full consultation with both Arabs and Jews."[11] This commitment was kept secret for two years. Nonetheless, the promise made to Ibn Saud at this juncture has been seen as the boundary marking the beginning of official American involvement in the Palestine issue.[12]

Soon after Roosevelt took this step, the White House embarked on a secret diplomatic effort to resolve the Palestine question through direct agreement between Arabs and Zionists. Significantly, the initiative began to take shape while the administration was still in the final stages of its abortive attempt to issue an Anglo-American call for a moratorium on Palestine-related political activities. There was nothing contradictory between the two courses followed by the White House. In the joint statement on Palestine, the president saw the possibility of placing a sensitive and difficult issue into abeyance until the end of the war. Through his effort to promote a definitive agreement between Arabs and Jews, he hoped to resolve the same problem with a minimum of Great Power involvement. In each case he sought to neutralize the effects of the Palestine problem upon what he perceived as the immediate, and central, requirements of American foreign policy.

ROOSEVELT AS MIDDLEMAN: APPEALING TO IBN SAUD

Roosevelt's initiative in the summer of 1943 aimed at enlisting Ibn Saud's support for a Zionist takeover in Palestine. The general idea was first formulated in 1939 by the Saudi ruler's British confidant, H. St. John Philby. As conceived by Philby, the plan called for Arab acceptance of a Jewish Palestine west of the River Jordan. In return, all Arab countries east of Suez, with the exception of Aden, would gain independence. Organized world Jewry was to provide Ibn Saud with 20 million pounds sterling. A final provision required the British and American governments to be instrumental in proposing the plan and in serving as guarantors should the Saudi king accept it.

In late 1939 Philby interested Chaim Weizmann in the scheme. By the end of the year Weizmann had spoken of Philby's plan to Winston Churchill, then first lord of the admiralty. Two months later, while on a visit to the United States, the Zionist leader also outlined the proposal to President Roosevelt. Nothing resulted from these conversations, and the matter was apparently allowed to lapse during the early war years.

Philby, however, returned to Arabia where he broached the subject to Ibn Saud. He later described the king's reaction:

> There was nothing whatsoever to prevent him telling me then and there that it was an impossible and unacceptable proposition. . . . But the King did not tell me that. He told me, on the contrary, that some such arrangements might be possible in appropriate future circumstances, that he would keep the matter in mind, that he would give me a definite answer at an appropriate time that meanwhile I should not breathe a word about the matter to anyone—least of all to an Arab—and finally, that if the proposals became the subject of public discussion with any suggestion of his approving them, he would have no hesitation whatsoever in denouncing me as having no authority to commit him in the matter. I was perfectly prepared to accept that position, and the King knew that I would communicate his answer to Dr. Weizmann. He did not forbid me to do so.[13]

In early 1943 the issue was revived by Chaim Weizmann, who suggested to the Department of State that it was now appropriate for Zionists to seek a direct agreement with Ibn Saud.[14] With some modifications the plan Weizmann advanced at this point paralleled the original Philby scheme.

By June, Weizmann was able to bring his proposal directly to the president. An account of the meeting, subsequently prepared by Weizmann, indicates that very little was actually explained to Roosevelt about the planned agreement with Ibn Saud. Indeed, Roosevelt seized the initiative by announcing almost as soon as Weizmann entered the room that "he had gotten Mr. Churchill to agree to the idea of calling together the Jews and the Arabs."[15] Weizmann, to whom this was unexpected news, understood that both Roosevelt and Churchill planned to be present at such a gathering.

It is difficult to determine what caused Roosevelt's remarks. No record exists of any such agreement between him and the British prime minister, and nothing further appears to have been done either in Washington or London to arrange for a summit conference of British, American, Zionist, and Arab leaders. However, by the end of Weizmann's visit to the Oval Office it had been decided to send Colonel Harold Hoskins, a man with wide experience in the Middle East, to Saudi Arabia.[16] The official instructions subsequently given to Hoskins by the State Department ordered that he confine himself exclusively to asking Ibn Saud whether the king would enter into discussions with representatives of the Jewish Agency "for the purpose of seeking a solution of the basic problems affecting Palestine."[17]

Since Hoskins' mission dealt with Palestine, it first had to be cleared with the British government. The War Cabinet raised no objection but noted it saw no reason "to suppose that Ibn Saud's attitude would be such as to facilitate agreement between Arabs and Jews."[18] By the end of August Hoskins learned that the British were correct. Ibn Saud unequivocally rejected any suggestion of a meeting with Zionists. In his report, the presidential emissary tried to explain the king's attitude:

> [His] refusals and his reasons seemed . . . entirely consistent with his character and with his policies as he explained them to me. . . . They are based on his own religious and patriotic principles and reflect his sound political sense in recognizing clearly his limitations, both spiritual and physical, in this matter. He realizes that, despite his position of leadership in the Arab world, he cannot, without prior consultation, speak for Palestine much less "deliver" Palestine to the Jews, even if he is willing for even an instant to consider such a proposal.[19]

Ibn Saud also related "the reason for his personal hatred of Dr. Weizmann." This was found in the king's version of the approach made to him by Philby in 1940. The plan, he said, was tantamount to an attempt to bribe him with 20 million pounds. He was convinced that the whole thing had been instigated by Weizmann.[20] What particularly infuriated him, he said, was that Roosevelt had been mentioned as guarantor of the bribe.[21]

This categorical refusal ended all further American involvement with the Weizmann-Philby scheme. However, a few months after Hoskins' return from Arabia, Weizmann tried to interest Roosevelt once more in the same approach. Receiving support from Philby, the Zionist leader argued that Ibn Saud's apparent anger was only feigned and could be overcome were the American and British governments to make a firm and official offer along the line of the Philby plan.[22] The president was unmoved, and it appears that he was personally convinced that the Saudi king's angry reaction, although perhaps baseless, had nonetheless been sincere.[23]

An interesting feature of the Weizmann-Philby plan was that it rested upon the expectation of a massive exodus of Palestinian Arabs. The 20 million pounds to be given by organized Jewry to Ibn Saud were, in Philby's view, to finance "considerable transfers of [the] Arab population of Palestine." Weizmann candidly revealed to Sumner Welles his own interest in this aspect of the plan.[24]

Although Zionists publicly maintained that the displacement of Palestine's Arab inhabitants was not one of their objectives, they exhibited a different attitude in contacts with government officials. Weizmann's involvement with the Philby scheme is but one of the more outstanding examples of this. In the last few years before the outbreak of World War II, Zionists had approved the efforts of an American financier, Edward A. Norman, to promote a plan that called for the transfer of Palestine's Arab population to Iraq.[25] In 1941 Moshe Shertok suggested yet another new home for Palestinian Arabs. Speaking to an American diplomat in London, Shertok brought up the subject of Syrian independence and proposed that in return for Jewish financial and technical assistance, the Syrians could "relieve Palestine of a load of several thousand Arabs."[26]

Zionist interest in relocating Palestinian Arabs was increased by the belief that massive Jewish emigration from Europe would occur at the end of the war.[27] A memorandum submitted by the Jewish Agency to the Bermuda Refugee Conference in 1943 estimated that as many as 2 million Jews would have to leave Europe after the war.[28]

While it is somewhat unclear whether Roosevelt fully appreciated the importance placed on Arab emigration by the Weizmann-Philby plan, there is no reason to suppose he would have been offended by the notion. In December 1942, upon advising Secretary of the Treasury Morgenthau to "go easy" on the Palestine question, Roosevelt added that he had already decided on an approach to that issue.[29] Saying that he would place Jerusalem under a religious administration, the president explained that he "actually would put a barbed wire around Palestine, and . . . would begin to move the Arabs out." When Morgenthau asked whether this would be accomplished by allowing Zionists to "buy up the land," Roosevelt replied that it would not; he would provide land for Palestinian Arabs in some other part of the Middle East. In this way, he concluded, 90 percent of Palestine's population would eventually be Jewish.[30]

During the same conversation Roosevelt indicated the distinction he maintained between the political problem of Palestine and the growing Jewish refugee problem. Explaining his idea of moving Arabs from Palestine to make room for Jews, he described that approach as necessary so that Zionists would not bring in more settlers than "they can economically support . . . and that point has been reached." When Morgenthau asked what was to happen to "the two or three million Jews . . . still in the heart of Europe," Roosevelt referred to the possibility of settling many of them in Colombia—and made it plain that he was also considering other possible relocation areas for European refugees.[31] Among the latter, the president at times fixed on Angola, Cyrenaica, and Venezuela's Orinoco Valley.[32] However, none of these ideas evolved into a coherent plan. Actually, Roosevelt appeared to feel that the Jewish refugee problem was best seen as part of the broader issue of refugees of all faiths and nationalities with which the world would have to cope at the end of the war.

Certainly it was only within the latter context that Roosevelt took any direct steps. In late 1942 he established the secret "M" Project, composed of a small group of academics headed by Dr. Isaiah Bowman. Working in unmarked offices hidden in the annex of the Congressional Library, the staff of "M" Project was given the enormous task of suggesting options for massive population resettlement on a global scale in the postwar period. The president felt the project would eventually help him make decisions that would avert future wars.[33] Although "M" Project was disbanded upon Roosevelt's death, and its studies and recommendations filed away and forgotten, it is probable that the president saw it as an active effort by his administration to prepare the groundwork for policies of subsequent benefit to both Jewish and non-Jewish refugees.

Roosevelt knew that Zionist leaders opposed Jewish immigration to countries other than Palestine.[34] Yet he never accepted the premise that Palestine could fully meet the postwar resettlement needs of European Jewry. This readiness to distinguish between the political problem in Palestine and the humanitarian problem of Jewish refugees contributed to the flexibility he showed upon learning that Ibn Saud had rebuffed Colonel Hoskins. When Hoskins delivered a personal report of his conversation with the Saudi monarch, Roosevelt was already entertaining an idea of a compromise in Palestine that would preclude either Arab or Jewish nationalists from holding sway over the country.

THE ADMINISTRATION'S VIEWS
ON A COMPROMISE IN PALESTINE

On September 27, 1943, Colonel Hoskins spent over an hour with Roosevelt relating the negative results of his talks with Ibn Saud. Undiscouraged by the report, the president immediately outlined a new approach that he felt might provide grounds for a comprehensive American policy toward Palestine. Referring to his hopes of reducing the Jewish refugee problem through emigration to Colombia, he informed Hoskins that his current thoughts

> leaned toward a wider use of the idea of a trusteeship for Palestine—of making Palestine a real Holy Land for all three religions, with a Jew, a Christian, and a Moslem as the three responsible trustees. He said he realized it might be difficult to get the agreement of the Jews to such a plan but if Moslems and Christians of the world were agreed he hoped the Jews could also be persuaded. This concept to be successful would, he also realized, have to be presented as a solution larger and more inclusive than the establishment of an Arab State or of a Jewish State. He realized that this idea of course required further thought and needed to be worked out in greater detail, but at least that was the line along which his mind was running.[35]

These remarks led directly to a great deal of activity in the Department of State, to the preparation of the first recorded official American suggestion of a political framework within which the Palestine problem might be resolved, and to the communication of the plan to British officials at the bureaucratic level. The impact of Roosevelt's suggestion has generally been misjudged. The following is a typical misinterpretation:

> Musing aloud one day in 1943, [Roosevelt] asked: Why not make a genuine Holy Land, to be administered by trustees representing the world's three major faiths? This was only a typical Roosevelt trial balloon, but whatever chance the scheme had of implementation was killed by a State Department underling who seized the opportunity to come up with so patently anti-Zionist a plan for administering the trusteeship as to render it ludicrous.[36]

The so-called underling was Gordon P. Merriam, the assistant chief of the Division of Near Eastern Affairs, who within weeks of Roosevelt's suggestion outlined an administrative plan for Palestine that attempted to structure the general idea broached by the president. Wallace Murray passed Merriam's views on to Assistant Secretary Berle and to Acting Secretary

Edward Stettinius.[37] A thorough reading of documentary evidence shows that the possibility of circumventing the exclusive claims of Arabs and Jews through creating a "real Holy Land" was neither accorded cavalier treatment nor simply considered by a sole functionary within the State Department. There is also firm evidence that Roosevelt was kept informed of the efforts to convert his suggestion into a practicable format for the future administration of Palestine.

Merriam's original effort assumed that the conclusion implicit in Roosevelt's remarks—that the Palestine mandate would remain a failure if it continued to be governed as in the past—was "entirely sound." He suggested tentatively that the president's idea of a religious trusteeship might also be sound and was, at any rate, worth exploring. As "a basis for thought and discussion," he advanced the following ideas:

1. That Great Britain continue to act as the mandatory power.

2. That the view that Britain's primary responsibility was to prepare Palestine for independence be abandoned pending more propitious conditions, and that Palestine instead be regarded "for the time being as a sacred repository of the interests of Christianity, Islam, and Judaism."

3. That the basic responsibility for Palestine be removed from the League of Nations "and reposed in interested Christian and Islamic nations and the Jews."

4. That Palestine be opened to Jewish immigration in accordance with its economic absorptive capacity—but with the proviso that the country's Jewish population not rise above that of the Arabs.

5. That a body representing "those nations which manifest a legitimate interest in Palestine" supervise the British administration, and that this body's composition reflect the interests of the three major religions in the Holy Land.[38]

Arguing that the general idea of administering Palestine within a religious framework was worthy of serious thought, Merriam offered this opinion:

Certainly the Christian (numerically the greatest) interest in Palestine, taken as a whole, is in the main religious. There is more alloy in the Moslem religious interest, but it is probable that the Moslem, and specifically Arab, political interest in Palestine . . . is more defensive against Zionist political ambitions than agressive furtherance of Arab political ambitions. As to the Jews, while the Zionists are much heard from at present, that is because of the compassion felt for the Jews in Europe, and there is ground for believing that even now the main interest of most Jews in Palestine is religious and humanitarian, not political.[39]

Both Berle and Stettinius felt these ideas touched on a subject too important for them to comment upon without the approval of Secretary of State Hull, who was then absent from the country. It was decided that detailed consideration of the proposal should await Hull's return. However, Stettinius did reveal that Roosevelt had once briefly mentioned to him the idea of a religious trusteeship for Palestine. The undersecretary promised Wallace Murray that if the opportunity arose he would discuss the matter further with the president.[40]

Sometime after Hull's return in November, the task of suggesting a political arrangement for Palestine compatible with American interests was taken up by the State Department's Interdivisional Area Committee on Arab Countries. This planning group included "M" Project's Dr. Bowman. After rejecting a variety of alternatives, the Interdivisional Committee eventually decided in favor of a refined version of Merriam's scheme.[41] Bowman, a personal friend of the president as well as his "geographic advisor," served as the link between the State Department planners and the White House. When Wallace Murray forwarded a summary of the Interdivisional Committee's plan to Stettinius, he referred to it as having been "prepared at the President's request by Dr. Bowman and his associates in the Department."[42] Bowman kept Roosevelt abreast of the plan's development during 1943 and 1944.[43]

The Interdivisional Committee proposed that the Palestine mandate be replaced by a trusteeship. The new arrangement was intended to last indefinitely but would nonetheless eventually lead to an independent Palestinian state. A religious (Christian, Moslem, Jewish) "board of overseers" would provide an acceptable moral purpose for international action to override the particular claims of Arab and Jewish nationalisms.

Among the more important modifications made to Merriam's original suggestions was the reduced status of the religious "overseers." Unlike Merriam, who had closely followed the president's basic idea by assigning the religious board significant powers, the Interdivisional Committee designed it as an advisory bureau linked to the trusteeship administration—which would remain in British hands. An equally significant departure from Merriam's plan was a provision for establishing the Palestinian Arab and Jewish communities as autonomous entities with broad powers of self-government. The Interdivisional Committee hoped that the combination of a strong trusteeship administration, communal autonomy, and an overall religious veneer would in time lead to an abatement of Arab-Zionist tensions.[44]

In April 1944, Murray and Bowman outlined this proposal to the British undersecretary of state for foreign affairs, Sir Maurice Peterson. Although Sir Maurice could not speak officially for the British government, he assured the Americans that the Foreign Office would "go all out" for such a solution.[45]

The trusteeship plan never became a feature of American policy toward Palestine. By the spring of 1944 the White House was under strong domestic pressure to support the establishment of a Jewish Commonwealth. In the years that followed, both the Roosevelt and Truman administrations found it more difficult to think of Palestine in long-range terms. However, the central idea behind the trusteeship scheme—that in lieu of a continuation of the status quo or any immediate form of independence it would be better for Palestine to be administered indefinitely by a third party while local autonomy was enjoyed by the Arab and Jewish communities—long continued to be visible in the State Department's approach.

By the end of 1943 the Roosevelt administration had failed to establish a clear policy. Although the previous aloofness of the United States had yielded to an undefined, but undeniable, acceptance of some degree of responsibility for Palestine's future, Washington had yet to clarify its attitude toward the question of that country's ultimate political disposition.

In the months ahead the difficulties of doing this intensified. On the one hand, American Zionists, looking to the national elections scheduled for the fall of 1944, redoubled their efforts to commit policy makers to the support of Jewish statehood. On the other hand, Arab governments began to take collective action to impress Washington with the Arab world's united opposition to Zionism.

The Roosevelt administration soon abandoned any attempt to initiate a long-range Palestine policy. With the United States more frequently reacting under the spur of dominant momentary pressures, there ensued a period during which Washington embarked on an unprecedented series of flagrantly contradictory steps.

7. A POLICY OF NO POLICY: 1943-45

Following the American Jewish Conference of August 1943, Zionists could look forward to the national elections of November 1944. Zionist leaders immediately began reinforcing the impression that the "Jewish vote" would be awarded to candidates whose records on Palestine were demonstrably friendly. With indispensable help from supporters in the leading ranks of both major political parties, Congress and the White House were encouraged to court Jewish favor by committing the United States to a pro-Zionist policy prior to the elections.

Soon after its reorganization in the fall of 1943, the American Zionist Emergency Council launched a carefully orchestrated campaign against Britain's White Paper policy as a prelude to its election-year activities. Viewed by the Zionist leadership as an "educational" campaign to develop and test the political skill of their movement within the United States, this initial effort aimed at mobilizing American public opinion against the 1939 White Paper under the provisions of which Jewish immigration into Palestine was to cease at the end of March 1944.

At the direction of AZEC, local Zionist committees throughout the nation contacted congressmen, influential members of the Republican and Democratic parties, and municipal and state officials. Within months these efforts helped secure anti-White Paper resolutions from all major Jewish organizations, important national civic groups, labor unions, and Christian religious associations. This grassroots activity, coupled with an upsurge of anti-White Paper mail pouring into Washington, quickly caught the attention of policy makers.[1]

Prominent among those warning the administration to take a firm stand against the White Paper was the Democratic congressman from New York, Emanuel Celler. As early as September 1943, Celler wrote to Roosevelt's secretary, Marvin McIntyre, repeating advice he had recently given Cordell Hull to the effect that the administration should act before the Republicans took the initiative in speaking out against the White Paper. According to Celler, this was the "nub" of the question. The congressman warned that if New York's Governor Thomas E. Dewey, the likely Republican presidential candidate, issued an anti-White Paper pronouncement in the near future, "as far as the race of Abraham, Isaac and Jacob is concerned, he would steal the show right from under our noses."[2]

Politically minded officials capable of influencing foreign policy were early advocates of securing Jewish support by responding favorably to Zionist pressures. By late November 1943, for example, Assistant Secretary of State Breckinridge Long was urging Cordell Hull to oppose the British White Paper. This advice rested solely on Long's conviction that neither Hull nor Roosevelt should incur the wrath of American Zionists.[3] Although Long was strenuously opposed by the career Foreign Service officials who dealt with Near Eastern Affairs, Hull, who had spent the greater portion of his years in public service as a dedicated congressional Democrat, was more receptive.[4] On December 13, 1943, the secretary of state discussed the White Paper with the British ambassador, Lord Halifax:

The President and myself, and other officials of this Government, in the light of our international interest in the Jewish situation, based primarily on the residence and citizenship of some five million Jews in this country, are in earnest sympathy with the proposal of the Jews that the immigration provision be extended by the British Government beyond March thirty-first.[5]

It turned out that the British were already on the verge of abrogating the deadline. Halifax pointed out that the White Paper not only established a terminal date for immigration but also an upper limit on the number of Jews to be allowed into Palestine. He informed Hull that London had "agreed or was in the act of agreeing" that Jewish immigration might continue after March to the full limit of the White Paper quota, a policy that would permit some 30,000 more Jews to land in Palestine.

In early February 1944, Hull learned from the American ambassador in London that the British government had formally adopted this step.[6] Although the decision temporarily defused the White Paper issue, it did not reduce Zionist activity in the United States. Having successfully conducted a nationwide campaign against the White Paper, Zionists began an equally energetic, and more sustained, effort to elicit official American support for the creation of a Jewish state in Palestine.

THE PALESTINE
RESOLUTION IN CONGRESS

On January 27, 1944, two identically worded resolutions were introduced in the House of Representatives. The proposed measures called for the United States to

> use its good offices and take appropriate measures, to the end that the doors of Palestine shall be opened for free entry of Jews into that country, and that there shall be full opportunity for colonization, so that the Jewish people may ultimately reconstitute Palestine as a free and democratic Jewish Commonwealth.[7]

A similar measure was introduced in the Senate four days later, jointly sponsored by Robert Wagner and Republican leader Robert Taft.

The resolutions placed the Roosevelt administration in a quandry. Still determined to avoid any commitment on Palestine, the White House could not ignore the adverse effect that its outright opposition might have on the Democratic Party in the November elections. The problem was exacerbated by the impending Allied invasion of Europe and the need to avoid any outbreak in the Middle East that would complicate the military situation. As a result of these factors, the administration embarked on a secret, well-coordinated campaign to prevent congressional approval of the Palestine resolutions. Slightly over six weeks after the measures were first introduced, these obstructive tactics were successful. However, the actions of the White House raised serious questions in the minds of leading Zionists about Roosevelt's attitude toward their cause.

The feeling of having been outmaneuvered that some American Zionist leaders retained once the Palestine resolutions were placed in abeyance was not without foundation. This was particularly true in the case of Rabbi Abba Hillel Silver, the cochairman of the American Zionist Emergency Council, who was most responsible for the decision to press for the resolutions. An ardent Zionist from his early youth, the Cleveland rabbi rejected what he termed the path of "backstairs diplomacy" and instead preferred public confrontation with government officials.[8] Unlike the coleader of AZEC, Stephen Wise, Silver had no lengthy association with Roosevelt. On the contrary, although Silver's supporters described him as apolitical in American domestic affairs, the rabbi's closest relation with a leading political figure appears to have been his friendship with Robert Taft, who as a senator from Ohio was known as "Mr. Republican."[9]

According to Nahum Goldmann, the question of seeking pro-Zionist congressional resolutions was debated for months within the upper levels of the Zionist leadership before the measures were finally introduced.[10]

Throughout the deliberations Silver demanded immediate efforts to obtain the resolutions. Supported by Rabbi Wise, Goldmann argued that the Allies' continuing military requirements in the Middle East would almost surely cause such resolutions to be blocked "by either the White House, the State Department or the War Department, or all three." Goldmann also cautioned his colleagues against believing assurances obtained from individual congressmen since "this was an election year and members of Congress and other politicians were ready to promise the Jews almost anything with the hope of getting votes."[11]

However, the decisive event allowing Silver's view to prevail in Zionist councils was not linked to promises of congressional support, but rather to what Silver took to be a definite indication from Cordell Hull that the Roosevelt administration would not oppose pro-Zionist resolutions in the House and Senate. The rabbi gained this impression when he asked Hull whether the State Department had reservations over the prospect of a congressional declaration on Palestine. When Hull responded that such a matter was entirely for Congress to decide, Silver concluded that his project had received the "green light" from the department and, by extension, from the Roosevelt administration.[12] Although Goldmann tried to temper Silver's enthusiastic appraisal by pointing out that Hull had simply and "in the best diplomatic tradition . . . limited his remarks to taking the completely correct position," the Cleveland rabbi now mustered sufficient backing to launch a campaign on behalf of the Palestine resolutions.[13]

Hull was less than frank in his conversation with Silver. In his *Memoirs* he describes the feeling of the Department of State as follows:

> The passage of these resolutions, although not binding on the Executive, might precipitate conflict in Palestine and other parts of the Arab World, endangering American troops and requiring the diversion of forces from European and other combat areas. It might prejudice or shatter pending negotiations with Ibn Saud for the construction of a pipeline across Saudi Arabia, which our military leaders felt was of utmost importance to our security. And it would stimulate other special interests to press for introduction of similar resolutions regarding controversial territorial issues relating to such areas as Poland and Italy.[14]

With this host of reasons for opposing the resolutions, the secretary of state nonetheless confined himself to answering Silver's query "in the best diplomatic tradition." His answer, of course, was also strictly in accord with the Roosevelt administration's policy of avoiding a direct clash with the Zionists. That policy would continue to be a fundamental feature of the government's approach to Palestine. Nowhere was it more evident than in the administration's carefully constructed, and equally carefully hidden, onslaught against the 1944 Palestine resolutions.

Silver's original approach to Hull was characteristic of the Rabbi's penchant for "confrontation politics." In asking the opinion of the secretary of state, the Zionist leader could scarcely have been ignorant of the true attitude prevailing in the State Department. Barely five months had passed since Zionists had singled out the so-called cabal in the department as responsible for the stillborn Anglo-American Palestine statement. By posing his question directly to Hull, Silver hoped to present the Roosevelt administration with a neatly packaged devil's choice: to admit its opposition to the Palestine resolution and be placed on the defensive in the eyes of American Jews at the beginning of an election year, or to disguise its opposition and thereby open the way for speedy congressional action favorable to Zionist aims. However, if Silver was attempting a clever political trick, he soon discovered that Hull was equally adept at that sort of game. With the close, but discreet, involvement of the president, the administration quickly mobilized its forces to bloc the Palestine resolutions under the one banner immune to Zionist attack: the claim of military necessity.

On January 28, the day after the resolutions were introduced in the House of Representatives, Congressman Sol Bloom, chairman of the House Committee on Foreign Affairs, informed Assistant Secretary of State Berle that his committee was preparing to consider the measures. Pointing out that the resolutions had been introduced by a Republican and a Democrat and had the support of the House majority and minority leaders, Bloom announced that he did not plan hearings. Instead, he would simply have his committee "report the resolution out favorably and let it go at that." At the congressman's request, Berle relayed this information to the British Embassy, adding his own opinion that the resolution would surely pass.[15]

According to comments later made by Bloom, it was the American Council for Judaism's demand for public hearings that prevented the House Committee on Foreign Affairs from dealing cursorily with the matter.[16] While this might have been true, it is likely that Bloom welcomed the opportunity to hold the hearings as a means of placating Zionists through the publicity that would be generated for their cause. For the truth is that Bloom knew of the administration's decision to prevent passage of the resolutions even before the hearings commenced. Thus, although Bloom was undoubtedly personally sympathetic to the measures, a fact he made abundantly evident during the committee's deliberations, his real role was to provide a degree of compensation to the Zionists for the disappointment that ultimately awaited them.

It is unclear at just what point Bloom learned of the administration's intentions. However, he must have known at least one day before the hearings opened. On that date, February 7, Secretary of War Stimson, a personal friend of the congressman, spoke with him about the pending resolution.[17] Although no record of this conversation exists, Stimson must have repeated what he wrote in a letter sent that day to the chairman of the Senate Foreign Relations Committee, Thomas Connally. In his message to Connally, Stimson referred to the proposed Senate Resolution as "a matter of deep military concern to the War Department," and added:

> I feel that passage of this resolution at the present time, or even any public hearing thereon, would be apt to provoke dangerous repercussions in areas where we have many vital military interests. Any conflict between Jews and Arabs would require the retention of troops in the affected areas and thus reduce the total forces that could otherwise be placed in combat against Germany. The consequent unrest in other portions in the Arab world would keep United Nations resources away from the combat zone. I believe therefore that our war effort would be seriously prejudiced by such action.[18]

Hull also wrote to Connally. Significantly, he based the State Department's opposition to the resolution completely on "military considerations advanced by the Secretary of War."[19] Hull did not mention any of the other factors described in his memoirs as having shaped the State Department's outlook on Palestine.

While the House Committee began its public hearings on schedule, the Senate Committee decided to consider the Palestine resolution in closed session. Meanwhile, Zionists pressed an intensive campaign to pressure both houses of Congress. The 1944 *Annual Report* of the Zionist Organization of America described the activities surrounding the Palestine resolutions in this way:

> The local committees performed magnificently. From large cities and hamlets, thousands of letters, postcards, and telegrams poured in upon the members of the Senate and the House. Every member of the Foreign Affairs Committee was contacted several times by his constituency. Congressmen were unanimous in exclaiming that they had seldom seen such amazing public interest in a piece of legislation.[20]

This agitation brought rapid reactions from Arab governments. Within days of the commencement of the Bloom Committee hearings, protests were made to the Department of State by Iraq and Egypt.[21] By the end of February, not only had these countries reiterated their views but further protests reached Washington from Lebanon, Syria, and Saudi Arabia.[22]

This diplomatic initiative marked the first concerted approach to Washington by Arab governments over the Palestine question. The gist of the Arab argument at this point may be gleaned from an aide memoire left with the State Department by the Egyptian minister. After expressing concern that the "demand for the abolition of the White Paper will hardly meet any opposition in Congress," the note went on to say:

It is useful to recall, in this connection, that the question of persecuted Jews and that of the Zionist problem are not one and the same thing. While the Arab people, in common with the rest of the world, bitterly condemn the barbarous treatment to which the Jews have been subjected, nevertheless, they feel that such oppression should not, under any circumstances, serve as a reason for persecuting, in turn, the people of Palestine, made up of Moslems, Christians and Jews, thus subjecting them to the tender mercies of the Zionists! For neither Palestine, nor the neighbouring Arab people, will accept such a situation with equanimity.

. . . Firmly united [the Arabs], find in the aggression on one of them, aggression on all; and will thus not tolerate politicians and Zionists denying Palestinians the benefits of the Atlantic Charter.[23]

Despite their formal protests, the pro-Western elites who controlled the Arab governments initially sought to minimize public awareness within their own countries of the proposed congressional resolutions.[24] However, such news could not be effectively suppressed. Spread by various media, including the Axis propaganda machine in the Middle East, it quickly began to stir passions in the Arab world. American diplomats in the Middle East registered concern over the uproar that passage of the resolution might cause.

From Baghdad the American minister, Loy Henderson, reported that interest in the Palestine resolutions was so intense it "crowded all other aspects of foreign affairs into the background." Henderson felt that passage of the resolutions would make it impossible "for the bulk of the politically conscious people of Iraq to reconcile the policies called for in the resolution with the pronouncements of the War aims of the United States and other members of the United Nations." He was also convinced that adoption of the resolutions would

greatly assist the efforts of the Axis to convince the Arabs of this area of the lack of sincerity and of the duplicity of the United States and would more than offset the good will which has been created . . . in this area by various American governmental organizations in recent years.[25]

State Department officials in Washington shared this alarm. With Roosevelt's approval, American diplomats in Arab capitals were instructed to explain to their host governments that American foreign policy formulation was the prerogative of the Executive Branch and that the proposed resolutions, even if passed, could not be considered binding upon the government.[26] The same point was made to Arab diplomats in Washington.[27] While Arab spokesmen acknowledged the technical validity of this explanation, they in turn pointed out that the distinction might be lost on the average Arab in the Middle East.[28]

At a cabinet meeting on February 17, ten days after Bloom opened hearings on the House resolutions, Roosevelt intervened directly. The president wanted to lay the issue to rest by having Stimson make public his letter of February 7 to the chairman of the Senate Foreign Relations Committee.[29] The secretary of war, however, demurred and suggested instead that the same result might be achieved by having military representatives testify secretly before Connally's committee in executive session.[30] Roosevelt agreed but made it clear that should this not kill further action on the resolutions Stimson's letter would have to be published.[31]

The fate of the Palestine resolutions was now sealed; but there remained the problem of having them shelved without embroiling the administration in a controversy with the Zionists. The White House and the State Department were determined to avoid as far as possible any onus of responsibility by making it appear that military considerations beyond their control were the sole issues in question. Stimson, still as reluctant to take responsibility for a move opposed by the Zionists as he had been in the earlier matter of the Anglo-American statement, hoped to satisfy the president by shifting responsibility onto the shoulders of his own high-ranking military subordinates. It was also doubtful whether members of Congress would be prepared to abandon the resolutions on the basis of military information that, if not made public, might raise difficulties for them with their own Jewish constituents. Finally, there was the problem of providing Sol Bloom, whose committee had ended its public hearings, with a plausible excuse for dropping the measure.

What ensued was a veritable scramble to avoid any appearance of responsibility for the demise of the Palestine resolutions. Within days of the February 18 cabinet meeting, Chief of Staff General Marshall appeared before Connally's Senate committee. During the supposedly "secret" session, Marshall outlined the military reasons that militated against proceeding with the resolutions. Marshall's comments were soon common knowledge on Capitol Hill.[32] However, nearly a month would pass before the Palestine resolutions were finally discarded.

In the interval, Bloom tried to arrange for representatives of the War Department to speak to his own committee, undoubtedly in an effort to cover himself with the Zionists.[33] The congressman also tentatively suggested that the administration compensate Zionists for the collapse of the original resolutions by allowing his committee to approve a much watered-down version.[34] However, when he failed to get any encouragement from either the Department of War or State, he did not pursue the issue.

Since Marshall's declaration had not killed the resolutions, there was greater pressure upon the luckless Stimson to publish his letter to Connally. Moreover, now that Bloom was also asking for testimony from the War Department, Stimson uneasily faced the prospect of being tagged as the sole obstacle to Zionist hopes. The Secretary of War, quite possibly at some cost in pride, made one last effort to avoid this uncomfortable position.

In early March Assistant Secretary of War John J. McCloy called at the State Department to discuss the status of the Palestine resolutions with Wallace Murray and Assistant Secretary of State James C. Dunn. McCloy's mission was to argue that the State Department should take a more active part in opposing the resolutions "since they had political as well as military implications."[35] Revelling in this classic opportunity for bureaucratic vengence, Murray reminded McCloy "of the earlier experience the Department had had in endeavoring to obtain the support of the War Department on the issue of a joint American-British declaration on Palestine and of the complete lack of cooperation of the War Department in that instance." Murray then piously added that the State Department now felt, "as was clear from the text of Mr. Stimson's letter to Senator Connally," that military considerations had come to "far outweigh political implications."[36]

Stimson bowed to the inevitable by making his opposition to the Palestine resolutions public on March 17. However, he did not publish his letter to Connally. This was not surprising since that letter was dated February 7, a fact that, if revealed at that stage, would have embarrassed Stimson, Connally, Bloom, and the entire Roosevelt administration. Instead, the secretary prepared another letter that he sent to Bloom. Without elaboration the letter simply stated that further action on the Palestine resolutions would prejudice the war effort.[37]

Zionists publicly responded to the deferment of the Palestine resolutions by claiming a limited success. Rabbi Silver announced a "moral victory" since the resolutions had not been adopted by Congress solely because of military considerations.[38] The American Zionist press also praised Congressman Bloom for his efforts on behalf of the measures.[39]

However, Zionist leaders were not so complacent in private. Near the end of February, Silver—who was by then aware of the true attitude of the War Department—complained to Assistant Secretary of State Long that "the Administration, having led him up to this point and having encouraged him, should now find a way for him to extricate himself."[40] Although Silver's agitation was partly over the misleading impression he had been given by Hull, it was at least equally rooted in his awareness that failure of the resolutions would place him in an extremely embarrassing position vis-a-vis his colleagues in the Zionist movement. Long described the Rabbi's demeanor as "calm and deliberate" but giving evidence of "resentment and smoldering anger."[41]

Within upper Zionist circles, despite the plaudits he received from the Zionist press, Sol Bloom did not escape blame for the collapse of the resolutions. In May 1944, Louis Lipsky—a close associate of Silver—told the congressman of a widespread suspicion that "while you seemed to favor the Resolution, you were in fact working all the while for its defeat."[42]

A by-product of the administration's sabotage of the congressional resolutions was an innocuous presidential endorsement of Jewish endeavors in

Palestine, given to Zionist leaders as a consolation. Six days before Stimson wrote his letter to Bloom on March 17, Roosevelt met with Wise and Silver. The president apparently promised that he would speak out clearly in support of Zionism at a later date.[43] In the meantime, he authorized them to make the following statement:

> The President authorized us to say that the American Government has never given its approval to the White Paper of 1939.
> The President is happy the doors of Palestine are today open to Jewish refugees, and that when future decisions are reached, full justice will be done to those who seek a Jewish National Home, for which our Government and the American people have always had the deepest sympathy and today more than ever, in view of the tragic plight of hundreds of thousands of homeless Jewish refugees.[44]

This revealed no new departure in American policy. The Zionist leadership, however, was eager to give the appearance of having salvaged something from the frustrated campaign for the Palestine resolutions. Roosevelt's authorized message was accordingly praised as "the first clear-cut expression of sympathy with Zionist aims" to be made during the war years.[45]

Nonetheless, Wise and Silver were under no illusions about its real significance. Four days after their reception at the White House, the Zionist leaders wrote to Roosevelt enclosing a draft statement they wished him to issue. The suggested declaration supported free and unrestricted entry of Jews into Palestine with "full opportunity for colonization," and also stated that the purpose and intent of American policy toward Palestine was to see a Jewish Commonwealth constituted in that country.[46]

Although Roosevelt did not comply with this request, the vague comments he permitted Silver and Wise to make in his name were sufficient to cause consternation in the Arab world. To allay these misgivings, Roosevelt immediately authorized American diplomats in Arab capitals to explain that while the U.S. government had never approved the White Paper, neither had it ever taken any position at all relative to that document.[47]

In an immediate sense the tactics adopted by the Roosevelt administration were successful. Defeat of the resolutions was secured without involving the government in an open quarrel with the Zionists; the American Jewish community had been mollified by a presidential statement; and the possibility of disturbances in the Arab world had been averted.

Viewed from a broader perspective, however, the administration's approach left much to be desired. Although it avoided the problem of defining American policy toward Palestine, it deliberately obscured the full extent of the administration's opposition to the pro-Zionist measures placed before Congress. By publicly basing its attitude entirely upon transient military factors, the administration strengthened the impression that U.S.-Arab relations were immaterial to the development of American policy toward

Palestine. In this manner the administration created complications that would haunt it once military requirements could no longer be invoked as the basis of its approach to Palestine.

For the Zionists, the collapse of the Palestine resolutions in March 1944 did not entail an unmitigated defeat. They drew comfort from the opportunity to obtain many expressions of support from individual congressmen.[48] Moreover, it could not have escaped the notice of Zionist leaders that the administration's drawn out and difficult strategy was indicative of the political strength attributed to the Zionist Movement.

INCREASED ZIONIST
PRESSURE ON THE WHITE HOUSE

After the congressional resolutions were shelved, Zionists wasted no time advising the Roosevelt administration of their dissatisfaction with its approach to Palestine. Near the end of April, Rabbi Silver wrote to Senator Wagner setting forth two steps that he considered necessary for the administration (and, by implication, the Democratic Party) to regain the goodwill of American Jews. First, said Silver, the president should issue "a clear-cut statement" in support of the Zionist cause. Second, he "should call off the 'hounds of war' " and give the "green light" for passage of the Palestine resolutions.[49]

A few days later Louis Lipsky urged Bloom to help the Zionists attain these two objectives. Lipsky frankly stated that the Zionist leadership could not be expected "to take a position of resignation" in view of "the fact that the Administration is determined to give us gestures instead of action."[50] After warning the Congressman that Rabbi Silver, whom he described as a man listened to "by vast sections of our people," was on the verge of concluding that the Roosevelt administration would do no more than "send . . . Rosh Hashonah greetings to Jews from time to time," Lipsky urged Bloom to persuade the president to issue a pro-Zionist statement. Lipsky stressed that unless this were done, the Republican Party could be expected to benefit in November. There would, he claimed, "break out a veritable storm of criticism against the Administration" which would be "highly undesirable in the critical months ahead." He added:

> The Republicans know what is going on very well. They are preparing to use the issue to the utmost. They can afford to make liberal promises and they are going to make them. . . . They will be used extensively among the Jews of New York, Chicago, Philadelphia, Boston, Cleveland, and elsewhere during the election campaign.[51]

Lipsky's prediction was well founded. In June the Republican National Convention approved a resolution that declared:

In order to give refuge to millions of distressed Jewish men, women and children driven from their homes by tyranny, we call for the opening of Palestine to their unrestricted immigration and land ownership, so that in accordance with the full intent and purpose of the Balfour Declaration of 1917, and the resolution of a Republican Congress in 1922, Palestine may be constituted as a free and democratic Commonwealth. We condemn the failure of the President to insist that the mandatory of Palestine carry out the provision of the Balfour Declaration and the mandate while he pretends to support them.[52]

With their own convention scheduled to open the following month, Democrats became increasingly anxious to counter the Republicans' bid for Jewish votes. Fears were raised that failure to have a competitive Palestine plank in the Democratic platform would seriously hurt the president in New York.[53]

Writing in the *Zionist Review*, Judge Bernard Rosenblatt expanded upon the reasons for concern:

New York is entitled to 47 electoral votes, while only 266 electoral votes are necessary to elect a President. Whether the vote of the State of New York goes to one party or another (and that may be by relatively few votes in a population of over 13 million) will make a difference of 94 votes in the electoral college, so that it may be readily understood why a presidential contest may hinge on the political struggle in the state of New York. . . . Only once during the last three-quarters of a century was a President elected who failed to carry the State of New York.[54]

Zionist sympathizers diligently repeated this argument to delegates at the Democratic Convention. In an exceptionally candid letter to Elmer Berger, Congressman Celler explained why he had so ardently argued before the convention's Platform and Resolution Committee that it would be "suicidal" to refrain from a pro-Zionist commitment on Palestine. As a "practical politician" he had addressed the committee "in the language that politicians understand":

One of the purposes of the Convention is to re-elect a democratic president of the United States. Only those who bury their heads in the sand fail to realize that there is a Jewish vote. Such a vote is not dissimilar to a "Catholic vote," or a "labor vote," or a "Daughters of the American Revolution vote."[55]

The congressman stressed why he felt it necessary to appeal for the Jewish vote in pro-Zionist terms:

I know Brooklyn. . . . It is the largest Jewish community in the world. Enough votes may have been lost by non-adoption of the Palestine plank to lose the borough to the Democrat Party. Loss of the Borough might have meant loss of the City which in turn might have meant the loss of the State and the defeat of the Democratic nominee.

You know the bit of doggerel, "For want of a nail a shoe was lost," etc. That was precisely the situation.[56]

Inspired by this reasoning, the convention adopted a Palestine Plank that clearly outdid the Republicans'. Although shorter, the Democrats' pronouncement called for a "Jewish Commonwealth" and was, therefore, more pleasing to Zionists:

We favor the opening of Palestine to unrestricted Jewish immigration and colonization, and such a policy as to result in the establishment of a free and democratic Jewish Commonwealth.[57]

Competition for the Jewish vote did not abate. By mid-September Samuel Rosenman warned Roosevelt that the Republican Party's pro-Zionist bid was having some effect.[58] In early October the Republican presidential candidate, Thomas Dewey, pledged that as president he would work toward opening Palestine to unlimited Jewish immigration and land ownership and for that country's "reconstitution . . . as a free and democratic Jewish Commonwealth."[59]

On October 15 Roosevelt sent Robert Wagner a message reinforcing the position taken by the Democratic Convention in July. After repeating the text of the Democrats' Palestine plank, the president's note promised:

Efforts will be made to find appropriate ways and means of effectuating this policy as soon as practicable. I know how long and ardently the Jewish people have worked and prayed for the establishment of Palestine as a free and democratic Jewish Commonwealth. I am convinced that the American people give their support to this aim and if re-elected I shall help to bring about its realization.[60]

The historian Frank E. Manuel has correctly appraised this statement as differing from all previous presidential salutations to Zionists in that "it was not a mere expression of sympathy or favor; it was a promise to find ways and means to fulfill a policy plank of the Presidential political party."[61] In Palestine the Arab community immediately protested the president's remarks by boycotting scheduled discussions with an official American economic mission.[62] Upon Roosevelt's reelection a few days later, both Zionists and their opponents eagerly awaited some sign of how he would treat his campaign promise of October 15.

ROOSEVELT AFTER THE ELECTION

With Roosevelt once more in the White House, Zionists immediately reopened their campaign for pro-Zionist congressional resolutions. On November 9, 1944, Rabbis Wise and Silver, accompanied by Nahum Goldmann, called on Edward Stettinius, who had recently replaced Cordell Hull as secretary of state, to inquire whether the department would oppose renewed action on the resolutions.[63] The Zionist leaders pointed out that according to a letter sent by Secretary Stimson to Senator Taft in early October, the War Department had now altered its obstructive position. Stimson had announced:

> I find that there is still strong feeling on the part of many officers in my department that the passage of [pro-Zionist Congressional resolutions] would interfere with our military effort. However, I do feel that the military considerations which led to my previous action in opposing the passage of this resolution are not as strong a factor as they were then.
>
> In my judgement, political considerations now outweigh military, and the issue should be determined upon the political rather than the military basis.[64]

Stettinius avoided a direct answer, saying only that he wished to discuss the matter with the president.[65] When the secretary of state brought up the question with Roosevelt a few days later, it was decided to inform Wise that the administration felt "it would be unwise to have the resolutions reconsidered at this time."[66] In the meantime, Congressman Bloom joined those who wanted to revive the Palestine resolutions.[67] Stettinius therefore also informed him of the administration's position.[68]

Zionist leaders were deeply divided over how to react to these ominous signs of official recalcitrance. On the one hand, Rabbi Wise and Nahum Goldmann felt it would do no good, and possibly quite a bit of harm, to antagonize the White House by seeking congressional action over its opposition.[69] On the other hand, Rabbi Silver called for a direct demand for passage of the resolutions and a comprehensive drive to mobilize public support behind the Zionist position.

The effects of this split were evident almost at once. The day after learning that Roosevelt opposed reintroduction of the Palestine resolutions, Wise sent Stettinius a cable that revealed some of the difficulties he faced. The Zionist leader's remarks indicate that the manner in which Stettinius relayed the president's views had left him with the impression that Roosevelt contemplated taking pro-Zionist action at a later date:

> Things would be made easier for me if I might have a word, however brief, stating what you said to me about the Chief's suggestion.[70]

When the secretary of state informed the president of this request, and asked for guidance, Roosevelt replied that nothing should be told to Wise "or anybody else" and concluded that the Zionists would simply "have to trust my judgement on this."[71] Whatever reasons Wise had for believing that the White House would subsequently reward Zionists for refraining at the moment from reopening the issue of the Palestine resolutions, Roosevelt was determined that they be kept secret.

Although this placed Wise at a disadvantage vis-a-vis more militant elements in Zionist ranks, he was unwilling to oppose the president's wishes. However, Silver and Senator Wagner pressed forward with demands for immediate action on the Palestine resolutions.

On November 28, Bloom, who had received encouragement from Silver, allowed the House Foreign Affairs Committee to report favorably a revised form of the resolution. The amended version dropped the word "Jewish" preceding "democratic Commonwealth," as well as the phrase calling upon the U.S. government to take "appropriate action" in support of the Zionist cause in Palestine. In the words of Richard Stevens, the altered measure was "almost as innocuous as the official declarations of pre-Biltmore days."[72] Although this rendered the resolution relatively impotent, Bloom had nonetheless gone against the president's desires as they had been relayed to him by Stettinius. When Roosevelt's outlook became generally known on Capitol Hill a few days later, Bloom came under heavy criticism from members of his own committee. In an apparent attempt to extricate himself from an embarrassing position, the congressman sent Stettinius a rambling and confused letter in which he tried to explain his reasons for leading his committee into precipitate action.[73] Despite the favorable report of the Foreign Affairs Committee, the House deferred to the White House by not dealing with the proposed resolution.

In the meantime, Silver and Wagner, apparently under the illusion that the House Resolution was safe, concentrated their attention on the Senate. On December 2 Wagner advised Roosevelt that the Senate Foreign Relations Committee had agreed "reluctantly and only after long discussion" to delay action on the Palestine resolution in order to allow the secretary of state to comment on the measure. Wagner warned that if Stettinius opposed the resolution "so soon after the Party Platform and your own [October 15] Declaration, a bad impression might be created not only among the Jewish people, but among non-Jewish people as well."[74]

While the future of the resolution before the Senate committee was still in question, Wagner and Silver called on Stettinius. Although by this time Roosevelt had personally told Wagner that no action should be taken on the Palestine measure, the senator refused to drop the matter. He continued to insist that American interests would not be harmed by the resolution as it would be only a congressional endorsement of a position already taken by the president.[75]

The administration had all along counted on the chairman of the Senate Foreign Relations Committee, Connally, to overcome Wagner's stand. Connally's loyalty to Roosevelt encouraged a belief that the resolution could be killed without the necessity of overt intervention by the administration. Reporting to Roosevelt on his interview with Wagner and Silver, Stettinius confidently predicted:

> Connally will be able to persuade the Committee not to take action at this time. He feels he has the situation in hand and that he will not have to ask me to testify.[76]

The committee chairman was far too sanguine about his own influence in the face of mounting Zionist pressure. Only 24 hours after offering his optimistic appraisal to Stettinius, Connally called the secretary to insist, "on five minutes notice," that the administration issue an official statement against the proposed resolutions.[77] He worried that were this not done immediately the resolution would be voted out favorably. Stettinius described the ensuing events to Roosevelt:

> I immediately went over and testified in secret session of the Committee, making clear that this was a highly delicate matter; that I would talk to them in absolute confidence; and that there might be serious repercussions if there was any violation of this confidence.
> I explained the delicate situation in the Arab world; that you, yourself, had not yet had an opportunity to deal with this question as exhaustively as you have in mind; and that we felt that passage of the Resolution now would tie your hands and not leave you in a flexible position. The general sentiment of the Committee was that they would be willing to leave the entire matter in the hands of the Executive for the time being and not report out the Resolution. However, they insist on a public statement from the Executive, saying that in our judgement the passage of this legislation at this time would be unwise from the standpoint of the general international situation.
> We must give Senator Connally a prompt answer. . . .
> Would you please advise me . . . whether, because of the broad issues involved, you would be willing to make the statement, or whether you prefer that the statement be issued from the State Department.[78]

Roosevelt preferred to stay in the background. Two days later the State Department publicly asked that no action be taken on the Palestine resolutions because of the current "general international situation."[79] The president congratulated Stettinius for an approach that was "just right."[80]

By the close of the 78th Congress, Zionists had failed to obtain the expression of support they sought from that body. With this, the Zionists' internal differences blew into a full-scale quarrel. The scope of the controversy was revealed in a letter written by Wise to Roosevelt only days after the State Department's intervention. After expressing his unhappiness over the fate of the Palestine resolutions, Wise disassociated himself and his chief supporters from Silver's confrontation tactics.[81] He also announced his resignation from the chair of the American Zionist Emergency Council.

Wise's departure from the Zionist leadership was short-lived. Under the shadow of his failure to obtain the congressional resolutions, Silver resigned as cochairman of the AZEC, as well as from the chair of that body's Executive Committee. Rabbi Wise assumed the post of chairman, which he occupied until Silver was reinstated some six months later.

Speaking on behalf of the Jewish Agency Executive to the Executive Committee of the American Zionist Organization, Nahum Goldmann clarified some of the reasons for the prevailing displeasure with Silver:

> The political effect of the deferment of the resolution on Palestine at the request of the Administration is grave indeed. Antagonizing the President of the United States is a serious matter. . . . The policies of the Zionist Emergency Committee during the last month were contrary to Zionist policy as conceived and carried out during the last twenty years. . . . If this fight against the President and this policy of attacking the Administration is continued it will lead us—and I choose my words very carefully—to complete political disaster.[82]

Goldmann's views were not based simply on the president's immense power in world affairs. The fundamental danger he perceived was that the White House might be antagonized to the point of articulating clearly and publicly the considerations that caused it to balk at Zionist demands.

The enduring and established Zionist policy to which Goldmann referred was that of working for long-range goals by consistently seeking limited commitments from the American government. Even when these efforts elicited no more than vague and essentially noncommittal responses, Zionist tactics required the most favorable interpretations to be placed on relations with Washington. Not only did this preserve a veneer of harmony between American policy makers and Zionist leaders, it also helped further the public claim that—with the exception of a few perverse individuals in the lower ranks of the State Department—there existed no substantive differences of opinion between Zionists and the final arbiters of American national interests.

The chief asset enjoyed by Zionists in the United States was the absence of significant public opposition. Rabbi Silver's tactics risked causing the government itself to offer such opposition. In the event that the administration opposed Zionists in a serious public debate over the question of whether, or to what extent, it was in the interests of the United States to further the creation of a Jewish state in Palestine, Zionists might find the congressional and popular support they had carefully cultivated over the past five years swept away. Goldmann had indeed chosen his words carefully when he raised the specter of "complete political disaster."

Stephen Wise shared Goldmann's concern. This is plainly evident in a telegram Wise sent to Stettinius the day before the secretary met with Senator Wagner and Rabbi Silver to discuss the future of the Palestine resolutions:

> We would all be happy if the Chief and you could see your way to give approval. . . . [However] . . . I . . . do not wish to have action taken to the contrary to your and the President's recommendations. Situation should under no circumstances be permitted to arise in which Senate Committee would be informed of Chief's opinion communicated through you to us in confidence. In that case it would be best for Senate Committee to postpone action throughout this session.[83]

Just what presidential opinion Wise was so anxious to keep from the Senate Foreign Relations Committee cannot be precisely ascertained. However, one strong possibility suggests itself. On December 3, the day before Wise's urgent cable to Stettinius, Roosevelt sent Senator Wagner an explanation of what he termed "the only trouble about additional action by either House in regard to Palestine at this time."

> There are about a half a million Jews there. Perhaps another million want to go. They are of all shades—good, bad and indifferent.
>
> On the other side of the picture there are approximately seventy million Mohammedans who want to cut their throats the day they land. The one thing I want to avoid is a massacre or a situation which cannot be resolved by talking things over.
>
> Anything said or done over here just now would add fuel to the flames, and I hope that at this juncture no branch of the Government will act. Everybody knows what American hopes are. If we talk about them too much we will hurt their fulfillment.[84]

This message was a significant sign of the seriousness with which the president viewed Arab opposition to Zionism. Moreover, it indicated that Roosevelt considered it an imperative of American foreign policy toward Palestine to avoid "a situation which cannot be resolved by talking things over." If Wise knew that the president was thinking along these lines, there would have been good reason for discomfort over the possibility that the Senate Foreign Relations Committee would become aware of it. Certainly, Wagner recognized the harmful implications contained in Roosevelt's message. When rumors concerning the letter began to circulate, the Senator's office flatly denied the communication's existence.[85] Zionist support in Congress might indeed have suffered greatly had it become known that Roosevelt held such a stark view of Arab opposition.

Roosevelt had kept abreast of the Arab unrest produced by pro-Zionist declarations of Republican and Democratic candidates during the elections and by the reintroduction of the congressional Palestine resolutions.[86] However, an additional factor that entered into the administration's calculations in the closing months of 1944 was the attitude of the Soviet Union. Evidence had been accumulating that pointed to growing Soviet interest in the Middle East. Much of it indicated that Moscow might base its diplomacy in the region on traditional Russian anti-Zionism.[87] In the State Department this raised fears that the Soviet Union might take advantage of the Palestine problem to win the support of the Arab world.[88]

In late November, as if to emphasize that Arab resentment could not be ignored by American policy makers, the president forwarded to Rabbis Wise and Silver copies of protests over the Palestine resolutions made by several Arab organizations then meeting in Cairo.[89] A month later, during a meeting with Stephen Wise, Roosevelt mentioned the possibility of Soviet opposition to Zionist aims in Palestine.[90] In answering criticism by Congressman Celler of his postelection policy on Palestine, the president again alluded to the Soviet factor. The reply to Celler, who had demanded to know whether there existed an acceptable explanation for the president's "retreat" from his promise of October 15, also implied that Roosevelt still retained an open mind on the Palestine issue:

> Give me an opportunity to talk with Stalin and Churchill. There are all kinds of schemes—crackpot and otherwise—being advanced. Perhaps some solution will come out of this whole matter. Naturally I do not want to see a war between a million or two people in Palestine against the whole Moslem World in that area—seventy million strong.[91]

The president's mention of Stalin and Churchill referred to his impending journey to Yalta. The tripartite summit meeting, held between February 4 and 11, brought forth Zionist demands for definitive action by the administration. Senator Wagner reminded the president that the discussions abroad might be "of fateful significance for the Palestine issue and the future of the Jews as a people." The senator argued that "if Arab consent is to be a prerequisite of any political settlement [in Palestine], there can be no hope of justice to the Jewish people." What had to be done, he said, was to establish a Jewish state with "determination and speed," for the Arabs would accept an "accomplished fact."[92]

Roosevelt had already come to conclusions that prevented him from falling into line with the strategy advocated by Wagner. Retaining a firm faith in his own diplomatic abilities, the president had decided to meet with Ibn Saud in order to explore possibilities for some agreed solution to the Palestine problem. In early January Roosevelt requested advice from James M. Landis, director of economic operations in the Middle East.[93] Landis stressed that nothing useful could be done unless it went to the "root" of the matter, which in Landis's view required distinguishing between a Jewish Commonwealth and a Jewish "National Home." Arguing that a compromise might be worked out on the basis of some conception of a National Home, Landis pointed out that the "one great stumbling bloc" was the question of Jewish immigration.

> [Immigration] at present possesses a significance that it should not possess because of its relationship to the political as distinguished from the economic future of Palestine. In other words, if the extent of immigration can be related to the economic absorptive capacity of Palestine rather than to the political issue of a Jewish minority or majority, there is hope of striking an acceptable compromise even on the immigration question. This is particularly true now for I believe that the economic absorptive capacity of Palestine has been grossly exaggerated.[94]

Having received this measure of encouragement, Roosevelt proceeded with his plans to meet Ibn Saud. At the end of the Yalta Conference, during which the topic of Palestine did not arise, the president went to Egypt, where without prior announcement he met Ibn Saud aboard the American warship *Quincy* on February 14, 1945.

Ibn Saud spoke plainly about his opposition to Zionism. When Roosevelt asked the king's advice on the problem of European refugees, Saud suggested they return to lands from which they had been driven. In his opinion, those who for various reasons could not do so should be given "living space in the Axis countries which oppressed them."[95] According to the official American memorandum of Roosevelt's conversation with Ibn Saud, the king then elaborated on the Palestine issue:

> His Majesty . . . expounded the case of the Arabs and their legitimate rights in their lands and stated that the Arabs and the Jews could never cooperate, neither in Palestine, nor in any other country. His Majesty called attention to the increasing threat to the existence of the Arabs and the crisis which has resulted from continued Jewish immigration and the purchase of land by the Jews. His Majesty further stated that the Arabs would rather die than yield their lands to the Jews.[96]

When Ibn Saud ended these remarks with an appeal for American support, Roosevelt replied that

> he wished to assure His Majesty that he would do nothing to assist the Jews against the Arabs and would make no move hostile to the Arab people. He

reminded His Majesty that it is impossible to prevent speeches and resolutions in Congress or in the press which may be made on any subject. His reassurance concerned his own future policy as Chief Executive of the United States.[97]

Roosevelt seemed deeply impressed by the firmness of Ibn Saud's views. The president later remarked that of "all the men he had talked to in his life, he had least satisfaction from this iron-willed monarch."[98] While returning to Washington, Roosevelt confided to Edward Stettinius that he hoped for a conference with congressional leaders to "re-examine our entire policy in Palestine."[99] He was also convinced that were bloodshed between Arab and Jew to be avoided, some "new formula" would have to be found.[100]

News of the surprise meeting with Ibn Saud dismayed Zionists. Emanuel Celler complained that the president had not arranged to meet any Palestinian Jewish leaders during his trip abroad.[101] Zionists' mortification increased on March 1, when the president reported to Congress on the Yalta Conference. Referring to his stop in Egypt, Roosevelt told his congressional audience:

Of the problems of Arabia, I learned more about the whole problem, the Muslim problem, the Jewish problem by talking with Ibn Saud for five minutes than I could have learned in an exchange of two or three dozen letters.[102]

Samuel Rosenman, who witnessed the president's address, felt "this was a thought that must have popped into his head just at that moment." According to Rosenman, the president's comments had to be understood in the context of the general character of his presentation to Congress, which Rosenman described as marred by a "halting, ineffective manner of delivery."[103]

On the other hand, Secretary of Labor Frances Perkins heard Roosevelt's speech with relief, feeling it laid to rest rumors that the president was in a weakened condition:

His speech was good. His delivery and appearance were those of a man in good health. All of us, I think, felt that whatever unspoken fears we might have were dissipated.[104]

Whatever impression Roosevelt may have given those who listened to him on March 1, the impact made upon him by Ibn Saud seems to have been profound. During an informal luncheon with Colonel Hoskins on March 3, the president referred several times to his meeting with the king. He also told Hoskins that a Zionist state "could be installed and maintained" in Palestine "only by force." When Mrs. Roosevelt remarked that Zionists were perhaps willing to risk conflict with the Arabs, Roosevelt argued that "there were

15,000,000 or 20,000,000 Arabs in and around Palestine and that, in the long run, he thought these numbers would win out."[105]

The president's public comments after his return from Yalta generated quite a bit of controversy. Edwin Johnson, Democratic senator from Colorado, lapsed into hyperbole that not only typified much of the reaction but also could not have been calculated to give more offense to the Arab world:

> With all due respect to the President and King Ibn Saud, I must say that the choice of the desert king as expert on the Jewish question is nothing short of amazing. . . . I imagine that even Fala [Roosevelt's pet dog] would be more of an expert.[106]

The reaction among Zionists led to rapidly mounting calls for the return of Dr. Silver and his more militant policies.[107] The furor subsided somewhat in mid-March when Rabbi Wise was received at the White House and authorized to issue the following statement in the President's name:

> I made my position on Zionism clear in October. That position I have not changed, and shall continue to seek to bring about its earliest realization.[108]

In turn, this statement provoked a spate of protests from the Arab world, among which was one from Ibn Saud.[109] In reply to the Saudi king, Roosevelt recalled their recent meeting in Egypt and reiterated the assurance he had given at that time promising to take no action that might prove hostile to the Arab people.[110] Similar replies were forwarded to Syrian and Iraqi leaders.[111]

On April 12, 1945, Roosevelt's death ended what, with particular reference to the last few months of his life, can perhaps be best described as a self-contradictory involvement in the Palestine question.

THE LEGACY OF ROOSEVELT

In the interval between the 1939 White Paper's promulgation and Roosevelt's death, the American government shifted its relation to the Palestine problem from that of an essentially disinterested spectator to that of an interested party. By implication of the promise to Ibn Saud and other Arab leaders that the United States would consult with Arabs and Jews before taking any decision affecting the basic situation in Palestine, Washington claimed a role in determining that country's final disposition. Even more strongly, of course, was the same claim entailed in Roosevelt's pro-Zionist campaign promise of October 15, 1944.

While American involvement in the Palestine issue was a reality at the end of Roosevelt's life, its implications were still unclear. The keystone of Roosevelt's approach was the avoidance of any decision on the long-range question of Palestine's eventual political fate. Somewhat ironically, American acceptance of a role in Palestine's future initially resulted from the administration's wish to avert the need for expressing its views on just that issue. The purpose, after all, of Roosevelt's promise to Ibn Saud in 1943 had been to reassure the Arabs that whatever levels of intensity might be reached by domestic pro-Zionist agitation, the American government would remain impartial toward the Arab-Zionist quarrel until the end of the war, when it would formulate a considered and definitive position on the basis of full information from both sides. The willingness of the Arab governments to accept this position helped pacify the Middle East during the war years.

In contrast to his dealings with the Arabs, the president was not frank with American Zionists about his desire to defer considerations of Palestine until after the war. Although the Zionist leadership was aware of the administration's preference for that approach, its opposition was strong enough to cause the president to abandon plans to place the Palestine question officially into abeyance. Nonetheless, the administration, with the direct involvement of the president, worked in various ways to frustrate attempts to commit the American government to a pro-Zionist policy. For much of the period between 1939 and 1945, the administration's evasive policy, and the adroit political maneuvering required to pursue it, was justifiable in terms of immediate military requirements. Because of this it was largely immune to Zionist attack.

As the tide of battle turned irreversibly in favor of the Allied powers, the Roosevelt administration's difficulties in coping with Zionist demands multiplied. Nonetheless, until the fall of 1944, the president showed—both through the intricacies of his ongoing, but subtle, struggle with American Zionists and his diplomacy with the Arabs—an unyielding purposefulness in avoiding pressures for a firm statement of American intentions toward Palestine. However, by October 1944, with the outcome of the war virtually assured, Roosevelt was caught firmly between the hammer of Zionist political strength on the domestic front and the anvil of Arab determination to block Zionist plans.

That the Pro-Zionist declaration made by Roosevelt on October 15, 1944, was an act of political expediency is clear from the circumstances that surrounded it. That it did not constitute a definitive statement of intent seems equally evident from the alacrity with which he retreated from the declaration after his reelection.

It is impossible to establish conclusively whether the contradictory actions taken by the president between October 1944 and his death six months later formed part of a premeditated tactical approach. It is clear, however, that the president's patent inconsistency formed a recognizable pattern. Cordell Hull's comment that Roosevelt "in general . . . at times talked both ways to Zionists and Arabs" was never more applicable than in this period.[112]

It is also obvious what the effect of the president's post-October approach must have been upon the protagonists in the Palestine drama. Neither Zionists, although publicly clinging to the October 15 statement, nor Arabs, although officially basing themselves on Roosevelt's promises, could have predicted with any certainty what the president might have ultimately supported in Palestine. Indeed, perhaps up to the time of his death Roosevelt himself did not know. Still, the effect of his last six months in office had been, either by design or chance, to preserve a condition that had long prevailed: The American government remained unidentified with any particular formula for Palestine's final political disposition.

Roosevelt should have known that he could not long sustain the frenetic pace of conflicting promises. A document taken to Yalta by the president's State Department advisors noted that the administration's policy had so far aimed "primarily at forestalling any action which would be likely to create a situation in the Near East that would endanger the war effort and jeopardize American interests in that area." It went on to warn: "this preventive policy cannot be continued indefinitely. The adoption of a more positive policy is clearly desirable."[113]

Although Roosevelt avoided defining Washington's aims in Palestine, he did so at the price of creating future difficulties. One drawback of his approach was that it left his successor the problem of coping with a string of contradictory commitments. Charges of betrayal and bad faith would be leveled against the United States by Arabs or Zionists—or by both—regardless of the course chosen by its government.

Second, neither Arabs nor Zionists could ignore Roosevelt's vacillation. The knowledge that American policy makers found it difficult to take a firm stand would in the future stimulate each group to adopt a rigid attitude in hope of exerting maximum influence in Washington. On the one hand, Zionists were aware that the declaration obtained from the president on October 15, 1944 had resulted from the Democratic Party's fear of the Jewish vote. On the other hand, Arabs could reflect upon their united protest against the Palestine resolution as a factor that helped undermine that measure in the spring of 1944. It is also likely that Ibn Saud and other Arab leaders perceived the conciliatory tone of Roosevelt's remarks aboard the *Quincy* as largely due to the stern position taken by the Saudi king.

Yet another, and more far-reaching, problem was posed by the fact that while Roosevelt's supportive comments to Zionists were publicly and widely disseminated, his pledges to Arab leaders were made discreetly in diplomatic communications. A related issue was that the president's reservations concerning the Zionist program for Palestine were never made public. To the rank and file of Americans, both Jewish and non-Jewish, the little official opposition to Zionists goals that surfaced to public view after 1939 was apparently related to transient requirements of military operations. Even in late 1944, when the administration opposed the congressional Palestine resolutions on the basis of the general "international situation," the State Department's declaration gave the impression that some particular and temporary political situation was responsible. Actually, as the records show, the president and his foreign policy advisors held serious doubts over some of the fundamental contentions advanced by Zionists as well as over the long-term implications of committing the United States to a pro-Zionist policy. The next president had to cope with this legacy of public statements while facing the same realities that produced Roosevelt's unpublicized reservations.

8.   THE PALESTINE PROBLEM AT THE END OF WORLD WAR II

In some ways, Palestine benefited considerably during the six years it took to crush the Axis powers. Early economic dislocations caused by the closure of the Mediterranean to commercial shipping were rapidly offset by the country's new role as a supply depot for Allied forces in the Middle East and North Africa. Palestinians, Arabs and Jews alike, found employment as laborers and technicians. Palestinian agriculture found a ready market in the military. Finally, the skills and energy of the Jewish community were put to lucrative use in establishing several war-related industries, which among other things produced industrial diamonds, textiles, automobile parts, armor plating, and medical supplies.[1]

Under the impetus of wartime prosperity, the Palestinian Arab community engaged in agricultural modernization and in the expansion of manufacturing and service enterprises. Although the Arab economy remained basically agricultural, native Palestinians were increasingly investing in urban businesses. By the summer of 1945, newly registered Arab corporations included an airline and an insurance company, and plans were well in progress for the establishment of cement and weaving industries.[2]

The generally improved economic situation did not dissipate an air of tension that hung over the country by the closing months of the war. Both Arabs and Zionists felt the moment approaching when the British government could no longer avoid a decisive policy. Both parties were also aware that the past six years had seen the international dimensions of the Palestine problem develop in ways that would exert a definite, although as yet unknown, influence on the outcome of their struggle.

THE JEWISH COMMUNITY
AT THE END OF THE WAR

The Yishuv emerged from the war greatly strengthened. Somewhat paradoxically, this situation reflected the Zionists' heightened sense of insecurity in the face of forces that appeared to be gathering to prevent the creation of a Jewish state. Thus, not the least of the enhanced resources enjoyed by the Jewish community was its military strength. During the war the Haganah had been purposefully developed into a well-organized and substantial force. By the end of 1944 it counted nearly 37,000 members, many of whom had been trained in the British Army.[3] Many more veterans were recruited at the end of hostilities in Europe.[4] The Zionist force had also amassed a considerable quantity of arms and other military supplies.[5] Despite occasional searches by mandatory authorities, the bulk of the illegally held arms and munitions were successfully concealed in caches scattered across Jewish-controlled areas of Palestine.

Following implementation of the Land Transfer Regulations foreseen by the 1939 White Paper, Jewish land purchases reflected the Zionists' determination to entrench themselves as strongly as possible before Palestine's final status was decided. Between September 1939 and September 1946, the Jewish National Fund increased its holdings from 473,000 to 835,000 dunums (a dunum is approximately one fourth of an acre). A variety of ingenious techniques permitted 79 percent of this expansion to occur in zones where the White Paper either prohibited or restricted land acquisition by non-Arabs.[6]

Zionist land policy had both political and military purposes. Ever since the abortive 1937 Peel partition scheme, Zionist holdings had been extended over as wide an area as possible in anticipation of an eventual decision to divide the country. Tracts were also purchased with an eye to their strategic importance. In 1943 the Zionist leadership began establishing settlements in key geographic points and manning them with units of Haganah's elite strike force, the Palmach.[7] The director of the Jewish National Fund's purchasing operations, A. J. Granott, later observed that "national policy, security and strategy" had been "linked through acquisition with the settlement objective, all being welded together into a united, systematic, purposeful, and far-seeing policy."[8]

While the Yishuv's position was being strengthened through such measures, dissident elements within the Jewish community were also becoming more powerful. Unwilling to accept the authority of Zionist agencies officially recognized by the mandatory, these factions engaged in terrorist activities against the British administration.

The largest of the two terrorist organizations, the Irgun Zvai Leumi, suspended operations during the early years of the war. However, soon after the Axis reversals at el-Alamein and Stalingrad, the Irgun command decided to start a terrorist campaign against the mandatory regime.[9] For various reasons the decision was not acted on until early 1944, when government offices in Jerusalem, Tel-Aviv, and Haifa were bombed. These attacks opened a confrontation between the British and the Irgun that did not really subside until the end of the mandate.

Unlike the Irgun, the terrorist "Stern Gang," known after its messianic founder, Abraham Stern, refused to cease anti-British activities even during the darkest days of the war in the Middle East. In Sternist eyes the White Paper placed Great Britain squarely in the ranks of enemies of the Jewish people.[10] Any compromise with the mandatory administration was considered tantamount to treason. Indeed, much of the Stern Gang's activity was devoted to terrorizing or assassinating opponents within Palestine's Jewish community.[11]

By the last year of the war, terrorism had led to a visible deterioration in relations between the mandatory and the Jewish Agency. Resentment in the Yishuv over the White Paper had been inflamed by a series of searches for illegal Haganah arms and by the confiscations and trials that attended the discoveries of some caches during 1943 and 1944. When the terrorist campaign escalated in the latter year, Yishuv spokesmen condemned the dissident factions. However, the official Zionist leadership took no active steps to aid in the suppression of terrorism.[12]

Still, leaders of the Zionist Movement worried that Jewish terrorism would undermine the political pursuit of statehood. They also viewed the Irgun as a grave threat to their own authority within the Yishuv.[13] In the summer of 1944, futile efforts were made to bring the Irgun under Jewish Agency control.[14] Had they been aware of this attempt, it is doubtful that British authorities would have been pleased. For the government of Palestine sought not merely a respite from terrorist attacks but the eradication of the threat to internal stability posed by the very existence of terrorist organizations.

The mandatory's dissatisfaction with official Zionism's reaction to terrorism was forcefully expressed in a joint statement issued in October by the commander-in-chief of British Middle East Forces and the Palestine government:

> Verbal condemnation . . . is not in itself enough. . . . Accordingly, . . . the Jewish community in Palestine, their leaders and representative bodies [are called upon] to . . . discharge their responsibilities and not to allow the good name of the Yishuv to be prejudiced by acts which can only bring . . . dishonour on the Jewish people as a whole.[15]

Motivated by both the desire to protect their authority within the Jewish community and the fear of seeing their political relations with the British government harmed beyond repair, the leaders of the Jewish Agency now decided to move against the Irgun.[16]

As initially conceived, the campaign was to have utilized the Haganah to compile information that could then be used to disrupt Irgun operations. To this end, a number of Irgunists were rounded up by Haganah agents and held for interrogation. However, before these measures could proceed very far, the assassination of the British minister resident in the Middle East, Lord Moyne, caused a drastic revision of the original plans.

Lord Moyne was gunned down by Palestinian Jewish terrorists just outside his Cairo residence on November 6, 1944. The murder of this highly respected member of the British war cabinet shocked the Zionist leadership. Things seemed to take a dire turn when Prime Minister Churchill reacted to the assassination by warning that terrorism might cause Zionist sympathizers to "reconsider the position we have maintained so consistently and so long in the past."[17]

In light of these events, the Jewish Agency expanded its opposition to the dissidents by cooperating actively with British authorities.[18] This new policy permitted the mandatory administration to detain some 200 suspected terrorists before the end of November.[19]

At the same time, the powerful labor organization, the Histadrut, took strong measures to isolate the terrorists from Jewish communal life. Conceived by David Ben Gurion, the new policy required members of the Yishuv to deny employment, shelter, or protection to known members of terrorist groups, to resist terrorist threats and extortion, and—most importantly—to cooperate with British authorities.[20]

Although Lord Moyne's assassins had belonged to the Stern Gang rather than to the Irgun, official Zionist efforts were directed almost exclusively against the latter organization. The cause of this appears to have been that the Sternists, shocked by the strength of the reaction to Moyne's murder, privately agreed to suspend their activities.[21]

Zionist cooperation with the British lasted for six months. During this period, the Irgun, crippled by the detention and deportation of many of its members, remained for the most part quiescent. However, by mid-June 1945 the official Zionist attitude had changed. The turnabout in policy seems to have been caused by political pressures at upper levels of the organized Yishuv.[22] Certainly, among the Yishuv as a whole there was a distaste for turning fellow Jews over to British authorities. The Jewish Agency's instructions that Irgunists be reported to the Haganah were generally unpopular:

> [It was] an order that many Jews who were far from the spirit of the Irgun or Stern found . . . impossible to obey. They knew that a denunciation to Haganah meant subsequent arrest by the Mandatory police, that it meant handing Jews over to Gentile punishment.[23]

The failure of official Zionist leaders to aid in the struggle against Jewish terrorists prior to the assassination of Lord Moyne, and the relatively brief duration of their cooperation after that event, were products of the growing militancy that gripped the Zionist Movement after 1939. Rooted in the White Paper, and exacerbated by revelations of the decimation of European Jewry, the conviction that Jewish statehood should be uncompromisingly and strenuously demanded had gained lodgement throughout the Yishuv.

This was illustrated by the reception accorded to Chaim Weizmann at the end of 1944 when he visited Palestine for the first time since 1939. Although Weizmann was treated warmly, he found his leadership eroded. A committed anglophile who persisted in hoping for British-Jewish cooperation, Weizmann was simply out of step with the Yishuv. He was disturbed to discover that certain negative features had developed within the Jewish community:

> here and there a relaxation of the old, traditional Zionist purity of ethics; a touch of militarisation, and a weakness for its trappings; here and there something worse—the tragic, futile, un-Jewish resort to terrorism, a perversion of the purely defensive function of the Haganah; and worst of all, in certain circles, a readiness to compound with the evil, to play politics with it, to condemn and not to condemn it, to treat it not as the thing it was, namely an unmitigated curse to the National Home, but as a phenomenon which might have its advantages.[24]

Weizmann did not fail to speak his mind while in Palestine. Through press conferences, public addresses, and private contacts with communal leaders, he advocated cooperation with the mandatory. In trying to promote his gradualist outlook, he also worked to dispel the idea that a Jewish state could be created immediately. However, his faith in the ultimate attainment of the Zionist goal was not shaken. Shortly before returning to Britain in March 1945, he spoke to the Jewish Agency's Inner General Council and declared that "the younger ones among you will yet be living in a Jewish state in Palestine."[25]

In direct contrast to this was the position taken by David Ben Gurion, who demanded a Jewish state "in our time."[26] Although no open quarrel developed between Weizmann and Ben Gurion prior to the former's departure from Palestine, it was clear that despite their agreement on ultimate objectives the two men stood for distinctly different tactical approaches. The American consul general at Jerusalem concluded that any serious confrontation between Weizmann and Ben Gurion would be resolved by the Yishuv in favor of the latter.[27]

By the end of World War II, Palestine's Jewish community was becoming increasingly intransigent. Although the option offered by terrorist groups—a full-scale revolt against the mandatory administration—was still overwhelmingly rejected, the political climate was such that the possibility of an eventual armed clash could not be discounted. Leadership had passed to those whom Weizmann characterized as seeing possible political leverage to be gained through terrorism. In the months ahead, events would lead to an alliance between the terrorist groups and the Yishuv's quasi government as they combined their efforts to force Britain's agreement to the establishment of a Jewish state.

THE ARAB COMMUNITY
IN PALESTINE

Zionists' inclination to view British, rather than Arab, opposition as the most important obstacle to their hopes was due to the continuing disorganization of Palestine's indigenous community. During the early years of the war the Palestinian Arabs' organizational stagnation had been virtually complete. The dominant faction of the prewar era, the Husseini clan's Palestine Arab Party, lay shattered. Its leaders had either fled the country or were detained in exile by the British. The party's ruin appeared assured by the activities of the mufti of Jerusalem, Haj Amin, who from his refuge in Berlin not only helped direct pro-Nazi intrigues in the Middle East but also took an active interest in the anti-Semitic policies of his benefactors.[28]

Those factions that at one time had rivaled the Husseinis were equally unable to provide leadership to Palestinian Arabs. In part this was due to the elimination of many anti-Husseini spokesmen by the mufti's henchmen during and immediately after the Arab rebellion. For example, the National Defense Party, the organ of the Nashashibi family—once the most prominent challenger to the mufti's power—virtually ceased to exist after its principal leader was assassinated in 1941. However, a more important factor inhibiting Arab political organization was the mandatory's policy of requiring Arab nationalists who had been exiled during the rebellion to refrain from political activity as a condition for repatriation. Not until the end of 1942 did the government remove its ban on Arab political activity.[29]

Even then, the Arab community was slow to take steps toward reorganization. Although there existed six recognizable political factions at the end of the war, they were unable to agree on a common front. As had been true in the past, the sources of discord among the various Palestinian Arab groups tended to lie in personal rivalries among the leaders rather than in questions of ideology. Despite their disunity, however, Palestinian spokesmen were of one mind in their utter rejection of Zionism, their denial of any historical, moral, or legal justification for that movement, and in their demand for the establishment of Palestine as an Arab state.[30]

By 1945 two major factions were vying for control of the Arab community. One of these was formed by a group of notables who had led the Istiqlal (Independence) Party after 1936. The second was composed of the followers of the Husseini family.[31] Although the mandatory permitted the latter to reconstitute the Palestine Arab Party in 1944, it continued to prohibit the return to Palestine of the party's former president, Jamal el-Husseini, who had been held in Rhodesia by the British since 1941. A senior member of the family, Tewfik al-Husseini, nominally occupied Jamal's place after 1944.[32]

Continuous internal bickering almost kept the Palestinians from being represented at the 1944 Alexandria Conference, the meeting that prepared the way for the creation of the Arab League several months later. Despite efforts by non-Palestinian—particularly Egyptian—leaders to encourage the formation of a multifactional Palestinian group to attend the conference, the Husseini Party's insistence on a controlling voice led to a deadlock that was not broken until the last-minute designation of Musa al-Alami as the sole delegate from Palestine. Scion of an aristocratic Palestinian family, al-Alami was a British-trained lawyer with impeccable nationalist credentials. Although previously associated with the Palestine Arab Party, al-Alami had kept above the bitter swirls of intra-Arab politics. It was his known commitment to the Palestinian cause, as well as his reputation as an individualist, that made him an acceptable choice to the various factions.[33]

The discussions in Alexandria boosted Palestinian Arab morale. At the conclusion of the conference a protocol, signed on behalf of Egypt, Syria, Lebanon, Iraq, Transjordan, Saudi Arabia, and Yemen, declared the intention of those countries to create a League of Arab States and announced their common support for the Palestinian Arabs. The protocol also called upon the British government to adhere to the provisions of the 1939 White Paper.[34] It linked Palestine to the overall interests of the Arab world in these terms:

> Palestine constitutes an important part of the Arab world and . . . the rights of the Arabs [in Palestine] cannot be touched without prejudice to peace and stability in the Arab world. . . . the promises binding the British Government and providing for the stoppage of Jewish immigration, the preservation of Arab lands, and the achievement of independence for Palestine are permanent Arab rights whose prompt execution would constitute a step toward the desired goal and toward the stabilization of peace and security.

Arguing that the Arabs were "second to none in regretting the woes . . . inflicted upon the Jews of Europe," the declaration concluded by denying that the Holocaust was relevant to Palestine's future:

> The question . . . should not be confused with Zionism, for there can be no greater injustice and aggression than solving the problem of the Jews of

Europe by another injustice, that is, by inflicting injustice on the Palestine Arabs.[35]

On March 22, 1945, the seven adherents to the Alexandria Protocol concluded a pact establishing the League of Arab States. An annex to the League Pact took the position that by virtue of its detachment from the Ottoman Empire after World War I, Palestine possessed an international existence that "cannot de jure be questioned any more than can the independence of any other Arab country."[36] Special provision was made for Palestinian representation on the Council of the Arab League, a body in which all member states were represented.

The formation of the Arab League served notice that the Arab states as a unit stood behind the Palestinian Arabs in their struggle against Zionism. In light of the initial success achieved by united Arab diplomacy in opposing American pro-Zionist congressional resolutions in the spring of 1944, this development raised optimism throughout the Arab world. However, while the Palestinian Arabs gained a significant avenue for the presentation of their case in foreign capitals, nothing concrete had been done toward achieving the political consolidation of their own community. This fundamental problem was to plague them throughout the final three years that led to Israel's creation.[37]

DIMENSIONS OF THE
PROBLEM OF IMMIGRATION

By the spring of 1945 the opposed nationalisms of Arabs and Jews in Palestine were embodied in the attitudes held by the two communities toward the question of immigration. The issue had always been central to the Palestine problem. Until Weizmann's "gradualist" policy was wrecked in 1939, Zionists were content to defer pressing ultimate political demands while Palestine's Jewish community grew through mass immigration. Recognition of this threat to their own nationalist aspirations provided the mainspring for the Arabs' opposition to the mandate and for the violent peak it reached between 1936 and 1939. Although the Biltmore Program clarified the political essence of the Arab-Zionist controversy, the question of immigration remained in the forefront of Palestinian affairs for most of the mandate's duration.

Two things lent urgency to the issue in the final months of the war. One of these was the imminent fulfillment of the quota of Jewish settlers to be permitted into Palestine under the White Paper. The British government's waiver of the original March 31, 1944, deadline for Jewish immigration had averted a crisis at that time, and the full force of Zionist outrage over the

White Paper had been dampened by assurances that Jews would continue to enjoy legal entry into Palestine—at least for some time to come. On the other hand, the protests emanating from Arab spokesmen over Britain's failure to adhere strictly to the original terms of the White Paper seemed more *pro forma* than substantive.[38] The real point at issue, so far as the Arabs were concerned, was the numerical limit on Jewish immigrants established in 1939. Arab determination to hold the mandatory to the White Paper's ceiling of 75,000 immigrants was made plain at the Alexandria Conference.

Zionists never concealed their willingness to resist, by force if necessary, strictures on Jewish immigration. While the initial bellicose statements made in 1939 by Zionist leaders were generally replaced by expressions of cooperation with the mandatory once the war in Europe began, Zionists had not modified their essential hostility to the White Paper. In March 1943, only months after the immediate Axis military threat to the Middle East was removed by the battle of el-Alamein, Ben Gurion called upon the youth of the Yishuv to prepare for the fighting that would come at the end of the war.[39]

The second factor contributing to the intensification of Arab and Jewish interest in postwar immigration was the plight of large numbers of European Jews. The Arab position, which Ibn Saud took care to explain to Roosevelt aboard the *Quincy*, was that humanitarian concern for Jewish survivors of European barbarism could not be allowed to dictate anti-Arab measures in Palestine.

Whatever inherent logic this argument may have had, the future of European Jewish survivors could not so easily be divorced from Palestine. The trauma undergone by world Jewry, and shared by concerned Gentiles, as the planned and extensive nature of Hitler's genocidal policy became known, gave compelling immediacy to the notion that Palestine should serve as the focal point for the reconstruction of Jewish life. Largely in lieu of a considered appraisal of the political basis of Arab-Zionist tensions, public opinion in the West—and particularly in the United States—emotionally supported the idea that Jews who had survived the Holocaust should not be denied entry into Palestine.

Zionist leaders did not overlook the political significance of humanitarian concern. Against the backdrop of restrictive immigration policies followed by the Western democracies, the Zionist contention that only a Jewish state would relieve the suffering of European Jews carried great weight. This was especially true after the Bermuda Conference of 1943 demonstrated that Washington was not prepared to modify existing American immigration laws.[40] Not until 1947 was a belated, and ultimately futile, effort made to relax American immigration policy with a view to aiding the growing numbers of Europeans of all faiths displaced from their homes by the war.

In keeping with their fundamental belief that only Palestine could, or should, serve as the homeland for the Jews of the world, Zionist leaders had little interest in encouraging liberal immigration policies in other lands. A memorandum submitted by the Jewish Agency to the Bermuda Conference, for example, merely noted that "unhappily" the possibility of large-scale emigration by Jews to countries other than Palestine was "for political and other reasons . . . limited in the extreme."[41] Advanced without condemnation or outrage, this conclusion served as the premise for an argument that "no greater contribution" could be made toward resolving the problem of European Jewry than "doing everything possible" to give practical effect to the Balfour Declaration.[42]

Much the same approach had been taken in an earlier memorandum submitted by Zionist leaders to the State Department and the British Embassy in Washington. On that occasion, however, the Zionists' lack of concern over the restrictive immigration policies of the Western democracies explicitly rested on the assumption that anti-Semitism was an inevitable feature of Jewish minority status. Even should European victims of anti-Semitism be permitted to emigrate in large numbers to places other than Palestine, the memorandum warned, "such a migration will in the end serve merely to transfer the problem from one country to another." At the same time, any suspicion that prevailing immigration laws in the West might be a disservice to European Jews was implicitly downgraded by the Zionists' claim that Palestine "should be capable of absorbing another three million inhabitants."[43]

This attitude could only have further reduced the chance that Western governments would lower the bars they had raised against immigration.[44] On at least one occasion a top Zionist leader actively encouraged resistance to the idea that Western democracies should receive even minimal numbers of European Jews after the war. This occurred in the spring of 1944, when Canadian Prime Minister MacKenzie King informed Nahum Goldmann that domestic conditions would prevent Canada from taking in even 10,000 Jewish refugees. Goldmann assured King that Zionists were not at all interested in having Jews go to Canada, but only to Palestine.[45] The Zionist leader later reported that when he also offered "to take some Jews from Canada to Palestine," King was "more than satisfied" and became an enthusiastic supporter of the call for Jewish statehood.[46]

The subordination of immediate humanitarian considerations to long-range political goals was not only evident in Zionism's lack of interest in Jewish emigration to lands other than Palestine. It was made even more starkly clear in the fall of 1944 by the official Zionist hierarchy's successful endeavor to block passage of a congressional resolution calling for the establishment of emergency shelters in Palestine for Hungarian Jews.

Events in Hungary caused worldwide concern over the fate of that country's 800,000 Jews in the spring of 1944.[47] Although Hungary had sided with the Third Reich, its government's enthusiasm for Hitler's policies waned visibly as Allied armies swung to the offensive. In March 1944, German troops installed a new government in Budapest. Although the new regime functioned under the continuing regency of Admiral Miklos Horthy, it was far more pro-Nazi than its predecessor.[48] Under German influence, Hungarian leaders embarked on a sweeping anti-Semitic program. The relative security previously enjoyed by the country's Jewish community rapidly collapsed. By summer the Allies were aware that Hungarian Jews were being deported en masse. The transferrals were partly for the purpose of carrying Jewish workers to forced labor in Germany; but they also carried thousands to Nazi death camps. By July it was estimated that some 12,000 Jews were being shipped daily to their deaths in Poland.[49]

As a result of a combination of factors—including Allied warnings that retribution would be exacted for crimes against the defenseless Jews of Hungary, the intercession of the Vatican and influential neutral states, and, possibly, also a desire on the part of Hungary's new leaders to assert some measure of independence from their German patrons—the Hungarian government decided in July to suspend the deportation of Jews.[50] At the same time, Budapest offered to allow the exit of Jews in possession of entry permits to other countries.[51] Through the Red Cross, the United States informed Hungary that it would accept responsibility for the care of all Jews who might reach neutral or Allied territory, and for finding "temporary shelters of refuge for such people."[52] Six days later this commitment was jointly, and publicly, reaffirmed by the British and American governments.

Tragically, serious and eventually insurmountable problems had to be faced before advantage could be taken of the Hungarian offer. The greatest of these was the attitude of the Germans, who still retained ultimate control over events in Hungary and whose cooperation would be necessary if Jewish emigration were to be possible. Since May, in fact, the British and American governments, along with the Jewish Agency, had been responding to secret overtures made by German representatives trying to bargain for the safety of Hungarian Jews.[53] The complex and tortuous path of those negotiations are of marginal interest here, although it should be noted that they proceeded concurrently with Budapest's offer to permit Jewish emigration. In mid-October 1944, Germany extended its occupation of Hungary, the regent was in effect deposed, and what had seemed to be a possibility for arranging a Jewish exodus from the country evaporated.[54]

Apart from the German factor, another problem that arose in the wake of the Hungarian government's offer was that of providing havens of refuge should the need arise. In June the Roosevelt administration circumvented American immigration laws by establishing a refuge for European war refugees on a temporary basis at Oswego, New York. Facilities at Oswego, however, were extremely limited and served only some 1,000 refugees by the end of the war. Although the Oswego experiment was widely approved in the

United States, Roosevelt announced later in the summer of 1944 that the government did not intend to establish further shelters along similar lines.[55] In view of the apparent possibility of extricating large numbers of Hungarian Jews, the British and American governments instead considered creating havens in North Africa and Italy.

On August 24, a week after Washington and London publicly accepted responsibility for refugees who might escape from Hungary, resolutions were introduced in Congress calling upon the president and the secretary of state to use their good offices

> to put into effect immediate establishment of mass emergency rescue shelters in the mandated territory of Palestine, similar to the emergency shelter at Oswego, New York, so that the Hebrews of Europe may find haven from the ordeals of persecution.[56]

The resolutions received bipartisan sponsorship in both the Senate and the House. House majority leader John McCormack publicly endorsed the measures. Robert Taft was one of the cosponsors in the Senate.[57] The inspiration for congressional action, as well as for the idea of seeking only temporary shelter in Palestine for Hungarian Jews in order to avoid violating the White Paper immigration quota, was provided by Peter Bergson, a Revisionist Zionist leader in the United States.[58]

Despite the significant support initially given to the resolutions, the measures quickly lapsed into obscurity. The reason for this was that official Zionists convinced the chairmen of the foreign relations committees of both houses to kill the legislation.[59] Nahum Goldmann subsequently described the reasons that prompted this step. Terming the resolutions "idiotic," Goldmann saw the whole affair as primarily an attempt by Revisionist Zionists to gain publicity. He gave the following justification for the official Zionists' approach to the resolutions:

> The entire proposal was of no use as a rescue measure since it was impossible for Jews from Hungary to reach Palestine . . . and . . . in any case the [official] Zionists were opposed to any scheme which would seek to place Jews in Palestine only temporarily and on the understanding that they would be sent elsewhere after the war.[60]

Although Goldmann's assessment of the chances of extricating Jews from Hungary ultimately proved almost completely correct, this could not have been known with certainty at the time official Zionists opposed the congressional resolutions. The determining factor in Zionist opposition appears, then, to have been a combination of hostility toward Revisionist Zionism and unyielding insistence on the principle that Jews entered Palestine "as of right and not on sufferance."

It is unfortunate that in the years ahead almost all parties to the Palestine controversy tended to approach the Jewish refugee problem in terms of its political rather than its humanitarian significance.

In 1945 thousands of European Jews fell into the category of "displaced persons," individuals who had been forced during the hostilities, either as refugees or captives, far from their prewar homes. For many of these survivors there was no question of trying to rebuild their lives anywhere but in Palestine. The psychological impact of first-hand experience with Hitler's attempted "final solution," the destruction of the communities among which they had once lived, and in many cases the loss of their immediate families produced an unbridgeable alienation from European society and a deep desire to emigrate to Palestine. Other displaced Jews, particularly those from Eastern Europe, returned to their homes after the war, only to confront a legacy of anti-Semitism. In many cases these too came to view Palestine as a possible place of resettlement.

The immediate aftermath of the war saw the beginning of large migrations of Jews within Europe. Many were trying to go to Palestine; many were seeking places where they might rebuild lives that had been shattered beyond repair in their countries of origin. Even before the end of the war, a Zionist organization was created to guide the growing numbers of potential immigrants to places where transport to Palestine might be most easily arranged. Although the original efforts of "Brichah," as the organization was known, were limited to aiding East European Jews reach Balkan ports, its activities in 1945 quickly expanded to include the creation of technically illegal "underground" routes into Italy and the Western-occupied sectors of Central Europe, where Jewish displaced persons could find shelter in camps run by Allied forces. As the movement of Jews continued unabated, the Jewish Agency worked through Brichah to "channel this flow intelligently into a reservoir that would turn the very misery of these people into a powerful weapon."[61] In the postwar years the expanding pool of Jewish refugees exercised growing pressure on behalf of Zionist aims in Palestine; a pressure whose focal point was the American government.

BRITAIN'S POSITION IN PALESTINE
AT THE CLOSE OF THE WAR

Throughout the war the British government was officially committed to the policy laid down by the 1939 White Paper. However, the Zionist leadership had cause to hope that the end of hostilities in Europe would bring London to support the establishment of a Jewish state. Winston Churchill had not altered his opinion of the White Paper, branded by him in 1939 as "a breach of faith."[62] In 1942 and 1943 Chaim Weizmann received "friendly assurances" from the prime minister that the Zionist cause would benefit from changes to be made in Britain's Palestine policy at war's end.[63] In the spring of 1944 Nahum Goldmann concluded that Churchill had become even more strongly in favor of Zionism.[64] Later that same year Churchill spoke to Weizmann in terms indicating a readiness to resolve the Palestine problem by dividing the country between Arabs and Jews. The possibility that Britain would extend substantial financial aid to a Jewish state was also spoken of by the prime minister.[65]

While Churchill was extending encouragement to Zionists, the British Labour Party adopted an even more pro-Zionist stance. In April 1944 the party's national executive declared:

> There is surely neither hope nor meaning in a Jewish National Home unless we are prepared to let the Jews, if they wish, enter [Palestine] in such numbers as to become a majority. There was a strong case for this before the war, and there is an irresistable case for it now. . . . Consideration should be given to enlarging the present boundaries of Palestine. Let the Arabs be encouraged to move out as the Jews move in. Let them be compensated handsomely for their land, and their settlement elsewhere be carefully planned and generously financed.[66]

This program was reaffirmed several months later by the general convention of the Labour Party.

By early 1945, British administrators were privately predicting the White Paper's demise. Lord Gort, high commissioner for Palestine, confided to the American consul general his belief that public opinion in the United States and Great Britain would make it impossible for the mandatory to end Jewish immigration once the White Paper quota was filled.[67] The high commissioner personally favored the mandate's continuation after the war. He was sure that a Jewish state created by partition against the will of the Arabs would be "a bridgehead which must either be extended or wiped out." In reporting these views to Washington, the American consul general concluded that London had not yet decided on a future policy toward Palestine.[68]

The assessment was correct. The British government had not settled on the policy it would pursue at the end of the war. Moreover, despite Churchill's assurances to Weizmann and the Labour Party's declared intent, it would become apparent that no postwar British government could easily pursue a pro-Zionist policy.

There were several reasons for this. On one level there was the awkwardness of replacing the supposedly "definitive" policy guidelines laid down in 1939. In itself, however, this would not have constituted an obstacle of sufficient proportions to dissuade the British government from a radically pro-Zionist departure at the end of the war. The checkered history of Britain's administration of the mandate had long since demonstrated that decisions were not apt to be unduly affected either by the moral weight of past commitments or by the embarrassment of embarking upon contradictory paths. A more compelling factor militating against any precipitous abrogation of the White Paper was Britain's political position in the Middle East as a whole at the end of World War II.

In a strictly regional context, British interests in the Middle East remained much the same as they were before 1939. Iraq, Persia, and the Persian Gulf region continued to be important as areas of British oil holdings. From London's point of view, the significance of Anglo-Egyptian relations similarly continued to revolve around the Suez Canal, that still-vital link with the oil fields to the East as well as with British territories in Africa, the subcontinent, and the Far East. However, by the summer of 1945 the political climate in which the British government labored to secure these interests was distinct from that which prevailed prior to the war. Britain, previously a creditor, was now deeply in debt to both Egypt and Iraq. As members of the sterling bloc, these countries had benefited from British war expenditures and amassed huge balances of sterling securities.[69] The liquidation of these assets posed a severe problem, particularly in view of London's postwar desire to guide British exports in directions that would earn scarce foreign currencies or raw materials. On the other hand, Egypt and Iraq were eager to obtain payment in much-needed capital goods and to convert the greatest possible amount of their sterling balances to other currencies. The problem was not settled until London concluded separate arrangements with Baghdad and Cairo in 1947. In the interim, however, this difficult issue was an incentive for the British government to maintain the goodwill of its Arab creditors.[70]

In both Egypt and Iraq, growing resentment had, in fact, developed over the dependent relationship these countries had with Britain. In Iraq, which since the collapse of the Rashid Ali al-Galani regime had been under the firm control of strongly pro-British elements, manifestations of dissatisfaction were suppressed during the war. Egyptian public opinion had been less constrained. Egypt was rife with agitation for a complete revision of the existing relationship with Britain. Strong calls were made for the withdrawal of British troops from all parts of the country as well as from the Anglo-Egyptian Sudan. Supported by the nationalistic Wafd Party, these demands were increasingly uncompromising. At the end of 1945 the Egyptian government initiated what proved to be a protracted and often bitter series of negotiations over these objectives.[71]

In trying to cope with Arab nationalism, British policy makers could not ignore the impact of Palestine. Moreover, Egyptian demands for the removal of British troops introduced a new element into British calculations. London soon began viewing Palestine as a possible alternative base for troops that might have to be pulled out of Egypt.[72] Naturally, this militated against any action that might provoke prolonged disturbances in that country.

The British government's concern over its economic and strategic interests in the Middle East did not arise mainly from the flow of political currents indigenous to the region. Rather, it was largely the product of incipient cold war tensions. By the spring of 1945 the wartime unity of the Allied powers had so deteriorated that Churchill decided "the Soviet menace . . . had already replaced the Nazi foe" as the chief problem of the Western democracies.[73] Even before the war's end, Moscow's intentions in the Middle East came into question as a result of Soviet policy toward Turkey and Iran. In the latter country the Soviet Union's administration of the territory occupied by its forces since 1941 cultivated Azerbaijani and Kurdish separatist movements. On the other hand, by June 1945 Moscow was advancing irredentist claims upon two Turkish provinces and demanding a military presence in the Dardanelles. These ominous trends in Turco-Soviet and Persian-Soviet relations were to develop into international crises formed by the attempted creation of a communist state in Azerbaijan in 1945 and the Soviet Union's ultimatum to Turkey in August 1946.

Mounting Cold War tensions increased the difficulties facing British policy makers in Palestine. George Kirk notes:

> The decline in Britain's material power as a result of the war had increased the importance for her of maintaining good relations in the strategic region of the Middle East . . . in the central third of which—from Egypt to Iraq inclusive—the politically conscious opinion of the Muslim Arab majority was as sensitive as ever on the subject of Palestine.[74]

Thus the British government faced the necessity of acting on a complex problem among whose chief dimensions could be cited: the continuing need to avoid alienating the Arab world, the rising danger of a Jewish rebellion, and the apparent influence of pro-Zionist forces on American foreign policy. It is significant that Churchill, despite his earlier affirmations of support to Chaim Weizmann, lost hope that Britain could handle the Palestine problem without undermining its own national interests. Less than two months after Hitler's downfall, Churchill confided to his colleagues:

> I do not think we should take the responsibility upon ourselves of managing this very difficult place while the Americans sit back and criticise. Have you ever addressed yourselves to the idea that we should ask them to take it over? I believe we should be the stronger the more they are drawn into the Mediterranean. At any rate, the fact that we show no desire to keep the mandate will be a great help. I am not aware of the slightest advantage which has ever accrued to Great Britain from this painful and thankless task. Somebody else should have their turn now.[75]

Churchill's idea was ill-timed. Events were to prove that the American government was not prepared to be drawn into an active role in Palestine. Yet Churchill indicated what was to become a cardinal feature of Britain's Palestine policy for most of the mandate's remaining life. With their country virtually bankrupt and psychologically weakened by six years of war, British leaders consistently attempted to enlist the United States as a partner in resolving the Palestine problem.

THE UNITED STATES AND THE EMERGING
FACTOR OF GREAT-POWER POLITICS IN PALESTINE

In 1944, Washington cocktail gossip had it that American officials would privately and frequently admit: "We don't quite know just what our interests in the Middle East are, but they're growing."[76] Whether or not the story is apocryphal, it mirrored a real situation. At the end of the war there was uncertainty among American policy makers as to the precise nature and extent of U.S. interests in the Middle East. However, there was no avoiding the fact that American involvement in the region had expanded immensely since 1939 and was likely to continue to do so.

Oil ranked first among American economic and commercial activities in the Middle East. The government's determination to preserve the American monopoly on Saudi Arabia's vast petroleum resources was demonstrated in 1943 by its efforts to gain control of ARAMCO and by its later plans for a pipeline to the Mediterranean. By 1944 the British government, potentially the strongest rival to the United States in Saudi Arabia, recognized that the American position in that country would henceforth predominate.[77]

By the end of the war American businessmen were broadening their ambitions in the Middle East beyond areas directly related to oil. A major and burgeoning field was commercial aviation. During the war American airlines considerably expanded their domestic and foreign operations.[78] The pool of technically trained men and the increased facilities for aircraft production that accumulated in the United States placed American companies in a position to lead in the development of international commercial aviation.[79] Linking Europe, Asia, and Africa, the Middle East figured prominently in all plans for global air routes.[80] It was not long before American airline executives began seeking overflight and landing rights in the area.[81]

Further opportunity for American involvement in all aspects of the commercial life of the Middle East was opened by a financial agreement negotiated between the United States and Britain in 1945. Under the terms of the Anglo-American agreement, Britain was pledged to abolish the dollar pool of the sterling area as a whole. This meant that by mid-1947 those countries previously dependent upon London for the conversion of local currencies to dollars would be able to engage in free exchange, thereby greatly facilitating trade with the United States.[82]

World War II emphasized that oil was not merely a valuable commercial commodity but also a vital strategic resource.[83] In early 1944 an expert team sent to the Middle East by the American government concluded that the center of world oil production had shifted from the Gulf of Mexico and the Caribbean to the Middle East-Persian Gulf region.[84] Washington could not ignore the need to preserve American access to Middle Eastern oil fields in the postwar world.

In the meantime, the American military developed an appreciation for the strategic importance of the Middle East and its resources. In 1945 the Saudi Arabian government permitted the establishment of an American airfield at Dahran, a facility that remained in operation after the war. Military strategists had also been early supporters of the American government's efforts to play a direct role in the exploitation of Middle Eastern oil. After Washington failed to obtain control of ARAMCO, the American Navy took the lead in advocating the short-lived proposal for the construction of a pipeline from the Persian Gulf to the Mediterranean. After the war, Secretary of Defense Forrestal repeatedly urged that the strategic importance of oil should guide the formulation of American policy toward the Middle East.[85]

The attention given to the Arab-Zionist problem by the entire Moslem world inevitably raised the prospect that these commercial and strategic interests might be adversely affected by the course of American involvement in Palestine. A related consideration was the possibility that some other Great Power might attempt to utilize the Palestine problem to undermine the U.S. position in the Middle East. By the end of the war, Washington policy makers viewed the Soviet Union as the most likely potential source of trouble in this respect.

In the latter years of the war, evidence began to mount that Moscow was anxious to increase its prestige in the Arab countries. Initial indications were confined to Soviet efforts to highlight cultural affinities between the USSR and the Arab world. In 1944, for example, Soviet Moslems were permitted to undertake the Haj for the first time in 20 years. Later that same year, invitations were issued to the Orthodox Christian Patriarchs of Jerusalem and Alexandria to attend the election of a new Russian Patriarch.[86] Efforts were also made to generate pro-Soviet sympathies among ethnic minorities in the Middle East. In the Levant, Soviet propaganda sought to impress the large Armenian community by dwelling at length on the anti-Nazi exploits of the Soviet Armenian war hero, General Bagramyan.[87] A similar purpose appeared to underlie the publication in Soviet Armenia of a Kurdish-language newspaper for distribution in Northern Iraq.[88]

In late 1944 the State Department requested the American Embassy in Moscow to assess Soviet intentions in the Middle East. The Embassy's report, prepared by Frances B. Stevens, strongly suggested that the Kremlin was opening a major campaign to secure a permanent and influential position in the political and economic life of the Middle East. A telegraphed summary of Stevens' analysis was considered sufficiently important to be forwarded promptly to President Roosevelt.[89]

One of the difficulties confronting American policy makers was the mystery that surrounded Moscow's attitude toward the Palestine problem. The Soviet government was traditionally opposed to Zionism on ideological grounds. In his assessment of Soviet policy, Stevens noted that he could observe "no sympathy with Zionism" on the part of Soviet authorities, and warned that Soviet leaders could "be counted upon" to use the Palestine issue to "increase Soviet influence in the Arab countries to the detriment of Great Britain and the United States." On the other hand, Stevens felt that official Soviet silence on the Palestine problem, as well as the absence of editorial comment on the subject in the Soviet press, indicated "that either the Soviet Government considers it premature to take a definite position or that a definite policy has not yet been formed on the highest level."[90]

The State Department was forced to rely on a variety of informal, and at times second-hand, sources in order to deduce Russian intentions. In September 1944, Nahum Goldmann reported "very definite indications" that the Soviet government was becoming more friendly to Zionism. According to Goldmann, he had noticed in conversations with Soviet diplomats a "definite sympathy toward the creation of a Jewish state in Palestine." However, the Zionist leader was careful to point out that his diplomatic contacts stressed "they were expressing their personal views rather than any policy of the Soviet Union." By way of supporting his opinion that a pro-Zionist Soviet shift was in the offing, Goldmann cited a reported conversation held between President Eduard Benes of Czechoslovakia and Joseph Stalin. Stalin, remarked Goldmann, was said to have told Benes that he had no objections to the establishment of a Jewish commonwealth.[91]

Information from other sources directly contradicted Goldmann's impressions. In 1944 Ira Hirschmann, an operative of the War Refugee Board in Turkey, discussed the Palestine problem with an official of the Soviet Embassy in Ankara. Hirschmann reported that the Soviet representative indicated that the USSR was firmly opposed to the establishment of a Jewish state in Palestine.[92] When the American Embassy in Moscow assessed the significance of Hirschmann's account, it tended to view the information as reliable.[93]

On balance, the State Department opted for the more conservative view of Soviet foreign policy: that ideological Soviet anti-Zionism would assert itself in Moscow's policy toward Palestine. When Roosevelt traveled to Yalta in early 1945, he carried a memorandum prepared by the Near East Division as a reference should he become involved in discussions of Palestine. Roosevelt was advised to refrain from taking a definite position on Palestine's future until consultations had been carried out with both the Arabs and Jews and with the British and Soviet governments. The president was particularly admonished against giving Moscow an "opportunity to augment its influence in the Near East by championing the cause of the Arabs at the expense of the United States."[94] During the next two and a half years, as the Soviet Union continued to avoid defining its policy, this attitude was at the heart of much of the State Department's approach to the Palestine problem.

At the time of Roosevelt's death there were clear indications that the Palestine problem might give rise to repercussions affecting American regional interests in the Middle East as well as the wider strategic position of the United States in the realm of global politics. However, in the summer of 1945 it was not clear just what importance the American government would attach to its influence with the governments of the Middle East, or how it would respond to Great Power tensions in the area. It was the problem of Roosevelt's successor to deal with both these questions and to handle the Palestine issue in a manner compatible with the answers he devised.

III: THE TRUMAN ADMINISTRATION AND PALESTINE

9. TRUMAN FACES THE PALESTINE PROBLEM

Harry S Truman was catapulted to the presidency by Roosevelt's death on April 12, 1945. The new president soon demonstrated a highly developed sense of political maneuver. However, unlike his predecessor—in whom political acumen combined with a sophisticated and cosmopolitan bearing—the "Man from Independence" brought an air of homespun simplicity to the White House.

Differences and similarities between Truman and Roosevelt emerged clearly in their handling of the Palestine problem. The strongest point of identity was their common realization that the task of formulating a definitive Palestine policy was complicated by contradictory implications of foreign and domestic political factors. Both men reacted to this situation by temporizing. For each president, delay regularly allowed events to outdistance policy decisions.

In retrospect, differences between them are equally apparent. The most important of these lay in the cumulative results of the dilatory approaches they followed. Roosevelt's pattern of opposed promises to Arabs and Zionists had so beclouded his position by the time of his death that he could have established almost any long-range policy on Palestine with virtually equal justification. During the three years Truman presided over America's involvement with the Palestine problem, he proved as anxious as Roosevelt had been to avoid defining Washington's position vis-a-vis the Arab-Zionist conflict. Yet to by-pass that central question, he resorted to a series of tentative and partial commitments. In the long run, these tactics did not permit Truman to escape sharing responsibility for Palestine's political fate.

Roosevelt and Truman were also differentiated by their abilities to appreciate the growing complexity of the Palestine problem's international ramifications. Between 1939 and 1945, Roosevelt's originally narrow outlook altered markedly. During his penultimate term in office he not only witnessed the growth of long-term American economic and strategic interests in the Arab world but also kept alive to their relevance to American policy in Palestine. Through contacts with Arab leaders, particularly with Ibn Saud, he apparently gained some personal insight into the depth of Arab opposition to Zionism. On the other hand, Truman came to the presidency with a highly limited perspective on Palestine. During the following three years he either chose to disregard, or could not adequately comprehend, the full dimensions of the issue.

Distinctions in the approaches taken by Roosevelt and Truman were to some degree reflections of their different personalities. Possessing a vibrant and expansive intellect, Roosevelt at times exhibited traits that might well be labeled visionary.[1] Elements of this sometimes surfaced in his various far-reaching schemes for arranging a settlement between Arabs and Jews in the Middle East and for defusing the growing problem of European Jewish refugees.

Roosevelt's political instincts caused him to perceive clearly the uncomfortable dilemma that foreign and domestic considerations created for a president attempting to decide upon a Palestine policy. He consciously opted for expedient measures designed to forestall a long-term definition of American objectives in Palestine. Yet this was not the limit of his response. In his many, varied, and ultimately stillborn schemes for dealing with Palestine and related issues, there can be discerned the response of Roosevelt's imaginative nature to a political dilemma. His conceptual gropings cannot simply be dismissed as flights of fancy borne by despair over finding an acceptable policy. Faced with a problem that placed the government in a no-win situation, Roosevelt—consciously or otherwise—appears to have relied upon his imaginative powers to find a way to alter the problem itself. In short, Roosevelt's mental search was directed toward finding some means of reducing the Palestine issue to amenable proportions; that is, to a level at which a decision could be made on Palestine's ultimate political future without incurring unacceptable domestic or international consequences. Thus,he hoped to rearrange the Palestine equation by resettling Jewish refugees in South America, or Africa, or Alaska; or perhaps by removing the Palestinian Arabs; or perhaps again by enlisting worldwide Christian support for an international Holy Land, thereby undercutting both Jewish and Arab nationalisms; or, as he told Stettinius, by discovering "some new formula."

If Roosevelt's vision sometimes extended almost to the realm of illusion, Truman's was strongly focused on immediate circumstances. A man of correspondingly restricted imagination, he found it difficult to conceive of innovative approaches. It was a fateful limitation. Unable to place his faith in a creative spark that might extricate him from the dilemma of Palestine, Truman could only perceive that issue as it reached the White House in its most elemental form. For him, far more than for Roosevelt, the "Palestine problem" was that of having to choose between the contradictory imperatives of domestic and international politics; the necessity of meeting the requirements of the Democratic Party or protecting the long-range foreign interests of the United States. Incapable of searching for a way out of this agonizing dilemma, Truman retreated into indecision. His administration lapsed into a paralysis on Palestine that was broken only periodically by spasmodic reactions to overriding momentary pressures.

TRUMAN'S PERSPECTIVE
ON PALESTINE

A. J. Granoff, a Kansas City lawyer, first became acquainted with Harry Truman in the summer of 1924.[2] During the following years he formed an informal friendship with the future president at poker parties hosted by Truman's intimate friend and haberdashery partner, Eddie Jacobson. On several occasions in 1947, Granoff accompanied Jacobson to Washington to urge their friend in the White House to support the Zionist cause.

Granoff did not feel that Truman knew much of the Palestine problem during his first years as president. Of his visits to the White House, he recalls:

> [Truman] knew next to nothing about Zionism, a Jewish state, a Jewish homeland, [the] Balfour Declaration. I think that, up to about August 1947, those terms were Greek to Harry S Truman.[3]

Granoff undoubtedly exaggerated. Truman's appreciation of the terms was certainly deficient, but he was well acquainted with their use. As a senator, Truman joined the long list of public figures who occasionally made pro-Zionist comments. He reacted to the 1939 Palestine White Paper by speaking out on the Senate floor against Britain's new policy as a clear violation of the Balfour Declaration.[4] In April 1943 he prominently participated in a pro-Zionist rally in Chicago.[5] Along with many of his Senate colleagues, Truman freely endorsed such Zionist projects as the Palestine Foundation Fund.[6] He also became a member of Peter Bergson's Committee for a Jewish Army, although initially he was apparently not aware that the committee was a Revisionist Zionist group strongly opposed by official Zionists. After Bergson ran an advertisement in the New York *Times* criticizing the Roosevelt administration's handling of the Bermuda Conference on Refugees, Truman angrily withdrew from the organization.[7] At the same time, however, he assured the official Zionist leader Stephen Wise of his continuing desire to help the Zionist cause.[8]

Despite friendly ties to American Zionists, Truman was visibly influenced by the Roosevelt administration's desire to downplay the Palestine issue during the early years of the war. Upon resigning from the Committee for a Jewish Army, Truman advised Wise that "when an ad such as Bergson put in the New York *Times* can be used to stir up trouble where our troops are fighting, it is certainly outside my policy to be mixed up in such an organization."[9] He also stressed his conviction that it would be impossible to help the Jewish people "at the expense of our military maneuvers."[10]

In a form letter developed to answer queries concerning his attitude toward the pro-Zionist Wagner-Taft Senate resolution in 1944, Senator Truman even more clearly revealed his desire to uphold the administration while retaining the support of his Zionist constituents. He explained:

> [The resolution] is one which affects the foreign relations program between Great Britain, the United States, and the Middle East. My sympathy of course is with the Jewish people, but I am of the opinion that a resolution such as this should be very circumspectly handled until we know just where we are going and why.
>
> With the difficulty looming up between Russia and Poland, and the Balkan states and Russia, and with Great Britain and Russia absolutely necessary to us in fighting the war I don't want to throw any bricks to upset the apple cart, although when the right time comes I am willing to help make the fight for a Jewish homeland in Palestine.[11]

Truman's account of his involvement with Palestine raises more questions than it answers about the motivations that governed his actions after he assumed the presidency. It does, however, reveal something of his limited perspective. His *Memoirs* indicate that he attached great importance to the "solemn promise" made to the Jews in the Balfour Declaration.[12] "This promise," he felt, "should be kept." However, he seems to have had no awareness of any ambiguity in the Balfour Declaration:

> I was fully aware of the Arabs' hostility to Jewish settlement in Palestine, but like many Americans, I was troubled by the plight of the Jewish people in Europe. The Balfour Declaration promising the Jews the opportunity to re-establish a homeland in Palestine, had always seemed to me to go hand in hand with the noble policies of Woodrow Wilson, especially the principle of self-determination.[13]

Critics of the president's outlook have aptly pointed out that "while applying self-determination to the Jewish people, he apparently did not apply it to the Arab majority of Palestine."[14]

A long-standing aspect of Truman's approach to the Palestine issue was the peculiar relationship he postulated between the Arab-Jewish political contest in Palestine and the problem of resettling European Jewish refugees. He apparently concluded that large-scale Jewish immigration into Palestine had no bearing on the political situation in that country.[15]

It is difficult to believe that Truman, despite the accumulated evidence available to him, despite the warnings of the State Department, and despite his various exchanges with British leaders, sincerely believed that Jewish immigration could be treated as an apolitical, "humanitarian" subject in the context of postwar Palestine. Yet, after averring in his *Memoirs* that his "primary concern" was the "basic problem"—"the fate of thousands of Jews in Europe"—Truman resorts to this sort of rationalization:

> It was my attitude that America could not stand by while the victims of Hitler's racial madness were denied the opportunities to build new homes. Neither, however, did I want to see a political structure imposed on the Near East that would result in conflict. My basic approach was that the long-range fate of Palestine was the kind of problem we had the U.N. for. For the immediate future, however, some aid was needed for the Jews in Europe to find a place to live in decency.[16]

In light of the record of Truman's three-year entanglement in the Palestine problem, it is almost superfluous to point out that he was hardly in the forefront of those advocating United Nations responsibility for Palestine. Nor—as will be seen—was he averse in principle to taking secret steps independently of the United Nations toward a political settlement in Palestine. Much more important is the fact that between 1945 and 1948 Truman took no effective action on what he claims was his "primary concern": the fate of the Jewish refugees.

The beginning of Truman's involvement with the Palestine issue in the spring and summer of 1945 did not substantially brighten the "immediate future" of the thousands of Jews in displaced persons camps. His failure to acknowledge the fundamental connection between the question of immigration and the Arab-Zionist conflict rendered sterile his insistence that European Jews be permitted to enter Palestine without reference to the political tensions that wracked the country. It is difficult to accept the contention that Truman did not perceive this. It is equally difficult not to believe that he made use of the mantle of single-minded humanitarianism to cloak his basic reluctance to define American policy toward Palestine.

At the end of World War II, the restrictive laws that since 1924 had drastically curtailed immigration into the United States effectively barred the entry of any large numbers of Jewish, or other, displaced persons. Not until 1946 did Truman tentatively acknowledge that special legislation might be necessary were the United States to accept some responsibility for solving the humanitarian problem posed by displaced persons of all faiths.[17] In the summer of 1947 Congress showed its reluctance to aid war victims by failing to act on a proposal to allow 400,000 displaced persons to enter the United States over a period of several years. Truman demonstrated his own unwillingness to challenge the prevailing restrictionist ethos by not supporting the suggested measure.

Despite congressional foot-dragging, the refugees posed a political problem for the United States in the aftermath of the war. Even before the end of hostilities in 1945, American occupation forces in Europe assumed responsibility for the physical care of thousands of newly freed concentration camp inmates. In the months after V.E. Day, additional thousands of displaced persons found shelter under American Army auspices. Apart from the moral onus created by these circumstances, more mundane factors helped remind American policy makers of the desirability of resettling the refugees. The not inconsiderable cost of supporting them could not be borne indefinitely. Then, too, the burden of meeting the needs of displaced persons proved a novel and difficult task for U.S. military authorities in occupied Europe.[18] Finally, it could have been anticipated in Washington that any patently callous disregard of the refugee issue would eventually expose the government to domestic as well as international criticism.

Thus, quite apart from the Palestine issue, the postwar Jewish displaced persons constituted a double problem for the Truman administration. On the one hand, their existence in European camps created mounting administrative, financial, and political difficulties. On the other hand, Washington's unwillingness to take decisive steps toward reducing the barriers to immigration into the United States left it with the problem of discovering some alternative for disposing of its homeless Jewish charges.

Truman's insistence that massive Jewish immigration be permitted into Palestine without reference to political considerations is therefore understandable as something more than simply a means of placating American pro-Zionist opinion while avoiding an active commitment that might have irrevocably antagonized the Arab world. In short, the president's desire to see the Jewish refugees relocated in Palestine is indisputable. However, it appears that whatever humanitarian inclinations motivated him were at least equally matched by the hope of relieving the United States of its unwelcome responsibility for thousands of displaced Jews.

This aspect of the American outlook on Palestine received minimal public attention between 1945 and 1948. Perhaps for fear that the results would prove embarrassing, the nature of American humanitarian interest in displaced Jews was not often probed by journalists, public figures, and government officials. Only occasionally were there instances of penetrating and outspoken commentary. In mid-October 1945, for example, Robert Gale Woolbert, associate editor of *Foreign Affairs*, charged that many Gentile Americans supported Zionism "because they don't want any more Jews in this country."[19] In mid-1946 an exasperated British foreign secretary, Ernest Bevin, spoke out in a moment of undiplomatic candor and attributed the intensity of agitation in the United States on behalf of massive Jewish immigration into Palestine to the fact that Americans "did not want too many of them in New York."[20]

The reluctance to accept Jewish immigration into the United States had also exerted an influence on the Roosevelt administration; but Roosevelt distinguished between the problem of displaced European Jews and the task of formulating a policy toward Palestine. This enabled him to consider alternatives other than Palestine or the United States as possible solutions to the refugee problem while simultaneously examining various political approaches to the Arab-Zionist controversy.

Truman, on the other hand, linked the refugees firmly to Palestine. However, he was unwilling to accept the inescapable political implications entailed by that position. Instead, he maintained that his administration had developed a "humanitarian" policy devoid of political content. It was a posture that left the United States incapable of taking effective action either to aid displaced Jews or to further a settlement in Palestine. While it enabled the U.S. government to delay defining its position on Palestine's political future, Truman's approach was hardly devoid of political impact. It exerted a far-reaching influence on the course of the Palestine problem.

Throughout Truman's first three years in the White House, Washington continued to face the problem of devising a purposeful Palestine policy in the light of contradictory domestic and international political considerations. The dilemma remained essentially the same as that which had afflicted the Roosevelt administration. Now, however, the domestic factors more visibly included both pro-Zionist sentiment and Washington's eagerness to accommodate the popular bias against relaxing limitations on immigration into the United States—a bias that had decidedly anti-Semitic overtones.[21] In this sense, two currents of public sentiment, pro-Zionism and anti-Semitism, combined as the proverbial strange bedfellows to influence the American approach to Palestine. Even so, domestic considerations struggled in Truman's mind with requirements imposed by prevailing conceptions of U.S. strategic and economic interests.

Although Truman could not ignore international considerations, he had little admiration for the men in the State Department who kept reminding him of them. Roosevelt had worked largely in tandem with his State Department advisors on the Palestine question. Under Truman this cooperation soon dwindled. Not only did the White House cease to welcome advice from the department, it also severely curtailed the amount of information given to department officials about the president's increasing personal involvement in matters relating to Palestine.

Truman records that when he became president, he was "skeptical" about some of the views and attitudes "assumed by the 'striped-pants boys' in the State Department." His feeling was that "they didn't care enough about what happened to the thousands of displaced persons."[22] However, he gives somewhat contradictory accounts of the effects of his differences with State Department officials. On the one hand, he has written:

> The Department of State's specialists on the Near East were, almost without exception, unfriendly to the idea of a Jewish State. . . .
>
> I was never convinced by arguments of the diplomats. I want to say, however, that in these differences of opinion between the White House and the State Department on the business of Palestine there was never any question as to who made the decisions and whose policies would be followed. Where some of our diplomats, and especially the gentlemen on the Near Eastern desks, differed was on the speed with which we should progress, not on the direction of the movement.[23]

And yet, with reference to the same differences of opinion, and obviously alluding to the State Department's Near East Division, Truman has also noted:

> The difficulty with many career officials in the government is that they regard themselves as the men who really make policy and run the government. They look upon the elected officials as just temporary occupants. Every President in our history has been faced with this problem: how to prevent career men from circumventing presidential policy. Too often career men seek to impose their own views instead of carrying out the established policy of the administration.[24]

These apparent discrepancies have done nothing to shed light on charges that the State Department, spearheaded by the Office of Near Eastern and African Affairs, engaged in a concerted effort to sabotage Truman's Palestine policy between 1945 and 1948.[25]

While the department attempted to remind Truman of Palestine's international implications, the president was also constantly faced with that issue's domestic significance. Zionist lobbyists, nationally known politicians, political commentators, and presidential assistants at various times, and in various ways, linked American policy toward Palestine to the political fortunes of the Democratic Party in general and to those of Harry Truman in particular. Three men in the last group who figured prominently were Samuel Rosenman, David Niles, and Clark Clifford.

At Truman's request, Rosenman stayed on after Roosevelt's death as special counsel to the president. Rosenman, who was affiliated with the non-Zionist American Jewish Committee, resigned his White House position in January 1946. Nonetheless, both during and after his tenure as special counsel, he advised Truman on various occasions to take steps that were in accord with Zionist desires. His suggestions were based on domestic political considerations.[26]

According to David B. Sachar, who had access to the papers of David Niles,

> no one in the White House, with the exception of President Truman, was more instrumental than Niles in shaping and influencing Administration policy toward the newly developing [Jewish] state, and every document that came to the White House pertaining to Palestine went to him for his information and approval.[27]

Niles first entered the Roosevelt White House as a presidential assistant dealing with minority groups. An ardent Zionist sympathizer, he quickly became involved with the Palestine issue. However, it was under Truman that Niles's influence became significant. He was well known to have a passionate distaste for publicity.[28] Sachar concludes that while psychological reasons may have been behind Niles's "mania" for anonymity, "the fact remains that his inconspicuousness was essential to his work. For it was only by wielding his influence behind the scenes that he could effectively maintain the position of power and confidence which he so highly cherished."[29] It was in "behind-the-scenes" maneuvers that Niles demonstrated his commitment to obtain American support for Zionist ambitions in Palestine. Niles was, of course, a staunch Democrat. He reportedly once explained his activities in regard to Palestine by telling a contemporary that "the most important and fundamental national interest of the United States was the re-election of the President."[30]

Clark Clifford seems to have shared this view. Having joined the Truman administration in the summer of 1945 as an assistant to the president's naval aide, Clifford's importance grew rapidly. By 1946 he was serving as counsel to the president. In that capacity he prepared a lengthy memorandum for Truman in 1947 outlining the general strategy for the Democratic Party in the 1948 presidential election. The memorandum held that "it may generally be assumed that the policy that is politically wise is also the best policy for the country."[31]

The tension created within the administration by the conflicting advice Truman received from the State Department and his White House advisors was a constant feature of the American approach to Palestine until 1948.

ZIONIST-BRITISH-ARAB TENSION:
THE SUMMER OF 1945

Zionist patience with Britain's White Paper policy was fast running out when Truman entered the White House. The looming final defeat of Hitler's armies released frustrations and tensions that, fed by memories of those slain

in Nazi death camps, had accumulated in the Yishuv during six years of re-
strictive British rule. Germany surrendered unconditionally to the Allies on
May 7. Ten days later Chaim Weizmann submitted a memorandum from the
Jewish Agency to Prime Minister Churchill.[32]

J. C. Hurewitz notes that while Weizmann continued to prefer moderation in the pursuit of Zionist goals, his "counsel for patience and faith in
Britain could have no further meaning after V.E. Day, unless Europe's Jewish survivors were soon allowed to enter Palestine freely."[33] The memorandum forwarded to Churchill bears out the truth of Hurewitz's observation. It
bluntly requested the establishment of Palestine as a Jewish state, and the
transfer to the Jewish Agency of authority to regulate immigration and development in the country. In early June, Churchill replied that Palestine
could not be "effectively considered until the victorious Allies are definitely
seated at the Peace table." The agency thereupon demanded that as an interim measure, pending a final Palestine settlement, the British government
immediately provide 100,000 immigration certificates for use by European
Jews.[34]

As the quota for Jewish immigration into Palestine set by the 1939
White Paper was expected to be filled by the end of summer, Zionist leaders
anxiously awaited a reply. However, London was not disposed to confront
the difficult question of Palestine so soon after the war. Churchill himself
had become uncertain over how to deal with the mandate.[35] Moreover, the
war cabinet had been dissolved at the end of May and preparations were under way for the first general elections in Britain since the outbreak of the war.
At the end of July a Labour government was swept into office with Clement
Attlee as prime minister and Ernest Bevin as foreign secretary. This immediately raised Zionist hopes. A month later these hopes were dashed when the
Labour government finally responded to the request for 100,000 immigration certificates.

Throughout the summer of 1945, Zionist leaders warned that rejection
of their demands for immediate and massive immigration and prompt statehood might produce violence in Palestine. In late June, Nahum Goldmann
called at the State Department, where he spoke with Loy Henderson, Evan
Wilson, and Gordon Merriam—all of whom dealt with Near Eastern affairs.
Goldmann warned that the "mood of the Jewish people was turning to desperation." Pointing out that "anything might happen where 60,000 young
men were fully trained and ready to take up arms in defense of their rights,"
he argued that Dr. Weizmann and other moderates would lose influence
within the Zionist movement unless Britain complied with Zionist demands.
This, he said, would mean that the "control would pass to those not averse to
violence."[36]

A few days later Goldmann returned to the department with David Ben
Gurion and Eliezer Kaplan. Speaking to the same officials, the Zionist

leaders repeated much of what Goldmann had said earlier. However, there was a difference in the tenor of their remarks. Ben Gurion, who took the lead in presenting the Zionists' view, spoke in uncompromising terms.

> Mr. Ben Gurion [said] that the Jews for the past few years had received promises from Allied leaders which had caused them to believe that they would eventually see the fruition of their aims in Palestine, if only they kept quiet during the European war. Now that that war was over the Jews were beginning to ask what was holding the implementation of those pledges. Mr. Ben Gurion said that the world must not underestimate the strength of the Jews' feelings on this point. The Jews had no desire to have any trouble with the British Government and they knew perfectly well that if worse came to worst, they would not last long against the combined might of the British Empire. They would, however, fight if necessary in defense of their rights and the consequences would be on Great Britain's head if the Jews were provoked into some action which no one wanted to see. In other words, the Jews were determined to have their demands met and if the British should decide otherwise, the fault would be that of the British Government.[37]

Henderson asked two questions. First, "whether the Arabs were not likely to make trouble in the event that the British should adopt a pro-Zionist solution in Palestine?" Second, he wished to know if "the immediate objective of the Zionists was to obtain a lowering of the bars to Jewish immigration into Palestine?" Ben Gurion responded to the first query:

> [He] said that he knew the Arabs well and that they would not really put up any kind of a fight. The Bedouins of the desert were, of course, good fighters but it was well known that they had no interest in the Palestine problem and so the leaders of the Arab States would not be successful in rallying their people to support of the Arab position on Palestine.

Henderson's second question was answered by all three Zionists:

> Mr. Ben Gurion, seconded by Dr. Goldmann and Mr. Kaplan, said that while it was, of course, imperative to reach a settlement on immigration at the earliest possible moment, they were opposed to any attempt to solve the Palestine problem by piecemeal methods. Their position was well known and they had come to the point where they could no longer accept anything less than the granting of all their demands, including the immediate establishment of a Jewish State.[38]

In early August a World Zionist Conference was held in London. It was the first such gathering since the hurried closing of the Twenty-First Congress on the eve of World War II. The delegates, divided into followers of the relatively moderate Weizmann and the activist Ben Gurion, passed a series of resolutions calling for the establishment of Palestine as a Jewish state and the abandonment of restrictive immigration policies by the mandatory.[39]

Almost simultaneously, the London branch of the Arab Office, the propaganda organ of the Arab League, reacted to the postwar increase in Zionist agitation by releasing a lengthy statement of the "Present Arab Attitude over the Palestine Question." The statement called on Britain to adhere to the provisions of the 1939 White Paper. It warned that the Arabs of Palestine "supported by public opinion throughout the Arab World," were "inexorably opposed" to Zionist aims. However it claimed:

> [The Arabs] are ready to accept all those Jews that have already come into Palestine (estimated now at 600,000) as a permanent part of the country's population and as full citizens (under adequate guarantees provided by the Arab League in conjunction with the World Organization) in an independent Arab Palestine, united with her sisters in the Arab League. They are ready to accept a Jewish cultural and spiritual home in Palestine, which has already come into being and is today a fact. But they will not abdicate their sovereign position as the rightful owners of the country. They regard the White Paper as a solemn guarantee of this prescriptive position and this elementary right, and any attempt to go back on it now would be viewed as another breach of faith by England—and would cause the utmost prejudice to Anglo-Arab relations.[40]

Alluding to the Jewish Agency's request for the establishment of a Jewish State and the immigration of 100,000 European Jews into Palestine, the Arab Office declaration argued that the Zionists' political offensive was coupled to a deceptive humanitarian appeal:

> On the humanitarian plane Palestine may not unreasonably be deemed to have contributed far more than its just share towards the solution of the Jewish problem. . . . It is extremely unfair to the Arabs to go on using the humanitarian argument, wittingly or unwittingly, in support of the political claims of Zionism. The political question was finally settled by the White Paper, and any attempt to force more refugees on Palestine now, on whatever grounds it is ostensibly made, would be a breach of that settlement. Would it be too much to ask other nations and particularly the British Commonwealth and the United States, with their enormous territories and great absorptive capacity, to contribute one-tenth of Palestine's share towards a settlement on what remains of the Jewish problem on purely humanitarian plane? On this plane the problem can and should be solved internationally.[41]

Confronted by the rigid positions of Zionists and Arabs, the Labour government set about trying to deal with Palestine. Initially this task was given to a special cabinet subcommittee chaired by Foreign Secretary Bevin. The subcommittee concluded that Britain could not by itself carry out a pro-Zionist solution in Palestine. As an interim measure it proposed that Jewish immigration be permitted at the rate of 1,500 per month after the expiration of the White Paper quota. This proposal was accepted by the cabinet. Weizmann was informed of the decision in late August. He rejected it as "entirely inadequate."[42]

The Labour cabinet's retreat from its preelection pro-Zionist stand showed that the new British government had no definite political formula to implement in Palestine. In the months ahead, British policy aimed at arranging some orderly settlement that would obtain at least tacit acquiescence from Zionists and Arabs, if not their formal agreement.

By the end of the summer of 1945, the Labour government appeared certain of only one thing in regard to Palestine: Britain wanted the help of the United States in promoting and implementing a long-term settlement between Arabs and Jews. Harold Laski privately tried to explain London's difficulties:

> No Government can alter in a brief ten weeks the whole contours of a foreign policy, the roots of which go down deep into the roots of the nation. . . .
> . . . On Palestine, it would certainly make the task of the British Government easier if the Americans would offer to share in the difficult responsibility of our mandate, instead of merely offering us advice by resolution. 5,000 American troops in Palestine are worth 100 resolutions from the United States Senate.[43]

The Labour government's vacillation emboldened Arabs and Zionists alike.[44] As it became apparent that Washington also remained undecided as to the type or extent of active responsibility it would accept for Palestine, the positions of extremists in both the Arab and Jewish camps seemed grounded even more firmly in sound political logic.

TRUMAN TAKES UP THE PALESTINE QUESTION

President Truman's first official contact with the Palestine issue occurred only days after he entered the White House when Secretary of State Stettinius warned that Zionists would soon seek "some commitments in favor of . . . unlimited Jewish immigration into Palestine and the establishment there of a Jewish state." Stettinius pointed out that the Palestine issue had extensive ramifications throughout the Near East that went "far beyond the plight of the Jews in Europe." The president was advised that the Palestine question touched on interests "vital to the United States," and that the "whole subject . . . should be handled with the greatest care and with a view to the long-range interests of this country."[45] Two weeks later Truman received a memorandum in which the State Department outlined the conflicting promises passed out by his predecessor.[46]

Truman initially appeared willing to accept the department's advice. On April 20 he received Rabbi Wise but made no specific commitments to the Zionist leader, assuring him only of his "agreement with the expressed policy of the Roosevelt administration on Palestine."[47] Shortly thereafter, demonstrating a readiness to pick up the unpublicized strands of Roosevelt's Palestine policy, Truman sent messages to the governments of Transjordan and Egypt, repeating Roosevelt's pledge to take no decision affecting the basic situation in Palestine prior to full consultations with both Arabs and Jews.[48] However, this initial even-handedness was quick to erode.

Prior to the president's departure on July 7 for the Potsdam Conference, American Zionists made a concerted effort to obtain White House support for their demands on the British government. While official Zionist organizations—led by the Zionist Emergency Council—supported the full program of the Jewish Agency, officially non-Zionist organizations, such as the American Jewish Committee, campaigned on behalf of the agency's demand for unrestricted immigration. It was later claimed that organizations representing more than 2 million persons telegraphed the president urging that his good offices be used at Potsdam on behalf of Jewish claims in Palestine.[49] Zionist supporters in Congress were also active. In mid-May Senators Wagner and Taft began gathering signatures on a petition urging immediate steps to open Palestine to Jewish immigration and pave the way for a democratic Jewish commonwealth. The message, signed by 54 senators and 251 representatives, was given to Truman on July 2.[50] A similar plea was cabled to the White House by 37 of the 48 state governors attending a conference in Michigan.[51]

Although Palestine was not officially discussed at Potsdam, Truman managed to bring up the problem with British leaders. The president sent Churchill a memorandum stating that restrictions on Jewish immigration into Palestine "continue to provoke passionate protest from Americans most interested in Palestine" and expressing hope that the mandatory would "find it possible without delay to lift the restriction."[52] Before he could reply, Churchill was replaced as prime minister by Attlee. The Labour leader acknowledged the note and promised to give it close attention.[53] However, Truman was unable to provide any definite answer to queries from both prime ministers as to what help might be expected from the United States should Britain permit massive Jewish immigration into Palestine.[54]

On August 16 Truman held a press conference, the first since his return from Potsdam, at which he described the American position on Palestine:

The American view on Palestine is that we want to let as many of the Jews into Palestine as it is possible to let into that country. Then the matter will have to be worked out diplomatically with the British and the Arabs, so that if a state can be set up there they may be able to set it up on a peaceful basis. I have no desire to send 500,000 American soldiers to make peace in Palestine.[55]

Truman's tendency to separate the question of Jewish immigration into Palestine from political tensions in that country was reinforced by a report he received in late August from Earl G. Harrison, whom the president had sent to investigate the European refugee problem.

Harrison felt that "on a purely humanitarian basis with no reference to ideological or political considerations so far as Palestine is concerned," there could be some "reasonable extension of the White Paper of 1939." Although admitting that there might be room to question the precise number of Jews that should be granted immediate entry into Palestine, he believed the Jewish Agency's figure of 100,000 was reasonable. Harrison argued that meeting the Zionist demand would promote a sound "solution for the future of Jews still in Germany and Austria." Harrison's report did not recommend radical action by the United States to help resolve the displaced persons problem, suggesting only that Washington "should, under existing immigration laws, permit reasonable numbers of such persons to come here . . . particularly those who have family ties in this country."[56]

Actually, the report was hardly compiled without "reference to ideological or political considerations." It was greatly influenced by two very active Zionists, Dr. Joseph J. Schwartz and Rabbi Abraham J. Klausner, who accompanied Harrison throughout most of his stay in Europe.[57] This probably explains why Harrison's tally of Jews under American and British administration in Germany and Austria confirmed the Jewish Agency's estimate of 100,000. In fact, this figure greatly exaggerated the actual total.[58]

Truman sent Prime Minister Attlee a copy of Harrison's report and urged prompt action on its recommendations. Attlee received this message at a very inopportune time. The British Colonial Office had only recently proposed that immigration into Palestine should not be stopped but rather limited to the rate of 1,500 a month until a final settlement could be devised. Although the Jewish Agency rejected the offer, negotiations between the British government and the Zionists continued through the middle of September. When the Jewish Agency's position remained unchanged, London unilaterally implemented the suggested interim immigration schedule.

In the meantime, Attlee was alarmed to learn on September 14 that Truman planned to release the Harrison Report the following day—along with an approving statement from the White House. The prime minister immediately asked for a delay.[59] Shortly afterward, Attlee sent Truman a detailed letter arguing that Britain could not at that time allow 100,000 Jewish immigrants into Palestine. He reminded the president that both the American and British governments were committed to consult with Arabs and Jews before determining any final policy toward Palestine, and that violation of those commitments might "set aflame the whole Middle East." Attlee also mentioned the Jewish Agency's rejection of the proposed interim immigration rate, and accused Zionists of "insisting upon the complete repudiation of the White Paper and the immediate grant of 100,000 certificates regardless of the effect on the situation in the Middle East this would have." Finally, he pointedly recalled that "as things are, the responsibility for preserving order, with all the consequences involved, rests entirely on this country."[60]

Truman held off for two weeks. However, he was clearly unmoved by Attlee's argument against the feasibility of immediate, massive Jewish immigration into Palestine. At the end of September the White House released the Harrison Report to the press. It also released a letter from Truman to General Eisenhower expressing the president's determination "to have the doors of Palestine opened for such of these displaced persons as wish to go there."[61]

INITIAL RESULTS OF TRUMAN'S
PALESTINE INVOLVEMENT

By the end of September, Truman's six-month involvement in the Palestine issue had created difficulties for himself and the American government both at home and abroad. His single-minded insistence that massive Jewish immigration into Palestine be permitted without reference to political factors had antagonized the British government. Zionists feared and resented the president's failure to clarify the nature of his contacts with Attlee. The Arab world, focusing on Truman's repeated comments in support of Jewish immigration into Palestine, was rapidly concluding that Washington was about to abandon Roosevelt's pledge of "full consultations."

Truman's comments at the August 16 press conference following his return from Potsdam generated much confusion. While the Iraqi government condemned the president's statements for their support of Zionism, the American consul general in Jerusalem reported that only mild protests had been received from Palestinian Arabs.[62] Indeed, some Arab leaders in Palestine interpreted Truman's reference to the necessity of peaceful settlement in Palestine as a sign that his verbal support for Jewish immigration was an empty gesture.[63] This view was echoed in the Palestinian Arab press, which pointed out that Jewish immigration and peace were incompatible.[64]

Zionist reaction was equally divided. On the one hand, the president's remarks were welcomed as placing the United States on record against the restrictive White Paper of 1939.[65] However, Truman's statement about not sending American troops to Palestine caused some alarm. Rabbi Silver termed the president's fears "fantastic" and sought Wagner's aid in trying to obtain an invitation to the White House so he could allay such worries.[66]

Despite their discomfort, Zionists were unable to see Truman during the next several weeks. On September 6 Silver again contacted Wagner:

> What our Government intends to do in the matter is still a mystery to us. The promises and the endorsements of the Zionist program are all there— but no action—no directives to our State Department. President Truman's recent statement on Palestine at the press conference on August 16 was very ambiguous and left the Jews of America baffled and confused. . . . The Zionist leaders have not had an opportunity to discuss the subject with the President since last April and then only for a few brief moments.[67]

During September, press reports of Truman's contacts with the British government provoked further alarm among Arabs and Jews. Zionist worries arose from a suspicion that the mysterious Anglo-American communications might presage some arrangement to permit 100,000 Jews into Palestine while giving political control of the country to its Arab population. In that case the Arabs would still retain a majority of some 600,000. Although Zionists never pretended that the entry of 100,000 refugees was a final demand, it has been argued that by concentrating propaganda so heavily on the refugee problem they became vulnerable to a political move of this sort.[68] The extent of Zionist distrust of the administration was apparent during a conversation in late September between Acting Secretary of State Acheson and three prominent Zionists: Emanuel Neumann, Louis Levinthal, and Benjamin Akzin.

Referring to reports of ongoing negotiations between Truman and British officials, the Zionist leaders asked Acheson to clarify the administration's intentions. Truman had kept the State Department so much in the dark about his activities that Acheson could only truthfully reply that "no one now in the Department was in a position to answer the question." The talk then developed into a tense encounter. Acheson's visitors pointed out that his reply left them in "a rather peculiar position." Obviously not believing that the undersecretary was himself in a peculiarly ignorant position, they recalled the 1944 Democratic and Republican platforms and warned that American Jews would not be satisfied with anything less than a Jewish Commonwealth in Palestine.

The hapless Acheson only intensified the misunderstanding by again professing ignorance of "what negotiations or conversations, if any, had been taking place between the American and British Governments with regard to Palestine," and coupling this with a personal expression of confidence that Washington would keep its promises. Emanuel Neumann was sufficiently agitated to drop virtually all pretense of diplomatic decorum. American Jews, he warned,

> would use every means at their disposal to force the appropriate officials of the American Government to live up to the pledges of two Presidents and of the two great political parties. The Jewish people had many weapons at their disposal, including the radio and the press and supporters in both houses of Congress. It was understood, for instance, that the American Government was planning to grant huge credits to Great Britain. The Jewish people might well oppose the granting of such credits in case the British Government failed to take the proper steps with regard to Palestine.

Neumann's threatening reference to the Truman administration's projected financial aid to Britain gave Acheson a chance to take the offensive:

> Mr. Acheson stated that he sympathized with and understood the desire of the Zionists to be given an opportunity to present their case to the American Government. . . . He could not, however, go along with some of the statements which Mr. Neumann had just made. He believed that it would be extremely foolish for the Zionist leaders to take a position that unless they could at once achieve their aims with regard to Palestine, Jewish groups in the United States would endeavor to injure the international position of the United States or to wreck general American Governmental policies. Such a course would be to the disadvantage of the Zionist leaders and would be unfair to the millions of loyal, patriotic Jews in the United States.

At this point Neumann's colleagues felt things were getting out of hand. Levinthal announced that "in his opinion Mr. Neumann had gone a little far." Neumann tried to explain away his remarks by saying "he had not intended to give the impression that the Zionist leaders would encourage the Jewish people to bloc the conduct of American foreign relations." He was, he said, merely stating the fact that "the Jewish people would be so outraged at the failure of the American Government to live up to its promises that they might strike back in ways which would be unwise and harmful to themselves as well as the United States."[69]

Although the Neumann-Acheson confrontation ended on a note of cordiality, Zionists had demonstrated the extent of their displeasure with the ambiguity of the president's position. The same point was made by the frequent calls for a pro-Zionist presidential statement that emanated from prominent Zionists during the late summer of 1945.[70]

On September 29, Truman responded to the mounting pressure by publishing the Harrison Report and his own letter to Eisenhower. According to

Sumner Welles, the president's action was inspired by worried managers of the Democratic Party.[71]

Rumors about Truman's contacts with the British government caused growing unease in the Middle East. The early optimistic interpretations of the president's post-Potsdam statements gave way to rising apprehension, which in the absence of clear information was sometimes based on gross distortions of fact. In Iraq the press reported that Truman was pressing for the immediate admission into Palestine of 1 million Jews.[72] Prince Abdallah of Transjordan indignantly voiced alarm over a rumor that the president was urging Attlee to grant 10,000 immigration certificates.[73]

Publication of the Harrison Report and the Eisenhower letter at the end of September exacerbated Arab unrest. On October 3 the ministers of Egypt, Iraq, Syria, and Lebanon called in a body at the State Department to present a formal request for assurances that the American government would live up to its promises of consultation. Acting Secretary Acheson replied that he was "not in a position to discuss the matter" and advised the ministers to make the request when Secretary Byrnes returned to Washington.[74]

At this juncture Ibn Saud decided to publish a letter sent to him by Roosevelt soon after the Yalta Conference. The letter reaffirmed the president's earlier pledge regarding consultations and promised that no action would be taken "which might prove hostile to the Arab people."[75] Hoping to minimize the embarrassment that would be caused to the administration by unilateral Saudi publication of the Roosevelt letter, Byrnes advised Truman to agree to simultaneous release of the document in Riyadh and Washington. Byrnes also urged Truman to issue an independent statement reaffirming his predecessor's promise.[76] Although the president agreed to release Roosevelt's letter, he refused to issue a statement of his own.

Perhaps those most mystified by Truman's actions in the summer and fall of 1945 were officials in the State Department, and particularly those in the Office of Near Eastern and African Affairs. It was painfully evident to these men that the president was unwilling to confide in them, or to give much weight to their suggestions.

Upon becoming secretary of state at the end of June 1945, James Byrnes received an analysis prepared by the Near East specialists. The document outlined the various long-range solutions for Palestine that had been under study in the department since 1943: a Jewish state, an Arab state, partition, and the communal autonomy trusteeship scheme.[77] It described the first two alternatives as inequitable and prejudicial to American interests. Although the Near East Division was skeptical about the feasibility of partition, it still felt that adequate support by the Great Powers might lead the Arabs to accept such a solution. However, the trusteeship proposal was clearly favored by the specialists. While admitting that the scheme would meet with disapproval from both Arabs and Jews, they argued that it would be less likely than others to injure American interests—and more likely to provide grounds for an eventual rapprochement among moderate Palestinian Arabs and Jews. The emphasis in the assessment given to Byrnes was on the need for international planning and coordination, and not on the specifics of the trusteeship arrangement itself. The Middle East analysts argued only that their hope for an orderly Palestine settlement rested on "some kind of solution similar to this [trusteeship] plan."

On the other hand, they were emphatic about the necessity of an internationally coordinated approach to Palestine:

> In our opinion, it is important that Great Britain, the United States, the Soviet Union and, if possible, France, should endeavor to reach an agreement among themselves with regard to the future of Palestine . . . otherwise there is a danger that one or more of these great powers might endeavor to pass on to the other powers the responsibility for the decisions made, with the result that both Arabs and Jews might have grounds to hope that with sufficient amount of agitation on their part the decision could be revised. Such a situation would almost inevitably lead to political instability in Palestine and the Near East.[78]

The gap between Truman's outlook and that of the State Department was shown by the president's outspoken support for massive Jewish immigration into Palestine at his August 16 press conference. A few days later the department ineffectually strove to narrow the disparity by offering Truman the following advice:

> No government should advocate a policy of mass immigration unless it is prepared to assist in making available the necessary security forces, shipping, housing, un-employment guarantees.

The president was flatly told that "the United States should refrain from supporting a policy of large-scale immigration into Palestine" until these issues were resolved.[79]

Truman preferred what he heard in other quarters. On September 7 Rosenman assured the president that there was "nothing inconsistent" between Roosevelt's promise to Ibn Saud to do nothing to assist the Jews against the Arabs and Truman's statement to the press on August 16. "I do not think," Rosenman continued, "that opening the doors to Palestine is in any sense an act which is a 'move hostile to the Arab people.' "[80]

While Truman was not swayed by the views of the State Department, those in charge of day-to-day American relations with Middle Eastern countries found their task becoming increasingly more difficult. At the end of September, the Office of Near Eastern and African Affairs still had no definite knowledge of Truman's dealings with the British, or of the objectives he was seeking, save what it gleaned from "newspapers and other sources."[81] Acting Secretary Acheson was in an identical situation. Acheson, in fact, concluded that Truman and the frequently absent Byrnes "were the only two Americans" who were in a position to know Washington's policy toward Palestine.[82] But if Byrnes was privy to Truman's dealings with the British, he was obviously under strict instructions not to relay the information to department officials.

Lack of communication with the White House left the department incapable of answering numerous queries from American diplomats in the Arab world who were being pressed by their host governments to explain Truman's intervention with London.[83] At the same time, the department began to fear that Truman might disregard promises to consult with Arabs and Jews before assuming any commitment on Palestine. On October 1, Loy Henderson brought the matter up with Dean Acheson:

> No matter what decision we might make, we should not overlook the assurances that we have given that we shall consult in advance the Arabs and Jews. Those assurances have been given in writing by both President Roosevelt and President Truman. There can be legitimate differences between the Arab peoples, the Zionists and ourselves as to what should be the future status of Palestine. There should not, however, be any differences as to the willingness of the United States Government to keep its word.[84]

On the following day Acheson forwarded Truman a memorandum entitled "Views of the Department of State concerning American Promises regarding Palestine." This was a remarkable document in which the State Department directly confronted the president with his responsibility to fulfill American commitments.[85]

After briefly reviewing the reactions of Jewish and Arab leaders to reports that Truman was urging Britain to permit the immediate entry of 100,000 Jewish refugees into Palestine, the memorandum stressed existing presidential pledges to delay a decision affecting Palestine's basic situation until after consultations with Arabs and Jews. It then referred to Truman's campaign on behalf of the 100,000 in the following blunt terms:

> The President's proposal would, if adopted, constitute a basic change in the Palestine situation, and it is already clear from the violent reaction of the Arabs that it would in fact make an immediate issue out of the Palestine question. The British White Paper, adopted in 1939, established a quota of 75,000 for Jewish immigration into Palestine during the following five years, after which time there was to be further Jewish immigration without Arab acquiescence. President Truman's proposal would involve the abrogation of a cardinal feature of the British White Paper policy.
>   The disposition on our part to fail to carry out our promises would constitute the severest kind of blow to American prestige not only in the

Near East but elsewhere. Much of the work done in the Near East in recent years in building up respect for, and confidence in the United States would be undone. Beyond the loss of prestige is the very serious threat to vital American interests in that area which would result from a hostile Arab world. Moreover, the smaller nations of the world, who have looked to the United States for leadership . . . would be sadly disillusioned if we violated our word in this conspicuous instance.[86]

Shortly before this message reached the White House, the demoralizing influence of Truman's actions on the State Department was visible in a marginal notation penned by George V. Allen, deputy director of the Office of Near Eastern and African Affairs, on another memorandum dealing with Palestine:

It seems apparent to me that the President (and perhaps Mr. Byrnes as well) have decided to have a go at Palestine negotiations without bringing NEA into the picture for the time being. . . . I see nothing further we can appropriately do for the moment except to carry on our current work, answering letters and telegrams, receiving callers, etc., as best we can, pending the time (which will come soon) when the whole thing will be dumped back in our laps.[87]

Allen was unduly optimistic. The "whole thing" was never returned to the lap of the Near Eastern Office. However, his unfounded aspiration appeared to have some grounds in mid-October, when the British government followed up earlier attempts to discover what the United States would contribute to an orderly settlement in Palestine by inviting American participation in a joint investigation as a first step toward devising a compromise solution to the Arab-Zionist conflict.

10. SEARCH FOR A POSITION: THE ANGLO-AMERICAN COMMITTEE OF INQUIRY

As Clement Attlee's government became more involved in formulating a postwar Middle East policy, it discovered the difficulties of trying to redefine traditional concepts of British interests. Although the Labour Party opposed the imperial format in which Britain's presence in the Middle East had grown, the new ministers of the crown could not avoid concluding that the security of the Suez Canal, continued access to Near Eastern oil deposits, and the retention of political influence in Middle Eastern capitals were important foreign policy objectives.[1]

By the fall of 1945 the Attlee cabinet had not sorted out its priorities in the Middle East. However, it realized that London's Palestine policy could not be isolated completely from considerations of larger strategic and political issues.[2] A symptom of this awareness was that the Foreign Office was far more involved than the Colonial Office (under which the mandate was administered) with the Palestine question. Uncertainty over the continued stationing of British troops in Egypt made Foreign Office planners anxious to secure an option for some sort of long-term presence in Palestine regardless of the final settlement that might be arranged in that country.

This, along with a desire to enlist active American participation in resolving the Arab-Zionist conflict, was the basis upon which Ernest Bevin hoped to build a Palestine policy when he wrote to Secretary Byrnes on October 19 suggesting a joint committee of inquiry.

PREPARATIONS FOR THE ANGLO-AMERICAN COMMITTEE

In view of Truman's refusal to consider the political implications of massive Jewish immigration into Palestine, it was not surprising that the original British proposal called for an investigation of the extent to which the refugee problem could be solved through means that would not exacerbate the Palestine issue. Bevin suggested the following terms of reference for a joint investigative committee:

I. To examine the position of the Jews in British and American occupied Europe. . . .

II. To make an estimate of the number of such Jews whom it may prove impossible to resettle in the country from which they originated.

III. To examine the possibility of relieving the situation in Europe through immigration into other countries outside Europe.

IV. To consider other available means of meeting the needs of the immediate situation.[3]

Under item III, Palestine was to be considered a possible place of resettlement, but only as one among several. The Labour government hoped the proposed investigation would discover an alternative to Palestine.

However, Truman was not prepared to have the search guided into other channels. When the Harrison Report was released, it had been made clear that the president favored the idea that 100,000 immigrants should be permitted into Palestine. Then, too, rumors of Truman's contacts with Attlee on behalf of the refugees had associated the White House with the Jewish Agency's demand for prompt immigration. It would have been difficult for the president to agree with London's conception of an inquiry without appearing to have reversed himself. Moreover, any inquiry whose purpose was to suggest possibilities other than Palestine for Jewish resettlement would inevitably have raised questions about American willingness to receive displaced persons.

Truman records his determination to make it "plain that I was not going to retreat from the position which I had taken in my letter to Attlee of August 31." He did not, he recalls, want the United States to become party to "dilatory tactics."[4] Byrnes was instructed to reply accordingly to the British initiative.

The president's reaction was colored by city elections in New York, scheduled for early November. Samuel Rosenman, who at Truman's direction had become increasingly involved with the Palestine issue, warned repeatedly that the Democratic Party could be harmed by American participation in the suggested inquiry.[5] Rosenman pointed out that Zionists were already angered by the recent publication of Roosevelt's 1945 letter to Ibn Saud.[6] While agreeing that the United States could not simply ignore its commitment to consult with Arabs as well as Jews before taking long-range decisions on Palestine, he advised Truman to treat such consultations as no more than an obligatory formality with no substantial bearing on policy.[7]

Preliminary discussion between British and American representatives quickly brought London to agree that a joint inquiry should focus more on the question of Jewish immigration into Palestine rather than on emigration to other countries. By October 29, Byrnes was convinced that a consensus over the purpose of the investigation could be reached within 48 hours. Nonetheless, when pressed by the British to conclude the agreement, Byrnes demurred on grounds that political reasons made it necessary to wait until after the New York elections.[8]

Meanwhile, Rosenman continued warning Truman against what Zionists considered Britain's stalling tactics.[9] Despite efforts to keep the negotiations over the inquiry committee secret, reports appeared in the American press. Zionists immediately accused the administration of permitting London to evade the obligations of the Balfour Declaration.[10]

On November 13 the British and American governments finally announced their intent to form the Anglo-American Committee of Inquiry. The terms of reference given to that body largely reflected Truman's wishes. The committee was charged with examining the impact of conditions in Palestine upon "the problem of Jewish immigration," and with investigating the European Jewish refugee problem with a view to estimating the numbers that might "migrate to Palestine or other countries." The committee was asked to take evidence from competent witnesses and to "consult with representative Arabs and Jews" before making policy recommendations to the two governments.[11]

By early December, Washington and London further agreed to limit the investigation to 120 days. This was done at the insistence of the Truman administration, which feared that absence of a deadline would increase domestic opposition to the project. Although the Foreign Office, hoping the committee would liberally interpret its instructions to consider possibilities of immigration to "Palestine or other countries," at first argued against the idea, it quickly conceded the point.[12]

British agreement at this stage was also influenced by renewed congressional interest in the Palestine resolutions originally introduced in 1944. As pressure built up in favor of a revised measure, Byrnes advised London's ambassador that congressional action could be delayed only by limiting the inquiry's duration.[13] However, British agreement did not have the desired result; nor did Truman's announcement that he opposed congressional action at this time on grounds that it would undermine the need for an inquiry on Palestine. On December 17 the pro-Zionist resolution was approved by the Senate. Two days later the House of Representatives followed suit. Although the 1945 Congressional Resolution differed from the 1944 version by referring to the need for a "democratic commonwealth" in Palestine, rather than a "democratic Jewish commonwealth," Zionists considered it a significant victory.[14]

As Washington and London began appointing members to the Committee of Inquiry, Truman announced that "within the existing immigration laws" he had asked responsible officials to allow refugees to enter the United States with all possible speed.[15] This had virtually no effect on the problem of displaced persons. Existing laws were such that ten months after the president's directive was issued, only 4,767 refugees—Jews as well as non-Jews—had been permitted into the United States.[16]

ARAB AND ZIONIST REACTION TO THE ANGLO-AMERICAN COMMITTEE OF INQUIRY

Arab and Jewish reaction to the Committee of Inquiry was conditioned by the seriously deteriorating situation in Palestine. Events were already validating the warnings issued by Zionist leaders in the summer of 1945. In September the commander of the Haganah, Moshe Sneh, initiated a series of meetings with representatives of the Stern and Irgun groups that led to a working coordination among the three forces.[17] By November a formal agreement was reached, placing the terrorists under the ultimate direction of the Jewish Agency.[18]

British intelligence services kept London informed of the movement toward a unified Jewish Resistance.[19] The news impelled the British Government to reinforce its military strength in Palestine with veteran combat troops, and to augment naval and air units in the area.[20] Despite these measures, the mandatory was unable to prevent the first coordinated Haganah-Stern-Irgun action on the night of October 31.[21] Nor, until it took the offensive several months later, was it able to curb the ensuing wave of Jewish terrorism in Palestine.

While the Jewish Agency added this military dimension to the political initiative it had undertaken at the end of the war, it also embarked on yet another venture. In October David Ben Gurion traveled to Europe, where he examined conditions in the displaced persons camps. Soon afterward he convinced Jewish Agency leaders to adopt a policy in Europe designed to obtain greater support from the United States.

When Ben Gurion arrived on the Continent, a steady stream of East European Jewish refugees was starting to flow into the occupied sectors of Western Europe. Unlike the original Jewish displaced persons who had remained under the care of Allied military authorities since their liberation from German camps, these new arrivals were either Jews who had escaped capture by the Nazis, but who were now determined to leave their native lands, or individuals who returned to their prewar homes after liberation only to encounter a residue of anti-Semitism.

Many migrants made their ways to the displaced persons camps, where they received preferential rations accorded to those officially categorized as

"DPs." Since this was technically illegal, the East Europeans were called "infiltrees." The American Army was uncertain over how to receive the infiltrees—or, indeed, whether to receive them at all.[22] In the fall of 1945 Washington had no stated policy, and for a time individual officers adopted different courses of action.[23]

While in Europe, Ben Gurion obtained personal assurances from Lt. General Walter Bedell Smith that the army would not hinder the movement of infiltrees. This pledge was subsequently strengthened by Major General John H. Hilldring, assistant secretary of state for occupied areas, who informed Jewish leaders that the army would assume responsibility for an additional 50,000 refugees. Although no formal decision on the matter was ever announced by Washington, it was informally arranged that all Jewish refugees wishing to enter American camps would be permitted to do so.[24]

On the basis of the information he gathered in Europe, Ben Gurion saw an opportunity to increase American pressure on Britain for a pro-Zionist settlement in Palestine. He explained his thoughts to the Jewish Agency Executive in Jerusalem:

> This will be a major factor for the Americans to demand their [Jewish displaced persons] removal to Palestine. . . . It is possible to bring there [American-occupied Europe] all the European Jews from everywhere, without any difficulty. . . . If we manage to concentrate a quarter of a million Jews in the U.S. Zone, it would increase the American pressure [on the British Government] not because of the economic problem—that does not play any role with [the Americans]—but because they see no future anywhere but in Palestine.[25]

The instrument for carrying out Ben Gurion's suggestion was already in existence: Brichah. Although that organization's efforts had hitherto been devoted primarily to transporting refugees to ports from which illegal immigrant ships sailed to Palestine, this was easily changed. Brichah was now given a new mandate

> to send the mass of the refugees into the U.S. Zone in Germany so as to create there a large reservoir of Jewish population that by its very existence would exercise a growing pressure on Palestine's closed doors; and . . . to send a continual trickle of would-be immigrants to France and Italy, whence most of the [illegal immigrant] ships sailed.[26]

In this way, by the end of 1945, Zionists adopted a tactic whose purpose was not only to drive home the plight of refugees to the American government but also to force the United States to become increasingly concerned with the final disposition of the displaced European Jews. Ben Gurion correctly reasoned that the United States would see no future for the refugees anywhere but in Palestine.

The Anglo-American Committee of Inquiry was perceived as a threat by Zionists, who feared that Britain might yet succeed in having the committee focus primarily on a search for some solution to the displaced persons problem other than mass emigration to Palestine. On November 15, Rabbis Silver and Wise sent a message to Truman regretting American involvement in the joint inquiry and interpreting that step as "the withdrawal, at any rate for the time being, of your request for 100,000 immigration certificates." Reminding the president that they spoke on behalf of millions of Americans, they urged him to "reconsider the whole matter."[27] When this failed to kill the inquiry, Silver called on the Inner Council of the Jewish Agency to boycott the Anglo-American Committee. Although his views received substantial support, agency leaders reluctantly decided that political wisdom required their cooperation with the British-American investigation.[28]

The Arab world was also divided over the impending inquiry. Various courses—ranging from a total boycott to full cooperation—were advocated within the Council of the Arab League.[29] In the end, the council agreed to testify before the committee, but it warned that its presence would not imply "recognition . . . of the right of the Anglo-American Committee . . . to decide the Palestine issue, nor . . . the right of Great Britain and the United States . . . to handle the problem exclusively."[30]

Palestine's Arab community remained splintered by factional infighting. However, signs that the mandatory was at last embarking on a search for a final settlement produced efforts to achieve Palestinian unity. In mid-November the president of the Arab League Council, Syria's Jamil Mardam, headed an inter-Arab delegation to Jerusalem in a temporarily successful bid to promote a united front. A new Palestinian Arab Higher Committee was formed one week after Mardam's arrival. Five of the twelve seats on the new body were allotted to the Husseinis' Palestine Arab Party. The remaining positions were given to five other prewar parties, and one went to the independent Palestinian notable, Musa al-Alami.[31]

In early December the Higher Committee officially responded to the news of the Anglo-American inquiry. Although its reaction stopped short of a refusal to cooperate with the committee, it did not disguise the extreme distaste with which the Arabs looked upon the whole affair. Particular exception was taken to American involvement in the inquiry:

> The American people and government have shown great partiality in favor of the Jews and Jewish aspirations. Both the Republicans and Democrats have declared that they support Zionism and the policy of establishing a Jewish State in Palestine. Many congressmen have also expressed their sympathies for the Jews and have supported the Jewish political program. Moreover, Mr. Harry Truman . . . has asked that 100,000 Jewish immigrants be immediately admitted into Palestine, and he still insists on this. It is not, therefore, logical that the United States should be a judge in a case in which it has already declared its views.[32]

Nonetheless, Palestinian Arabs ultimately agreed to cooperate with the inquiry. The decision was almost entirely due to the influence of Jamal al-Husseini, who in late December was released from internment in Rhodesia. Although barred from Palestine until February 1946, he publicly argued from his temporary headquarters in Cairo against the idea of a boycott.[33] Jamal al-Husseini's prestige as chief assistant of the mufti of Jerusalem—who was now detained in France—won the Higher Committee's grudging acceptance of his advice.[34]

By the end of 1945, Arabs and Zionists were at least willing to tolerate the Anglo-American inquiry. However, both sides perceived the British-American effort as just another obstacle to their maximum political ambitions. In each camp the influence of extremists was bolstered by knowledge that neither London nor Washington was quite sure of what it could realistically hope to accomplish in Palestine. Arabs as well as Zionists concluded that uncompromising postures were most likely to influence the indecisive Great Powers.

THE ANGLO-AMERICAN COMMITTEE OF INQUIRY IN OPERATION

When the British and American governments simultaneously announced the planned joint inquiry into the Palestine situation, it was evident that each party favored a different approach. In London, where the announcement was made to Parliament, Ernest Bevin antagonized Zionists by arguing that Palestine might contribute toward settling the Jewish refugee question, but that it could not "provide sufficient opportunity for grappling with the whole problem."[35] Zionists were further offended by remarks Bevin made distinguishing between a Jewish state, which he maintained Britain had no obligation to establish, and a Jewish home in Palestine, which he agreed was a British commitment. With much justice, Zionist leaders charged that Bevin had prejudged the inquiry.[36]

When Truman announced American participation in the joint committee, he also prejudged the inquiry by releasing the text of the letter he sent to Attlee in August commending the prime minister's attention to the Harrison Report's support of the demand that 100,000 Jews be allowed into Palestine.[37]

The committee, composed of six British and six American members under a rotating chairmanship, began its investigation in early January 1946. In the interval since the inquiry was first announced, Zionists and their supporters had worked hard to ensure that individuals favorable to their cause were on the American delegation. Congressman Celler reminded Truman of the Democratic Party's Palestine plank and argued that some of the committee's members should reflect that position.[38] Samuel Rosenman offered the president a list of possible appointees, restricting his suggestions to persons well known for pro-Zionist inclinations.[39]

The group finally chosen to represent the United States largely met Zionist wishes. Apart from Frank Aydelotte and William Phillips, who joined the committee free from past commitments on Palestine, the remaining American delegates were associated with pro-Zionist positions. The American cochairman, Judge Joseph Hutchison, had lent his name to a pro-Zionist advertisement that appeared in the New York *Times* in late 1942.[40] Although Hutchison adopted an impartial position on the committee and demonstrated an open mind on the Palestine issue, three other members of the American group proved stoutly committed to the Zionist cause. These were James G. McDonald, formerly an advisor to Roosevelt on refugee affairs[41], Frank W. Buxton, a Boston newspaper editor[42], and Bartley C. Crum, a California lawyer.[43]

The committee first convened in Washington. It then proceeded to London, to the displaced persons camps on the Continent, and finally to the Middle East. Throughout the deliberations, committee members were handicapped by uncertainty over their governments' objectives in Palestine. Richard Crossman, who served on the British delegation, noted that all those on the committee found it difficult to recommend specific courses of action:

> The biggest unknowns . . . were the policies and intentions of our two governments. Here we remained on our own guesswork even after we had established what Arabs and Jews and what British and American public opinion desired.[44]

Bartley Crum concluded that most of his British colleagues primarily feared the growth of Soviet influence in the Arab world because they believed that Russia was dedicated to "reducing Britain to a fourth-rate power in the Middle East."[45] Conceding that "there might be points at which British imperial and Russian nationalistic interests did not coincide," Crum was convinced that "surely the United States and Russia had few points at which their basic interests were in conflict."[46]

Despite their differing approaches, committee members managed to produce a unanimous report, complete with recommendations, well in advance of the 120-day deadline. Their efforts to achieve a consensus were spurred by a comment made at the investigation's outset by Ernest Bevin, who promised to support a report backed unanimously by the committee. Submitted in late April 1946, the report has since gained general recognition as "an honest effort to deal with a difficult problem."[47]

The tenor of the recommendations was set by the committee's initial appraisal of the Palestine issue.

> The Jews have a historic connection with the country. The Jewish National Home, though embodying a minority of the population, is today a reality

established under international guarantee. It has a right to continued existence, protection and development.

Yet Palestine is not, and can never be a purely Jewish land. It lies at the crossroads of the Arab world. Its Arab population, descended from long-time inhabitants of the area, rightly look upon Palestine as their homeland.[48]

Having equated the Arab and Jewish positions, the committee concluded:

[It would be] neither just nor practicable that Palestine should become either an Arab state, in which an Arab majority would control the destiny of a Jewish minority, or a Jewish state, in which a Jewish majority would control that of an Arab minority. In neither case would minority guarantees afford adequate protection for the subordinated group.[49]

On this basis the Anglo-American Committee report advanced considerations reminiscent of those that led to the religious trusteeship scheme unofficially discussed between State Department and Foreign Office officials in 1944. Noting that "the great interest of the Christian world in Palestine has . . . been completely overlooked, glossed over, or brushed aside," the committee "emphatically declared":

Palestine is a Holy Land sacred to Christian, to Jew, and Moslem alike; and because it is a Holy Land, Palestine is not, and can never become, a land which any race or religion can justly claim as its very own . . . [and] the fact that it is the Holy Land sets Palestine completely apart from other lands and dedicates it to the precepts and practices of the brotherhood of man, not those of narrow nationalism.[50]

Underlying the idealistic rhetoric was a belief that the form of government ultimately established in Palestine should ensure—with international guarantees—that neither Arab nor Jew dominate politically. What was needed was replacement of the mandate by a trusteeship under the United Nations. Since the committee felt any immediate attempt to grant sovereignty either to a single binational Palestinian state or to separate Arab and Jewish states would "result in civil strife such as might threaten the peace of the world," the trusteeship arrangement was to last indefinitely pending the abatement of intercommunal tensions.[51]

Supplementing this central proposal were several suggestions for the country's future administration. Each recommendation was made with the goal of reducing Arab-Jewish friction, largely by emphasizing the role of the trustee. In this vein, for example, it was suggested that the Administering Power supervise education, equalize social disparities by aiding the Arab community in certain fields, and initiate large-scale development projects.

The committee also recommended constitutional and legal measures. It suggested overcoming the political significance of immigration by guaranteeing Arabs and Jews equal representation in any future government. It also called for the abrogation of restrictions on Jewish land purchases in Palestine, but tried to balance this by urging an end to the practice of excluding Arab labor from Jewish lands.[52]

All of this was in line with the committee's attempt to remain even-handed. Yet, even had the general formula that shaped the report been accepted by all parties, there would have still remained the need to devise a specific political arrangement for Palestine. Since this would have involved negotiations to produce a workable Arab-Zionist consensus, modifications and refinements of the committee's proposal would almost inevitably have been required. However, the essential thrust of the Anglo-American Committee's approach never became the object of serious attention by the protagonists in the Palestine conflict.

Instead, the aspect of the report that received the most public attention in 1946—and that has since been the most misunderstood of the committee's conclusions—dealt with Jewish immigration. The report advocated the admission of at least 100,000 additional Jewish immigrants into Palestine. However, the committee's position has commonly been misrepresented as having called for "immediate action [for] . . . the grant of one hundred thousand immigration permits";[53] or as having urged that "the doors [of Palestine] be opened to allow 100,000 Jewish refugees to enter immediately";[54] or as having called upon Britain "immediately [to] issue 100,000 immigration certificates."[55]

Although the committee did call for immediate action by the mandatory government, it did not call for the immediate entry of 100,000 Jewish immigrants. The report carefully distinguished among the "authorization" of immigrant certificates, the "awarding" or "issuing" of them, and actual immigration.[56] Unqualified immediate action by the mandatory was requested only in relation to the authorization of certificates. With regard to the awarding of certificates, the pertinent recommendation was designed to allow the mandatory government to exercise its own judgment.[57]

This distinction was not accidental. Throughout the latter part of 1945, the British government had stressed its opposition to demands that large-scale immigration be permitted before it could be incorporated into a comprehensive plan. Had the committee's report demanded the immediate entry of the 100,000, it would have stood little chance of acceptance in London regardless of its merits when considered as a whole.

The report was purposefully vague in commenting on immigration after the admission of an additional 100,000 Jews. It offered only one broad guideline for future policy:

> The well-being of both [Arab and Jew], the economic situation of Palestine as a whole, the degree of execution of plans for further development,

all have to be carefully considered in deciding the number of immigrants for any particular period.[58]

The committee's study of the Jewish refugee problem convinced it that many Jews would remain in Europe. It could not, however, ignore the real dilemma of Jews "wishing or impelled" to leave. For while accepting the view that Palestine alone could not meet Jewish emigration needs, the committee was forced to admit that information from other countries "gave no hope of substantial assistance." Its report called on the United States and Great Britain, in association with other countries, to find new homes for all displaced persons "irrespective of creed and nationality."[59] It is notable that here again the committee requested action "immediately."[60]

Acknowledging that its proposals would not win acceptance from Arab and Jewish extremists, the committee urged the administering power in Palestine to ensure that violence or terrorism would be "resolutely suppressed."[61] Still, the Anglo-American investigators gave little idea as to how their recommendations might be implemented—or how the responsibilities for doing so should be divided between Great Britain and the United States.

Any review of the Committee of Inquiry must keep in mind the impossibility of knowing whether by 1946 there still existed any chance for an orderly resolution of Arab-Jewish tensions in Palestine. It has often been noted that neither Zionists nor Arabs demonstrated any willingness—either during or in the immediate aftermath of World War II—to modify their political goals in the interest of an enduring peace. This has commonly led the Anglo-American report to be dismissed as a visionary—though balanced—exercise in futility. Christopher Sykes sums up this attitude by stating that the committee made "the familiar mistake of supposing that fairness was relevant to post-Balfour Palestine."[62]

However, it can be argued that the political rigidity that Arabs and Zionists exhibited by 1945 was to a great extent a product of British and American indecision. The end of World War II forced Washington and London to deal directly with the question of Palestine and so to confirm what had become obvious much earlier: that neither power had any firm, long-term policy. The Labour government quickly revealed the depth of British reluctance to formulate, much less to implement, an approach to Palestine without the active involvement of the United States. On the other hand, Washington's continued refusal to clarify its own position seemed to guarantee that the mandatory would not hit upon a decisive course in the near future.

In effect, this led to a situation that not only permitted, but indeed virtually demanded, that Arabs and Zionists outbid one another in extremist posturing. Anglo-American indecision allowed both protagonists to make maximum claims without directly challenging either Great Power, while also issuing threats of extreme retaliation should those claims be denied. Under the circumstances, Arab and Zionist spokesmen found ample opportunity to indulge in dire warnings of self-destructive warfare against any party seeking to implement a solution that failed to meet their maximum demands.[63]

In this light, the true significance of the report of the Anglo-American Committee of Inquiry lay in the fact that it was the first officially sanctioned effort by the United States and Britain to define acceptable parameters within which Palestine's future would be considered. Although the committee's recommendations were more in the nature of general principles than a specific constitutional program, they did offer London and Washington an opportunity to indicate specific demands that would not be entertained.

The Attlee government's desire for the inquiry was predicated on the assumption that a closely coordinated Anglo-American approach would automatically introduce a new set of political dynamics into the Palestine equation; one that would lead Arabs and Zionists into a process of redefining their objectives in optimum, rather than maximum, terms. This, it was hoped, might yet permit some orderly settlement to be arranged. Whatever merits that outlook may have had will never be known, for the central requirement for testing it—Anglo-American cooperation—failed to materialize.

AMERICAN AND BRITISH REACTION TO THE COMMITTEE'S REPORT

The British and American governments received copies of the report on April 20, 1946. Ten days later the document was made public. Initial reaction in Washington was generally favorable. The consensus reached by officers of the State Department's Office of Near Eastern and African Affairs was that the proposals formed "a set of general recommendations which constitute a reasonable and intelligently defined compromise."[64] President Truman felt the report was "careful and complete" and pointed "in the right direction."[65]

The spiral of violence in Palestine lent urgency to the British government's consideration of the report. During February and March, assaults on installations of the mandatory administration had been made by Stern, Irgun, and Haganah units.[66] Five days after London received the Anglo-American Committee's proposals, the situation dramatically worsened. On the night of April 25, Jewish terrorists raided an army motor pool in Tel-Aviv and killed seven British soldiers. On the next night the first breakdown of military discipline in the history of the mandate occurred as British troops wreaked revenge on a small Jewish village, causing extensive property damage and maltreating numbers of inhabitants.[67]

These events were very much on Ernest Bevin's mind when he discussed the Anglo-American Committee's conclusions with Secretary Byrnes, whom he met in Paris at the Council of Foreign Ministers. Significantly, Bevin stated that Britain was prepared to permit 100,000 refugees to enter Palestine as recommended by the committee. However, he added that it would be impossible for them all to immigrate into the country at once. The foreign secretary wanted to know what role the United States would accept in Palestine. He expressed alarm over the "aggressive frame of mind" of the Jewish Agency, and claimed that Palestinian Jewry was amassing large quantities of arms with money supplied by Jews in the United States. The possibility that massive immigration would increase the Yishuv's military strength caused Bevin great concern. He hoped the United States would share the burden of keeping order by furnishing troops. The foreign secretary also revealed that the pressures faced by his government were overcoming his personal desire to retain a British presence in Palestine. The point had nearly been reached, he said, where he had "to consider the possibility of a complete British withdrawal."[68]

Byrnes was unable to specify what the United states might contribute to a Palestine settlement. Nonetheless, London's willingness to accept the recommendations regarding 100,000 Jewish refugees appeared to offer hope that a joint approach could be worked out. The British government was convinced that the Anglo-American report should be treated as a whole, and it received support for this view from the American ambassador in London, Averell Harriman.[69] Bevin, however, was somewhat alarmed by Byrnes' inability to clarify American intentions. He therefore asked that Washington make no policy statement on the Anglo-American report without first consulting the British government.[70] Truman was not willing to grant this request.

On April 30 the report of the Anglo-American Committee was simultaneously released in Britain and the United States. Truman took the occasion to issue a statement completely at variance with the British view of the report as a comprehensive, unitary proposal. London was informed of the president's intention to do this only hours before the event.[71]

Truman's statement made direct reference solely to those parts of the report that could be expected to please Zionists, and only vaguely noted that the Anglo-American Committee had also made recommendations for the protection of Palestinian Arabs' civil and religious rights and economic welfare.[72] Although it made no mention of the report's call for international action to resettle displaced Jews, Truman's statement emphasized the necessity of solving the refugee problem. The president singled out the recommendation concerning immigration: "I am happy," he said, "that the request which I made for the immediate admission of 100,000 Jews into Palestine has been unanimously endorsed." As for the other proposals, Truman remarked that they dealt "with many other questions of long range policies" which he would take under advisement.[73]

The statement was tantamount to a declaration that Truman had not altered his original view of refugee immigration as something apart from the political problem of Palestine's future. It also seems to have been the origin of the common misconception that the Inquiry Committee recommended immediate admission of 100,000 Jews into Palestine.

On the following day, Clement Attlee discussed the Anglo-American report in the House of Commons.[74] The prime minister was highly critical of Truman's efforts to isolate certain recommendations. He pointed out that the report "must be considered as a whole in all its implications." Since execution of the committee's recommendations would entail heavy and enduring commitments, his government was anxious to learn the extent of American willingness to share "the resulting military and financial responsibilities."

Although Attlee carefully mentioned that with reference to the 100,000 the report called for actual immigration to be pushed forward "as rapidly as conditions permit," he did not make an issue of the matter by challenging Truman's interpretation. Instead, recalling that the Anglo-American Committee had condemned the existence of "private armies" in Palestine, he declared that no massive immigration could be permitted unless and until such forces were disbanded.

Of all the points in the prime minister's speech, this last condition caused the greatest amount of controversy. By demanding the dissolution of "private armies," Attlee had clearly referred not only to recognized terrorist groups but also to the Haganah. At the time, American and British public opinion mistakenly maintained a sharp distinction between the Irgun and Stern groups and the Haganah.[75] Furthermore, the condition Atlee attempted to impose went beyond the recommendations of the Committee of Inquiry.[76]

Attlee's demand was a blunder. Yet his mistake appears to have been more in making a fixed and public condition for implementation of the inquiry report rather than in his notion of the military danger that might result from massive immigration were the Haganah not somehow neutralized. Even without additional manpower, the strength of Zionist forces by 1946 was sufficient to threaten the mandatory's authority. Richard Crossman records that the Inquiry Committee had been "deeply impressed" by Britain's general officer commanding (GOC), who offered a stark assessment of Zionist military capabilities at a briefing where the difficulties of a partition settlement were discussed:

The G.O.C. was quite explicit that Haganah would be able without difficulty to hold any area allocated to the Jews . . . whereas large British reinforcements would be required to police any pro-Arab solution which involved suppression of the Haganah.[77]

It was understandable that the British government, which would bear the burden of implementing any compromise settlement in Palestine, was anxious to have the threat posed by Jewish forces removed prior to massive immigration. Attlee's error was that the manner of his public demand smacked of an ultimatum that was little more than a ruthless attempt to barter refugees for political concessions. It might have been wiser for the prime minister to have delayed elaborating his government's position on the question of private armies until it became more clear whether any grounds existed for Britain and the United States to promote jointly the type of overall settlement envisaged by the Inquiry Committee. As it was, his inept comments in Parliament only provided fuel for renewed Zionist charges of British betrayal. In turn, these increased Truman's domestic difficulties in dealing with Palestine.

The conflicting reactions of Truman and Attlee appeared to indicate an even greater gap between the British and American governments than had existed when the Committee of Inquiry was first launched. This, however, was not true. It was somewhat paradoxical that in the following months Washington and London would come closer to establishing a joint long-range policy toward Palestine than at any other time between 1939 and 1948.

II. SEARCH FOR A POLICY: THE AFTERMATH OF THE INQUIRY

Arabs and Zionists reacted bitterly to the Anglo-American Committee report. By the time the British and American governments formally requested written comments from the various interested parties on May 20, general dissatisfaction with the committee's conclusions was already evident.[1]

When the report was made public, protest strikes were held by the Arabs of Palestine, the Levant states, Iraq, and Egypt. Individual Arab leaders suggested that action might be taken against British and American economic interests should the report form the basis of future Great Power policy toward Palestine.[2]

Azzam Pasha, secretary-general of the Arab League—known for his generally moderate political views—warned that "Arabs were united in their complete opposition to the policy of the report." He was not impressed by the Inquiry Committee's specific rejection of Jewish statehood in Palestine since he felt that

> only three things mattered: Immigration, land and future government. The report gave Zionists two things which could lead only to [a] Jewish state: Immigration and [the] right to purchase unlimited land while [its] denial of [the Palestinian Arabs'] right to control immigration and land transfer was [a] denial of all Arab rights.[3]

Arab diplomats in Washington jointly called on the secretary of state to stress their united opposition to the results of the inquiry.[4] Before the end of May, a conference of Arab states led to further expressions of solidarity against the Anglo-American report.[5]

The Inquiry Committee's report also gave renewed vigor to calls for unity within the Palestinian Arab community, where the united front achieved in November 1945 with the aid of Syria's Jamil Mardam had collapsed. It fell, once more, to the Arab League to forge some degree of cooperation among the quarreling Palestinian factions, which by June were divided into the Husseini-dominated Higher Committee and a new rival group known as the Arab Higher Front. The task of unification was now facilitated by the arrival in Egypt of Haj Amin al-Husseini after his escape in May from French detention. Under pressure from the Arab League, both the Higher Committee and the dissident Higher Front were replaced by the Arab Higher Executive. This group included Haj Amin as chairman, his cousin Jamal as vice-chairman, and members of the anti-Husseini factions.[6]

Zionists were no less opposed than Arabs to the Anglo-American Committee's compromise proposal. However, their reaction was more circumspect than the heated outrage of Arab spokesmen. At a meeting of top Jewish Agency leaders, Ben Gurion flatly labeled the committee's report "a disguised new edition of the White Paper." Ben Gurion was not only angered because the solution advanced by the Anglo-American Committee precluded the creation of a Jewish state but also because he felt the report as a whole vested exceedingly broad powers in the administration that was to construe and implement its recommendations.[7]

Unlike Ben Gurion, other agency leaders balked at the idea of publicly rejecting the report. David Horowitz, who was present at the meeting, has explained their reasoning:

> They believed that outright rejection was extremely risky and would permit Great Britain to maintain the status quo [in Palestine] while arousing adverse public opinion in the United States. After all, they pointed out, the report had been passed unanimously by the committeemen, and defiance of it would be taken as directed against public opinion in America as well as in Britain, and would destroy immediate prospects, including the proposal of one hundred thousand [immigration] certificates.[8]

The debate was resolved 24 hours later by Attlee's demand for the disarming of private armies in Palestine. Zionist leaders claimed that Attlee's statement constituted an implicit rejection of the Anglo-American report since it made its implementation contingent upon "conditions that would not be met." This, it was held, released the Jewish Agency from having to take any firm stand.[9]

In effect, the agency adopted the position articulated by Truman on May 1, denying the unity of the report and distinguishing between so-called immediate and long-term proposals for Palestine. This enabled the Zionists to accuse the British government of sabotaging the work of the Anglo-American Committee, while they themselves did not risk alienating American and British public opinion by flatly rejecting the report. At the same time, Zionists continued to demand the unconditional entry of 100,000 Jewish refugees into Palestine.[10] Thus, the Jewish Agency refused to respond formally to the report, announcing instead that it would discuss the full range of recommendations arising from the Anglo-American inquiry only after the mandatory took steps to permit unrestricted immigration of 100,000 Jews into Palestine.[11]

Other Jewish organizations followed the agency's lead. On May 28, the American Jewish Conference declared that discussion of "long-term recommendations" would be "premature and harmful," since it would delay the admission into Palestine of the 100,000. The Zionist Emergency Council took a similar stance.[12]

During the early summer, American Zionists launched an anti-British campaign in conjunction with their ongoing and highly visible publicity drive on behalf of massive immigration into Palestine. The British Embassy in Washington and British consulates throughout the country were picketed, the Attlee government was denounced at mass meetings and protest marches, and thousands of anti-British postcards, letters, and telegrams descended upon Congress and the White House. The threat made to Dean Acheson by Emanuel Neumann several months earlier was carried out: The immediate target of the campaign was the proposed postwar American loan to the United Kingdom. Rabbi Silver urged American citizens to ask their representatives in Congress whether "the United States can afford to make a loan to a government whose pledged word seems to be worthless."[13] By July, when hearings on the loan—which had received Senate approval in May—opened in the House of Representatives, the British government feared that the project might be voted down.[14]

The Jewish Resistance answered Attlee's demand for its disbandment by stepping up activities against the mandatory administration in what appeared to be a "conscious and concerted effort to establish a Jewish state by force and drive the British from Palestine."[15] This heightened wave of violence, conducted in concert by the Haganah and Jewish terrorist groups, culminated in massive attacks against the country's highway and railway networks. It did not abate until the British government finally ordered a full-scale military offensive against Jewish forces.

TRUMAN'S TWO-TIERED APPROACH
TO THE ANGLO-AMERICAN REPORT

Publication of the Anglo-American Committee of Inquiry report led to a division of opinion within the Truman administration. This conflict resulted in contradictory suggestions being passed on to the president. Without apparent consideration for the likely consequences of his actions, Truman responded by simultaneously launching two Palestine policies, each tailored to suit one of the conflicting sets of advice he had received.

The problem facing the administration at the beginning of May 1946 was to determine its position toward the Anglo-American report. Upon receiving the report, Truman had reinforced his standing commitment to the unqualified entry into Palestine of 100,000 refugee Jews. Nonetheless, he also indicated that he would take the bulk of the committee's recommendations "under advisement." At some point, then, the president would have to respond openly to the overall solution advocated by the committee. The question was whether Truman could delay consideration of long-term political factors in Palestine until his demand for Jewish immigration was fulfilled. The root of the conflict within the administration lay in the different answers offered to the president.

On the one hand, David Niles and General John H. Hilldring, who was still serving as assistant secretary of state for occupied areas, encouraged Truman to forego consideration of a political settlement and concentrate on pressuring the British government to admit the 100,000 into Palestine. On the other hand, the State Department's Near East specialists, supported by the highest levels of the department, tried to persuade the president to explore with the British some of the substantive issues involved in a political solution in Palestine.

On May 3, Hilldring submitted a memorandum to Undersecretary Acheson in which he proposed a strategy to force Britain's hand on the 100,000 "immediately and without reference to future action on any other aspects of the [Inquiry Committee's] Report."[16] It seems beyond doubt that the president was informed of Hilldring's plan. Hilldring maintained constant contact with David Niles on matters pertaining to Palestine. Since Hilldring was known to be strongly pro-Zionist, it was natural that he developed a sense of mutual interest with Niles.[17] Moreover, only a few days after Hilldring first broached his scheme to Acheson, the Office of Near Eastern and African Affairs countered with a blunt challenge to the General's views.[18] Faced by directly conflicting opinions within the department, Acheson decided to suspend any action until the secretary of state and the president decided "on our total attitude toward the Report and the obligations which may arise from it."[19] Finally, it must be noted that during May, June, and July, Truman adopted a course that fulfilled each of the main parts of Hilldring's plan.

The considerations upon which Hilldring based his counsel were not related to the situation in Palestine, of which he made no mention. Instead, the general linked his advice to American "military and political interests in Germany and Austria."

> In order to further our interests in Germany and Austria, i.e., to resettle the Jewish displaced persons as expeditiously as possible, I think that all the Jewish pressure should be directed against the British rather than against the U.S. and British Governments jointly. This result . . . can be achieved only if this Government pursues an aggressive public policy of needling the British to implement the Committee's recommendation for entry of 100,000 immediately and without reference to future action on any other aspects of the Report.

Hilldring urged immediate action:

a. A public statement by the President stressing the urgent necessity of immediate implementation of the Committee's recommendation for issuance of 100,000 immigration visas.

b. A public offer of the U.S. Government to assume primary responsibility for movement of the 100,000 from Europe to Palestine.[20]

David Niles was simultaneously encouraging Truman to continue pressuring the British government over the 100,000 without considering Palestine's political problems. A good example of Niles' activities was his analysis of a letter sent to the White House at this time by Myron Taylor, the president's personal representative to the Pope. Taylor, who had worked with Dr. Isaiah Bowman of the State Department's Territorial Committee for Post War Studies, advised Truman to return to the plan formulated by that group in 1943-44 for establishing Palestine as an international trusteeship within a religious framework.[21]

Either consciously or simply out of ignorance, the analysis Niles submitted to Truman was riddled with half-truths, unsupported allegations, and outright distortions of fact. For example, Niles implicitly ridiculed the notion of a religious trusteeship for Palestine by stating:

> It is . . . obvious to point out that Christians, particularly Catholics, have more to fear from the Moslems than from any other competitive religious groups. The Jews have always gotten along well with the Christians in the Middle East which is something that cannot be said about the Moslem group.[22]

Niles also attacked Taylor's fears that a pro-Zionist policy would unite Moslem sentiment against the United States by assuring the president that "the danger of unifying the Moslem world can be discounted because a good part of the Moslem world follows Gandhi and his philosophy of non-resistance."

However, Niles' main argument against Taylor's advice was in the form of a gentle reminder that the administration was committed to the unconditional entry of 100,000 Jews into Palestine.

> May I again respectfully point out that you are concerning yourself now only with the transference of 100,000 Jews. The other parts of the report you, yourself, publicly said that you take under consideration for future study.[23]

The position of the Office of Near Eastern and African Affairs was in direct contrast to that of Hilldring and Niles. Here it was argued that the entire Inquiry Committee report should be considered in determining an overall American policy toward the Palestine issue. It was suggested that the report be used to discover whether grounds existed for further Anglo-American cooperation on Palestine. A three-stage plan to accomplish this was prepared by Loy Henderson and submitted to Acheson in early May. Essentially, Henderson proposed:

1. That the American and British governments carry out concurrent but separate "consultations" with Arabs and Jews, thus fulfilling the obligations held by each government in this respect.

2. That in light of whatever emerged from their respective consultations with Arabs and Jews, the British and American governments consult each other "as to the policy which they will adopt toward the report as a whole."

3. That the British and American governments issue a public announcement of that policy.[24]

Truman formally approved Henderson's approach. The president then wrote directly to Attlee seeking London's agreement and suggesting that consultations with Arabs and Jews begin promptly and conclude within a two-week period.[25]

Attlee agreed with the outlines of the plan but asked that the initial consultations with Arabs and Jews be delayed until May 20, in order to avoid complicating delicate negotiations then in progress with Egypt over the Suez Canal. He also advised setting a one-month deadline for receipt of Arab and Jewish views, and suggested that a conference be held eventually among the United States, Britain, the Arabs, and the Zionists. In this way, he felt, London and Washington would have the best chance "of promoting the largest possible measure of agreement between the other interested parties."[26] Attlee was obviously still hopeful that a firm British-American front would produce moderation in Palestine.

Finally, and in order to ensure the greatest possible agreement between the British and American governments prior to any multilateral conference, Attlee proposed a meeting of "experts" from each country to discuss the military and financial aspects of a Palestine settlement. Following further communications between the president and the prime minister, most of Attlee's views were adopted. However the question of official American participation in a general Palestine conference was not resolved.

In the meantime, the president apparently also gave serious consideration to the role the United States might assume in any Palestine settlement. He requested the Joint Chiefs of Staff (JCS) to appraise the possibility of an American military commitment. On the basis of strictly military considerations, the Joint Chiefs reported that only a very limited number of American troops could be spared for duty in the Middle East. Although such forces might be sufficient to help maintain order, it was feared that the presence of American soldiers in Palestine would touch off disturbances throughout the region "far out of proportion to any local . . . difficulties." The JCS analysis recommended that nothing be done in Palestine "that would cause repercussions . . . beyond the capabilities of British troops to control."[27]

As had been agreed between Truman and Attlee, preliminary talks between U.S. and British experts commenced in mid-June. The deliberations, held in London, focused on the details of a massive transfer of refugees from Europe to Palestine.[28]

Truman now instructed the secretaries of state, war, and the treasury to form a Cabinet Committee to carry out the second stage of the State Department plan, holding consultations with the British in light of Arab and Jewish views on the Anglo-American report. The bulk of the Cabinet Committee's work was to be done by a group of alternates, headed by former Assistant Secretary of State Henry F. Grady. Attlee's eagerness to proceed quickly with high-level discussions of long-range policy caused Truman to send Grady and other cabinet alternates to London on July 10, a week earlier than originally planned.

Although it was widely known that the two governments had been in fairly regular contact since the end of the Anglo-American inquiry, the purpose and substance of the communications between Washington and London were kept secret. Moreover, the fact that the United States had joined Britain in a search for a long-range Palestine policy based on the Anglo-American report as a whole was obscured by the public posture taken by Truman in the three months from May to July. On this level the president followed Hilldring's suggestion of "needling" Britain over the immigration question.

For example, at press conferences on June 6 and 14, Truman reiterated his support for the admission of 100,000 refugees into Palestine and indicated that he had not deviated from his original position on the matter.[29]

On July 2 the president also publicly promised Zionist leaders that the United States would assume "technical and financial responsibility for transporting the refugees to Palestine."[30] Truman's promises regarding the 100,000 were unqualified. They entailed a commitment to obtain the immediate entry of the refugees into Palestine without allowing any scope for a timetable—however short—that might be part of an overall political settlement in Palestine.[31]

Not surprisingly, the differences in Truman's policy at the public and diplomatic levels were mirrored in relations between the United States and Britain. Official relations between the two countries progressed smoothly toward erecting a joint policy that could be pursued in an effort to settle the Palestine dispute. Yet there was an increasingly strained public atmosphere between the two governments as Truman continued to insist upon the unconditional entry of the 100,000 and British spokesmen continued to insist that such a movement could not be divorced from a political formula for Palestine. The deterioration in public relations culminated on June 12, when Ernest Bevin blurted his famous charge that Americans favored Jewish immigration into Palestine because "they did not want too many of them in New York."[32]

The outcry in the United States was immediate. Typical was the reaction of *Washington Post* columnist Barnet Nover, who claimed Bevin had reached a "low and despicable . . . level" unmatched by British statesmen in modern history.[33]

Within the confines of the administration, however, such reactions to Bevin's comments must have appeared naive. Two weeks before the British foreign minister voiced his irritating opinion, David Niles reminded Truman of the Jewish refugee problem and added that

> there would be terrific resistance if we attempted at this time to bring even
> a small portion into our own country beyond the present quota limitations.
> I don't see how we could ask other countries to do what we ourselves are
> unable to do.[34]

When Truman was publicly asked whether he had given consideration to improving relations with the British by making "some generous gesture" toward welcoming a few displaced Jews into the United States, he cited the necessity of complying with existing immigration laws and stated that he had no intention of recommending any change in legislation.[35]

On the diplomatic level, however, the president demonstrated an awareness that it might indeed be worthwhile to make a "generous gesture." His hidden diplomatic posture opened the way for the first, and only, comprehensive plan by the United States and Britain for a coordinated attempt to produce a settlement in Palestine. That the plan was stillborn was largely due to the domestically uncomfortable situation in which Truman had placed himself by his repeated public demands for unconditional and immediate immigration of 100,000 Jewish refugees into Palestine.

THE MORRISON-GRADY PLAN

On June 29, British troops in Palestine launched an offensive against the Jewish Resistance. Since Jewish forces offered no armed opposition, the operation did not lead to bloodshed. Over a period of several days, arms searches and arrests were carried out in Tel Aviv and the Jewish sections of Jerusalem and Haifa as well as in rural Jewish settlements.[36] British troops also occupied the offices of the Jewish Agency, seizing evidence that established the agency's complicity in the wave of terrorism that had swept Palestine.[37]

Although many Jewish leaders, including David Ben Gurion, avoided arrest by being absent from the country, most ranking Zionists who remained behind were taken into custody. Among these were the head of the Jewish Agency's Political Department, Moshe Shertok, and his assistant, Dr. Bernard Joseph.[38]

The offensive was prematurely halted after some two weeks, a decision apparently taken because London feared the incensed Zionist reaction in the United States might kill the projected American loan to Britain.[39] Nonetheless, the mandatory dealt a severe blow to the Zionist military structure. Armed with "amazingly accurate" lists of members of the Haganah and its elite shock troops, the Palmach, and equally accurate knowledge of the communal villages in which Jewish forces were stationed, British troops arrested nearly half the Palmach and much of the Haganah leadership.[40]

This plunged Palestine's Jewish community, and the Zionist movement in general, into confusion.[41] On July 25, the sudden revelation of an impending Anglo-American agreement over a political formula for Palestine marked the "peak" of the crisis facing Zionism.[42]

In the meantime, the Truman administration had been embarrassed by the domestic outcry attending Britain's unexpected offensive in Palestine. In an effort to mitigate growing Zionist criticism of the government's continuing unexplained diplomatic contacts with Britain, Truman issued a statement on July 2 affirming that the mandatory's anti-Zionist measures had been taken without his prior knowledge and expressing hope that the arrested leaders would be quickly released.[43]

These events occurred while the president's specially appointed Cabinet Committee and its Board of Alternates were quietly reviewing the requirements and problems of formulating an overall Palestine policy. Inevitably, the problem boiled down to determining specific actions that the United

States would be prepared to take in light of the foreign and domestic objectives of the Truman administration. As the three cabinet members and their alternates considered this issue, they were faced by contradictory international and domestic pressures that had shaped the responses of two administrations to the Palestine problem since 1939.

With congressional elections scheduled for November 1946, Democratic Party leaders warned the president against antagonizing American Jewish voters. In late June, for example, Truman initially refused Congressman Sol Bloom's invitation to discuss Palestine with the entire congressional delegation from New York State.[44] Celler immediately wrote to Matthew J. Connelly, Truman's appointments secretary:

> I am hesitant about telling this to the Delegation. It certainly will give political ammunition to the upstate Republicans who wanted to attend and you remember New York faces a very crucial election. Frankly, it is my opinion that it is bad politics for the President not to meet with them—even if it is on the Palestine question.[45]

Celler's aroused political instincts were soothed when the president agreed to meet the New York legislators before the end of July.[46]

Zionist leaders steadily reminded Truman of his commitment to obtain immigration of 100,000 Jewish refugees into Palestine without reference to political conditions in that country. In early July the president received the four American members of the executive of the Jewish Agency in order to reiterate the position he had taken upon receipt of the Anglo-American Committee's report.[47]

While Zionist lobbying kept the Truman administration aware of domestic forces as it struggled to define an approach that could be taken by the Cabinet Committee during the upcoming talks in London, reports from the Middle East kept Washington abreast of possible international repercussions. Fears that the Arabs would retaliate economically against a pro-Zionist policy were reinforced when Saudi Arabia suspended discussions with American commercial airline companies over landing and overflight rights.[48] The American minister in Jeddah, William Eddy, was informed of the Saudi decision by Foreign Minister Feisal. "You will understand," said Feisal, "that no action can be taken by [the] Saudi Government on projects of cooperation such as [airline] proposals . . . so long as we are in doubt about the intentions of your Government toward us." The prince continued:

> I personally still hope that your gov[ernment] will not sacrifice the good will and the considerable investment of the American people in the Middle East in favor of Zionism. Surely the mutual best interests in this area of 140,000,000 Americans and 45,000,000 Arabs will prevail against the spe-

cial pleading of almost 5,000,000 Jewish lobbyists. It is precisely America's
total interest in the Middle East that would be sacrificed.[49]

Almost simultaneously, the American chargé at Damascus reported that
negotiations between a group of private Syrian businessmen and representatives of Pan American Airlines had, for similar reasons, become "worthless."[50] The American diplomatic agent and consul general at Beirut noted in
early June that he had rarely heard Syrian President Shukri Quwaitly "speak
with more conviction" than during a recent conversation. The latter had
said:

> [the] Palestine problem touches us all very closely. We fear [the] great in-
> fluence wielded by Jews everywhere notably, in [the] United States. We
> truly believe that unless [a] full stop is put to their machinations . . . to
> further Zionist immigration [into Palestine], Palestine Arabs will eventu-
> ally be reduced to economic and political serfdom and [the] Arab world cut
> in two.[51]

While these signs were ominous, American diplomats were aware that
verbal threats, and even such relatively minor actions as the suspension of
talks over commercial air rights, would not necessarily lead to Arab reactions against the United States in the major fields of oil and Great Power
diplomacy.

By refraining from direct threats against American oil concessions during his conversation with William Eddy, Feisal had given clear indication that
the Saudi regime was uncertain of the extent to which it might retaliate
against a pro-Zionist policy in Washington. However, the mystery of Saudi
intentions was not cleared up until October, when Eddy's successor in Jeddah
was officially informed of Ibn Saud's determination not to allow Palestine to
impair the "friendliest [of] relations" with the United States.[52]

Other Arab elites took similar stands. When negotiations between
ARAMCO and Transjordan collapsed after the Anglo-American inquiry,
King Abdullah secretly confessed to the American consul general at Jerusalem that popular feeling in his country temporarily "had tied his hands," but
he promised to come to terms with the oil company "at the earliest opportunity."[53]

Throughout the Arab world many government leaders were torn between sincere opposition to Zionism and a reluctance to enter into political
conflict with the West, particularly with the United States. In Washington it
was hoped that this ambivalence would lead to only a token anti-American
reaction by the Arab states should the United States support Zionist ambitions in Palestine. On the other hand, American policy makers realized that
the personal hesitancy of individual Arab leaders to make Palestine the cru-

cible of Arab-American relations might be overridden by the more intense feelings rampant at all levels of Arab society. Even should this not prove immediately true, American diplomatic observers felt that a pro-Zionist policy would eventually produce a bitter political estrangement between the United States and the Arab world.[54]

During early June these views formed the substance of a report prepared by Philip Ireland, of the American Legation in Cairo, who returned from a trip of some 3,000 miles through Palestine, Syria, Transjordan, and Iraq. Particularly worrisome to Ireland was his discovery that many members of the ruling and land-owning classes were hoping for Soviet support against what they perceived as pro-Zionist trends in London and Washington. Gloomily concluding that American and British policies had so far done little to alleviate this problem, Ireland suggested that Soviet penetration of the Middle East no longer depended so much upon Arab attitudes as on the degree to which "the Russians will push."[55]

After reviewing the difficulties of formulating a policy toward the Arab-Zionist conflict, the Cabinet Committee and its Board of Alternates concluded that no approach could avoid American insistence on the transferral of 100,000 Jewish displaced persons to Palestine. This was accepted in a spirit of uneasy resignation. Aware of the potentially explosive consequences of mass immigration, and concerned over the possibility that it would trigger an Arab-Soviet rapprochement, the American position was seen as a " 'calculated risk' without any satisfactory formula for making the calculation." Nonetheless, the Board of Alternates decided that "our relationship to the Palestinian situation and the commitments of the President are such that we should take this course."[56]

On July 9, one day before Henry Grady and his colleagues were scheduled to depart for London, Truman approved the instructions given to the negotiating team.[57] Unlike the president's public posture, the directive dealt concretely with specific issues relevant to an overall Arab-Zionist settlement. For the first time, a framework was set for a comprehensive official explanation to the British government of what the United States would contribute to a political settlement in Palestine.

Grady and the other alternates were to inform London that Washington would not be willing to employ military forces or to act as trustee or cotrustee in Palestine. Having established this, the negotiators were authorized to take positive positions on other issues that had previously been studiously avoided by the president. Exclusive of the cost of transporting displaced persons to Palestine (which the United States was already pledged to pay), Truman was willing to ask Congress for a grant-in-aid of from $25 to 50 million for "improving conditions of the people of Palestine," to support the admission of Palestine to the International Bank and a loan of up to $200 million by that organization to the government of Palestine—or, failing that, to support a loan of up to $100 million from the Export-Import Bank—and, finally, to ask both those banks to make available "substantial funds for development" to other Middle Eastern countries.[58]

Grady's instructions also reveal that Truman was fully aware that a compromise in Palestine could not be predicated on the assumption that all Jewish refugees go to that country. In an abrupt reversal of his previous restrictive outlook on immigration into the United States—which only three weeks earlier he had reaffirmed to the press—Truman agreed to request congressional approval for the admission of "say 50,000 non quota victims of Nazi persecution" into the United States. The president was also willing to "end preferential displaced persons care for future infiltrees in Europe."

Truman was obviously hoping that these two steps, when coupled with the transferral of 100,000 displaced Jews to Palestine, would eliminate the Jewish refugee problem, thus removing a major obstacle to Arab-Zionist compromise. By the end of June 1946 there were, in all probability, less than 110,000 Jews living in European displaced persons camps.[59] It must also have been anticipated that terminating the preferential treatment accorded to infiltrees would at least retard further growth of the refugee problem in Central Europe.

Grady was also to inform the British government that the United States would support the Anglo-American Committee report "as a whole, including 'No Jewish, no Arab state.'"

The task of the American negotiators was to discover whether within the boundaries set by these instructions there existed some formula for Palestine that Britain would be willing to implement with financial and political support from the United States.

The Truman administration's position during the London discussions was clearly intended to mark a profound change in the course followed by American involvement with Palestine since 1939. The administration's willingness to come out in favor of a compromise arrangement that would fully satisfy neither Arab nor Zionist demands was significant. The same was true of its readiness to indicate specific ways in which the United States would help promote an Arab-Zionist settlement. Equally important was Truman's intention to acknowledge publicly that future U.S. policy toward Palestine would be conditioned by American interests in the Arab world. This political fact of life had, of course, long been a basic part of the dilemma that American policy makers faced over Palestine. Yet Washington had so far refrained from answering domestic pro-Zionist demands with a frank exposition of the international considerations that entered into foreign policy formulation. Now, however, Grady was to inform the British that

> any future announcements of our policy [should] contain some emphasis
> of our interest in the Palestine situation as part of our larger interest in the

peoples of the Middle East, their regained political equality and their economic development, and of our understanding at any rate of their points of view.[60]

The Grady team was surprised by the British government's enthusiasm over the proposed American role. Although Washington had anticipated that its decision against the use of American troops would create some difficulties, Grady found that Attlee's government had already accepted as inevitable the American refusal to assume active responsibility in Palestine. The subject of U.S. military involvement was not even raised during the talks.[61]

Two weeks of negotiation produced agreement on a common strategy. The scheme, which became known as the Morrison-Grady Plan, called for the mandate's conversion into a trusteeship and the creation of an interim federal structure composed of autonomous Arab and Jewish provinces and a central government administered by the Trustee Power. The proposed provincial boundaries were purposely drawn to include in the Jewish province "the best land in Palestine, practically all citrus and industry, most of the coastline, and Haifa port."[62]

The federalized trusteeship was to be of indefinite duration, pending Palestine's final independence. It was designed to provide a period of grace during which communal passions might cool and, it was hoped, the authorities of the autonomous Jewish and Arab provinces might experience the benefits of cooperative action with the central government. The plan did not prejudge the country's final political disposition, but rather looked to the evolution of some agreement between Arabs and Zionists under the open-ended trusteeship. The proposal forwarded by Grady to his superiors in Washington described these essential considerations as follows:

[The plan] makes it possible to give practical [effect] to the principles of government enunciated in . . . the Anglo-American Committee [report]; and it offers a prospect of development towards self-government of which there is less hope in a unitary Palestine. It provides a means of segregating Jew and Arab to an extent which should substantially reduce the risk of a continuation of widespread violence and disorder in Palestine. In the long term, the plan leaves the way open for constitutional development whether towards partition or towards federal unity. The association of representatives of the two provinces in the administration of central subjects may lead ultimately to a fully developed federal constitution. On the contrary if the centrifugal forces prove too strong, the way is open toward partition. The provincial plan does not prejudge this issue either way. The administering authority will be prepared to hand over the government to the people of the country as soon as the two communities express a common desire to that end and present an agreed schedule which will ensure its stable administration.[63]

The central government, to be administered by Britain as trustee, would exercise direct control over Jerusalem and the Negev Desert, pending their ultimate status. It would also retain exclusive authority over Palestine's foreign relations, defense, customs, and "initially" over the police, Haifa harbor, communications, railways and civil aviation, as well as over provincial development projects. Although in strictly local affairs the provincial governments would exercise wide powers, the central government retained the right to appoint the presidents of provincial legislative bodies during the first five years of the plan's execution.

The plan sought to defuse the immigration issue by allowing 100,000 displaced persons into the Jewish province within 12 months after a decision was taken to implement the scheme as a whole. Subsequent immigration into each province would be regulated by local governments, although the central administration reserved the power to impose limitations should Palestine's economic absorptive capacity become strained. Still, it was intended that "under ordinary circumstances" immigration into the Jewish province would proceed "on whatever scale is desired by its government." The precise conditions under which the central government might establish immigration quotas were to be set forth in the instrument that created the new trusteeship system. That agreement would also provide for direct appeal to the United Nations by Palestinian provincial authorities in case of a dispute with the central government over immigration quotas.

The British and American negotiators in London accepted the validity of the Anglo-American Committee's finding that Palestine alone could not provide for the emigration needs of all Jewish victims of persecution. The Morrison-Grady Plan outlined an approach for handling the problem of Jewish refugees within the context of the broader problem of displaced persons of all faiths.

As part of this approach, Truman would "seek the approval of Congress for special legislation for the entry into the United States of 50,000 displaced persons, including Jews." Second, the British and U.S. governments would give strong support to an appeal in the UN General Assembly calling on all member states "to receive in territories under their control a proportion of the displaced persons in Europe, including Jews." London and Washington would also continue to support the efforts of existing international organizations, such as the Intergovernmental Committee on Refugees, to resettle displaced persons. Finally, simultaneous, though separate, overtures would be made by Britain and the United States to the British Dominions. In seeking aid from these countries, the British government would "stress the relations between the settlement of displaced persons and the problem of Jewish immigration into Palestine." Washington, on the other hand, would argue that its own efforts to establish emergency immigration quotas "would be favorably influenced if assurances [were] given that a number of displaced persons would be re-settled in the British Commonwealth."[64]

In the realm of finance and economic development, the Morrison-Grady Plan followed the approach envisaged in the instructions given to the American negotiating team. The Truman administration would seek congressional approval for extensive financial aid to Palestine. Financial inducements would also be offered to the Arab states in order to obtain their support for a federal compromise between Palestinian Arabs and Jews.[65]

The British and American planners realized that their proposal would not please all parties. Under the projected trusteeship scheme, Palestine's central government would have strong powers to deal with terrorist activities. However, the Morrison-Grady approach deviated from Prime Minister Attlee's earlier demand for the unconditional dissolution of all "private armies" in Palestine by calling for such forces to submit themselves to the control of the central government.

In summary, then, the Anglo-American negotiations resulted in a proposal that tried to strike a responsive chord among Arabs and Jews by relying upon a carefully designed "carrot and stick" approach to convince each group that it stood to benefit more by accepting the plan than by opposing it:

1. The Jews of Palestine would benefit from development of the national home; internal communal autonomy within specified territorial limits; the immigration of 100,000 Jews within 12 months after a decision was taken to put the plan as a whole into effect; the prompt resolution of the Jewish refugee problem; control over future immigration into the Jewish province in accordance with Palestine's absorptive capacity; and the possibility, if desired, of an eventual sovereign Jewish state.

2. The Arabs of Palestine would benefit from internal autonomy and control over immigration within specified territorial limits; massive aid for social and economic development; and the eventual option to choose sovereign statehood in part of Palestine.

3. The Arab states would benefit from the possibility of massive economic aid and the political friendship of Great Britain and the United States.

The sanctions to devolve upon parties rejecting the interim federal trusteeship scheme were not so clearly stated. It is true that outright violent resistance was to be met with force; but this was not actually the major sanction envisaged by the British and American teams who formulated the proposal. During the talks, the British had repeatedly specified their unwillingness to implement the solution sheerly through force. The Morrison-Grady proposal acknowledged that "in view of the existing situation in Palestine, any policy for that country will probably have to be introduced without the willing consent of either community." However, it also recognized that "there is a degree of sustained and determined resistance . . . beyond which no policy could be enforced."[66] Political, rather than military, sanctions were relied upon to inhibit Arabs and Jews from offering such a degree of resistance. It was for this reason that such a high value was placed upon Anglo-American coordination by the authors of the Morrison-Grady Plan.

The basic problem to be overcome in arriving at any settlement was the extremism that gripped Arabs and Jews. The immediate task was to convince each side that adamant opposition to the proposed new approach would plunge it into an unrewarding political conflict with the United States and Britain that could only benefit its antagonist. The assumption was that a joint Anglo-American front might make this threat credible and lead Arabs and Zionists into competing for an accord with the Great Powers. The logic of the Morrison-Grady Plan rested on the hope that, once started, such a process of competitive moderation could lead to an orderly resolution of the Palestine affair.

The British government did not insist upon formal acceptance of the proposal by the two communities in Palestine. Instead, London believed that a combination of its own military power and political suasion on the part of the United States might produce a sufficient degree of "acquiescence" from Arabs and Jews to allow the plan to be put into effect.[67]

London hoped to achieve this at a general conference during which the federal trusteeship plan would be presented to the Arabs and Zionists. However, British policy makers had no intention of offering the proposal as an ultimatum. Rather, it would serve as a "basis for discussion."[68] Although U.S. participation in the projected conference remained problematical when the Morrison-Grady Plan was formulated, the British counted heavily upon presenting Arabs and Zionists with a firm Anglo-American commitment to a compromise in Palestine.

On July 24 Grady informed Washington of the outcome of his negotiations with the British. He also notified the State Department that he saw "no practical alternatives to [the] recommendations."[69] The American representative praised his British counterparts, saying they had been "most reasonable and cooperative," but cautioned that Britain would be unwilling to "renegotiate" the matter. Grady correctly sensed the British government's growing impatience with the burden of Palestine.

Whether the federal structure devised in London, or any variation of it that might have emerged from subsequent negotiations with Arabs and Jews, would have ultimately led to an orderly resolution of the Palestine problem is a moot point. This was assured by Truman's prompt rejection of the plan submitted by Grady.

12.   THE END OF
ANGLO-AMERICAN PLANNING

On July 22, members of the Irgun Zvai Leumi detonated a powerful bomb under one wing of Jerusalem's King David Hotel. Their objective was to destroy documents taken from the Jewish Agency headquarters to British military and administrative offices that occupied part of the hotel.[1] The blast destroyed much of the King David and killed nearly 100 people. The attack, the worst instance of terrorism since the beginning of the mandate, was a sign of the growing depression that gripped the Zionist leadership in the summer of 1946.[2] In Palestine the immediate cause of this was the military offensive launched by the mandatory in mid-June. Although the British initiative had been cut short, many Palestinian Jewish leaders remained in custody. The confusion and unease that dominated the Yishuv during July and August 1946 is seen in David Horowitz's description of a meeting of Zionist leaders who had escaped arrest:

> The deliberations . . . were stamped by the consciousness of the grave juncture and the absence of any clear line to follow. It was an imbroglio of confusion and frustration, a resolute desire to defend ourselves, the need to give a firm demonstration of devotion and identity with those who were penned behind the barbed wire of [the detention camps at] Latrun and Rafa, and the lack of any plan for practical action.[3]

However, underlying the tensions created by immediate conditions in Palestine were Zionists' fears over the import of the continuing contacts between the American and British governments.

Prior to the King David bombing, there had already been indications that many Zionists were worried by the militant policies of their leaders.[4] The mandatory's strong reaction to the King David incident, and the revulsion of public opinion in Great Britain that the act occasioned, further convinced

197

moderate Zionists that their movement was courting disaster. These fears, and the bankruptcy of extremism, seemed confirmed three days after the King David attack by news of an impending British-American agreement over the Morrison-Grady Plan. With this, the most serious crisis faced by Zionism since 1939 came to a head.

Efforts to keep secret the substance of the Anglo-American talks in London were successful until shortly before the text of the Morrison-Grady Plan was cabled to Washington on July 24. However, when unofficial, but essentially accurate summaries of the proposal appeared in the press, a storm of Zionist outrage immediately broke out in the United States. Rabbi Silver termed the proposed settlement a "conscienceless act of treachery."[5] Nahum Goldmann tried to influence the American delegates in London by writing directly to Grady. Goldmann's letter succinctly pointed to the problem that confronted Truman. He reminded Grady of the Jewish Agency's consistent demand that immigration "proceed immediately and without awaiting decision on major policy."

> From the very first days after the publication of the Inquiry Committee's report, President Truman has taken the same position, and has given expression to his views in various public statements.[6]

The effects of the protests were quickly felt in Washington. On July 26 Secretary of the Navy James V. Forrestal recorded the situation as he learned it from a discussion with the members of the Cabinet Committee on Palestine:

> Jews are injecting vigorous and active propaganda to force the President's hand with reference to the immediate immigration of Jews into Palestine. Two areas have been agreed upon—one for the Arabs and one for the Jews, with the Arabs getting the less desirable land. The problem is complicated by the fact that the President went out on the limb in endorsing the [Anglo-American] report saying that a hundred thousand Jews should be permitted entry into Palestine.[7]

In the meantime, Washington was unsure of how to deal with the Zionists and their supporters. To complicate the administration's difficulties, important parts of the Morrison-Grady scheme were garbled during its original transmission. Not until the night of July 25 was Grady asked to clarify the timing envisaged for the transfer of 100,000 displaced Jews to Palestine.[8] Grady's reply stressed that the plan did not require suspending immigration until actual implementation of its constitutional provisions, but that, on the contrary, immigration would be initiated immediately once a decision had been taken to put the plan as a whole into effect. Grady emphasized that the British government did not expect formal approval of the compromise formula from either Arabs or Jews, but hoped to obtain "a measure of acquiescence" from both parties. Finally, he assured Secretary Byrnes that there was not "the slightest doubt that the British Government will give the green light to the 100,000 at the earliest possible moment."[9]

The unease felt by Grady's superiors was not dispelled. Zionist charges of betrayal were making Truman increasingly reluctant to become committed to any plan that would undercut his previous stand on behalf of the unconditional entry of 100,000 Jews into Palestine. On July 26, Byrnes again communicated with Grady, this time more explicitly describing the administration's difficult situation:

> We can appreciate the British position. Nevertheless after the stand that the President has taken we do not see how we can enter into an arrangement which would prevent us from continuing to take the position that the 100,000 should move without awaiting from agreement on the part of Arabs and Jews. That agreement might be delayed for months or years and we would have to be silent. . . . Any arrangement that might be made between us and the British should leave us free to insist on the transfer of the 100,000 beginning at once. We feel that we should be able to announce that we have not abandoned the position taken by the President in this regard.[10]

The message was answered by Ambassador Harriman who tried to allay Washington's suspicions:

> I am convinced [the] President can rely on the good faith of [the] British Government to move with the greatest speed in the consultations [with Arabs and Jews] . . . [the] British can see the solution of the problem of Jewish immigration only through their provincial plan. . . . I know [the] British are as anxious for speed as we are.[11]

While Harriman may have somewhat soothed the doubts over Britain's willingness to expedite the transfer of Jewish refugees, he offered the president no escape from the fundamental dilemma. Indeed, no such avenue existed. Truman had to choose, on the one hand, to adhere to his earlier position supporting massive immigration without reference to political considerations—a stand that held no hope of alleviating the plight of Jewish refugees or of resolving the Palestine problem—or, on the other hand, to follow the path advocated by Grady—an option that held out a possibility of resolving both the Jewish refugee and Palestine issues, but that would also incur the wrath of American Zionists.

Unable to decide, Truman opted to wait until Secretary Byrnes, who was scheduled to be in Paris, could discuss the matter with Grady and Prime Minister Attlee. After holding these consultations on July 29, Byrnes immediately advised the president to support the Morrison-Grady scheme. The secretary of state also suggested a lengthy statement, jointly drafted by Byrnes and Grady, that he urged Truman to issue on July 31, the day Attlee would discuss the Morrison-Grady Plan in the House of Commons.[12]

Byrnes's draft statement would have had the president describe briefly the substance of the overall approach embodied in the Morrison-Grady Plan, stressing the projected American financial aid to Palestine and other Middle Eastern countries, as well as the administration's intention to seek special legislation permitting 50,000 nonquota immigrants into the United States. The president was then to address the problem created by his earlier position supporting the entry of 100,000 Jews into Palestine. Byrnes suggested a realistic explanation of the factors that had all along made the question of immigration a difficult and complex political issue:

> I want to say an additional word about the immigration into Palestine of 100,000 persecuted Jews from the centers in Germany, Austria and Italy which was one of the recommendations of the Anglo-American Committee of Inquiry. The U.S. has been urging the promptest possible beginning of this immigration. It has joined in active preparations for the movement. There are two things which must be remembered. First, we are not the mandatory for Palestine and cannot make a unilateral decision on the matter. Second, every effort should be made to create conditions such that these people will not open a new chapter in their tragic lot by immigration into a violent and strife-torn Palestine. . . .
>
> The situation as it has developed is such that this immigration can in the judgement of both the United States and Great Britain be peacefully and speedily effected as an immediate part of a general plan as has now been formulated.[13]

The statement drafted by Byrnes also referred to British hopes of using the Morrison-Grady Plan as a basis for discussion with Arabs and Zionists. The president was to request "prompt and generous cooperation" from those parties in "discussing and effecting the new proposals."[14]

Finally, the suggested statement revealed that Byrnes had elicited a far-reaching concession from Attlee. The president was to point to this as proof that he was not abetting British procrastination:

> I am given the personal assurance of Mr. Attlee that [British-Arab-Zionist] consultations will be expedited to the utmost. I am convinced from what Mr. Attlee tells me that the consultations can be completed and the decision of His Majesty's Government can be reached no later than September 15, and that immigration will proceed as rapidly as the immigrants can be absorbed. . . . I believe that the plan proposed is the best solution to this difficult problem that can now be secured.[15]

Although the new twist in British policy indicated the depth of Attlee's desire to proceed with the Morrison-Grady Plan, it is unclear just what induced him to accept a virtual six-week deadline for a final decision by the British government. The most obvious explanation, of course, is that Byrnes suggested this as the only possible way to secure Washington's support. Actually, such a tentative and conditional American commitment to the Morrison-Grady approach would have seriously jeopardized London's chances of finding the "measure of acquiescence" it required to implement the provisional autonomy plan. With the final U.S. position contingent upon the conclusion of an Anglo-Arab-Zionist accord prior to September 15, opponents of the scheme could only view extremist tactics as eminently logical.

In any case, the value of this final gesture by Attlee remains academic. On July 30, after discussions with members of his cabinet and various congressmen, the president decided against making the statement suggested by Byrnes. On the same day, Acting Secretary Acheson told the British ambassador that Truman had taken the decision "with the greatest reluctance and regret," but that "the extreme intensity of feeling in centers of Jewish population" in the United States prevented either of the major political parties from upholding the plan.[16]

Nonetheless, the president soon informed Attlee that no final decision on the Morrison-Grady scheme had been reached. Claiming that he did not feel able to offer such support "in present circumstances," Truman advised the prime minister to expect a more definite statement "in the not too distant future."[17] On July 31 the White House released a noncommittal announcement to the effect that Truman was considering certain recommendations produced by the Anglo-American talks on Palestine but wished to reserve any decision until the American negotiators returned from London.[18]

British leaders were dismayed. Attlee complained that his government's confidence in the success of the provincial autonomy plan had rested entirely on the belief that Washington would give "moral as well as financial support." Ambassador Harriman reported that the prime minister appeared to have fallen into confusion over how to handle the Palestine issue.[19]

With Attlee required in Paris for an international conference, and Bevin temporarily ill, it fell to Herbert Morrison to explain the provincial autonomy plan to the House of Commons on July 31. Morrison argued that the proposal offered a reasonable chance to resolve the Palestine problem. Although he admitted the plan did not have American backing, he was guardedly hopeful that an affirmative reply would yet be received from Washington.[20]

Uncertainty over the American attitude prompted a change in British plans to meet with Arabs and Zionists. Attlee, who had wanted to convene the conference in London by mid-August, now decided to delay until the end of the month. On August 9 the prime minister made a last attempt to influence Truman. In a personal message to the president, Attlee referred to the plan as "in all circumstances the best that can be devised and the most likely to lead to a settlement in Palestine." It was, he said, the only solution permitting the introduction of a substantial number of refugees into Palestine without imposing a military burden that Britain would be "quite unable to discharge." The prime minister pointed out that in the absence of American support the British government would try its best in the coming negotiations with Arabs and Zionists to arrange some agreement on a modified form of the Morrison-Grady Plan. Such modification, however, would probably relate to the "tempo and extent" of Jewish immigration. Attlee's message closed with an emotional plea for Truman's active support.

> You will, I am sure, realize that we have to deal with the actual situation with all its difficulties and dangers. The lives of the British, Jews and Arabs are imperilled and I more than hope that you may see your way clear to assist us in a final and permanent solution.[21]

Attlee's hopes were in vain. By this time the president's initial reaction had been reinforced by the American members of the Anglo-American Committee of Inquiry, who rejected the Morrison-Grady scheme on grounds that it did not provide for a unitary state.[22] On August 12 Truman informed the prime minister that domestic opposition prevented him from extending formal support to the provincial autonomy proposal "in its present form as a joint Anglo-American plan."[23]

IMPLICATIONS OF TRUMAN'S
REJECTION OF THE MORRISON-GRADY PLAN

American Zionists could justifiably feel that their intense opposition was instrumental in causing Truman's refusal to support the Morrison-Grady formula. Truman had personally been in favor of the proposal. A year after he yielded to Zionist pressure over the Morrison-Grady Plan, the president was contacted by a personal friend, obviously a newly interested observer of the Palestine problem, who suggested solving the Arab-Zionist conflict by using "the Constitution of the United States as the basis of the solution," and creating in Palestine "a federated state, with certain matters such as immigration, tariff, and other things given to the federated state, and the autonomy that our [American] states enjoy given to the contesting elements in that troubled country."[24] In reply to this well-intentioned advice, Truman sent the following note:

The report of the American Commission, which was made more than a year ago, and which should have been adopted, made the very recommendation you referred to in your letter but neither the Jews nor Arabs seemed to want it.[25]

Despite the president's evident confusion between the Anglo-American Committee of Inquiry and the Cabinet Committee's Board of Alternates, his sympathy with the Morrison-Grady formula was obvious.[26] For the president to have argued that the possibility of a settlement in Palestine along federal lines collapsed, because "neither the Jews nor Arabs seemed to want it," was an unfortunate effort to obscure the significance of his own actions. The Morrison-Grady Plan was formulated on the assumption that Arabs and Zionists would be initially opposed to the idea of provincial autonomy. It was precisely because of the need to reduce the extent to which resistance would have to be overcome by force that the Morrison-Grady Plan presumed the closest possible political cooperation between London and Washington. Truman's rejection of the policy suggested by Grady and his colleagues prevented any serious exploration of the provincial autonomy scheme.

It cannot be known whether the Morrison-Grady Plan was realistic or not. There are, however, indications that by the summer of 1946, moderate Arab and Zionist leaders were turning more to the concept of a federal settlement in Palestine. In March 1946 the leading political figure of Iraq, Nuri as-Said, informed Edwin G. Wilson, the American ambassador in Ankara, that he personally "favored [a] moderate solution [in Palestine] on lines of [a] federated state."[27] Nuri as-Said's counterpart among Zionist leaders was Chaim Weizmann. In early August the American chargé in London reported what he had learned of a conversation held the previous day between Weizmann and British Colonial Secretary George Hall:

Hall told me of his private talk yesterday with Dr. Weizmann. Weizmann indicated that he considered a provincial plan the best solution but with qualifications on the present [Morrison-Grady] proposal, (A) that the trusteeship should have a limit of three to five years before which partition would probably be desirable; (B) that more autonomy should be given the provincial governments and (C) more territory particularly the Negeb area should be included in [the] Jewish province. Weizmann agreed [that] the proposals gave a basis for discussion. Incidentally, Dr. Weizmann called on me on personal [business] last week. He commented on the press discussion of the plan and indicated similar views to those quoted by Hall, but said that he could not speak for extreme Zionists.[28]

Truman's rejection of the Morrison-Grady Plan ensured that the dynamics of political confrontation in Palestine would continue to promote extremism. Arabs as well as Jews would continue to see a possibility of forcing the mandatory to comply with their respective maximum demands by resorting to extreme tactics. Under such conditions, there was little chance that Zionist and Arab moderates could discover whether they shared a workable notion of a federal settlement.

THE BREAKDOWN OF
ANGLO-AMERICAN COOPERATION

Truman's rejection of the Morrison-Grady Plan did not immediately produce an open rift between the United States and Britain. On the contrary, the president's decision was not publicly announced until early October. In the meantime, Washington endeavored to keep alive the myth that the Morrison-Grady Plan was still under consideration.

This bit of deviousness served several purposes, not the least of which was to obscure the fact that the United States was now left with no Palestine policy, nor any guidelines for formulating one. Truman's decision destroyed the credibility of what had ostensibly formed the cornerstone of his Palestine policy for nearly one and a half years: obtaining the immigration into Palestine of 100,000 displaced Jews. Having failed to support Britain's willingness to attempt implementation of a scheme designed to fulfill this objective, it was now far more difficult for the Truman administration to avoid the central issue of the Arab-Zionist conflict by expressing itself in humanitarian terms. Truman's humanitarian approach to the Palestine problem had all along been little more than an expedient method of placating domestic Jewish opinion while avoiding the uncomfortable problem of defining an American position on the Palestine problem in any meaningful political sense. With that gambit now played to its fullest, the administration once again directly faced the need to clarify its stand on Palestine's political future. Claiming to have the Morrison-Grady Plan still under review allowed American policy makers to delay acting on this difficult issue.

The tactic also permitted the president to make some amends to Attlee, who was deeply angered at having been denied support despite his agreement to each of the conditions laid down by the United States. The British, forced to proceed alone with plans for a conference with Arabs and Zionists, would bitterly resent further "needling." Byrnes advised the White House to refrain "for the present" from insisting on Jewish immigration into Palestine.[29] Washington initially even gave limited aid to Britain's solitary effort. As London began planning to lay the provincial autonomy plan before Arabs and Zionists, Foreign Secretary Bevin grew convinced that Arab acquiescence would not materialize unless other nations agreed to absorb some of Europe's displaced Jews. In mid-August, Bevin quietly requested a presidential statement in favor of permitting Jewish refugees into the United States.[30]

The White House responded with a carefully constructed public declaration strongly hinting that Truman might seek special legislation to allow an unspecified number of displaced persons, "including Jews," into the country.[31]

The Truman administration's reluctance to publicize its decision on the Morrison-Grady Plan was enhanced by an apparent shift in the Zionist position. The revelation in late July of a possibly imminent Anglo-American commitment to the establishment of a federal regime in Palestine tended to undermine the prestige of Zionist militants. Under the circumstances, moderate leaders regained some of their ebbing influence. The dramatic outcome came on August 5 at a meeting of the Jewish Agency Executive held in Paris. Prodded by Chaim Weizmann, agency leaders decided upon drastic policy changes. The most significant initiative was a secret executive resolution proposing the creation of a sovereign Jewish state in a part of Palestine. The agency's partition proposal called for a Jewish state in a territory far larger than that suggested as a Jewish province by the Morrison-Grady Plan.[32] It was also larger than the Jewish state later recommended by the United Nations partition plan. Nonetheless, it was a concrete piece of evidence that Zionist leaders were not irrevocably tied to the Biltmore Program.

The same Jewish Agency Executive meeting also decided to terminate the alliance between Haganah and Jewish terrorists in Palestine. This step was taken only after Weizmann threatened to resign publicly from the agency unless all ties with terrorist groups were severed. To ensure a complete break with past policy, the elderly Zionist demanded, and obtained, the removal of the militant Moshe Sneh from the Haganah leadership.[33]

The agency's partition proposal was prompted by a desire to prevent Truman from supporting the provincial autonomy scheme. On August 6, Nahum Goldmann carried the plan to the United States in hope of obtaining Washington's approval.[34] Over a span of several days he held a series of conferences with Loy Henderson and Dean Acheson.[35] He did not, however, gain an American commitment to the Zionist partition plan.[36]

Nevertheless, State Department officials were impressed. Acheson informed Ambassador Harriman in London of the department's feeling that the proposal "as elaborated upon by Goldmann might be regarded as certain alternations and extensions in various provisions [of the] Morrison [-Grady] plan rather than outlines of an entirely new plan."[37] The department thought the Zionist initiative offered "hope that [the] Jewish Agency will realistically join [the] search for [a] practicable solution."[38] Harriman was instructed to suggest to the British government that this possibility might be realized if Whitehall "let it be known" that the upcoming London Conference would not focus exclusively on any one plan—that is, on the provincial autonomy plan.

While American policy makers were guardedly hopeful that the Jewish Agency and the British government might find some way to reconcile their respective plans, it was evident that the Zionists' proposal differed in several essential respects from the provincial autonomy scheme. The most striking of these was that the agency's plan looked to the definite establishment of a Jewish state, while the provincial autonomy plan saw that as one of several options to be decided upon in the indefinite future. Second, the Jewish Agency sought control over a far greater portion of Palestine than the British seemed prepared to grant to a Jewish province. Moreover, Zionists demanded that no more than "two or three years" be allowed to pass before the final establishment of a Jewish state. Finally, the Jewish Agency plan failed to specify what would become of the Arab remnant of Palestine. While Zionists might be excused from concern over that question, the same was hardly true of the British government.

Actually, the text of the secret resolution passed by the Jewish Agency Executive on August 5 raised serious questions about the extent of Zionist willingness to resolve the differences between themselves and the British, or the Arabs, through negotiations. Containing three paragraphs, the resolution first labeled the plan "announced by Mr. Morrison in the House of Commons as unacceptable as a basis of discussion."[39] The second paragraph declared that the Jewish Agency Executive was "prepared to discuss a proposal for the establishment of a viable Jewish State in an adequate area of Palestine." The final paragraph, however, made it plain that Zionists would "discuss" partition only once the British government agreed to such a solution and took the following definite steps toward its implementation:

a) the immediate grant of 100,000 certificates and the immediate beginning of the transportation of the 100,000 to Palestine;

b) the grant of immediate full autonomy (in appointing its administration and in the economic field) to that area of Palestine to be designated to become a Jewish State;

c) the grant of the right of control of immigration to the administration of that area in Palestine designated to be a Jewish State.[40]

That Acheson and his colleagues felt a chance existed for Zionists and the British to resolve their differences through discussion—and thereby possibly arrive at a proposal that enjoyed the support of two of the three protagonists in Palestine—can be attributed more to the conciliatory demeanor of Nahum Goldmann than to the text of the Jewish Agency plan. For example, during an interview with Dean Acheson on August 7, Goldmann suggested some flexibility in the agency's territorial demands. Zionist leaders, he thought, would "be willing . . . to work out a compromise in Galilee." He also stated that Zionists were willing to allay Arab fears of a Jewish state as a "spearhead of Western imperialism" by proposing the inclusion of such a state in a confederation with its Arab neighbors. Acheson recorded Goldmann's description of the new Zionist orientation:

> He said that the Agency recognized the desperate position in which the Jews were now placed. If they insisted on a unitary Palestine, they would not achieve it. Neither the 100,000 nor any other number of Jews would come to Palestine. This would lead to frustration and disorder and the disintegration of the whole Zionist movement. Its only hope lay in some constructive future. It could not survive if its activities were restricted to those of the extremists in Palestine and to Madison Square Garden meetings in New York. They recognized that the U.S. Government might well become disgusted with the whole matter and wash its hands of the affair. The Jews would thus lose their only support. They were willing to accept finally a greatly reduced Jewish State if that meant that they could immediately turn to the problems of transporting the Jews whose place in Europe was becoming acute both for them and for us every day and that they could also turn to development in Palestine and away from political agitation.[41]

Events would soon show that the abrupt ascendancy in August 1946 of relatively moderate leaders, such as Weizmann and Goldmann, was made possible only by the Zionists' fear that the United States would support a non-Zionist solution in Palestine. As that fear dissipated, an equally abrupt return to militancy occurred.

The Truman administration's public insistence that the Morrison-Grady Plan had not been completely foreclosed as a policy option was undoubtedly a factor that prevented the Jewish Agency from returning immediately to the demands of the Biltmore Program. However, with congressional elections scheduled for November, Truman was coming under growing pressure to make some pro-Zionist gesture. By early September the president was wavering in his resolve to avoid officially revealing his rejection of the Morrison-Grady Plan. At a press conference on September 5 Truman reaffirmed his commitment to obtain the entry of the 100,000 into Palestine; claimed that the United States was still considering the Morrison-Grady Plan; and, somewhat incongruously, appeared to confirm rumors of that scheme's collapse by admitting that the "substance" of his reply to Attlee the previous month had become public.[42]

In the meantime, the British government was struggling to launch the London Conference, now certain that the United States would not join the proceedings.[43] In mid-August invitations were extended to the Arab states, the Jewish Agency, the Arab League Secretariat, and the Palestinian Arabs to meet early the following month. Difficulties immediately arose over the attendance of the Jewish Agency and the Palestinian Arabs.

The difficulty with the Arabs once again involved representation. The Arab Higher Executive, actually under the leadership of Haj Amin al-

Husseini, who remained in Egypt, demanded that the mufti and other members of the Higher Executive attend as delegates of the Palestinian Arab community. When Britain rejected this, the Palestinian Arabs decided to boycott the meeting.[44]

On the other hand, Zionist leaders indicated that the Jewish Agency's attendance was contingent upon its own partition proposal being the sole item of discussion. Colonial Secretary George Hall explained to Nahum Goldmann and Stephen Wise that such a condition was unacceptable, but he added that "the British Government would propose the original [provincial autonomy] plan but were fully ready to consider the Jewish Agency proposals and proposals from the Arabs as well." Goldmann and Wise carried this message to Paris where they consulted with other members of the Jewish Agency Executive. Hall was left with the impression that the Zionists would ultimately accept the invitation.[45]

However, the influence of Weizmann, Goldmann, and Wise was already beginning to wane as it became clear that the United States had decided to withhold support from the Morrison-Grady Plan. On September 5 the agency's representative in Washington, Eliahu Epstein, informed Loy Henderson that Zionists would not attend the London Conference. Epstein explained that Zionist leaders felt it impossible to "participate in a conference on any other basis than that of a Jewish state in at least a part of Palestine." Epstein acknowledged that "the Agency was unwilling to be placed in a position where it might have to compromise between the Morrison-Grady proposals on the one hand and its own partition plan on the other." He stressed that the decision "had been unanimous and had included Dr. Weizmann and Dr. Goldmann."[46]

Actually, it seems very likely that these leaders acquiesced in the decision only to preserve an appearance of unanimity. This, at least, was certainly true in Weizmann's case. David Niles learned from a secret source in Jerusalem that Weizmann was so disturbed over the agency's attitude that he was threatening to resign from the Executive were the decision on the London Conference not reversed.[47] This time, however, his threat had no impact.

The talks that began in London on September 10 between representatives of the Arab states and the British government were a far cry from what Bevin and Attlee had envisaged when a general conference was first suggested. Without the presence of the United States, the Palestinian Arabs, and the Jewish Agency, there was little chance of accomplishing anything meaningful. Nonetheless, London advanced the provincial autonomy plan. This was countered by the Arabs with a proposal for a unitary, self-governing Palestine in which Jews would be recognized as a religious community and guaranteed one-third of the new state's parliamentary seats. Until it recessed in early October, the so-called conference showed no signs of leading to any agreement.[48]

In the meantime, the British government was holding informal discussions with Zionists in an effort to bring about Jewish Agency participation. These contacts were considered of major importance. British policy makers obviously hoped that any hint of a likely meeting of minds between themselves and the Zionists would increase Arab willingness to compromise—something that in turn might cause the Jewish Agency to reduce the differences between its partition plan and the provincial autonomy formula. London had not yet abandoned the idea that the Jewish Agency's presence at the Conference might still permit some orderly settlement to be devised.

By mid-September the informal Anglo-Zionist talks resulted in visible progress. Nahum Goldmann informed Bevin and Colonial Secretary Hall that the Jewish Agency "was now prepared to attend [the] Conference to state its views."[49] However, having in this way dropped their demand that partition be the sole point of discussion, Zionists continued to insist that no restrictions be placed on the agency's power to name its delegates. Initially the British forbade the attendance of Zionist leaders directly implicated in terrorist activities.[50]

Nonetheless, Attlee's government tried to encourage a spirit of compromise on the Zionist side by appointing as colonial secretary Arthur Creech-Jones, the strongest Zionist sympathizer among the Labour Party's leadership.[51] On October 1 the British attempted to break the impasse over Jewish Agency representation by suggesting that a "truce" be arranged in Palestine under which the agency would actively work to curb terrorism. For its part the mandatory would release all Jewish detainees. Weizmann, who received this offer during an interview with Attlee, did not reject it, but he took no immediate position other than to agree that the subject should be pursued in later talks with the colonial secretary.[52]

The dialogue between British officials and Zionist leaders had so far concentrated strictly on procedural issues relating to the agency's participation in the London Conference. Now, however, Bevin tried to establish substantive grounds for Anglo-Zionist negotiations by telling Zionists that the British government was prepared to consider an interim arrangement of between three and ten years that would end with the self-government of Palestine. Bevin later claimed that the Zionists' reaction to this retreat from the indefinite interim period proposed by the Morrison-Grady Plan made him hope that a settlement might yet be arranged.[53]

At this point even Zionist leaders believed that the Jewish Agency Executive would soon join the London Conference. On October 3 Eliahu Epstein told Loy Henderson that he had been advised by agency members in London that "informal conversations with the British were proceeding rather well and that they had been discussing matters of agenda for later negotiations."[54]

Meanwhile, London requested a two-month adjournment of the conference. Publicly, this was justified by the excuse that the government needed time to consider a newly drafted version of the earlier Arab proposal for a unitary state. Actually, the British felt it would be unwise to allow the Conference to proceed further without the Jewish Agency. This was frankly explained to the Arab delegates. At their request it was not revealed to the press.[55]

British satisfaction with the events of the past few weeks was suddenly shattered by President Truman, whose fear that Jewish voters would turn against the Democratic Party in the upcoming congressional elections drove him to issue a strongly pro-Zionist statement on October 4. Throughout September, American Zionists had demanded that Truman support the Jewish Agency's partition proposal. However, Secretary Byrnes and Ambassador Harriman cautioned the president against taking any action that might upset the ongoing negotiations in London.[56] The State Department also warned against yielding to organized Zionist pressure to support "their policies of the moment" since that would "merely be encouraging them to make fresh demands and to apply pressure in the future."[57]

Truman initially heeded the department's advice.[58] However, domestic political considerations soon made him decide that a pro-Zionist declaration was vital. Democratic candidates were pressing strongly for such a step. At the end of September, over 100 leading Zionists sponsored a blistering "Open Letter to the Democratic National Committee" in the New York *Times*:

> The Jewish people has had enough of promises. It wants . . . action. We are approaching an election and we know that many of your spokesmen will again affirm adherence to American policy on Palestine as enunciated by Congress and our political parties. We will not be content with these speeches.[59]

Secretary of State Byrnes later singled out Samuel Rosenman and David Niles as having been chiefly responsible for the president's decision to issue a pro-Zionist statement on October 4. They had convinced Truman that New York would otherwise be lost to the Democratic Party.[60]

On October 3 Truman sent Attlee a copy of the statement he would make the following day.[61] The prime minister immediately asked for a delay sufficient to allow him to consult with Bevin, who was then in Paris.[62] Truman denied the request, noting that it was "imperative" to issue the statement on schedule.[63]

In fact, Byrnes had already spoken with Bevin. Bevin had been assured that it would be impossible to alter the president's decision since it was necessary to forestall "a competitive statement" from the Republican Party.[64]

Attlee's answer to Truman on October 4 deserves to be quoted in full:

> When just on midnight last night I received the text of your proposed statement on Palestine, I asked you at least to postpone its issue for a few hours

in order that I might communicate with Mr. Bevin in Paris. He has been handling the difficult negotiations with Jews and Arabs to arrive at a solution of this very complicated problem.

I have received with great regret your letter refusing even a few hours grace to the Prime Minister of the country which has the actual responsibility for the government of Palestine in order that he might acquaint you with the actual situation and the probable results of your action. These may well include the frustration of the patient efforts to achieve a settlement and the loss of still more lives in Palestine.

I am astonished that you did not wait to acquaint yourself with the reasons for the suspension of the conference with the Arabs. You do not seem to have been informed that so far from negotiations having been broken off, conversations with leading Zionists with a view to their entering the conference were proceeding with good prospects of success.

I shall await with interest to hear what were the imperative reasons which compelled this precipitancy.[65]

Attlee knew what caused the president's "precipitancy." October 4 fell on the Jewish holy day of Yom Kippur, a fact that Truman considered vital for the timing of his statement.

The Yom Kippur statement reviewed the Truman administration's public involvement with the Palestine issue, stressing the president's repeated calls for the entry into Palestine of 100,000 displaced Jews. It implicitly castigated the British government for seeking an overall settlement before acceding to Truman's pleas on behalf of the 100,000 and strongly reaffirmed the American position that "substantial immigration can not await a solution to the Palestine problem and should begin at once."[66]

The statement also declared Truman's readiness to recommend liberalization of American immigration laws so that the United States could collaborate with other nations in solving the "whole problem of displaced persons." However, no mention was made of any possible action to obtain special legislation permitting a limited number of nonquota immigrants into the United States.

Turning to the current state of the Palestine issue, Truman noted that the British government had offered the "so-called Morrison Plan" as a solution to the Arab-Zionist conflict. He then outlined the Jewish Agency scheme:

The Jewish Agency proposed a solution of the Palestine problem by means of the creation of a viable Jewish state in control of its own immigration and economic policies in an adequate area of Palestine instead of in the whole of Palestine. It proposed furthermore the immediate issuance of certificates for 100,000 Jewish immigrants. This proposal received widespread attention in the United States, both in the press and in public forums. From the discussion which has ensued it is my belief that a solution along these lines would command the support of public opinion in the United States.

Truman stopped just short of committing Washington to the Zionist partition scheme. He called for a synthesis of the Zionist and British plans:

> I cannot believe that the gap between the proposals which have been put forward is too great to be bridged by men of reason and goodwill. To such a solution our Government could lend support.

It was plain that Truman's October 4 statement would prevent the American government from supporting any British proposal with which Zionists were not in agreement. In effect, Truman's position now left Zionists free to reject any arrangement not to their liking while still enjoying American support on the immigration question. Thus, Zionists could maintain their maximum political demands without fear of damaging their relations with the United States. With Britain once again bearing sole responsibility for charting Palestine's political future, this could only cause the Arabs to adhere rigidly to their own maximalist demand: the immediate conversion of Palestine to a unified Arab state. The Attlee government was now even more deeply into the dilemma from which it had been trying to escape since 1945. So long as London remained responsible for Palestine, the British government could hope to settle the conflict there only by sponsoring and implementing the demands of one or another of the communal contestants.

This, of course, was precisely what the British had long sought to avoid. The other alternative was to surrender responsibility for the mandate. Under the impact of Truman's statement and the events that followed, it was not long before steps were initiated in pursuit of the second option.

The domestic impact of the Yom Kippur statement was not what Truman had hoped. Although the American press was generally pro-Zionists, political commentary tended to describe the president's action as an empty gesture made in hope of strengthening the Democratic Party. Writing in the New York *Times*, James Reston observed that "the President went against his political advisors and chose to follow the promptings of those who were primarily interested in retaining Democratic majorities in Congress."[67] Nor did the president's statement prevent a Republican landslide in the 1946 congressional elections, a victory that included the state of New York. It is ironic that with the exception of a letter to Ibn Saud written later in October, the Yom Kippur statement was virtually the last expression of Truman's interest in promoting massive, immediate Jewish immigration into Palestine.[68]

Zionists were almost universally pleased by Truman's Yom Kippur remarks. There was, however, some minor initial dissatisfaction with parts of the message. Eliahu Epstein reported on this to Nahum Goldmann. Epstein's report also reveals the slanted interpretation given to the Yom Kippur statement by the American press.

After the publication of the statement, I found necessary to express freely to our friend [David Niles] disappointment over some parts of it, especially where it comes out for "bridging the gap" between our plan and the Morrison Plan, instead of supporting our plan completely. . . . I must say, however, that not a single newspaper has pointed to this part of the statement and all headlines carried by the papers read "Truman's Support of a Jewish State."[69]

The full significance of the Yom Kippur statement soon began to dawn on responsible Zionist officials. In mid-October, Lionel Gelber, a Canadian on the staff of the Jewish Agency's New York office, analyzed the political impact of Truman's statement. Gelber was not unduly worried over the fact that the president had been motivated by partisan domestic considerations, and he noted that "even a child begotten in sin may, when nurtured with care, grow into virtuous manhood." The thrust of his analysis is revealed in the following excerpt:

President Truman, out of domestic political exigencies, has gone very far in verbal diplomatic support of a full program of political Zionism. No British Government can deal with an American President as cavalierly as with the Jewish Agency. Mr. Truman has engaged himself in our cause more heavily than ever before and not only over matters such as immigration, but in the basic political aim of Jewish statehood. The standing of his administration at home and abroad is involved to an extent without precedent. Under these new conditions, an affront to the Jewish Agency in London could easily become an affront to the President, to the Government and to the people of the United States. The primacy of Anglo-American friendship in the present posture of world affairs is a factor which, once having tended to our detriment, may thus now shift in our favor. So too, if any of these comments are valid, the consternation of the British must far transcend mere contempt for American electoral practices. For the bargaining power of the Jewish Agency, still far from massive, may have been augmented by President Truman to a degree we ourselves do not yet appreciate.[70]

It was not long before the altered conditions created by the Yom Kippur statement visibly affected the dynamics of the Palestine problem. First, however, the truce suggested by Attlee to Weizmann went into effect, and the Inner General Zionist Council, the leading organ of the Jewish community in Palestine, passed a resolution calling upon all Jews in the country to deny the terrorists "all encouragement, support and assistance."[71] In return, the British freed the Zionist leaders still in detention and allowed 2,800 illegal immigrants being held on Cyprus to enter Palestine.[72] Yet this flicker of conciliation rapidly died as militant elements regained control of the Zionist Movement.

Soon after the Yom Kippur statement, the original adjournment of the London Conference was extended until the beginning of the new year. This was done at the request of Chaim Weizmann, who now wished to allow the Twenty-Second Zionist Congress, which was to convene at Basle in December, to decide the question of Jewish Agency participation. The Basle meeting was the first general Zionist Congress since the end of World War II. With the mass of East European Jewry liquidated, American Zionists took a leading role in the proceedings. By 1946, two-thirds of the budget for development in Palestine was contributed by American Jews; and of 385 delegates to the Congress, 121 were Americans.[73] The largest single bloc at the meeting was that of the Zionist Organization of America, led by the militant Rabbi Silver.[74]

The resolutions passed at Basle shattered the moderate trend that Weizmann had attempted to foster since the summer.[75] Urged on by Rabbi Silver and David Ben Gurion, the delegates repudiated the partition plan that Goldmann had carried to Washington, and in its place reinstituted the Biltmore Program. Over Weizmann's objections, the Jewish Agency was barred from attending the London Conference. The militants delivered a final and symbolic blow by not reelecting Weizmann to the presidency of the Zionist Organization. However, in a minimal gesture of appreciation for his past service, the post was left vacant. The congress also decided to allow the Jewish Agency to maintain informal contact with the British government.[76]

The London Conference reopened on January 27, 1947. This time the Palestinian Arabs were present.[77] However, the Arabs quickly made it clear that they would not consider acquiescing to the partition of Palestine. If anything, their attitude had hardened during the months since September.[78] The Zionists, of course, absented themselves. Representatives of the Jewish Agency did carry on informal talks with British officials, but with the Biltmore Program once more serving as the official Zionist position there was no indication that any agreement on Palestine's future would be reached.

On February 14 the conference, the informal talks, and London's effort to arrange a compromise came to an abrupt end with an announcement that the British government would refer the whole Palestine issue—without recommendation—to the United Nations.

During this period the Truman administration maintained an uncharacteristic reserve—a new attitude that would become familiar in the months ahead. In the State Department, efforts were made to draw lessons from the preceding one and a half years of American involvement with Palestine. At the end of 1946 the chief of the Division of Near Eastern Affairs, Gordon P. Merriam, formulated his conclusions in typical diplomatic understatement:

It seems true to say that our policy has gradually taken form, though it is still somewhat indefinite, as the result of the pressures that have been applied to us from various directions. . . . The main point . . . is that our policy, as it stands, is one of expediency, not one of principle. Time after time we have been maneuvered into acceptance of more or less specific propositions: 100,000 immigrants; a compromise between the Goldmann and British Government schemes, and then we have had the task—not always easy—of finding principles to justify them. We ought to proceed from principle to the specific, not vice versa.

This analysis ended with a timely warning:

Operating a policy of expediency is an uncomfortable and dangerous business which we ought to get out of with all possible speed.[79]

13. PALESTINE IN THE INTERNATIONAL FORUM

The decision to deposit Palestine at the United Nations meant that Washington could no longer ignore fundamental political aspects of the Arab-Zionist conflict. As London's determination to abandon the mandate became increasingly obvious, the Truman administration uncomfortably contemplated the harm that unchecked international action could wreak upon vital American interests in the Middle East. Of particular importance were crystallizing global tensions between the Soviet and Western blocs. While the Soviet factor had not been overlooked by American policy makers since the days of Roosevelt, the realization that UN intervention might lead to an active Soviet role in Palestine was now at the heart of Washington's concern.

The significance of Cold War frictions to the Middle East became apparent soon after George Marshall's appointment as secretary of state in early 1947. Two months later, in March 1947, the Truman Doctrine indicated the high strategic value assigned to the region.[1]

In mid-February Dean Acheson and Loy Henderson considered the implications of Palestine's date with the United Nations. Acheson delineated the central problem:

> If the British make no proposal and take no leadership [at the United Nations] and we do not I presume that the Russians will take the ball and start off with an immense propaganda advantage. Therefore, it is hard to see how we can escape the responsibility for leadership.[2]

Acheson saw this as an obligation of the Executive Branch and feared that "if the administration does not give a lead . . . the Congress will undertake to do so with rather disastrous results."[3] Henderson agreed, but stressed the necessity of a carefully formulated policy that would not be subject to essential change once the government became committed to it internationally.[4]

State Department officials had long pressed for a comprehensive policy. However, that could only be established by the president. Under the impact of the heightened international political problems created by UN involvement with Palestine, the White House adopted an uncharacteristic reticence. The administration's silence lasted until the fall of 1947, when the American government finally revealed its views on Palestine's political destiny. Even then, as would become apparent by the spring of 1948, the administration had failed to settle upon a firm approach.

In the meantime, Truman all but abandoned his previous interest in the Jewish refugees. Their abrupt departure from Washington's artificial limelight did not mean they had been removed from the cast. They were there, in masses, still filling—but now with a new variation—the role of political pawn to more powerful actors.

THE JEWISH REFUGEE
PROBLEM IN 1947

By early 1947 the number of displaced Jews in American-occupied areas of Germany, Austria, and Italy had swelled as a result of an anti-Semitic outburst the previous summer in Kielce, Poland.[5] Although the panic created by the Kielce events subsided in the spring of 1947, the movement of East European Jews to the West continued, with Rumania becoming the primary source of refugees. Aided by Brichah, most of these found their way into American displaced persons (DP) camps in Germany and Austria.[6] The financial and administrative burden imposed upon military authorities caused the American Army to announce that no new refugees would be admitted into DP centers after April 21, 1947.[7] However, the decision was not rigidly enforced and within weeks was completely ignored.[8] In the summer of 1948, official estimates put the total of displaced Jews in Western Europe at roughly 200,000, of which approximately 125,000 resided in American-controlled facilities.[9]

Those who formed this constantly increasing mass perhaps suffered most from the circumstances surrounding the Palestine problem. By 1947 some had spent more than two years in DP camps. While many may have been passionately anxious to enter Palestine, the long waiting period exacted a toll. Some—for example, the majority of Rumanian Jews—had no wish to settle in Palestine.[10] Among those who originally intended to emigrate to

Palestine, many came to place their hopes elsewhere. By the fall of 1947, more than 55,000 applications for immigration into the United States had been made by displaced Jews in the American Zone of Germany.[11] In May 1948 the New York *Times* cited a "dramatic shift" in the attitude of Jewish refugees in Germany, claiming that 80 percent of them "now say they want to go to the United States and they specifically add that they do not want to go to the Holy Land."[12] A report submitted to the American Jewish Conference by Rabbi Abraham Klausner argued that Zionists had a mistaken image of the refugees:

> The thinking of our leadership has been that no matter what problems persist in Germany, they will be solved in the eventual solution of the Palestine problem. There is a basic error in this pattern of thought. The Jew as a group is not overwhelmingly desirous of going to Palestine. This statement requires qualification. It is difficult to suggest what people will do under duress. Judging from recent experiences such as recruitment for Haganah and registration for immigration to Palestine, we may predict that perhaps 30% of the people will go to Palestine.[13]

William Haber, advisor on Jewish Affairs to the American high commissioner in Germany, disputed Klausner's estimate, although he admitted to "doubts on this issue." Haber noted that by 1948 a "great number of the people who registered for migration to Palestine also registered for migration to other countries." This was hardly surprising. As Haber pointed out, displaced Jews sought emigration to any country "just so that they may quit Germany."[14] Had opportunities for emigration existed, many Jewish refugees would not have endured the long wait before it became possible for them to enter Palestine.

The refugees were to have no choice. By 1947 they were the focal point of four forces that pinned them to the DP camps of Western Europe: the lingering anti-Semitism in their countries of origin; the circumstances that caused the British government to refuse to fling open the doors to Palestine; the reluctance of the Western democracies, notably the United States, to open their own doors; and the unwillingness of powerful Zionist pressure groups to campaign for DP emigration to any place but Palestine.

So long as Washington continued to act as ardent champion of refugee emigration to Palestine, its own slackness in lowering barriers to immigration was obscured though not entirely hidden. Bevin's impolitic remarks at Bournemouth jarred American sensibilities, but the element of truth they contained was shunted aside by the enraged outcries that followed. In his State of the Union Message on January 6, 1947, the president referred to the general issue of displaced persons of all faiths, pointing out that the United States had not "done its part" to help solve that problem. Noting that new legislation was required, he recommended no particular program and only urged Congress to turn its attention to the matter.[15]

The moral influence of American demands for mass Jewish immigration into Palestine had already been weakened when Truman made this suggestion. However, it was not until later in 1947 that the limitations on American humanitarianism became more evident.

On April 1, 1947, Illinois Congressman William Stratton introduced legislation to allow refugees into the United States. The Stratton Bill was designed to permit 400,000 displaced persons of all faiths to enter the country over a period of four years.[16] The proposal drew little support, and some strong denunciations, when the House Judiciary Committee opened hearings in early June. Stratton's supporters argued that the legislation was morally necessary. They pointed out that Britain was permitting Jewish immigration into Palestine at the rate of 18,000 per year while the total of immigrants who entered the vastly larger United States in 1946 was only 40,000.[17] Opponents of the measure retorted that the proportion of foreign-born Americans was already too high. From the remarks of some congressmen it was clear that a major cause of opposition was the fear that large numbers of Jews would enter the country.[18] The June hearings ended inconclusively, and further consideration of the bill was delayed until the next session of Congress.

The Stratton Bill received little backing from Zionist and non-Zionist Jewish groups. During the 11-day hearings, only one witness, New York's ex-Governor Herbert Lehman, appeared for all major American Jewish organizations. Alfred Lilienthal has brought out the pertinent fact that Jewish organizations provided only 11 of 693 pages of testimony heard by the Judiciary Committee. This was in contrast to the 500 pages of testimony, nearly all of which emanated from American Zionists and their supporters, on behalf of the 1944 Palestine resolutions.[19]

Truman stayed carefully away from the debate over the Stratton Bill. In mid-May he took pains to dispel a rumor that the White House was contemplating a message to Congress about the issue.[20] Only in early July—once it was clear that the battle for new immigration legislation could not continue until the next congressional session—did the president call for the enactment of "suitable" laws dealing with displaced persons "as speedily as possible."[21]

However, not until June 1948, one month after Israel's creation, was Truman presented with a new immigration act—a law so different from the Stratton Bill that it was widely branded anti-Semitic.[22] Columnist Anne O'Hare McCormick's comment on the opposition incurred by even this highly restrictive legislation was a revealing statement on the extent of Zionist publicity during the postwar years, and on the impact it had on the American attitude toward receiving displaced persons:

> Although it has been explained a thousand times, Americans are slow to realize that more than 80% of the displaced persons waiting in Germany to be disposed of are non-Jews.[23]

The continuing plight of Jewish displaced persons was a major theme of Zionist propaganda during 1947. Funds were openly solicited by various organizations to aid the burgeoning movement of European Jews attempting to enter Palestine illegally, usually in ships purchased or chartered secretly by Zionist agents. Having abandoned some time earlier the practice of simply deducting the numbers of illegal immigrants from subsequent quotas for legal Jewish immigration, the mandatory was now interning those apprehended entering Palestine without official permission in detention camps on Cyprus.[24]

During 1947 the British government also vigorously pressed a standing request (first made in the summer of 1946) that Washington reappraise the tax-exempt status of contributions to organizations openly sponsoring illegal immigration and the Jewish Resistance in Palestine.[25] The State Department passed the matter on to the Department of the Treasury and the issue eventually lapsed with no firm decision.[26] However, in June 1947 Truman obviously had the British request in mind when he took the unusual step of asking American citizens to refrain from "engaging in or facilitating any activities which tend further to inflame the passions of the inhabitants of Palestine."[27] A month later the futility of the president's action was made obvious by the formation of a group called Americans for Haganah under the chairmanship of Bartley Crum, the former member of the Anglo-American Committee of Inquiry.[28]

UNSCOP

On April 2, 1947, the British government formally asked the United Nations to take up the Palestine question. UN Secretary-General Trygve Lie called a Special Session of the General Assembly to form a committee that would prepare the way for consideration of the Palestine issue at the General Assembly's next regular session in the fall.

American intentions were obscure throughout the deliberations that produced the United Nations Special Committee on Palestine (UNSCOP). However, while Washington continued to equivocate on Palestine's political disposition, it could not ignore the form in which the United Nations would confront the problem. In view of British and American desires to minimize Soviet involvement in the Middle East, procedural questions were of utmost importance.

The Special Session convened on May 9. It was soon apparent that Moscow hoped for a major role. The Soviet delegate proposed that the projected Special Committee include the five permanent Security Council members. This, of course, ran into Anglo-American opposition. The American delegation favored establishing a committee from which Security Council members would be specifically excluded. This position was eventually upheld. UNSCOP members were finally drawn from the delegations of Australia, Canada, Czechoslovakia, Guatemala, India, Iran, the Netherlands, Peru, Sweden, Uruguay, and Yugoslavia.[29]

Although there was some talk of allowing representatives of the Jewish Agency and the Palestinian Arab Higher Executive to address the Special Session, the idea was ultimately rejected.[30] However, Jewish and Palestinian Arab spokesmen were permitted to speak to the Assembly's First (Political) Committee.[31] Both sides devoted much of their presentations to the terms of reference that would guide UNSCOP's activities. Supported by the Arab states, Palestinian Arabs demanded that the UN investigative committee not consider the problem of Jewish refugees in Europe and focus solely on conditions in Palestine. The Jewish Agency naturally took a contrary view.[32] In keeping with its newly cautious approach, the United States did not press for specific instructions requiring UNSCOP to visit Europe. However, the American delegation did oppose the Arab position as prejudging the issue. In the end, it was left to the Special Committee's discretion whether or not to conduct on-site investigations in Europe.

Throughout this period the British government did not specify whether it would act on the UN recommendations that might eventually be forthcoming.[33] This was typical of the ambiguity that had marked British policy since London first announced that it would resort to the world body. During the spring of 1947, Foreign Secretary Bevin seemed eager for a prompt withdrawal from Palestine. Yet other government spokesmen, notably Colonial Secretary Creech-Jones, indicated that London did not intend to surrender the mandate but simply to obtain advice from the United Nations.[34] Many observers perceived this apparent uncertainty as a calculated effort to force the United States into assuming a share of direct responsibility in Palestine. Others felt that Attlee's cabinet hoped to scare Arabs and Jews into asking the British to stay on and save the country from chaos.[35]

Both analyses probably contained elements of truth. By 1947 the financial and psychological burdens of its role in Palestine were sorely trying the British government. On the other hand, Attlee and his colleagues may well have hoped to generate pressures that would lead to conditions permitting a long-term British presence in Palestine. Yet it appears that they were also sincerely prepared to withdraw should that gambit fail. This was evident from the consistency with which British representatives stressed London's refusal to accept sole responsibility for imposing any settlement not acceptable to Arabs and Jews.[36]

Zionists were apprehensive from the outset over the treatment they would receive at the United Nations. Although initial statements by Zionist leaders did not disguise their hopes of creating a Jewish state in an undivided Palestine, efforts were now made to show flexibility. It became known that the Jewish Agency would probably allow its representatives to explore possibilities for a settlement based on partition.[37] The tentative reemergence of the relatively moderate position defeated at the Basle Congress was directly related to the uncertain atmosphere at the United Nations.

However, the shift was hardly definite. The Zionist Organization was still committed to the Biltmore Program. In Palestine, prior to departing for the Special Session at Lake Success, Ben Gurion declared that "neither political talk nor even a United Nations decision will decide the fate of the Jewish people."[38] Moshe Shertok said much the same upon arriving in New York for the UN deliberations.[39]

When it was learned that the United Nations would consider the Palestine question, the Arab states and the Palestinian Higher Executive emphasized their refusal to accept anything less than a unified Arab state. The Higher Executive, still under the influence of Haj Amin al-Husseini, was represented in New York by Emil Ghuri, a Palestinian Christian who displayed a totally uncompromising attitude in his speech to the First Committee.[40]

As soon as UNSCOP was empowered to consider the Jewish refugee issue, the Higher Executive announced it would not cooperate with the UN investigation. This step was also taken because the Special Session had declined to include on its agenda an Arab demand for Palestine's immediate independence.[41] Although the boycott was opposed by the Husseini's Arab adversaries in Palestine, as well as by the Arab League, the mufti eventually had his way.

The careful vagueness that characterized the Soviet Union's approach to Palestine was not dispelled during the UN proceedings. Observers noted Moscow's obvious ambivalence that blandly supported "everything the Zionists asked for and everything the Arabs asked for."[42] However, on the final day of the Special Session, Soviet Representative Andrei Gromyko spoke in terms that seemed to herald a change in the Kremlin's position. Arguing that the "legitimate interests" of Arabs and Jews could be served only by the creation "of an independent, dual, democratic, homogenous Arab-Jewish state," Gromyko added that if this alternative proved unworkable, it would be necessary to consider "the partition of Palestine into two autonomous states."[43] The apparent inconsistency of advocating at once binationalism as the only proper solution and partition as a possible settlement was widely noted. Gromyko's speech was interpreted by some analysts as an effort to establish grounds for eventual Soviet support of partition.[44]

The purposes behind Soviet policy cannot be conclusively determined. Ideologically, the Soviet government had long opposed Zionism as a reactionary nationalistic movement. However, in retrospect it appears that at this point Moscow was motivated primarily by its objectives in the Middle East—which included reducing Britain's presence in the region. In an immediate sense, then, Russian policy toward Palestine probably aimed at terminating the country's tutelary status—and for this it made no great difference whether independence took the form of partition or binationalism. Unencumbered by past commitments, the Soviet Union was in an enviable position to support whatever course seemed likely to end the mandate soonest. Gromyko's final remarks at the Special Session preserved this flexibility. It was with no little concern that Dean Rusk, then director of the State Department's Office of Special Political Affairs, commented on this. Although Rusk still expected Moscow to support the Arab position (once it could "reap the greatest benefits in the Moslem world"), he ruefully noted at the end of May that Soviet policy "appeared to leave the USSR in an excellent tactical position for the future."[45]

Throughout the spring and summer of 1947, the Truman administration remained cautious and noncommittal. In early May, George Marshall rejected a request by 30 pro-Zionist Republican congressmen for a statement of American policy toward Palestine on the grounds that Washington did not wish to prejudice the findings of UNSCOP.[46] The president also refused to make any statement on Palestine during the UNSCOP investigation. At a cabinet meeting on August 8, Truman remarked that he "had stuck his neck out on this delicate question once, and he did not propose to do it again."[47]

By the end of August UNSCOP had held public and private hearings at Lake Success, Jerusalem, Beirut, and Geneva. Some members of the Special Committee also visited Jordan and DP camps in Europe. On August 31 the committee submitted its report.

Unable to agree on a single plan for settling the Palestine dispute, UNSCOP produced two proposals. The majority plan was supported by seven delegates (Canada, Czechoslovakia, Guatemala, the Netherlands, Peru, Sweden, and Uruguay), the minority plan by three (India, Iran, and Yugoslavia). One member (Australia) abstained.[48]

The majority proposal called for a complicated division of Palestine into seven areas, six of which would form two separate Arab and Jewish states while the seventh, in the midst of Arab territory, would be the internationalized city of Jerusalem. The parts of the proposed Arab and Jewish states were intertwined in rather serpentine fashion and linked through a peculiar system of borders that allowed each polity to enjoy continuous territorial limits.

It was clear that the suggested division was designed more in hope of satisfying the longings of Arabs and Jews for statehood than with the idea of creating two fully independent states. Significantly, UNSCOP unanimously agreed that Palestine's economic unity was "indispensable to the life and development of the country and its people." Thus, the majority plan proposed a ten-year treaty between the two states that would provide for common customs, currencies, and communications, as well as for joint economic development programs, "especially in respect of irrigation, land reclamation and soil conservation."[49]

The UNSCOP members who rejected partition argued that it was unworkable, and that the well-being of the country and its people should take precedence over the aspirations of the Jews for sovereignty. The minority plan proposed the transformation of Palestine into a sovereign federal state composed of Arab and Jewish provinces within which the respective communities would have broad authority over local affairs. The federal government was to have a bicameral legislature, one house of which would be equally divided between Arabs and Jews while membership in the other would be based on proportional representation. Legislation could be enacted by the central government only with the approval of majorities in each house.[50]

The Jewish refugee problem and the related question of immigration into Palestine figured prominently in the UNSCOP report. The part of the report that received unanimous UNSCOP approval requested the General Assembly to initiate and execute immediately an international arrangement for resolving the plight of Europe's displaced Jews.[51] With the exception of two dissenting votes, UNSCOP "accepted as incontrovertible that any solution for Palestine cannot be considered a solution to the Jewish problem in general."[52] The UNSCOP majority plan, postulating a two-year transition period during which Palestine would be administered by Britain (and possibly other members of the United Nations), called for immigration into the anticipated Jewish state at the rate of 75,000 per year. No immigration rate was set by the minority plan, although it proposed a three-year interim UN administration under which Jews would be allowed into the country "in such numbers as to not exceed . . . absorptive capacity."[53]

Perhaps the major inconsistency of the partition proposal was that the area it assigned to a Jewish state contained an approximately equal number of Arabs and Jews.[54] Although the Jewish community would have retained initial control of any democratic government, the higher Arab birthrate promised to reverse the political balance promptly.[55] This could have been prevented only by massive Jewish immigration or by an Arab exodus from Jewish Palestine.

The Jewish Agency reacted cautiously to the report. In early September the Zionist General Council, meeting at Geneva, dismissed the minority federal plan as "wholly unacceptable." It expressed satisfaction with the partition proposal while reserving final judgment "until the General Assembly has taken a decision."[56] However, on October 2 the agency abandoned this caveat and Rabbi Silver announced its acceptance of the partition plan—at the same time rejecting any contention that Palestine alone could not resolve the Jewish problem.[57] Meanwhile, dissident Zionist organizations, heatedly opposing both partition and federalism, continued to demand the conversion of all Palestine into a Jewish state.[58]

The Arab states and the Palestinian Higher Executive rejected both UNSCOP proposals.[59] Since each plan presupposed a degree of cooperation between Arabs and Jews, and since UNSCOP had offered no suggestion for implementing a solution in the absence of such cooperation, the Arabs appear to have reasoned that an inflexible attitude would reduce any likelihood of the United Nations as a whole accepting either of the Special Committee's recommendations. Not until October did growing misgivings over the political climate at the General Assembly prompt the Arab states to begin modifying their stance.

TENSIONS AND INDECISION
IN THE WAKE OF UNSCOP

During the summer and fall of 1947, Palestine witnessed an increase of violence that threatened to push the country into a triangular war among Arabs, Jews, and British troops. The mandatory's restrictive immigration policy, and particularly the deportation of illegal immigrants to Cyprus, continued to provoke outrage within the Jewish community. The Irgun and Stern groups stepped up activities, carrying out various attacks against railway installations, police posts, arms depots, and British personnel.[60] Jewish anger was raised to fever pitch in July by the British government's treatment of some 4,000 would-be immigrants apprehended in Palestinian waters aboard the *Exodus*. With internment camps on Cyprus filled to capacity, and the *Exodus* refugees unwilling to return to their point of embarkation in France, London ordered the ship escorted to Hamburg, where British troops forcibly removed the passengers.[61]

At the end of July the Irgun murdered two British soldiers in reprisal for the execution of three of its members.[62] A group of British soldiers and police countered this atrocity with another—shooting up a section of Tel-Aviv. Five Jews died and 15 were wounded in the incident.[63] Yet another element was added to Anglo-Zionist tensions when a military court rendered a questionable acquittal in the case of a British officer charged with kidnapping and murdering a Jewish youth.[64]

Jewish-Arab relations were rapidly deteriorating. In June a paramilitary Palestinian youth organization was formed under auspices of the Higher Executive, which appointed a former Egyptian Army officer as the group's commander.[65] In early August Arab attacks sparked a series of bloody confrontations at the Jaffa-Tel-Aviv boundary. In five days of intermittent clashes, 12 persons were killed and over 60 injured.[66]

Reports reaching Washington from the American consul general at Jerusalem, R. B. Macatee, emphasized that violent tendencies were beginning to reign unchecked in both the Arab and Jewish camps. Commenting on the Yishuv's reaction to UNSCOP, Macatee wrote:

> I have been unable to discover (except in the cases of the testimony given by Dr. Chaim Weiztman [sic] and Dr. Judah Magnes, neither of whom is typical) a single word showing on the Jewish side recognition or even realization that the primary interest of the UN in the Palestine problem is the preservation of peace. The Arab side was treated as non-existent, except when prodded into existence by UNSCOP delegates.[67]

At the same time, while acknowledging that "the Jewish community now publicly expresses horror of terrorist acts and disowns them," Macatee believed that Palestinian Jews were largely sympathetic to the Irgun and Stern groups.[68]

In the Arab community, opponents of the mufti's policies were subject to intimidation and murder. Sami Taha, secretary-general of the Arab Workers Society, and a follower of Musa al-Alami, suffered this last fate in September. Macatee learned through reliable Arab sources that the High Executive had ordered the assassination.[69] Musa al-Alami probably escaped a similar end only because of his absence from the country.[70]

Neither in Palestine nor in the surrounding states did the UNSCOP report stem the growing popular readiness to settle the Arab-Zionist dispute by war. Extremists of all sorts seized the opportunity to whip up emotions. In Damascus, fanatical members of the Moslem Brotherhood chanted approval in the streets while their leaders called for a "Jihad" against the Jews of Palestine, the establishment of that country as a sovereign Arab state, and the expulsion of Jewish immigrants who had entered after World War I.[71] Revisionist Zionist leaders urged Jews to confront the world, "and the Arabs in particular," with a *fait accompli* as soon as the United Nations accepted the principle of a Jewish state.[72]

Although Arab governments lagged behind popular sentiment in eagerness to resort to arms, it was becoming obvious that public pressure might force their intervention should an attempt be made to establish a Jewish state.[73] Meanwhile, leaders of the Jewish Agency, although not as skeptical as the Revisionists over prospects for an orderly settlement, were also preparing for war. By early October, the government of Palestine confirmed that the Haganah "was mobilizing at top speed."[74]

While these events were in progress, the United Nations was attempting to deal with the UNSCOP proposals. On September 23, 1947, the General Assembly began to review the UNSCOP report. An Ad Hoc Committee, composed of representatives of each member nation, was created to consider UNSCOP's recommendations.[75] This committee was informed by Colonial Secretary Creech-Jones that his government was now definitely committed to an early withdrawal from Palestine. At the same time, London stressed that it would in no circumstances be responsible for implementing a UN-sponsored settlement not fully acceptable to Arabs and Zionists alike.[76]

The British decision was announced only days after Secretary Marshall indicated on September 17 that the United States gave "great weight" to UNSCOP's partition proposal.[77] With Britain determined to surrender the mandate, the essential requirement of any suggested settlement was to provide for its implementation. In Washington this raised the uncomfortable possibility that the United States might incur direct and active responsibility for imposing any proposal it upheld at the United Nations.

By the fall of 1947 the United States—despite the vigorous disclaimers of American officials—was already widely held responsible for the critical situation in Palestine. Early in the year Ernest Bevin had spoken to Parliament in a vein leaving no doubt that the British government bitterly blamed the Truman administration for the conditions impelling it to submit the Palestine issue to the United Nations. Nor did the abrupt silence that characterized Washington's approach after the collapse of the 1947 London Conference prevent the Arab world from faulting the United States. In March the Council of the Arab League unanimously resolved to hold the British and American governments "jointly and severally responsible" for the threat to peace in Palestine.[78] Shortly afterward, Iraq formally conveyed a similar view to Washington.[79] The American ambassador in Baghdad was ordered to respond that the United States could accept no responsibility for a situation that had "arisen from circumstances entirely beyond its control."[80]

While Washington might self-righteously deny the exacerbating influence of its actions on Palestinian tensions prior to Britain's appeal to the United Nations, it still faced the necessity of adopting a clear position on the UNSCOP report. Two days before Secretary of State Marshall indicated tentative American support of partition, he discussed the difficulties of formulating a policy with the U.S. delegation to the United Nations. The essential source of Marshall's disquiet was the possibility that a stand in favor of partition would require the United States to "follow through." "We will," he brooded, "have to be ready to put troops into Palestine."[81]

As the General Assembly began to consider UNSCOP's report, the American government was deeply divided. As late as September 22, Loy Henderson sent Marshall a sweeping critique of the UNSCOP majority plan. Claiming that "nearly every member of the Foreign Service or of the Department who has worked to any appreciable extent on Near Eastern problems" shared his view, Henderson advanced a wide-ranging argument against supporting partition. His analysis was not limited to the current worries over American military involvement or a Soviet-Arab rapprochement, although these were viewed as eminently valid concerns. It also referred to the various investigations that in past years had held partition to be unworkable in practice. Henderson concluded that bisecting Palestine would not resolve the Arab-Zionist problem but instead cause the issue to become "permanent and more complicated in the future." Finally, he strongly criticized the majority plan on grounds that it contravened "generally accepted" American concepts by flouting such principles as self-determination and majority rule.[82]

Since Washington had so far only indicated that it gave "great weight" to the UNSCOP partition plan, Henderson urged issuance of another statement "making it . . . clear that our minds are by no means closed and that we shall also give due weight to the views of other nations and . . . the interested parties." This, he argued, would permit the government to maintain a more detached stand during the upcoming UN debate over UNSCOP's recommendations.[83]

Henderson and his colleagues in the Office of Near Eastern and African Affairs were convinced that the time was not ripe for a permanent settlement of the Palestine problem. They felt that any effort to implement a definitive political formula for the country in the near future would be "bound to result in failure, involving much loss of property and bloodshed and loss of prestige to supporters and executors of the plan." Thus, in their view, Washington's objective at the United Nations should be the establishment of a trusteeship that would provide an indefinite "cooling off" period before a final political arrangement was devised under the General Assembly's auspices.[84]

Marshall was not fully persuaded by these arguments. The secretary of state remained personally uncommitted to any specific solution in Palestine.[85] His indecision was apparent at a series of conferences held with the American delegation at the United Nations during September and October to map out an approach to the UNSCOP report. Faced on the one hand by warnings from the Middle East experts, and on the other by the strongly propartitionist positions of two members of the delegation—Eleanor

Roosevelt and General Hilldring—Marshall hit upon a course he apparently hoped would reconcile, or at least mute, the differences in American ranks.[86]

Meeting with the delegation on October 3, the secretary outlined his views. Washington would support the majority proposal "in principle," but certain modifications of the existing UNSCOP plan would be sought. These were to be "of a pro-Arab nature, concerning *inter alia* boundary changes and adjustments of the plan for economic union."[87] The following policy guidelines emerged from the ensuing discussion:

1. Were partition accepted by the General Assembly, the United States "should be willing to play its appropriate part in any enforcement of this plan. However, . . . it would be unwise to employ organized US military units for this purpose."

2. The majority plan's failure to win General Assembly approval would be "particularly probable" should the United States decline to help enforce it.

3. The United States should "not attempt to persuade other members of the General assembly to vote for the majority plan."

4. Should the partition plan fail at the United Nations, "some form of UN trusteeship for Palestine might be desireable."[88]

At this point Marshall apparently hoped to create an image of policy in the absence of any firm decision on Palestine's future. On one level, of course, such token support of partition might—for a short period—placate pro-Zionist domestic opinion while minimizing offense to Arab sensibilities. However, its real value lay in its seeming promise to remove the United States as far as possible from the onus of responsibility for Palestine. The Truman administration would now, finally, take a position on the Palestine issue, but it was determined to play a minimal role in any ultimate decision affecting that country.

This new tactical approach was responsible for the willful blindness of American policy makers toward the problem of implementing any UN recommendation. For to have linked their position to proposals for action and to have seriously discussed such issues before the General Assembly would have increased chances that Washington would be unable to resist calls for active involvement in Palestine. It was not surprising that Marshall felt no great need to deal with implementation during his conversation with the American delegation on October 3.[89]

A few days after that strategy session, Ambassador Herschel V. Johnson informed the Ad Hoc Committee on Palestine that Washington supported UNSCOP's partition plan, subject to "certain amendments and modifications." He did not explain how partition might be accomplished, although he vaguely noted that a volunteer "constabulary" might be required. Johnson seemed to assume that Britain would retain administrative responsibility in Palestine until some alternative regime could be established in accordance with the General Assembly's wishes.[90]

The last point was promptly challenged by the British ambassador who called on Undersecretary Lovett to reiterate London's refusal to impose a settlement upon either Arab or Jew. Britain, he insisted, would continue to administer Palestine only if the two communities reached an accord. In the meantime, plans were proceeding for a total withdrawal of troops and civilian personnel. Turning directly to Johnson's statement, the ambassador wondered if Washington "had given full consideration to the implementation of the proposed majority solution." Lovett carefully replied that "this phase of the Palestine problem had been given the most careful consideration."[91]

Lovett, of course, knew that Washington had no idea of how an orderly partition might be accomplished. Johnson's murky reference to a constabulary (which had not at all favorably impressed the British ambassador) was a case in point. The White House had specifically approved Johnson's mention of a constabulary, but only with qualifications that confused both the nature of that force and the possible role of the United States in its creation. On October 9 Truman had ordered Lovett to give the following instructions to the American Delegation in New York:

> We are not going to pick up the present United Kingdom responsibility for the maintenance of law and order in Palestine . . . any contribution we might make to law and order . . . would be a contribution under our United Nations obligations and as part of a United Nations police force or constabulary. . . .
> . . . likewise with respect to any commitment in the use of United States forces these again could only be made available as part of a United Nations force made necessary by any obligation we might have as a member of the United Nations.[92]

Since it failed to specify the administration's views of its "United Nations obligation" to uphold order in Palestine, none of this clarified American intentions. Lovett must have further confused the delegation by describing the "constabulary" approved by Truman as a local police force, not "organized troop units."[93]

The pretense of a firm policy was becoming costly as skepticism about the American position began to spread. However, the liabilities seemed suddenly to increase drastically two days after Johnson's statement when the Soviet Union unexpectedly announced it would support UNSCOP's majority plan. The Russian move was a surprise to the British and American governments, where dominant opinion had counted on Moscow's ambivalence being eventually replaced by open espousal of the Arab cause.[94] In Washington there began to develop the conviction that Soviet moves were carefully calculated to reap long-term benefits from the chaos that would attend any effort to partition Palestine.[95] The dilemma that swirled up from this hypothesis was clear and acute: Washington supported partition with no wish to become involved in Palestine, yet it had to presume that the Soviet position entailed more than a verbal commitment. "Implementation" was starkly thrust to the fore of Washington's problems.

In the first instance the magnitude of the situation left the State Department at loose ends, its erstwhile approach left suddenly hanging by useless and unattractive—if not dangerous—strands. A week passed before Robert McClintock, assistant to the director of special political affairs, discovered an avenue that might yet be viable; that is, a policy taking into account the British withdrawal while still precluding the United States and the Soviet Union from entering Palestine under the UN banner. It was a simple and logical solution that asked only that Palestine pay the price.

In McClintock's view, practical considerations—the British withdrawal and the new Soviet posture—required more forceful action on behalf of partition. Efforts should be made to secure a partition resolution that would be implemented coincidentally with Britain's withdrawal. This, he argued, would ensure that London "would perforce have to be the administering authority."[96] The mechanics required for this were relatively simple. McClintock had carefully estimated the earliest date by which Britain's administrative machinery could quit Palestine: July 1, 1948. By the expedient process of obtaining a UN resolution establishing that date as the official end of the mandate, London would "perforce" be left holding the bag.

An additional feature of McClintock's plan was designed to cover "the potential embarrassment which our constabulary suggestion still involves" (and presumably to assure London that nobody seriously expected it to act upon its unwelcome juridical responsibility). The scheme suggested that actual implementation of partition be left in the hands of Arabs and Jews, from whose ranks separate "Arab and Jewish Constabularies" could be created for this purpose.

Behind this approach was the desire to secure a legal status for Palestine that would prevent Soviet or American involvement in that country. McClintock shied away from the obvious conclusion that his suggested communal "constabularies" could be expected to turn their guns upon each other, and instead chose to maintain that there could "result . . . an uneasy, but nevertheless actual, balance of power as between the Jewish and the Arab

States."[97] However, it was clear that McClintock was not concerned with consequences in Palestine so long as the plan fulfilled its primary purpose.

The reaction to this suggestion was not long in coming. Loy Henderson, using the occasion to argue once more on behalf of a trusteeship in Palestine, attacked McClintock's central thesis:

> An unenforced partition would lead to outside intervention from the Arab states, the Soviet Union and, eventually, ourselves, in one form or another.[98]

The controversy wound up in the lap of Assistant Secretary of State Norman Armour. Armour decided against McClintock's proposal, "unless Mr. McClintock particularly desires to have his views brought to the Under Secretary's attention."[99] Despite Armour's correct procedure, the seeds of McClintock's idea had already fallen on fertile ground.

In the meantime, the American delegation at the United Nations was having great difficulty representing the United States. The delegates' discomfort increased when the press began publicizing charges that they were acting in bad faith by not strenuously lobbying for partition.[100] Such frontline burdens fostered dissatisfaction and complaints over the lack of direction being given by Washington, criticisms that were well-rooted in an appreciation of political realities. For example, on October 18 the delegation's advisor on security council affairs wrote to Ambassador Johnson:

> The Department is so anxious that the U.S. should not replace the British as the power most directly responsible for solving the Palestine question, that it does not want the U.S. to adopt clear-cut attitudes . . . as clear-cut attitudes might lead to responsibility for implementation.[101]

This analysis, valid when written, was on the verge of obsolescence. Within a short while, American delegates to the United Nations would find themselves strongly directed by Washington, although not always in directions they would have preferred.

ORIGINS OF A COMMITMENT:
DECISION FOR ANARCHY

Shortly after the American and Soviet positions were clarified, the General Assembly's Ad Hoc Committee created two subcommittees to prepare detailed proposals for settlements based on the UNSCOP recommendations. The Soviet Union and the United States were represented on the subcommittee dealing with the majority plan.

Now confronted with the urgent necessity of formulating a clear blueprint for partition, and for the American contribution toward such a settlement, Marshall met the UN delegation on October 23 to plan a policy.[102] It was decided that the United States would urge the partition subcommittee to make various modifications in the original UNSCOP majority plan. These were largely concerned with boundary alterations—including the reassignment of the Negev Desert—of benefit to the proposed Arab state. The proposed territorial adjustments would have reduced the area of the projected Jewish state from 6,000 to 5,500 square miles—that is, to about 55 percent of Palestine.[103]

However, by far the most significant change to be sought in the original partition proposal was designed to free Washington from the difficult problem of implementation. McClintock's recommendations, far from having been slain by Armour's rejection, reemerged bursting with life.

It was decided that the United States would press for a reduction of the transition period postulated by UNSCOP as a necessary first step in the creation of Arab and Jewish states. Rather than uphold UNSCOP's suggested two-year interim, Washington would ask that complete independence be accorded to Palestine's severed parts on July 1, 1948.[104]

The American plan provided for the establishment of a UN commission to serve as the "agency" responsible for transforming Palestine from a mandate into two sovereign states. The commission was to be small, to rely upon the "moral authority" of the United Nations, and to be charged simply with advising "Jews, Arabs and the mandatory power." Its real purpose, of course, was to symbolize the sole responsibility of the United Nations for Palestine's partition. American policy makers somehow imagined London might be persuaded that this facade would permit it to preside over the partition without incurring responsibility in the eyes of the Arab world.[105]

Actually, the Truman administration was not particularly worried about a British refusal to implement partition under such a transparent disguise. It was not accidental that July 1 was singled out as the mandate's terminal date. The full consideration given to McClintock's original idea emerges clearly in a secret memorandum prepared by Ambassador Johnson:

It is technically impossible for the British to evacuate their troops and supplies from Palestine in a shorter period than the one contemplated. It is conceivable that the British government may reject the suggestion regarding the date for termination of the mandate and may institute a policy of "scuttle and run." This may cause civil strife and chaos in Palestine and would present the United Nations with a very serious problem, one concerning which it might feel a moral obligation to take some action of a pacifying nature, although its legal powers to do more than make recommendations are by no means established. . . .

... It is apparent that the setting of an early and specific date for independence is the best way to avoid saddling the United Nations with the responsibility for administering the area and for implementing the recommendations, and hence is the best way to make sure that neither American troops nor Russian troops, nor any form of voluntary constabulary be employed.[106]

By the end of October, then, the Truman administration embarked on a policy that it fully realized was likely to result in bloody intercommunal warfare in Palestine. It is true that the American government had no active desire to promote an Arab-Jewish war, and in fact clung feebly to the hope that Britain might be maneuvered into officiating at the partition. Yet the decision to press for prompt establishment of Jewish and Arab states was taken despite a suspicion, indeed a virtual expectation, that London would "scuttle and run" rather than risk its interests in the Arab world. This did not cause much alarm in Washington since, after all, the ability of the United Nations—the most likely channel through which the Soviet Union or the United States might become directly involved in Palestine—to "do more than make recommendations" was a moot point. There were, in other words, grounds for the United States to resist any pressures that a precipitate British withdrawal might generate for Soviet or American intervention under UN auspices.

The dominant characteristic of America's Palestine policy since 1939 had been its development in response to factors other than the central conflict between Arabs and Jews. For nearly a decade this insidious pattern helped fuel tensions between Arabs and Jews, reduce prospects for an orderly political settlement, and increase the British government's willingness to abandon the mandate. It now culminated in a policy carefully and meticulously arrived at in full knowledge that it would almost certainly plunge Palestine into a bloodbath.

Two days after the finishing touches were laid on the American plan, Acting Secretary Lovett urgently instructed the American ambassador in London to learn whether, and to what extent, the British would cooperate with a UN commission in effecting a partition settlement that would become operative immediately upon a British withdrawal.[107] The ambassador's report was discouraging. Obviously wary of American intentions, Foreign Secretary Bevin had emphasized that London would make no commitment to help implement any recommendations of the General Assembly until they were carefully examined. However, it was clear that Bevin was not disposed to see Britain assume the role intended for it by the United States. The American suggestions, he said, implied "British assistance in carrying out a program for Palestine which . . . [would] lead to disturbances, if not in fact, to violence, the latter of which [appeared] to be certain."[108]

On October 31 the United States presented its plan to the partition subcommittee. Speaking at a press conference later in the day, Johnson offered this explanation for public consumption:

The most we can do is to lay down a plan which we hope is fair, and we want to be fair to everybody concerned, even if it does not give everybody everything they ask for. With a certain amount of good will and with some wise counsel on the part of competent people, the difficult transition period will be bridged and the two states become viable, both politically and economically, in a very short time. We feel strongly that the placing on the shoulders of the Jewish and Arab leaders in their states the full responsibility for their own future will be in some ways the best guarantee of its success.[109]

The Soviet member of the partition subcommittee welcomed the suggestion for a quick end to the mandate, although he criticized the American plan's reliance upon the British. As an alternative, the Soviets proposed an approach that differed in several important respects from Washington's. The Soviet option called for formal termination of the mandate on January 1, 1948 and for the withdrawal of all British troops within four months of that date. During a transition period that would endure at most for a year, Palestine would come under a UN administration to be exercised by a special commission formed of members of the Security Council.[110]

Washington saw this as a design to give Moscow "negative control" over developments in Palestine through use of the veto in the Security Council.[111] It was also feared that the chaos created by a sudden British withdrawal under these circumstances would give the Soviet Union an excellent opportunity to become even more directly involved in the affairs of that country.[112]

The different Soviet and American plans produced a deadlock in the subcommittee. Negotiations between the two powers produced a common proposal. Under the new plan, the mandate would end officially on May 1, 1948 while the proposed UN Commission would be chosen by the General Assembly but guided by the Security Council.[113] This compromise laid the basis for the General Assembly's subsequent partition resolution, which although containing further modifications (primarily the establishment of August 1, 1948 as the final possible terminal date for the mandate and a proposed two month interim between Britain's evacuation and the devolution of sovereignty upon the projected Palestinian states), retained American and Soviet support. American acceptance of this new deadline for the mandate's termination was undoubtedly influenced by the British representative, Sir Alexander Cadogan, who on November 13 informed the subcommittee that a complete British withdrawal would be effected at latest by August 1, 1948.[114] Britain, it seemed, was still destined to serve as primary international steward of the brewing chaos in Palestine.

THE PARTITION RESOLUTION

By November 19 the General Assembly's Ad Hoc Committee was in receipt of detailed plans prepared by the subcommittees that had considered the two UNSCOP proposals. On November 24 the Ad Hoc Committee rejected the minority plan; the following day it approved the partition proposal. The issue then became whether the General Assembly would favor the partition of Palestine.

At this point, despite Soviet and American support, Zionists faced an impending defeat. The Ad Hoc Committee had supported partition by a vote of 25 to 13. A similar division in the General Assembly would have killed the partition proposal. However, on November 29 the General Assembly approved a resolution recommending the partition of Palestine into Arab and Jewish states and the internationalization of Jerusalem by a margin of 33 to 13.[115] Only three more negative votes would have prevented the measure from obtaining the required two-thirds majority.

The exact role played by the American government, and particularly by President Truman, in securing this outcome is a matter of debate. There is no doubt that American representatives at the United Nations, acting on direct orders from the White House, strongly urged other delegations to support partition in the final days before the vote was taken. What is obscure is whether the White House directive caused American diplomats to use threats against the interests of other governments.

Truman had remained aloof from the Palestine issue throughout most of the debates over the UNSCOP report. However, he was kept informed of events at the United Nations, as well as of misgivings in the State Department over the course of American policy. Shortly before the final vote on partition, Lovett read aloud in Truman's presence a memorandum prepared by Loy Henderson:

> I wonder if the President realizes that the plan which we are supporting for Palestine leaves no force other than local law enforcement organizations for preserving order in Palestine. It is quite clear that there will be wide-scale violence in that country, both from the Jewish and Arab sides, with which the local authorities will not be able to cope.[116]

During much of the period that led to the crystallization of American policy behind partition, Truman reacted angrily to the intense pressures directed at the White House by Zionists. When he received a message from Senator Wagner in late September exhorting him not to be swayed "by Arab threats to 'break with the West,' " he retorted: "I know of no pressure except the pressure of the Jews, which has always been extensive and continuous."[117]

Despite his irritation, the president was eventually induced to take an active interest in pro-Zionist steps at the United Nations. In accordance with the plan approved by Marshall on October 23, the American delegation advocated the assignment of the Negev Desert to the projected Arab state in

Palestine. The region was valued by Zionists because of its potential for land reclamation. On November 19 Weizmann met with Truman and convinced him of the reasonableness of Zionist claims.[118] Truman immediately telephoned General Hilldring at the United Nations to say that "he . . . personally agreed with Wizemann's [sic] views."[119] The proponents of Jewish statehood saw this timely intervention as responsible for the Negev's ultimate inclusion in the area assigned to Jews.[120]

On November 24, the day the partition resolution was approved by the Ad Hoc Committee, Lovett met with the president and received instructions for the American delegation at the United Nations. Truman did not wish the use of "threats or improper pressure of any kind" in mustering support for Washington's position.[121] Within days, the White House would issue new instructions.

Shortly before the final UN vote, Loy Henderson began receiving complaints from various foreign diplomats in Washington about the activities of the U.S. delegation in New York. After an encounter with the Greek ambassador, who protested against strong American pressure, Henderson telephoned Herschel Johnson to learn how the delegation was handling Palestine. Confronted with this question, Johnson—a close personal friend of Henderson—burst into tears and replied substantially as follows:

> Loy, it's out of my hands. I have received a call from the President telling me that come what may he wants that resolution to succeed, and that we had just better make sure that it does.[122]

Asked whether Truman had personally delivered the new instructions, Johnson replied that the call had come from David Niles, "but he was speaking at the request of the President."

Sumner Welles offered this description of the sudden American departure at the United Nations:

> By direct order of the White House every form of pressure, direct and indirect, was brought to bear upon those countries outside of the Moslem World that were known to be uncertain or opposed to the partition.[123]

James Byrnes referred to November 1947 as a period during which the American government advocated the partition of Palestine "and brought pressure to bear on other governments to agree with us."[124]

On the other hand, several sources deny that the United States attempted to coerce other nations. General Hilldring agreed that the delegation in New York attempted "to persuade" other countries of the value of partition but denied that intimidation was used.[125] Jorge Garcia Granados, a strongly pro-Zionist Guatemalan representative, recalled only that shortly before the final partition vote, American delegates began "to suggest mildly that partition was worthy of support."[126]

The preponderance of evidence indicates that the Truman administration exerted strong pressure on other governments to obtain the necessary support for the partition resolution. Much of the debate over American actions during the United Nations' review of Palestine hinges on the question of whether "proper" or "improper" pressure was exerted; whether "persuasion" or "coercion" was utilized by American delegates. As no full record exists of the intercourse between American and other representatives at the General Assembly, no firm conclusion can be reached. On the other hand, the effects of American action are beyond question. David Horowitz, who was among the Jewish Agency observers at the United Nations, described what occurred in the days that led to November 29:

> America's line of action had swung in a new direction. As a result of instructions from the President, the State Department now embarked on a helpful course of great importance to our interests.
>
> The improved atmosphere swayed a number of wavering countries. The United States exerted the weight of its influence almost at the last hour, and the way the final vote turned out must be ascribed to this fact. Its intervention sidetracked the manipulation of the fringe vote against us.[127]

Passage of the partition resolution demonstrated with finality the bankruptcy of the rigid and unimaginative diplomacy pursued by the Arab states. Throughout virtually all of the UN deliberations, the Arab states publicly maintained their uncompromising demand for a unitary, Arab-dominated state. Only hours before the decisive General Assembly vote did the Arabs openly reveal any spirit of compromise. At that time, Arab representatives attempted to revive the General Assembly's interest in a federal settlement that would leave the Arab and Jewish communities of Palestine largely autonomous. It was, however, by then far too late for such an eleventh-hour proposal, and the Arab initiative—opposed by both the Soviet Union and the United States—was not even discussed.[128]

Ironically, the Arab delegations had in fact long since been prepared to accept a federal, or provincial autonomy, settlement in Palestine. In early October the head of the Iraqi delegation, Nuri as-Said, suggested to Saudi Arabia's Prince Feisal that the Arab states jointly seek a cantonal arrangement in Palestine. The plan hinged on an Arab-American agreement "at the highest level." He convinced Feisal that only Ibn Saud could induce the Palestinian Arabs to modify their position sufficiently to make the approach workable. Feisal obtained Ibn Saud's agreement to the Iraqi plan "on condition that it and his intervention have the full, unequivocal support of all the Arab delegations" as well as their commitment to abide by "any agreement" he might conclude with the United States.[129]

By late October these requirements had been met and the Arabs were anxious to open negotiations with the United States. Fearful that Washington might already be too committed to partition to show interest in alternative possibilities, and wishing to avoid the embarrassment of an outright rejection, the Arabs decided to make their initial approach through the good offices of the British delegation at the United Nations. Accordingly, the British were confidentially informed of the plan and asked to pass it on to the Americans. In the event that Secretary Marshall wished the matter to be pursued further, Nuri as-Said and Feisal would journey to Washington and propose the scheme directly to American officials. Should preliminary contacts indicate that the possibility of a cantonal arrangement might be explored in greater depth, the Arabs proposed that "the American Government should charge its Minister at Jeddah . . . with receiving King Saud's personal assurances in the matter and with discussing it in detail with him."[130]

In late October, Harold Beeley, a Middle East expert on the British delegation, outlined the Arab proposal to George Wadsworth, American minister to Syria and Lebanon. Wadsworth relayed the information to Herschel Johnson, who presumably transmitted it to the secretary of state. Although no record is available of Marshall's thoughts on the matter, they were obviously negative. The United States did not reply to the Arab demarche.

Having failed in this first effort to promote a cantonal settlement, the Arabs launched a subdued campaign to interest the United Nations in the project. Informally, Arab diplomats let it be known that while the "Arab states would not themselves propose cantonization in Palestine, they would not oppose it if it were proposed by some other nations."[131] The reluctance of Arab governments to advocate openly the solution they hoped to promote privately was linked to domestic considerations. Acquiescence to a compromise settlement advanced by the United Nations could have been more easily justified to the Arab masses than active lobbying on behalf of a solution that fell short of an Arab state in Palestine. Given the narrow margin of victory ultimately gained by proponents of partition in the General Assembly, this preference for indirection must be seen as a possibly fatal flaw in the Arab approach.

In mid-December the British government announced that it would consider its responsibility for the mandate terminated on May 15, 1948. With this the stage was set for the final scene of the Palestine drama.

14.   COLLAPSE INTO CHAOS:
WASHINGTON AND PALESTINE

For a short while, Washington appeared to have weathered the political storm generated by the partition resolution. The British government, while still disavowing responsibility for partition, would exercise its mandate over Palestine until mid-May, thus greatly lessening the possibility of third parties—particularly the Soviet Union—becoming involved in carrying out the resolution. At the same time, there were growing indications that American economic interests in the Middle East would not suffer as a result of Palestine. In early December the American minister in Jeddah was personally assured by Ibn Saud that the monarch saw no situation in which his country would be drawn into conflict with the West. Although the king admitted to differing "enormously" with Washington over Palestine, he realized "that we have our own mutual interests and friendship to safeguard."[1]

American policy makers quickly began to stress their eagerness to develop harmonious relations with the Arab world. Arab leaders were encouraged to take a broad view of Palestine and concentrate on establishing mutually advantageous relations. With President Truman's approval, diplomats in Arab countries were instructed to give the following explanation for Washington's pro-Zionist stance at the United Nations:

> After reviewing statements and expressions of policy by responsible American officials, resolutions of Congress and Party platforms of [the] last thirty years, [the American government] came to the conclusion that unless there was some unanticipated factor in [the] situation the trend of public opinion and policy based thereon practically forced it to support partition.[2]

Whatever hope Washington may have had that Arab governments could be so easily induced to abandon their interest in Palestine was quickly shattered. Between December 1947 and May 1948, war broke out between Arabs and Jews in Palestine. By the end of this period the Arab countries surrounding Palestine entered the fray. The ramifications of that chaotic situation produced a parallel measure of chaos in Washington.

WAR IN PALESTINE

Widespread fighting broke out in Palestine soon after the partition vote. Bloody clashes between Arabs and Jews took place in Jerusalem. The Irgun attacked an Arab village near Jaffa. Arabs ambushed Jewish traffic on the Jerusalem-Hebron road. Skirmishes between the two communities erupted in Haifa. By mid-December, 65 Jews and 38 Arabs had died. Over 130 Jews and nearly 380 Arabs were wounded during the first eleven days of the month.[3]

On January 20, 1948, Creech-Jones informed the House of Commons that His Majesty's government would permit the Arab and Jewish communities in Palestine to provide security arrangements in their own territories. The mandatory would concentrate British forces in Jerusalem and other centers of mixed population.[4] The colonial secretary revealed that the Jewish Agency had already been assured that the Haganah would not be hampered if it engaged in defensive operations and that the mandatory would no longer carry out arms searches.[5] This merely acknowledged the obvious fact that the mandatory was already in the process of surrendering its authority. As early as December 15, the Palestine government had officially handed over the policing of Tel-Aviv and Petah Tikvah, two entirely Jewish areas, to the Jewish Agency.[6]

In late January the first units of the Arab Liberation Army, formed by the Arab League with volunteers from various parts of the Arab world, entered Palestine without British opposition and took up positions in the predominantly Arab-populated Nablus-Jenin-Tulkarm triangle.[7] The Liberation Army, commanded by Fauzi al-Qawuqji, a prominent guerilla leader during the 1936–39 revolt, eventually numbered almost 4,000 men, including some 1,500 Palestinians.[8] Other Arab forces in Palestine totalled approximately 2,500 men by the end of the mandate.[9]

The Arab-Jewish War blossomed apace with the collapse of the mandate administration. The mandatory's occasional efforts to separate the combatants caused Jews as well as Arabs to accuse Britain of working on behalf of their adversary.[10] In fact, London was anxious only to enforce the minimal amount of order required for an unhampered withdrawal of British forces.[11]

During the first three months of 1948, Arab forces demonstrated a high level of capability in their engagements against Jews, although David Ben

Gurion later remarked that "until the British left, no Jewish settlement, however remote, was entered or seized by the Arabs."[12] However, at the end of March—with the approval of the Soviet Union—Jewish forces received the first of several large arms shipments from Czechoslovakia.[13] From that point on, the battle for Palestine turned rapidly and decisively in their favor.[14]

In March 1948 the Haganah High Command completed a comprehensive plan for a military offensive to secure the establishment of a Jewish state. Designated Plan "D," the scheme involved 13 large-scale operations by May 15.[15] Eight of these aimed at obtaining control of areas allocated to the Arab state by the UN partition plan.[16] The value of the painstaking care taken by the Zionist leadership since 1939 to nurture and expand the semiunderground Jewish fighting force was now evident. To implement Plan "D," nearly 30,000 front-line troops were called into service by May 1.[17] Launched at the beginning of April, the offensive quickly established the Zionists' military supremacy. By the last week of April, with the completion of only three of the 13 operations called for by Plan "D," UN observers in Palestine reported that "partition was an accomplished fact."[18]

As the fighting escalated, so did the price paid by each community. Both sides suffered mounting civilian casualties. The single largest outrage against noncombatants was perpetrated by the Irgun on the night of April 9, 1948, at the Arab village of Deir Yassin. Some 250 inhabitants, including more than 100 women and children, were systematically massacred and their corpses mutilated.[19] A few days later, Arabs ambushed a Jewish medical column in the environs of Jerusalem, killing nearly 40 doctors and nurses.[20] The memory of these and similar atrocities was to become an enduring element of Arab-Zionist relations.

An equally lasting problem began to take form in April as thousands of Palestinian Arabs fled before the victorious Zionist forces. In a manner reminiscent of scenes already familiar in outlying villages, Haifa and Jaffa were virtually emptied of their Arab inhabitants when they fell to Jewish troops. Although Zionist officials denied any premeditated plan to expel Arabs from Jewish-controlled areas, the balance of evidence leaves little doubt that official as well as dissident Jewish forces frequently exerted physical and psychological pressure to force Arab peasants and townsmen from their homes.[21] By the end of 1948, some 750,000 Arabs were destitute refugees.[22]

WASHINGTON: SECOND THOUGHTS, THIRD THOUGHTS

The Truman administration was initially widely praised by American Zionists for its position at the United Nations. Weizmann wrote to the White House expressing appreciation for the president's "initiative and leadership" in bringing about the historic UN resolution.[23] Henry Morgenthau, Jr. thanked Truman for having led the way to the General Assembly's "favorable action."[24] Emanuel Celler offered gratitude for Truman's "effective work."[25] Emanuel Neumann claimed the partition resolution was due "in large measure, perhaps in the largest measure, to the sustained interest and unflagging efforts of Harry S Truman."[26]

This halcyon period did not last long. In early December the American government announced an embargo on arms shipments to the Middle East.[27] Without success, American Zionists immediately urged Truman to rescind the action.[28]

Washington hoped the embargo might reduce, or at least contain, the volume of violence in Palestine. However, with both Arabs and Jews already fairly well equipped, and with both sides still able to obtain arms from other sources, the measure did not have a significant impact. The intensification of fighting soon raised the possibility that the United Nations, the Soviet Union, or the American government—or all three—might, according to their own lights, be dragged, or leap, into the conflict.

Near East specialists in the State Department and the Pentagon had, in any case, all along been disturbed by the administration's support of partition.[29] As early as January 1948, a State Department planning staff prepared a critical appraisal that suggested that the policy was harmful to American interests.[30] In mid-February the National Security Council (NSC) sent its assessment, along with policy recommendations, to the White House.

The NSC analysis developed the considerations that led to Washington's eventual abandonment of the partition plan. Arguing that the United States had incurred a "moral responsibility" by supporting partition at the United Nations, the document nonetheless suggested that a new approach would be justified were the existing policy shown to be incompatible with national security. It then schematized the current situation in a way that left no doubt of the NSC's belief that the national interests were imperiled. Most of the arguments were not new, having been advanced at various times by State Department officials. However, their presentation in a comprehensive format neatly captured the dilemma felt in upper Washington circles: the Middle East and Eastern Mediterranean were "vital" to the security of the United States, as was Arab oil; the greatest danger to the United States stemmed from the Soviet Union's policy of "Communist aggression"; the American government could not disregard the importance of "a friendly or at least neutral attitude by the Arab peoples toward the U.S. and its interests"; it could be assumed that Moscow intended to exploit the situation in Palestine to its advantage, and particularly to try to introduce into the Middle East "Soviet or Soviet-controlled forces under the guise of some U.N. action"; the most unfavorable eventuality for the United States would be the intrusion of Soviet troops into Palestine and "second only to that, the introduction of U.S. troops in opposition to possible Arab resistance"; increasing Arab animosity toward the United States would probably attend "each further manifestation of U.S. leadership in or support of the implementation of . . . partition."

Included in this catalog of policy imperatives were two relatively novel points. On the one hand, the NSC urged that consideration be given to the fact that "the Arab people sincerely believe in the righteousness of their opposition to Palestine's partition, which imposes upon them the major initial cost of attempting a solution of the international problem of Zionism." Second, the analysis suggested that the economic unity of Palestine called for by the UN partition plan was probably impossible to achieve. In an obvious effort to understate its outlook, the NSC concluded that "grave doubts" existed as to whether the partition option was "the most conducive to the security of the U.S., the increased prestige of the U.N., and to the peace of the world."[31]

Having set forth a framework implicitly critical of the administration's policy, the NSC examined alternatives that remained open to the United States. Four possibilities were developed:

1. Full support of the partition plan "with all means at our disposal, including the use of armed forces under the United Nations."

2. Continuation of support for partition at the United Nations by all measures short of "the use of outside force to impose the plan upon the people of Palestine."

3. A passive or neutral role toward events in Palestine that would involve "no further steps to aid in the implementation of partition."

4. Abandon partition "and seek another solution."

After reviewing the merits of each option, the NSC offered several policy guidelines. The civilian members of the group refrained from explicitly calling for a reversal of existing policy, although their advice implicitly raised that possibility:

1. Any solution of the Palestine problem which invites direct Soviet participation in administration, policing, or military operations . . . is a danger to the security of the United States.

2. Any solution . . . which results in the continuing hostility of the Arab world toward the United States will bring about conditions which endanger the security of the United States.

3. The U.S. should continue support for the partition plan in the U.N. by all measures short of the use of outside armed force to impose the plan upon the people of Palestine.[32]

The question, of course, was whether this final recommendation could be followed without incurring the dangers warned against in the first two points. Taken together, the advice proffered by the NSC's civilian members rested on the increasingly questionable assumption that an Arab-Jewish war in Palestine was not necessarily prejudicial to American interests since Washington might find ways to prevent direct Soviet involvement in the region as well as to avoid becoming itself the object of Arab hostility.

The NSC's military members were wary of this premise. Dissenting from Recommendation Three, they substituted the following:

> The United States should alter its previous policy of support for partition and seek another solution. . . . In the event of a reconsideration of the Palestine problem by the General Assembly, the United States should propose the creation of a trusteeship in Palestine with the U.N. Trusteeship Council as the administering authority. If necessary, this proposal should include provision for an international force to maintain order.[33]

Secretary of Defense Forrestal took utmost interest in such analyses. Deeply disturbed by the nature of American involvement with Palestine, Forrestal approached Democratic and Republican leaders to urge that the issue be treated in a bipartisan spirit. He was quickly disillusioned. Principal figures in each party rejected his advice. Republican Senator Arthur Vandenberg argued "that there was a feeling among most Republicans that the Democratic party had used the Palestine question politically, and the Republicans felt they were entitled to make similar use of the issue." By February, rebuffed on all sides, the frustrated secretary of defense abandoned his efforts to remove Palestine from the domestic political arena.[34]

The upcoming presidential election of 1948 guaranteed Washington's sensitivity to public opinion. In November 1947 Clark Clifford, special counsel to the president, prepared a lengthy memorandum outlining a political strategy for Truman's 1948 campaign.[35] He noted that "the Jewish vote, insofar as it can be thought of as a bloc, is important only in New York."[36] However, he also warned that with the sole exception of Woodrow Wilson in 1916, "no candidate since 1876 has lost New York and won the Presidency." With 47 electoral votes, Clifford concluded, New York was "naturally the first prize in any election." Clifford assessed the Jewish vote in the following way:

> [It] is normally Democratic and, if large enough, is sufficient to counteract the upstate [Republican] vote and deliver the state to President Truman. Today the Jewish bloc is interested primarily in Palestine and will continue to be an uncertain quantity right up to the time of election.[37]

American Zionists were steadily reminding Democratic Party leaders of the importance of the Jewish vote. Zionists were not only disgruntled over the embargo on Middle East arms shipments; by January 1948 they were becoming apprehensive that the American government might drop its support of partition. Leading Democrats across the country urged the president to restore Jewish confidence in the administration by standing firmly behind partition, and by ending the embargo.[38]

The most serious manifestation of Jewish displeasure came in mid-February 1948, when the Democratic candidate in a congressional by-election in the Bronx lost to Leo Isaacson. Isaacson was the candidate of the influential American Labor Party, whose support had been instrumental in securing New York's 47 electoral votes for Roosevelt in 1944.[39] Political observers attributed the Democrat's defeat to growing doubts among Jewish voters over Washington's commitment to partition.[40] The administration's alarm was heightened by the fact that Isaacson had been supported by former Vice-President Henry A. Wallace, whose declared candidacy for president was already causing fears that the New York Democratic vote would be split in the fall of 1948.[41]

While domestic considerations gave Truman cause to maintain, and perhaps even to pursue more forcefully, his support of partition, international factors were rapidly giving him grounds for considering a reversal of policy on Palestine. When it approved partition, the General Assembly had also created a five-nation commission to preside over the divison of Palestine.[42] The British government, however, arguing that the presence of that body would only further complicate the already deteriorating situation in Palestine, announced that the committee would not be allowed into the country until after May 1.[43] Nonetheless, the UN Commission kept abreast of developments in Palestine.[44] On February 16 the Palestine Commission formally requested armed assistance from the UN Security Council.[45]

This was precisely the contingency most feared in Washington since it provided the Soviet Union with a chance to assume some degree of responsibility in any UN action. Moreover, the United States was still not prepared to send American troops to Palestine. On February 18 the chairman of the Joint Chiefs of Staff advised Truman that implementation of the partition scheme would require from 80,000 to 160,000 men. American military planners pointed out that existing troop levels were so low that the United States was already badly strained to meet its existing commitments.[46] The apparent effectiveness of Arab forces in Palestine caused some American policy makers to fear the developing chaos in the Holy Land might lead to massacres on a scale that would force American military intervention.[47]

Finally, the general international situation in February and March 1948 seemed to enhance the dangers in the Middle East. At the end of February, a Communist coup in Czechoslovakia seriously strained East-West relations. In early March, General Lucius Clay in Berlin sent a top-secret message to Washington warning that war "may come with dramatic suddenness."[48]

In short, international factors—stemming from events in the Middle East and other parts of the world—were increasingly undermining the sanguine belief that underlay the propartition policy worked out by Marshall and the American delegation to the United Nations in late October: that vital American interests in the Middle East might with relative ease be shielded from the repercussions of an Arab-Jewish war in Palestine. As confidence in this premise faded within the higher ranks of the administration, renewed interest was taken in the trusteeship proposal advanced earlier as an alternative to partition.

Torn by the conflicting pressures, Truman vacillated and then reacted against the Zionists. On March 6 he answered a pro-Zionist appeal with a complaint:

> There are so many people in this country who know more about how the [Palestine] situation can be handled than do those in authority. It has made the situation exceedingly difficult and is not contributing in any manner to its solution.
>
> Of course, I appreciate the emotional feeling of you and your friends in regard to this . . . problem. . . . However, . . . so much lobbying and outside interference has been going on in this question that it is almost impossible to get a fair minded approach to this subject.[49]

When this letter was written, the administration had already embarked on a retreat from its support of partition. Truman was protected, at least partly, from the outraged cries of Zionist spokesmen by the White House staff, who had orders to refuse all requests for appointments concerning Palestine.[50]

The first concrete indication of a restructuring of policy was a statement made to the Security Council by Ambassador Austin on February 24. Addressing himself to the UN Commission's request for UN forces to implement partition, Austin argued that no legal basis existed for action by the Security Council:

> The Charter of the United Nations does not empower the Security Council to enforce a political settlement whether it is pursuant to a recommendation of the General Assembly, or of the Council itself. What this means is this: the Council . . . can take action to prevent a threat to international peace and security from inside Palestine. But this action must be directed solely to the maintenance of international peace. The Council's action, in other words, is directed to keeping peace, and not to enforcing partition.[51]

Zionist reaction was bitter, going so far at times as to condemn the Truman administration for being "anti-Semitic."[52] On March 8 the publicity director of the Democratic National Committee, Jack Redding, told Truman that "we have Zionist Jews in the office every day . . . and the pressure is building up a terrific head of steam." "It's no use putting pressure on the committee," the president replied, "the Palestine issue will be handled here and there'll be no politics."[53]

Despite these strong words, Truman was unable to commit himself to a firm policy. He did, however, manage to hide his personal indecision sufficiently to approve a course suggested by Marshall in early March. As a result of Truman's approval, the final step in reversing the administration's support for the partition of Palestine was taken on March 19, 1948. On that date, in what the New York *Times* described as an atmosphere of "pin-drop silence and bewilderment," the Security Council heard Warren Austin call for the abandonment of efforts to implement partition and for the conversion of Palestine into a UN trusteeship.[54]

Austin argued that since it was now impossible to conceive of the partition plan being implemented in all its parts, a trusteeship would "afford the Jews and Arabs of Palestine, who must live together, further opportunity to reach an agreement regarding the future of that country."[55] The American reversal was made complete by Austin's insistence that a trusteeship "would be without prejudice to the character of an eventual political settlement."[56]

There is a well-worn theory that the Department of State executed this reversal independently of the White House in a conscious effort to force the president into an anti-Zionist commitment.[57] That interpretation is not supported by the evidence. What is true is that Truman was angered and dismayed by Austin's statement. However, the president's reaction can be attributed to a breakdown in communication between the White House and the State Department—an unhappy situation that resulted directly from Truman's failure to keep the department fully apprised of his own vacillation.

At Truman's request, Clark Clifford became the "chief inquisitor" in a secret postmortem investigation to determine who held responsibility for Austin's statement.[58] The trail led to the president.

On March 8 Truman approved a draft of the statement subsequently delivered by Austin. While the text sanctioned by the president was not identical in every respect to Austin's remarks before the Security Council, "it was the same substance." Secretary Marshall immediately forwarded the approved draft to Austin at the United Nations. Eight days later, Marshall directed that the speech be delivered "as soon as Austin believes appropriate." Neither Marshall nor Undersecretary Lovett gave any indication to the American representative in New York that the president was to be informed of the timing of Austin's speech.[59]

In short, the highest officials of the State Department obviously believed Truman had approved the reversal.[60] This impression was transmitted in good faith to Ambassador Austin, who was granted discretion to announce the new policy at an "appropriate" time.

If one dismisses the possibility of calculated duplicity on the part of Marshall and Lovett, there appear to be three possible explanations, which are not mutually exclusive, for Truman's surprised agitation over Austin's statement. First, the president may have misapprehended the substance of the draft he approved prior to March 8. However, in view of the issue's domestic and international importance, this seems hardly likely. Second, Truman may have felt his approval was only tentative and that the matter would be referred to the White House before any action was taken. Since it would have been uncharacteristic for Marshall and Lovett to proceed so decisively had they felt the president's commitment was tentative, the probability in this case appears to be that Truman failed to clarify his attitude to the State Department.[61] Finally, the president may simply have undergone a change of heart after March 8. If this is true, Truman's former haberdashery partner, Eddie Jacobson, may have been instrumental in causing the president to renew his commitment to partition.

By late February, as evidence indicating a possible U.S. policy reversal mounted, Zionists became desperately anxious for an interview with the president. However, Truman adamantly refused to meet with Zionist spokesmen. Eddie Jacobson emerged as the Zionists' only avenue to the White House. In early March the president of B'nai B'rith, Frank Goldman, convinced Jacobson to go to Washington in an effort to arrange a meeting between Truman and Chaim Weizmann.[62] On March 13 Jacobson persuaded Truman to receive Weizmann.[63]

The meeting between the president and Weizmann occurred on March 18. At White House insistence, it was shrouded in secrecy and was strictly "off the record." Truman records only that the encounter was cordial and that it left him with the conviction that the Zionist leader "had reached a full understanding" of his policy.[64] In fact, the president appears to have assured Weizmann that Washington would not cease to support partition. According to Jonathan Daniels, Truman later told Clark Clifford that he "assured Chaim Weizmann that we were for partition and would stick to it."[65] Margaret Truman reveals that on March 19, 1948, her father furiously noted in his daily calendar that Austin's statement placed him "in the position of a liar and a double-crosser."[66] In the same diary entry, Truman complained that the State Department had "pulled the rug" from under him and brooded that "there are people on the third and fourth levels of the State Dept. who have always wanted to cut my throat."[67]

An intimate glimpse of the effect Austin's statement had upon the Truman administration is found in the papers of Truman's press secretary and boyhood friend, Charles G. Ross. Ross was deeply involved in Clifford's inquiry to determine the origins of the statement and kept extensive notes on what transpired immediately after March 19. Upon learning of Austin's statement, Truman's first impulse was to call a special cabinet meeting. However, the idea was dropped for fear that the press might discover and publicize the confusion then reigning in Washington. At this point the president asked Clifford, Ross, and White House appointments secretary Matt Connelly "to get the facts." The three White House men then met with Charles E. Bohlen, counselor of the State Department, and Dean Rusk, director of the Office of Special Political Affairs, to learn the State Department's justification for Austin's statement.[68]

After the factual background to Austin's presentation had been ascertained by Clifford, Ross, and Connelly, a second meeting was held to discuss the options open to the president in light of the reversal at the United Nations. This time Truman himself presided. In addition to Clifford, Ross, and Connelly, the White House was also represented by Oscar Ewing, Howard McGrath, and David Niles.[69] Representing the State Department were Secretary Marshall, Bohlen, and Henderson. The meeting developed into a direct confrontation between those who viewed Palestine primarily as a domestic problem for the Democratic Party and those who perceived it as an international problem for the United States. Ross' notes do not record any remarks by Truman, leaving the impression that the president was content to listen to the discussion among his subordinates. Marshall also appears to have preserved silence, except to declare his readiness to support any course desired by Truman.

The meeting was dominated by the lower-ranking White House and State Department spokesmen. Although the former had no grounds for accusing the department of impropriety in the matter of Austin's statement, signs of deep-seated hostility between the two groups emerged as the meeting turned into a general review of the Palestine problem. Particularly sharp exchanges occurred between Henderson and Niles.

> The whole Palestine problem was reviewed. It seemed clear to us of the P[resident's] Gang that the Dept. had consistently, from whatever motives, dragged its feet (to put it mildly) with respect to the P[resident]'s policy re Palestine. There was keener sensitivity to the British internal situation than to ours. Dave Niles showed his feelings toward Henderson—the atmosphere was charged with the dislike between the two as they exchanged words.[70]

The frustrated anger of Truman's pro-Zionist advisors arose from the realization that the administration would be unable to resume its support of partition. Moreover, Clifford's inquiry had shown that the State Department could not be accused of having acted without proper authorization. Despite Truman's apparent unhappiness, the administration was now committed to press for a trusteeship in Palestine. It was a situation that could be traced directly to Truman's own vacillation. Ross described the problem as seen from the White House:

It was unthinkable that there should be another reversal. He [Truman] had to accept the accomplished fact forced upon him by the precipitate State Department-Austin action. The truth of the matter could not be told. Telling it would have made out the P[resident] as vacillating or ignorant of something of the most vital importance, or both; and the truth, moreover, could only have been accompanied with a wholesale repudiation of the State Department. What a dilemma.[71]

On March 25 Truman issued a carefully drafted statement that offered the following explanation of the administration's new policy:

Unfortunately, it has become clear that the partition plan cannot be carried out at this time by peaceful means. We could not undertake to impose this solution on the people of Palestine by the use of American troops, both on Charter grounds and as a matter of national policy.[72]

In an effort to soothe the outrage he knew would engulf Zionists, Truman declared that Washington was not proposing trusteeship "as a substitute for the partition plan but as an effort to fill the vacuum soon to be created by the termination of the mandate on May 15."[73]

Not surprisingly, this did nothing to reduce the Zionist's sense of betrayal. Rabbi Silver condemned all attempts to retreat from partition and warned that any other form of settlement in Palestine could only be imposed by force.[74] Thirty Republican Representatives demanded a congressional inquiry into the policy reversal.[75] American public opinion strongly disapproved of the indecisiveness that now glaringly characterized the administration's approach.[76]

Under these inauspicious circumstances, the U.S. delegation at the United Nations proceeded to work for the establishment of a trusteeship. On March 30 the United States introduced two resolutions in the Security Council. One called for Arabs and Jews to meet with the Security Council to arrange a truce. The other requested a special session of the General Assembly to consider the Palestine problem. Both were promptly passed.[77] On April 20 the American delegation submitted a draft trusteeship proposal to the General Assembly.[78]

John Fletcher-Cooke, an advisor to the British delegation, recalls that the American plan "never had a chance of getting through the General Assembly."[79] Washington's reversal had antagonized the smaller states whose votes had been so sedulously sought in November. More importantly, the British government was unwilling to assume responsibility for establishing a trusteeship, and the Soviet Union denounced the American reversal as a blow to the authority of the United Nations.[80] Moreover, the Arab countries rejected the American plan as a plot to ensure the eventual establishment of a Jewish state.[81] Finally, most members of the General Assembly were convinced that the United States would not use its own troops to impose a trusteeship.[82] Between the end of April and May 15, the American delegation advanced six more draft resolutions.[83] None received significant support in the General Assembly.

In the meantime, Washington attempted to encourage a truce between Arabs and Zionists as a necessary first step toward the establishment of a trusteeship. Since no compromise was possible between the two antagonists over the question of Jewish statehood, this endeavor failed as well.[84] In early May the Truman administration proposed that the New York representatives of the Jewish Agency, together with the representatives of the United States, France, Belgium, and the Arab states at the United Nations, fly to Palestine for a round-table conference on the Arab-Zionist problem.[85] The president offered his private airplane to transport the entire party to the Middle East.[86] This plan was also rejected by the Arabs and Zionists.

During the six weeks immediately preceding the end of the mandate, Truman's popularity with American Zionists and their supporters plummeted steadily. Democratic Party leaders began to worry that the reversal might destroy Truman's usefulness as the party's standard bearer in 1948.[87] In mid-April the New York Democratic State Committee was unable to say whether or not it would support the president's nomination.[88] Clark Clifford kept in touch with leading Democrats who seemed convinced that the administration's pursuit of a trusteeship would cost Truman the presidency in November.[89]

On April 19 Chaim Weizmann wrote to Truman in an effort to convince him that partition was inevitable. "The clock," cautioned the Zionist leader, "cannot be put back to the situation which existed before November 29."[90] The Zionist military offensive in Palestine seemed to give concrete meaning to Weizmann's words. By the end of April, Zionists and their supporters were urging the administration to act on the basis of the emerging reality in Palestine. Clifford's assistant, Max Lowenthal, prepared a lengthy memorandum arguing that a realistic and domestically fruitful policy for the administration would be the extension of recognition to the Jewish state that would arise in Palestine once British rule ended. Lowenthal urged that the following points merited consideration:

> Present conditions represent a basic change from four and five weeks ago. At that time it was thought American and other troops might be needed to get the Jewish areas [delineated in the UN partition resolution] for the Jews. Now outside troops would be needed only to take away from them what they have already obtained for themselves. As for preventing future attacks by outside Arab states against the Jews, the latter say they can take care of themselves.[91]

Lowenthal suggested that "an announcement, even prior to May 15, that the Government of the United States intends to recognize the new [Jewish] government might bring our country a useful ally and supporter, diminish violence, help [the] U.N.—and at the same time free the Administration of a serious and unfair [domestic political] disadvantage."[92]

On May 13 Weizmann formally informed Truman that the Zionists would proclaim a Jewish state in Palestine. He asked that prompt recognition be given to the provisional government, which would be established at midnight May 15.[93] Leading American Zionists contacted Washington officials with identical requests.[94]

By early May Truman had become visibly irritated by the demands of American Zionists. When a congressional supporter of Zionism urged the White House to take action against Loy Henderson and other State Department officials who, it was claimed, had fallen "into the incredible web of Arabian monopoly and intrigue which has frustrated American high policy," Truman responded sharply:

> Of course, it seems to me that what's sauce for the goose ought to be sauce for the gander. As far as I'm concerned, I don't think there has ever been any more lobbying and pulling and hauling than has been carried by the Jews in this Palestine difficulty. . . . I have no objection to their lobbying—neither have I any objection to the Arabs doing so if they feel like it but, in neither case, does it affect my decisions or judgement.[95]

Despite his growing exasperation, Truman could not ignore the impending proclamation of a Jewish state. On May 12 he summoned domestic and foreign policy advisors to discuss the question of American recognition. Marshall, Lovett, Robert McClintock, and Fraser Wilkins represented the State Department, while Clifford and Niles spoke for the president's staff. The White House men predictably argued on the basis of domestic politics and urged a prompt announcement of intent to recognize the emerging polity. Equally predictable was the position of State Department officials, who advocated a "wait and see" approach that would allow the Jewish regime in Palestine to meet the same test "applied to any new government."[96]

Truman did not make his final decision until sometime on May 14. In the Truman Library is a copy of a letter presumably sent by the president in answer to Weizmann's plea for recognition. Probably typed by a White House secretary on May 14, but advance dated to the 15th, it says simply:

> I appreciated very much your letter of May thirteenth and sincerely hope that the Palestine situation will eventually work out on an equitable and peaceful basis.[97]

At precisely midnight Palestine time, May 14–15, and 6 p.m. Washington time, May 14, the state of Israel was proclaimed and a provisional government assumed office in Tel-Aviv. Eleven minutes later, Truman announced Washington's recognition of the new government as the *de facto* authority of Israel. Almost simultaneously, troops from the countries bordering Palestine began moving against Israeli forces.

The modern involvement of the West in Palestine began ingloriously on the wings of insincere and conflicting promises given by the British government for purposes of political expediency. For Britain, it ended with similar, though more visible, ignominy in the quiet official death of the mandate:

> At nine o'clock the High Commissioner, General Sir Alan Cunningham
> . . . inspected the troops, said good-bye to the Jew and Arab [mayor and deputy mayor of Haifa] and ten minutes later was on his way in a convoy to the port of Haifa. There was no crowd along the route; no one cheered—or jeered. In the port area the Irish Guards were drawn up. The general inspected them. They played God Save the King. The Union Jack was lowered and with the speed of an execution and the silence of a ship that passes in the night British rule in Palestine had come to an end.[98]

American involvement in the Palestine problem was equally without credit. It began and it grew without purpose or direction, nurtured in its tortuous way by shifting appraisals of transitory circumstances. Its end was almost poetically erratic. At the very moment Truman announced Washington's recognition of Israel, American diplomats at the United Nations—who had not been informed of this latest shift in policy—were urging the General Assembly to accept yet another limited trusteeship proposal.[99] It was only when the news was received over a press ticker-tape that the American delegates learned of Truman's action.

15.   CONCLUSION

The gory end of the Palestine mandate produced a legacy of emotional bitterness and conflicting political stands that has colored most of the ensuing history of the Middle East. Added to the basic controversy over the justice of Jewish statehood, there now also exist problems of territory, boundaries, rights of passage, and—above all—the future of a large and politically conscious Palestinian Arab population. Each of these issues serves today as a focal point for conflicting attitudes on the part of Israel, Arab actors, and Great Powers.

It is no exaggeration to say that the past three decades have seen the Middle East develop into one of the most volatile, confused, and confusing political theaters in the world. While by no means all of the area's ills can be ascribed to the Arab-Zionist struggle, not many have escaped its influence. Even the most cursory survey of the Middle East since 1948 demonstrates that few major political, social, or economic trends in Israel or the Arab world can be understood in isolation from Arab-Israeli frictions. The same, of course, is true of the complex network of international relations that has the Middle East as its epicenter.

ROOTS OF AMERICAN RESPONSIBILITY

For the United States, the legacy of Palestine has become an enduring problem of foreign affairs. In the years after 1948, despite the eagerness of American policy makers and the willingness of many Arab leaders to open a new chapter in Arab-American relations, it became evident that the past could not be exorcised. Influenced by partisan recollections, the pressures of the various elements of hostility between Israel and the Arab states, and the development of an acknowledged "special relationship" between the United

States and Israel, the Arab world came to believe that Washington's approach to Palestine had all along been calculated to result in a Jewish state.

To a large extent a similar distortion of history occurred in the United States. The generally close relations between Washington and Israel, a spate of early selective accounts of U.S. policy prior to 1948, and the pro-Israel bias that has colored the American press helped popularize the notion that the American people and government—save for a handful of recalcitrant military and diplomatic functionaries—were committed to the creation of a Jewish state in Palestine.

The inaccuracy of such interpretations is patent and furthers the false assumption that long-term purposefulness underlay American involvement with Palestine. The record, of course, shows that Washington's response to the Arab-Zionist struggle was actually a classic example of short-term policy formulation.

Why was this so? How was it that over a ten-year period the American government failed to settle upon a firm objective or a clear-cut and consistent orientation toward a problem that increasingly demanded attention?

At a relatively high level of generality the answer is that policy makers did not react to the Palestine problem in terms of its essential quality: the struggle for sovereignty between Arabs and Jews. Rather, they were more concerned with the actual and potential ramifications of that issue.

The course of U.S. policy toward Palestine in the decade before Israel's creation can be partly understood in terms of two variables. These are the overall political environment—both foreign and domestic—in which decisions were formulated, and the idiosyncratic elements injected by Roosevelt and Truman into foreign policy.

The international context in which the Roosevelt administration reacted to Palestine was formed by World War II. The overriding, and popularly unassailable, goal of victory was a constant touchstone that lent purposefulness to the administration's open and disguised efforts to defer consideration of Palestine. On the other hand, after Roosevelt's death the American government ceased to enjoy the shelter of a single-track national objective. Not only was Truman more exposed to the pressures that surrounded Palestine, he was also forced to cope with them at the very time that initially ambiguous demands of the Cold War severely complicated the ordering of foreign policy objectives.

In domestic terms both presidents were confronted by rising levels of pro-Zionist agitation that took place without significant public challenge. Even World War II did not allow Roosevelt to escape this. Again, the situation was made more difficult for Truman as pro-Zionist passions spiraled at the war's end, fueled both by revelations of the enormity of Hitler's genocidal campaign and the plight of displaced European Jewish survivors.

The reactions of Roosevelt and Truman to Palestine were influenced by their personalities. Self-confident, patrician, and pragmatic, Roosevelt simultaneously viewed the Palestine problem through the dispassionate eyes of a political realist and the imaginative perspective of a visionary. These traits visibly combined in his efforts to avoid a clear position on Arab-Zionist political tensions and in his attempts to hit upon some formula that would reduce the Palestine issue to less intractable proportions.

Truman not only lacked the protective aura of prestige accumulated by Roosevelt, but also the latter's intellectual gifts. Hearkening back to his rural roots, the "Man from Missouri" took pride in an elemental approach to politics. Unlike his predecessor, he found it difficult to conceive of possible alternatives to existing situations. More than Roosevelt, Truman may have also been influenced by a basic sympathy for the Jewish cause. Although available evidence indicates that he was not committed to the establishment of a Jewish state, it is clear that he exhibited far more interest in and sensitivity to the Zionist case than to the Arab position. Certainly—and here Truman also differed from Roosevelt—his involvement with Palestine is remarkable because of its failure to reveal a single occasion on which he exhibited any appreciation of the Arabs' view of Palestine. Thus, Truman's receptivity to arguments advanced by Eddie Jacobson, his willingness to meet Weizmann "off the record," and to be persuaded by that elderly Zionist's eloquence at a critical moment, and—to some extent—his declared concern for the welfare of European Jewish refugees become intelligible as aspects of a man not motivated solely by political expedience but also by personal sympathy.

Yet American policy toward Palestine between 1939 and 1948 cannot be adequately explained simply by reference to the general political context in which it proceeded and to the personalities of Roosevelt and Truman. It is essential to take into account the American foreign policy process. Without undue simplification, this can be described as occurring within a pyramidal structure having at its base the great mass of the voting public and at its apex the presidency. Between these two extremes fall interest groups, political parties, government organs, and public officials whose function it is to translate political desires into decisions of policy. A review of the values and underlying perspectives brought to bear upon Palestine by these actors leads to several conclusions.

It is evident that the general American public was largely uninformed about, and apathetic toward, the political conflict between Arabs and Jews in Palestine. Only American Zionists and their supporters constituted a group of any consequence primarily interested in Palestine's future. On the other hand, American anti-Zionists were numerically small, politically insignificant, and unable to spark any widespread controversy over the nature of American involvement with Palestine.

As an organized interest group, American Zionism followed a carefully arranged pattern of developing political support. Highly aware of the need to avoid positions that might provide grounds for public opposition, Zionist leaders refrained from requesting active American support in Palestine. Instead, the Zionist Movement worked to bolster its political position vis-a-vis Britain and the Arabs by eliciting limited, but progressively more significant, commitments and endorsements from the American government.

Congress reflected the attitudes of professional party strategists to Zionist pleas. Guided by domestic considerations, members of Congress generally made little effort to understand the conflict in Palestine but proved demonstrably eager to extend political help to American Zionists.

The perspective and the values that determined the reactions of diplomatic and military planners were quite different. Primarily concerned with Palestine's implications for international political and strategic questions, these men constituted the major source of opposition to Zionists. It must be kept in mind, however, that the dominant attitudes of the State Department and Pentagon did not question the intrinsic worth of Jewish sovereignty over Palestine, but only its implications for the United States at particular points in time. Not only did this approach usually not challenge historic and moral arguments advanced by pro-Zionist spokesmen, it also at times led to divisions among the planners themselves. Finally, of course, it was impossible for career Foreign Service or military officers to carry their opinions to any large segment of the public. What debate was kindled by anti-Zionist views in these quarters tended to be confined to the cloistered offices of the White House and, occasionally, to congressional forums.

Near the top of the pyramidal foreign policy process stand cabinet officers and others with ready access to the person ultimately responsible for foreign affairs. In general, the attitudes of presidential advisors speaking out on Palestine varied according to their responsibilities. Personal advisors on international affairs such as Roosevelt's representatives Colonel Hoskins and General Hurley urged that primacy be granted to the long-range value of Arab friendship. Secretaries of State Hull, Stettinius, and Byrnes also advised against supporting Zionism on grounds of the Arab world's strategic and political importance. Secretary Marshall, perhaps recalling Truman's disregard of his predecessors' opinions, took no such clear position on Palestine, although he regularly transmitted his subordinates' warnings to the White House and ultimately opposed the president's early recognition of the Jewish state.

Those more removed from international considerations tended to be more tolerant of possible American support for Zionism. Roosevelt's secretary of the interior and secretary of the treasury were outspoken pro-

Zionists. However, the most consistent and strong supporters of the Zionist cause within the upper levels of policy making were presidential assistants dealing with public relations and domestic political strategy. Thus, Samuel Rosenman, David Niles, and Clark Clifford were prominent spokesmen for the idea that the Democratic Party as well as the president would suffer from a policy opposed by Zionist sentiment.

There was no lessening of this division in the higher ranks of government prior to 1948. It is hardly surprising that the bitter, lengthy, and largely unpublicized contest between the two groups failed to produce a consensus over an approach to Palestine. What was, after all, at issue was not simply a question of alternative responses to a given problem, but rather the definition of the problem itself.

This official impasse formed the immediate context of White House involvement with the Palestine problem. Standing at the pinnacle of the American foreign policy process, the president had the responsibility of adjudicating between the opposing viewpoints and, in doing so, setting forth clear objectives around which a consistent policy might be built. Neither Roosevelt nor Truman accomplished this. In the absence of established priorities between domestic and international considerations, American policy toward Palestine unfolded as a series of discrete responses to whichever set of factors demanded immediate attention. Not only did this provide for the continuation of a divided outlook within the government, it also lay at the root of the inconsistency that marred American involvement with the Palestine problem.

By virtue of their office, Roosevelt and Truman may be held accountable for the course followed by the United States between 1939 and 1948. Yet, given the magnitude of the problem they faced, it is hard to fault their indecisiveness as individuals. Armchair criticism must be tempered by an awareness that neither man reacted to Palestine in a vacuum. Both were saddled with the weight of decision while regularly subjected to contradictory interpretations of political necessity and mutually exclusive concepts of political interest. The problem was only compounded by the fact that the conflicting trends of advice were often propounded by men of established personal integrity and lengthy experience in government.

It is not difficult to imagine that under similar circumstances any occupant of the White House would be tempted to shun the burden of decision in favor of limited steps that might at least reduce the possibility of irrevocable commitment should his choice prove false. That the sequence of such steps in the case of Palestine ultimately led to irreversible consequences does not detract from the compelling properties of the logic that produced them. It is, in other words, one thing to conclude that the American approach to Palestine stands as an example of flawed foreign policy largely because the presidency did not fulfill its role in the foreign policy process, and quite another to explain this simply by "blaming" Roosevelt and Truman.

The indecision that afflicted the presidency was influenced by conditions at lower levels of the pyramidal foreign policy process. It was not in itself unusual that a clash of perspectives, values, and consequent preferences developed over the Palestine question. Generally a recognized feature of policy making in the United States, such confrontations are considered to have the salutary effect of clarifying options and, ultimately, leading to the establishment of firm priorities. In the Palestine case, this was not the outcome. Differences over policy tended to produce only confusion and a prolonged, acrimonious division within government circles. The immediate cause of this was that the chief protagonists, primarily political party strategists on the one hand, and diplomatic and military planners on the other, shared no common ground for discussion. Moreover, each side seemed convinced that its outlook defined the best interests of the United States.

What becomes apparent at this point is the importance to the American decision-making process of an informed and interested public. For it is evident that the burden of the presidency was increased by the absence of popular debate over, and the large amount of apathy toward, Palestine and the developing American role in that country's affairs. As a political group, Zionists functioned efficiently within the boundaries of established procedure in the political system. However, Zionists faced no significant public test; the strategic and political questions that their requests for support raised in the Pentagon and State Department were barely explored in the public light.

As a result, Congress could find little reason to be receptive to State Department and Pentagon arguments. On the other hand, the priorities that the latter two institutions tried to impose upon American policy toward Palestine also remained unchallenged on a broad scale. The president was left facing a static, but vehement, controversy that gave him no guidelines for making decisions, nor any basis other than transitory circumstances for choosing between the opposed suggested perspectives. It is likely that more careful and more extensive public discussion of the Palestine problem and American involvement with that issue would have lent more consistency and purpose to the development of policy between 1939 and 1948.

An assessment of the American approach to Palestine in terms of its consequences for the United States yields mixed results. In certain respects both the Roosevelt and Truman administrations achieved some of the limited objectives that at times motivated them. In his relations with Zionists, Roosevelt proved tactically proficient at placating pro-Zionist domestic sentiment and at hindering the efforts of Zionist leaders to make Palestine a major concern of the government. Through his contacts with Arab leaders, he also did much to allay growing suspicions in the Arab world over American intentions toward Palestine. In the short run, Roosevelt's approach protected his administration's ability to concentrate on the military struggle against the Axis without being seriously distracted by the Palestine problem.

However, in a broader sense his actions were fraught with weighty drawbacks. The conflicting promises given to Arabs and Zionists created future difficulties for the American government. Moreover, the evidence of Roosevelt's basic uncertainty over Palestine was not hidden from Arab and Zionist leaders. In the promises they received from the White House, both sides saw proof that uncompromising positions could be productive in Washington. Finally, the disparity between Roosevelt's private and public attitudes portended future complications.

After 1944 the president's doubts over the wisdom of supporting Zionism were fueled more by the growth of long-term American political, economic, and strategic interests in the Middle East than by tactical wartime requirements. Yet his refusals to countenance Zionist requests were publicly explained in terms of immediate military necessity. The administration never gave a full, open account of the more far-reaching considerations that influenced it. Not only did this lend credibility to Zionist efforts to popularize the belief that the government was basically in favor of a Jewish state in Palestine, it also left Harry Truman in a difficult position when he had to confront the same international factors that had concerned Roosevelt.

As did his predecessor, Truman enjoyed partial success in attaining some of the objectives that at times determined his actions on Palestine. For a short while, for example, the president's ostensibly unadulterated preoccupation with Jewish refugees shielded him from the central political issues around which the Arab-Zionist controversy revolved. Benefitting from a Congress and public that obligingly refused to question the consistency of his approach, Truman propounded a view of Palestine rhetorically based upon an overriding concern for the welfare of displaced Jews without, however, seriously pursuing legislation to alleviate their plight through emigration to the United States. Thus,he avoided embroiling his administration in a controversy over the delicate question of relaxing American immigration laws. Although the president may have personally favored a more liberal immigration policy, his mild and infrequent suggestions along these lines did not really challenge the restrictionist ethos that gave pro-Zionist opinion in the United States a racist tint.

These achievements rather quickly made it even more difficult for the administration to deal with Palestine. The president's demands for massive and unqualified Jewish immigration into that country promptly reduced Washington's flexibility. By late 1946 Truman had become so ensnared by his commitment to press for immigration that the British government lost all hope of coordinating its approach to Palestine with the United States. This led directly to Britain's abandonment of the mandate. On the other hand, the Truman administration's essential acquiescence in the restrictive policies governing immigration into the United States constituted not only an obstacle to Washington's active participation in efforts to promote a comprehensive Palestine settlement, but also a not insignificant irritant in its relations with Britain and the Arab world.

To reiterate that American policy was inconsistent is only to belabor the obvious. Yet one striking instance of self-contradiction must be singled out for special mention. During most of the period reviewed in this book, the American government, at first in terms of immediate requirements and then in light of more extended calculations, viewed the outbreak of an Arab-Jewish war over Palestine as detrimental to the interests of the United States. This perspective, however, was shunted aside during the final crucial months of 1947 and replaced by a willingness to accept an Arab-Zionist explosion as a sad, but not overly significant, event. Washington, it is true, did not look with favor upon war as the price of partitioning Palestine. The United States, in fact, maintained a tenuous hope that Britain might be maneuvered into presiding over partition. Nonetheless, in supporting the UN partition resolution, Washington accepted the probability that London would prefer to abandon Palestine to chaos rather than risk its own interests.

There was a decided air of desperation about this decision to label chaos in Palestine acceptable. It stemmed from the administration's feeling that it could no longer avoid a clear position on Palestine's political future and its fear that any serious effort to provide an orderly conclusion to the mandate would jeopardize American interests. Dazzled by the dilemma, Washington chose to gamble that a breakdown in Palestine would not significantly increase the prospect of a Soviet incursion into the Middle East.

American responsibility for the 1948 outcome of the Arab-Zionist conflict cannot be quantified. Still, it is clear that Washington bore little direct responsibility for the creation of the Jewish state. Although the United States indirectly contributed in various ways to the development of conditions that eventually made Israel a reality, the Jewish state resulted directly from the perseverance, determination, and sacrifice of Palestine's Jewish community that—with the aid of Zionists throughout the world—was able to realize Herzl's ambition.

It is impossible to determine whether partition might have been effected under less anarchic terms or whether between 1939 and 1948 the Palestine problem might have been laid to rest through some ending other than partition. However, this does not alter the fact that the United States bore a significant degree of responsibility for the chaos that gripped Palestine at the end of the mandate. On one level, this responsibility is linked to American policy toward the UN partition plan. Here one must recall both Washington's active role in promoting partition before the General Assembly and its subsequent reversal of policy in early 1948. While the former stemmed from a calculated acceptance of probable anarchy, the latter could only have increased the willingness of the protagonists in the Middle East to disregard the terms of the UN resolution.

On a deeper level, American responsibility for the conflagration that swept Palestine was even more extensive, although perhaps less immediately obvious. Throughout the period considered in this work, American vacillation helped make extremism on the part of Arabs and Jews politically logical. It must be recalled that the uncompromising positions usually assumed by these parties were not immutable. Thus, for example, Zionists reacted to what seemed an impending Anglo-American agreement over a non-Zionist settlement by abandoning the Biltmore Program. Arab spokesmen, on the other hand, responded to their looming defeat at the United Nations by endorsing a federal settlement for Palestine that would have given the country's Jewish community a significant amount of autonomy within specified territorial limits.

Apart from these occasions, Arabs and Zionists acted within a fluid context created by the uncertainty of the two Great Powers most directly involved with Palestine. This attracted each protagonist to fanatical posturing not only as a means of encouraging Great Power support for itself, but at least equally as a defensive tactic to reduce the possibility of support being extended to its opponent.

It was this process of competitive extremism that the British government hoped to reverse with American aid. Sadly, the U.S. approach to Palestine did not permit testing of London's belief that a joint Anglo-American front could provide grounds for some orderly settlement. By the end of 1946 it was plain that Washington had precluded itself from any useful role in a partnership with Britain toward this end.

Between 1939 and 1948, then, the influence of the United States on Palestine was one that exacerbated the explosive trends already existing in that country. Comprising both sins of commission and omission, it was an unfortunate, and ultimately tragic, phenomenon. It was also one that might have been averted had American policy makers been more concerned with the probable repercussions of their actions upon Palestine.

THE PAST AS PRELUDE

The end of the first Arab-Israeli War fostered among the unwary and the wishful-thinking an illusion that the Palestine issue had been resolved. To be sure, Arab-Israeli tensions retained a high visibility in the politics of the Middle East. However, at least the festering structure of the mandate had been removed. The Jewish state, significantly larger than that proposed by the United Nations, demonstrated its vitality. The Arab states on Israel's periphery, although full of vitriol toward their unwelcome neighbor, faced a reality that would not easily be altered. There were, moreover, serious questions as to whether the Arab governments most immediately involved in the war possessed the will or capacity to sustain a prolonged state of hostility with the Jewish polity.

Viewed from abroad, the Middle East in 1949 seemed much like a recently lanced boil, still tender, still sensitive and painful, but at least now open to healing. Time appeared to have lost the threatening quality it carried in the last years of the mandate, when policy toward Palestine seemed forever formulated under the spur of imminent crisis. There was, of course, the considerable problem of Palestinian Arab refugees; but this, initially, also had the aspect of a sore that time would cure.

In Washington the new situation was taken to offer hope of dealing with more important and immediate issues in the Middle East: the incorporation of the Arab world in Western Cold War lines against the Soviet bloc, the preservation and expansion of economic interests, and the development of American political influence. Goodwill (expressed primarily through foreign aid and refugee relief) and patience were optimistically considered the necessary prescription for securing the American position in the Middle East.

It was not long before a comprehensive approach was devised that aimed at permitting the United States to fulfill its commitment to Israel's right to exist (an indisputable moral obligation after 1948) while simultaneously pursuing its ambitions in the Arab world. Essentially, the strategy was to dichotomize American relations with the Middle East so that ties with Israel would not impede those with the Arabs. The two wings of this new policy were given organic unity by the concept of "territorial integrity."

Enshrined in the Tripartite Declaration issued by the United States, Britain, and France in 1950, this principle cast Washington in the role of the Middle East's "territorial policeman." From an American perspective, it allowed power, principle, and fairness at last to be all happily combined in a single broad stance. "Power" was finally put to the service of American interests by virtue of the deterring threat to aggression from any quarter: any party violating "territorial integrity" would challenge the United States. "Principle" was involved in the approach and could serve as a standard for consistent decision making: "territorial integrity," after all, not only enjoyed a positive connotation in international law, before the United Nations, and in the popular vocabulary, but also seemed a secure and objective guide to deterrence. "Fairness," of course, seemed to well from the depths of the self-assumed assignment: a stand in favor of "territorial integrity" promised support to all victims of violation and retribution to all violators of the sacrosanct principle.

For a long while the policy succeeded. Compartmentalizing its approach to the Middle East, despite the vicissitudes of its relations with Israel and the Arab states during the 1950s and 1960s, permitted the United States to gain credible ground. On the one hand, Washington's commitment to Israel's existence was shown to be firm. On the other, despite the failure of early hopes to enlist the Arab world in military arrangements against the Soviet Union, American relations with individual Arab countries progressed rather productively. Even after the regional upheavals of the late 1950s, Washington retained significant political leverage in Egypt, while its influence grew steadily in Saudi Arabia, Jordan, and Lebanon.

After a decade of service as linchpin of the American approach to the Middle East, the Territorial Integrity Formula was basically untarnished. It is true that early, and tentative, efforts by Washington to expand its role of "policeman" into the realm of "peacemaker" by promoting limited or functional rapprochement between the Arabs and Israelis (for example, the "Johnston Plan" and the "Anderson Mission") foundered on the rocks of suspicion and discord.[1] Yet American policy makers could draw comfort from the thought that the projects appeared to have received respectful hearings. Only time, it seemed, was required before passions cooled sufficiently to allow Arab and Israeli self-interest to remove the need for the separate containers into which Washington's Middle East policy was divided.

This conviction remained unshaken when the Territorial Integrity Formula met its test at Suez in 1956. With the other policemen having deserted the force in hope of looting the canal, Washington retained its own badge, and its policy, by requiring the aggressors to withdraw.

Yet only 11 years after the Suez War the Territorial Integrity Formula was suddenly shown up as meaningless. The reasons for this are found on two levels. At the most shallow of these not-so-profound depths, it is clear that the 1967 Arab-Israeli War erupted because three key assumptions of the Territorial Integrity Formula were falsified by events. The first of these was the belief that time was beneficial, that Arab-Israeli tensions, if prevented from bursting into open warfare, would eventually abate to the point of permitting overall diplomatic harmony in the Middle East. What was, in fact, demonstrated throughout the period 1948–67 was that day-to-day relations between the two sides, whether conducted on the basis of border raids, retaliatory strikes, or verbal posturing, offered no scope for a diminution of hostile feelings.

Second, it was held that sponsorship of "territorial integrity" would cause Washington to be perceived as a concerned neutral in terms of the Arab-Israeli quarrel. This, on the one hand, could not ring true to the Arabs, who saw in the American position more of a commitment to an unjust status quo than to a matter of principle. By the same token, various aspects of

American-Israeli relations between 1950 and 1967—prominently including foreign aid and UN voting patterns—left no doubt about the true nature of American sympathies in the Middle East.

The third false assumption underlying the pre-1967 approach was that it established grounds for the objective identification of "aggression." This was finally proved false by the cycles of raid-counterraid that heralded the war of 1967. Simply put, in the climate of violence between Arabs and Israelis, the distinction between the intention and the act of territorial violation all but evaporated.

It is not overly difficult to discover why the underpinnings of the Territorial Integrity Formula gave way. One has only to descend to a slightly deeper level of analysis to see that the approach was consciously devised to shield Washington from the essential problem that remained at the source of Arab-Zionist enmity: Palestine's political future. Thus, in consequence of the "territorial integrity" strategy, the problematical issues of borders (the lines separating Israel from its Arab neighbors after 1949 were actually only armistice lines), the implications of the unborn Palestinian Arab state called for by the 1947 partition resolution, the definitive status of supposedly internationalized Jerusalem, and—above all—the future of the Palestinian Arab people were essentially placed beyond Washington's official consideration.

In retrospect the lesson of 1967 is clear. The 1948 Arab-Jewish War may have lanced the Middle East boil, but it did not touch the root infection. The question of whether Arab or Jew, or whether in some way both, would prevail in Palestine remained very much alive. The relative "stability" provided until 1967 by the Territorial Integrity Formula had only masked the rising inflammation in the Middle East. Neither Arabs, many of whom clung to the goal of undoing the Jewish state, nor Israelis, among whom significant numbers hoped to extend their control to the remnant of Palestine in Arab hands after 1949, did much to defuse the situation.

It is no coincidence that after 1967 the Palestinian Arabs burst forth upon the Middle East in a way that would not have been expected a few years earlier. The passage of time had allowed the Palestinians to overcome the trauma of their original displacement. By 1967 the dispossessed, confused, and fearful refugees had laid the foundations of a purposeful, committed, and organized national movement.

Washington did not recognize the political significance of Palestinian consciousness and organization in its response to the 1967 war. It was, however, quick to acknowledge the more superficial flaws of "territorial integrity." This was evident only days after the cessation of hostilities when President Lyndon Johnson announced a five-point package of principles for peace that constituted a new American approach to the Middle East. The import of Johnson's message was that the United States had abandoned its long-held goal of stabilizing the Arab-Israeli quarrel and would, instead, seek a definitive solution to the problem. However, only one of the five points alluded to the Palestinians—and this merely upheld the need to grant justice to "the refugees." The bulk of the White House message focused on points of contention between Israel and the Arab states. While claiming the new role of "honest broker"—to replace the collapsed one of "territorial policeman"—Washington assumed that the Middle East problem was confined to the context of interactions among sovereign states. From the outset this view implicitly relegated the Palestinian Arabs to the status of objects of, rather than subjects in, any political process that might lead to a settlement.

Much of the tangled political maneuvering among parties to the Middle East conflict, and most of the running series of bloody incidents that have riddled the region since 1967, can be linked to the Palestinians' insistence on recognition as a primordial participant group enjoying the right to pursue its demands on Palestine as best it may. The implications of that notion have not only met with predictable Israeli resistance but also with opposition from Great Powers and Arab regimes that perceived Palestinian nationalism as a threat to the regional status quo.

The results of the Palestinians' campaign are not yet fully in. Still, their offensive has achieved some undeniable success. With the Rabat Conference of 1974, the Arab world acknowledged the Palestine Liberation Organization (PLO) as the legitimate representative of the Palestinian people. Many states the world over have since followed suit. West European nations have urged the PLO's association with any peace process in the Middle East. In short, the Palestinian Arabs have managed to step from the darkened recesses of refugee hovels and gain significant recognition as political actors in their own right. It is notable that these limited political advances have been accompanied by a growing PLO reliance on diplomatic means to further its cause.

Whether this still-developing political identity is to mature in a way that will permit a peaceful solution in the Middle East—that is, to the point of recognizing and accepting Israel's sovereignty—remains problematical. The answer will depend upon many things, among which—if the past is in any sense actually a prelude—three are key. These are, first, the dynamics of internal Palestinian politics, which in the final analysis will be determined by the confluence of political ambitions and objective appraisals of political reality. The second determinant will be the policies adopted by Israel—policies that have so far left no doubt that expansionist visions vie with dreams of peace as the final arbiter of that country's destiny. Finally, there are the policies of third parties, whose attitudes may or may not help establish clear limits that will discredit the maximum goals of both principals and thereby encourage each to search out some ground for accommodation.

While Palestinians have been emerging from the shadows after 1967, the United States has been trying to serve as "peace broker," a facilitator of negotiated settlements between Israel and the Arab states. American policy makers have emphasized a commitment to Israel's security and well-being, but have remained notably vague on the nature of the settlement they wish to see evolve. Specifically, of course, this has cast doubt upon the nature and extent of Israeli concessions that Washington feels are required by American interests.

To date, apparently significant progress toward peace has occurred only between Israel and Egypt. While the importance of this should not be minimized, neither should it be exaggerated. It is worth recalling that American diplomacy first moved toward a clearer definition of what it sought in— and what the United States would contribute toward—an Egyptian-Israeli settlement only when prodded by the limited war Cairo launched in 1973. On the other hand, progress toward peace on the Egyptian-Israeli front has been possible only because Egypt, Israel, and the United States agreed to defer consideration of the issues at the heart of the Middle East dispute: the final territorial limits of Israel and the political future of the Palestinian Arabs.

It cannot be doubted that the new Egyptian-Israeli relationship may ultimately be overturned by failure of the two governments to reach a firm accord on these central problems. It seems equally probable that if this threat is to be averted it will become increasingly necessary for Washington to specify the parameters of its own vision of a comprehensive Middle East settlement. This can be done only by establishing—in far more precise terms than have yet been used—an American position regarding territorial questions and the Palestinians' political future.

The fact that American diplomacy since the June (1967) War has been characterized by a refusal to confront these issues raises disturbing parallels between the present and two earlier periods of U.S. involvement with the Middle East conflict. Just as the Territorial Integrity Formula erected a barrier between Washington and the basic political tensions between Arabs and Jews prior to 1967, so too did the various tactics adopted after 1939 by the administrations reviewed in this book. In neither case were American interests ultimately served.

If there is a major lesson to be gleaned from the history of American involvement with the Palestine problem, it is that power—whether defined in terms of moral suasion and prestige, political or economic leverage, or military resources—is apt to be nullified in the absence of a concrete and specific objective. Great Powers that failed to relate their objectives in Palestine directly to the points at issue between Zionists and the Arab world have in the past been dragged along by the flow of events into situations that were quite literally of the "no-win" variety. There is no reason to suspect that this peril has been eliminated.

Almost as these lines are written the lesson is being driven home with particular ferocity, and there emerge incipient signs that Washington may at last heed history's stern instruction. The 1982 Israeli-PLO War in Lebanon may mark a watershed in the U.S. approach to the Palestine problem. Certainly, Israel's invasion of Lebanon—with its high cost in civilian lives—and the ensuing massacre of unarmed Palestinian refugees in Israeli-occupied Beirut have, for the moment, highlighted Washington's lack of influence over events for which it must share responsibility. Articulate public opinion in the United States has reacted largely in a spirit that questions the policies that led to this situation. President Ronald Reagan's announcement in September of a new departure in American policy reflected a growing disillusionment with a "peacemaking" strategy that has given so little indication of the nature of the peace supposedly being pursued.

The Reagan initiative followed guidelines set by earlier administrations by rejecting *a priori* the creation of a Palestinian Arab state. Nonetheless, it seemed to move the United States closer to a firm concept of the territorial outlines within which a Palestinian-Israeli peace must evolve as well as toward a clear willingness to recognize Palestinian nationalism as a force that must be dealt with politically. At almost the same time, another harbinger of what perhaps is a changing Middle East equation was found in the extensive domestic Israeli opposition to the war in Lebanon. To its profound credit, a large segment of Israel's population reacted with horrified outrage to the possibility that its government could only see Palestinian national consciousness as an obstacle to be eliminated regardless of the human cost.

Both phenomena, the apparent American shift to a more specific statement of the political values that must be upheld in a Middle East settlement and the Israeli outcry against any hint that brute force and tactics bordering on the genocidal have become the Jewish State's only recourse, give hope that key protagonists in the Middle East drama will ultimately accept the Palestinian Arab people as a nation to whom the principle of self determination should be applied.

Yet the depressing history of the Zionist-Arab struggle is sufficient to engender caution. Moderation has frequently been the victim of extremism, and American policy has not been marked by determination or consistency.

The re-emergence of the Palestinian Arabs underscores the endurance of the problem that destroyed the mandate in chaotic bloodshed: whether one or the other, or somehow both, of the two peoples claiming Palestine will achieve unquestionable political dominance in that ancient land. The continued failure of involved third parties to answer this query in meaningful terms is likely to further circumstances that once again will entail only suffering for

Arabs and Israelis alike. It is also impossible to ignore the additional danger that further explosions in the Middle East may eventually engulf vastly larger areas of the world.

Pinned among his daily, immediate concerns, Eliot's Prufrock shied from overwhelming questions and measured his span in coffee spoons—all the while predicting:

> And time yet for a hundred indecisions,
> And for a hundred visions and revisions,
> Before the taking of a toast and tea.

Straining for optimism, one casts doubtful mental glances at the contemporary Middle East and wonders . . . is there?

NOTES

NOTES TO CHAPTER 1

1. Frank E. Manuel, *The Realities of American-Palestine Relations* (Washington, D.C.: Public Affairs Press, 1949), p. 169.

2. Esco Foundation for Palestine, Inc., *Palestine, A Study of Jewish, Arab and British Policies*, 2 vols. (New Haven, Conn.: Yale University Press, 1947), I:107–08.

3. A brief exception to the general aloofness that characterized the American approach to Palestine was the King-Crane Commission of 1919. The most comprehensive account of this episode in early U.S. policy toward Palestine can be found in Harry N. Howard, *The King-Crane Commission* (Beirut: Khayat, 1963).

4. Early sympathetic, but essentially noncommittal, pronouncements on Zionism by American policy makers can be found in Reuben Fink, ed., *America and Palestine* (New York: American Zionist Emergency Council, 1944).

5. U.S. Congress, *Congressional Record*, Proceedings and Debates, 67th Cong., 2d Sess., June 30, 1922, p. 9799.

6. Convention between the United States and Great Britain, reproduced in Fink, p. 485.

7. For a detailed exposition of the view that guided Washington's assessment of the 1924 Anglo-American Convention on Palestine, see Wallace Murray to Cordell Hull, June 17, 1940, 867n.01/1714, National Archives of the United States, General Records of the Department of State, Record Group 59, 1940–44. (Hereafter cited as N.A.)

8. Manuel, p. 307.

9. Robert L. Daniels, *American Philanthropy in the Near East* (Athens: Ohio University Press, 1970), pp. 17–40.

10. John De Novo, *American Interests and Politics in the Middle East* (Minneapolis: University of Minnesota Press, 1963), pp. 197–99.

11. The original name of the American operation in Saudi Arabia was the California-Texas Company (Caltex). This was altered to Arabian-American Oil Company in 1943. Benjamin Shwadran, *The Middle East, Oil and the Great Powers* (New York: Council for Middle Eastern Affairs Press, 1959), p. 320.

12. De Novo, pp. 204–06, 384–89.

13. Ibid., pp. 361–63.

14. Karl Twitchell, *Saudi Arabia* (Princeton, N. J.: Princeton University Press, 1947), p. 154; De Novo, pp. 363–64.

15. Barnet Litvinoff, *To the House of Their Fathers: A History of Zionism* (New York: Frederick A. Praeger, 1965), p. 81; Israel Cohen, *A Short History of Zionism* (London: Frederick Muller, 1951), pp. 40–56.

16. Esco Foundation, I:82; Leonard Stein, *The Balfour Declaration* (London: Vallentine Mitchell, 1961), pp. 117–30.

17. Stein, pp. 237–39.

18. Esco Foundation, I:75.

19. J. M. N. Jeffries, *The Balfour Declaration* (Beirut: Institute for Palestine

Studies, 1969), p. 9.

20. Great Britain, Parliament, *Parliamentary Debates* (House of Commons), 5th Series, Vol. 433, col. 1915. Address by Ernest Bevin.

21. Mandate for Palestine, reproduced in The Royal Institute of International Affairs, *Great Britain and Palestine 1915-1944*, Information Papers No. 20, 3rd ed. (London: Oxford University Press, 1946), Appendix II, pp. 151-55.

22. J. C. Hurewitz, *The Struggle for Palestine* (New York: W. W. Norton, 1950), p. 41.

23. Joseph B. Schechtman, *The United States and the Jewish State Movement* (New York: Herzl Press, 1966), p. 59.

24. Walid Khalidi, ed., *From Haven to Conquest* (Beirut: The Institute for Palestine Studies, 1971), Appendix I, "Population, Immigration, and Land Statistics, 1919-1946"; Litvinoff, p. 186.

25. Cohen, p. 135.

26. Hurewitz, pp. 41-42.

27. Albert Hourani, *Arabic Thought in the Liberal Age, 1798-1939* (London: Oxford University Press, 1962), pp. 285-87.

28. George Antonious, *The Arab Awakening* (London: Hamish Hamilton, 1938), pp. 130-34; Anthony Nutting, *The Arabs* (New York: Mentor Books, 1964), p. 276.

29. Nutting, p. 290. For an interesting, involved, and ultimately unconvincing attempt to establish the opposing view, see Isaiah Friedman, *The Question of Palestine, 1914-1918* (London: Routledge & Kegan Paul, 1973), pp. 65-96.

30. Nutting, p. 293.

31. Khalidi, "Memorandum by Mr. Balfour Respecting Syria, Palestine and Mesopotamia, 1919," p. 208.

32. Text of resolutions reproduced in Antonious, Appendix G.

33. Fannie Fern Andrews, *The Holy Land Under the Mandate*, 2 vols. (Boston: Houghton Mifflin, 1931), I:74-75.

34. Ibid. See also Yehoshua Porath, *The Emergence of the Palestinian-Arab National Movement 1918-1929* (London: Frank Cass, 1974), pp. 70-122.

35. Great Britain, cmd. 1540, 1921, Palestine, "Disturbances in May, 1921. Report of the Commission of Inquiry with Correspondence Relating thereto," Appendix B, "Medical Statistics."

36. Ibid., Appendix A, Resume, p. 59.

37. Great Britain, Correspondence with the Palestinian Arab Delegation and the Zionist Organization, presented to Parliament by Command of His Majesty, June 1922. See also Andrews, II:83-188.

38. Hurewitz, p. 60.

39. Ibid., pp. 57-63.

40. Great Britain, Report of the Commission on the Palestine Disturbances of August, 1929, Cmd. 3530 (London: His Majesty's Stationery Office, 1930), p. 129.

41. Esco Foundation, I:341, 360; Hurewitz, p. 31.

42. Great Britain, Palestine, Report on Immigration, Land Settlement, and Development, Sir John Hope Simpson, Cmd. 3686 (London: His Majesty's Stationery Office, 1930), pp. 54-55.

43. Nevill Barbour, *Nisi Dominus* (London: George G. Harrap, 1946), pp. 151–64.

44. Great Britain, Report of the Commission on the Palestine Disturbances of August, 1929, Cmd. 3530 (London: His Majesty's Stationery Office, 1930), p. 155.

45. Ibid., pp. 130–31.

46. Great Britain, Palestine, Report on Immigration, p. 56.

47. Hurewitz, p. 22.

48. Samuel Halperin, *The Political World of American Zionism* (Detroit: Wayne State University Press, 1961), p. 331.

49. Hurewitz, pp. 67–68.

50. David Waines, *The Unholy War* (Montreal: Chateau Books, 1971), pp. 84–87.

51. John Marlowe's description of the Arab revolt is worth repeating in this connection:

> Somehow or other, whether as a result of propaganda by Haj Amin and his minions, or of more complex and less identifiable forces, the last dying embers of the spirit of Jihad were . . . fanned into a flame which was, for a few short years, to glow. . . . Although instigated, and to some extent guided, and certainly used, by the political leaders of Arab Palestine, the Arab rebellion was in fact a peasant revolt, drawing its enthusiasm, its heroism, its organization and its persistence from sources within itself which have never been properly understood.

The Seat of Pilate (London: The Cresset Press, 1959), p. 137.

52. Waines, p. 90.

53. Government of Palestine, *A Survey of Palestine*, 3 vols. (Palestine: Government Printer, 1946), II:49.

54. Waines, p. 81; Hurewitz, p. 83. The revolt's degeneration into bloody confrontations among Arab factions is particularly well chronicled in Yehoshua Porath, *The Palestinian Arab National Movement; From Riots to Rebellion.* (London: Frank Cass, 1977), pp. 249–60.

55. Hurewitz places the upper range of Arabs killed during this period at approximately 5,000 (p. 112). Khalidi estimates the total as 5,032 (Appendix IV).

56. Wadsworth to the Secretary of State, January 8, 1940, Despatch 1187, 867n.01/1685, N.A., 1940–44.

57. Hurewitz, p. 73.

58. Ibid., pp. 78–80.

59. Christopher Sykes, *Crossroads to Israel* (London: Collins, 1965), pp. 211–13.

60. Ibid.

61. Hurewitz, p. 96.

62. Chaim Weizmann, *Trial and Error* (New York: Harper and Brothers, 1949), pp. 401–02.

63. Esco Foundation, II:891–92.

64. Ibid.

65. Great Britain, *Parliamentary Papers 1938–39*, Cmd. Paper 6019 (London: His Majesty's Stationery Office, 1939).

NOTES TO CHAPTER 2

1. Schechtman, p. 93.

2. Saul Friedman, *No Haven for the Oppressed* (Detroit: Wayne State University Press, 1973), pp. 17–83; Robert Silverberg, *If I Forget Thee O Jerusalem* (New York: William Morrow, 1970), pp. 158–59; Schechtman, pp. 93–95.

3. Michael A. Dohse, "American Periodicals and the Palestine Triangle April 1936 to February 1947" (Ph.D. dissertation, Mississippi State University, 1966). See especially pp. 241–43.

4. New York *Times*, January 16, 1939.

5. Ibid.

6. New York *Times*, February 28, 1939.

7. New York *Times*, March 9, 13, 16; April 9, 1939.

8. John Morton Blum, *Roosevelt and Morgenthau* (Boston: Houghton Mifflin, 1970), pp. 518–19.

9. New York *Times*, January 3, 1947. Funds collected by the United Jewish Appeal (UJA) were allocated for both Zionist and non-Zionist purposes. After 1942 the proportion of UJA funds assigned to the official Zionists grew steadily and rapidly—expanding from 29.2 percent in 1942 to 45.5 percent in 1948. In 1947 alone, Zionists received $56 million from the UJA. In 1948 the same source provided Zinoists with $70 million. Halperin, pp. 212–13.

10. New York *Times*, January 24, 1938.

11. New York *Times*, December 19, 1938.

12. Ickes to George M. Barakat, April 29, 1941, Private Papers of George M. Barakat, Centerville, Massachusetts.

13. Helen Shirley Thomas, *Felix Frankfurter* (Baltimore: Johns Hopkins University Press, 1960), pp. 23–26.

14. Liva Baker, *Felix Frankfurter* (New York: Coward-McCann, 1969), pp. 83–100.

15. Frankfurter to Roosevelt, November 25, 1938, in *Roosevelt and Frankfurter: Their Correspondence, 1928–1945*, annotated by Max Freedman (Boston: Little Brown, 1967), p. 466.

16. For some unexplained reason, Frankfurter destroyed the extensive correspondence he engaged in with the president during the spring and summer of 1939.

17. Freedman, p. 451. See also Charles A. Madison, *Eminent American Jews* (New York: Federick Unger, 1970), p. 300.

18. David Ben Gurion, "What Roosevelt Told Us," *Jewish Observer and Middle East Review* 12, no. 36 (September 6, 1963):14.

19. Esco Foundation, II:899–900.

20. Brandeis to Roosevelt, March 16, 1939, Franklin Delano Roosevelt Library, Hyde Park, New York (hereafter cited as FDRL) President's Secretary's File (PSF), Box 62.

21. Roosevelt to Brandeis, March 23, 1939, in ibid.

22. United States, Department of State, *Foreign Relations of the United States, 1939-1947* (Washington D.C.: U.S. Government Printing Office, 1955–73), 1939, vol. IV, p. 737. (Hereafter cited as FRUS.)

23. Ibid., p. 738.

24. Paul L. Hanna, *British Policy in Palestine* (Washington, D.C.: American Council on Public Affairs, 1942), p. 147.

25. The Royal Institute, *Great Britain and Palestine, 1915-1944*, p. 124.

26. Such, for example, was the assessment of Bert Fish, the American minister in Cairo. See Bert Fish to the Secretary of State, April 20, 1939, 867n.01/562, N.A., 1930-39.

27. Ben Gurion, "What Roosevelt Told Us," p. 14.

28. Unsigned cable from the Jewish Agency, London, to American Zionists, April 16, 1939, PSF Palestine, Box 62, FDRL.

29. Brandeis to Roosevelt, April 17, 1939, in ibid.

30. Ben Gurion, "What Roosevelt Told Us," p. 15.

31. Ibid.

32. Ibid.

33. Ibid.

34. Orville H. Bullitt, ed., *For the President, Personal and Secret: Correspondence Between Franklin D. Roosevelt and William C. Bullitt* (Boston: Houghton Mifflin, 1972), pp. 347-48.

35. Weizmann to Roosevelt, May 8, 1939, 867n.01/1542B, N.A., 1930-39.

36. Brandeis to Roosevelt, May 4, 1939, 867n.01/1548, N.A., 1930-39.

37. Weizmann to Roosevelt, May 8, 1939, 867n.01/1542B, N.A., 1930-39.

38. Manuel, p. 276.

39. Hurewitz, p. 226.

40. U.S. Congress, *Congressional Record*, Proceedings and Debates of the 76th Congress, First Session, Vol. 84, Part 3, Senate (Washington, D.C.: U.S. Government Printing Office, 1939), March 16, 1939, p. 2799.

41. Ibid., March 17, 1939, p. 2915.

42. Ibid., May 19, 1939, pp. 5798-5806.

43. Ibid., House, May 22, 1939, p. 5901; May 23, 1939, p. 5997.

44. Ibid., May 22, 1939, pp. 5930-31.

45. Ibid., May 25, 1939, p. 6167.

46. Ben Gurion, "What Roosevelt Told Us," p. 14.

47. Ibid.

48. A good description of the major factors that tended to generate popular resistance to liberalization of restrictive American immigration laws on the eve of World War II is found in David S. Wyman, *Paper Walls* (Amherst: The University of Massachusetts Press, 1968), pp. 3-27. See also Saul Friedman, pp. 17-36.

49. Ibid., p. 31.

50. Fink, p. 129.

51. Ibid., p. 369.

52. Ibid., p. 210.

53. Murray to Hull and Welles, February 9, 1939, 867n.01/1431 1/2, N.A., 1930-39.

54. Hull to Kennedy, March 2, 1939, 867n.01/1458, N.A., 1930-39.

55. Welles to Murray, May 5, 1939, 867n.01/1431 1/2, N.A., 1930-39. Welles described his views on Zionism in his book, *We Need Not Fail* (Cambridge, Mass.: Riverside Press, 1948).

56. Cordell Hull, *Memoirs*, 2 vols. (New York: Macmillan, 1948), II:1528.

57. Murray to Hull, March 25, 1939, 867n.01/1595, N.A., 1930-39.

58. Berle to Roosevelt, May 25, 1939, 867n.01/1602 1/2, N.A., 1930-39.

59. Hull, II, p. 1537.

60. Walter Millis and E. S. Duffield, eds, *The Forrestal Diaries* (New York: Viking Press, 1951), p. 346.

61. Weizmann, pp. 431-32.

62. Ibid.; Bartley Crum, *Behind the Silken Curtain* (New York: Simon and Schuster, 1947), p. 36.

63. Weizmann, p. 425.

64. See Dean Acheson's account of the "old" State Department as he experienced it in 1941 upon becoming assistant secretary of state: *Present at the Creation* (New York: W. W. Norton, 1969), Chapter II, particularly pp. 17-18.

65. See, for example, New York *Times*, August 22, 1946; and June 23, 1948. Interview with Loy W. Henderson, October 22, 1973, Washington, D.C.

66. Evan M. Wilson, "The Palestine Papers, 1943-1947," *Journal of Palestine Studies* 2, no. 4 (Summer 1973):45.

67. Ibid., p. 35.

68. A revealing aspect of Murray's involvement with the Palestine question was the supportive role he played in a rather curious scheme set in motion by Edward A. Norman, a retired Jewish-American businessman. Norman's elaborate plan, first formulated in the mid-1930s, sought to promote a massive migration of Palestinian Arabs to Iraq. As a first step, Norman hoped to implant the idea in the minds of Iraqi leaders. By 1938 Norman had enlisted the aid of various prominent persons in the United States and Britain, as well as the interest of Zionist leaders. He had also dispatched a privately employed "secret agent" to Iraq for the purpose of subliminally convincing Iraqi leaders of the value of massive Palestinian Arab immigration. After 1938, Norman regularly kept the White House and the State Department informed of his maneuvers. After the 1939 London Conference, Norman reported that leading members of Arab delegations had suggested to him the outlines of his own plan. At the close of the conference, Norman was invited to Iraq for further consultations. However, the outbreak of the war ended Norman's efforts on behalf of his scheme.

Had Murray and his colleagues been basically opposed to a Jewish state, they could have been expected to deal roughly with Norman's bizarre plan. Yet their reports on Norman's endeavors were remarkably free of criticism. A review of documentary evidence of Norman's plan indicates that Murray and his subordinates felt no harm could come from encouraging Norman on the off chance that he might strike upon an effective formula to resolve Arab-Zionist tensions in Palestine. "First Report on Iraq Scheme, May 5, 1938, by Edward A. Norman," 867n.01/1618; Memorandum of Conversation Between Edward A. Norman and Paul Alling, November 16, 1938, 867n.01/1618; "Second Report on Iraq Scheme, May 15, 1939, by Edward A. Norman," 867n.01/1618; Memorandum of Conversation Among Wallace Murray, Paul Alling and Edward A. Norman, June 7, 1939, 867n.01/1618; Wallace Murray to Sumner Welles, June 15, 1939, 867n.01/1618; Sumner Welles to Edward A. Norman, August 3, 1939, 867n.01/1649, N.A., 1930-39.

69. Roosevelt to Hull and Welles, May 10, 1939, 867n.01/1542B, N.A., 1930-39.

70. Welles to Roosevelt, May 6, 1939, 867n.01/1548, N.A., 1930–39.

71. Roosevelt to Brandeis, May 9, 1939, 867n.01/1548, N.A., 1930–39.

72. FRUS, 1939, Vol. IV, p. 757.

73. Actually, between 1920 and 1939, 306,049 Jews immigrated into Palestine, while during the same period the figure for Arab immigration was 18,630. *Survey of Palestine*, I:185.

NOTES TO CHAPTER 3

1. Weizmann, p. 418.

2. David Ben Gurion, "We Look to America," *Jewish Observer and Middle East Review*, January 31, 1964.

3. Halperin, pp. 50–51.

4. Ibid., p. 48; Harry S. Linfield, "The Jewish Population in the United States," *The American Jewish Yearbook, 1942–43* (Philadelphia: Jewish Publication Society, 1942), pp. 419–25.

5. *New Palestine*, July 7, 1939.

6. Weizmann, pp. 420–21.

7. Ibid.

8. Ibid.

9. Ben Gurion, "We Look to America."

10. Ibid., original emphasis.

11. Ibid.

12. Halperin, p.8.

13. Ben Halpern, *The Idea of the Jewish State* (Cambridge, Mass: Harvard University Press, 1961), p. 20.

14. Alan Taylor, *Prelude to Israel* (New York: Philosophical Library, 1959), p. viii.

15. James Yaffe, *The American Jews* (New York: Random House, 1968), pp. 4–19; Halperin, pp. 10–11.

16. Ibid.

17. Ibid., Appendix I, pp. 318–20.

18. Cohen, p. 125.

19. Halpern, p. 198.

20. Schechtman, p. 59.

21. Halperin, p. 155.

22. Ibid., p. 119.

23. Halpern, p. 205.

24. Between 1922 and 1929 Americans constituted only 3% of Jewish immigrants into Palestine. During the next decade the proportion fell to less than 2% and after 1939 averaged less than 1%. *Survey of Palestine*, I, p. 186.

25. Halperin, pp. 209–20.

26. Nahum Goldmann, *The Autobiography of Nahum Goldmann* (New York: Holt, Rinehart and Winston, 1969), p. 200.

27. Ben Gurion, "What Roosevelt Told Us," p. 16.

28. Ben Gurion, "We Look to America."

29. Ibid, original emphasis.

30. Goldmann, p. 221.

31. Richard P. Stevens, *American Zionism and U.S. Foreign Policy, 1942–1947* (Beirut: Institute for Palestine Studies, 1970), p. 25.

32. Halperin, p. 269.

33. Silverberg, pp. 193–94.

34. David Ben Gurion, *Ben Gurion Looks Back in Talks with Moshe Pearlman* (New York: Simon and Schuster, 1965), pp. 111–12.

35. Silverberg, p. 195.

36. Morris D. Waldman, *Nor by Power* (New York: International Universities Press, 1953), pp. 210–24.

37. Goldmann, p. 222.

38. Stevens, pp. 10–11.

39. Ibid.

40. Ibid., pp. 30–31; Halperin pp. 270–72.

41. An earlier version of the APC existed for a short while in 1932.

42. Stevens, p. 29.

43. Memorandum of Telephone Conversation, October 14, 1938, OF 700, FDRL.

44. Wise to Wagner, January 26, 1941; Wagner to Wise, January 28, 1941, Robert F. Wagner Collection, Georgetown University Library, Box 104. (Hereafter cited as Wagner Papers.)

45. Wagner to Senator W. J. Bulow, February 5, 1941, Wagner Papers.

46. Neumann to Levy, March 9, 1941, Wagner Papers.

47. Halperin, pp. 182–83; New York *Times*, March 28, 1941.

48. New York *Times*, May 1, 1941.

49. Halperin, p. 182.

50. Neumann to Levy, May 21, 1942, Wagner Papers.

51. Wagner to Bishop C. Ven Pilcher, May 17, 1945, Wagner Papers.

52. *Plan for Cooperation of World Pro-Palestine Committees* (Washington, D.C.: International Conference for Palestine, 1945).

53. Minutes of the World Committee for Palestine, January 11, 1946, Wagner Papers.

54. Director of Finances of the Jewish Agency.

55. Member of the Executive of the Jewish Agency; Comptroller of the Jewish National Fund.

56. Personal Political Representative of Chaim Weizmann in the United States; Secretary-General of the Jewish Agency's "American Section," 1943–46.

57. Member of the Jewish Agency Executive; Head of the Jewish Agency's Middle East Division, Political Department (1934–45); Director of the Jewish Agency Political Department, Washington, 1945–48.

58. The minutes of the WPC meeting record the presence of "Moshe Toff," undoubtedly a misspelling of Moshe Tov. Tov was a leading Latin American Zionist based in Argentina. Between 1945 and 1948 he served as Director of the Latin American Section of the Jewish Agency.

59. Neumann to Levy, May 21, 1942, Wagner Papers.

60. Louis E. Levinthal to R. Szold, December 18, 1942; Lilan Mond to David Delman, October 16, 1944, Wagner Papers.

61. A. S. Magida to David Delman, October 16, 1944, Wagner Papers.

62. Arthur Lourie to Philip Levy, December 31, 1942; see also unsigned note from AZEC offices attached to J. Grew to Wagner, February 3, 1945, Wagner Papers.

63. Unsigned letter from Zionist Organization of America Headquarters to Philip Levy, May 21, 1942, Wagner Papers.

64. LeSourd to Wagner, March 16, 1946, Wagner Papers.

65. Manson to Delman, August 25, 1944; Delman to Manson, August 29, 1944; Wagner to LeSourd, November 20, 1946, Wagner Papers.

66. Khalidi to Wagner, June 10, 1946, Wagner Papers.

67. Wagner to Roosevelt, May 22, 1942, Wagner Papers.

68. Cited in Stevens, p. 24.

69. Halperin, p. 260.

70. At times form letters were distributed that required only the addition of a signature before being mailed.

71. Silverberg, p. 370.

72. Andie Knutson to Philleo Nash, July 24, 1951, "Report on Unsolicited Telegrams on Palestine Situation Stored in Room 65"; see also Knutson to Nash, August 6, 1951, "Unsolicited Mail on the Palestine Situation," Philleo Nash File, ll-WH-O, Harry S Truman Library. (Hereafter cited as HSTL.)

73. Ben Edidin, *Jewish Community Life in America* (New York: Hebrew Publishing Co., 1954), p. 84.

74. Stevens, p. 21.

75. Zionist Organization of America, *48th Annual Report* (Washington, D.C.: Zionist Organization of America, 1945), p. 33.

76. Halperin, p. 258. On the contrary, American press coverage of the unfolding Palestine drama in the years 1939–48 was generally biased in favor of the Zionist position. See Dohse, passim.

77. Washington, D.C.: Public Affairs Press, 1944.

78. New York: D. Appleton Century Co., 1946.

79. Zionist Organization of America, *47th Annual Report* (Washington, D.C.: Zionist Organization of America, 1944), pp. 50–51.

80. Inis Claude, Jr., *National Minorities: An International Problem* (Cambridge, Mass: Harvard University Press, 1955), pp. 106–09.

81. Frank Gervasi, *To Whom Palestine* (New York: D. Appleton Century Co., 1946), pp. 10–11; Bernard Joseph, *British Rule in Palestine* (Washington, D.C.: Public Affairs Press, 1948), passim; A. S. Lyrique, "Motives Behind the Balfour Declaration," in J. E. Johnsen, ed., *Palestine Jewish Homeland* (New York: H. W. Wilson, 1946), pp. 115–17; Louis E. Levinthal, "The Case for a Jewish Commonwealth in Palestine," in ibid., pp. 137–39.

82. Gervasi, pp. 82–85; William B. Ziff, *The Rape of Palestine* (New York: Longmanns, Green, 1938), pp. 366–409; Levinthal, p. 139; Albert Einstein, "The Arabs and Palestine," in Johnsen, pp. 152–53; Wendell Phillips, "Before the Bar of History," in ibid., pp. 160–63; Samuel Schor, *Palestine and the Bible* (London: The

Book Society, 1934), pp. 115-20.

83. Ziff, pp. 366-84.

84. Ibid., pp. 366-409; Gervasi, pp. 125-42.

85. Ziff, pp. 10-11; Phillips, pp. 156-57.

86. Ziff, p. 402; Levinthal, p. 139; Phillips, pp. 157-67.

87. Milton Steinberg, "The Creed of an American Zionist," in Johnsen, pp. 132-34; James Parkes, "The Jewish World Since 1939," *International Affairs* 21, no. 1 (January 1945): 96-99.

88. Alfred Lilienthal, *What Price Israel* (Chicago: Henry Regnery, 1953), pp. 124-36; Richard Crossman, *Palestine Mission: A Personal Record* (New York: Harper and Brothers, 1947), p. 43; Dohse, p. 243; Halperin, p. 258.

89. Crossman, p. 43.

90. Charles Stember, et al., *Jews in the Mind of America* (New York: Basic Books, 1966), p. 173.

91. Ibid.

92. Ibid., p. 179.

93. "American Opinion, Current Popular Opinion on U.S. Palestine Policy," Papers of Clark M. Clifford (hereafter cited as Clifford Papers), HSTL.

94. Ibid.

95. Stember, p. 180.

96. Virginia Gildersleeve, *Many a Good Crusade* (New York: Macmillan, 1954), p. 85.

NOTES TO CHAPTER 4

1. Halperin, pp. 67-78.

2. Dearborn Independent, *The International Jew: The World's Foremost Problem* (Dearborn Independent, n.d.), II, p. 123.

3. "Report of Rabbi Elmer Berger to the Executive Committee Meeting," November 13, 1943. Executive Committee File, Files of the American Council for Judaism, Madison State Historical Library, Madison, Wisconsin. (Hereafter cited as ACJF.)

4. Elmer Berger, "The Council's Positive Program," unpublished paper, Annual Conference File (1946), ACJF; H. F. Schachtel, "The Council's Positive Program," unpublished paper, Annual Conference File (1946), ACJF; Berger to Sidney Wallach, April 26, 1946, Sidney Wallach File, ACJF.

5. Irving Reichert to Berger, December 22, 1944, Irving Reichert File, ACJF; Interview with Rabbi Elmer Berger, New York City, October 23, 1973.

6. Berger to David Ades, March 2, 1945, Lexington, Kentucky File, ACJF; American Council for Judaism, *A Program for the Post-War Status of Jews*, 1944; "Rosenwald Presents Palestine Plan to Truman," *Information Bulletin of the American Council for Judaism*, December 15, 1945.

7. Berger interview.

8. *A Program for the Post-War Status of Jews; Information Bulletin of the American Council for Judaism*, "Rosenwald Presents Palestine Plan to Truman."

9. Halperin, p. 291.

10. Berger to J. B. Moses, September 8, 1944, Radio File, ACJF; Berger to John Fitch, May 11, 1945, Non-Jewish Requests for Membership File, ACFJ.

11. J. C. Burnell to Berger, September 20, 1944; H. R. Evans to Berger, September 7, 1944; John Fitzpatrick to Berger, n.d., Radio File, ACJF. See also Christian Opinion 1944 File, ACJF.

12. New York *Times*, November 23, 1944.

13. Morroe Berger, "Americans from the Arab World," in James Kritzeck and R. Bayly Winder, eds., *Studies in Honour of Philip K. Hitti* (London: Macmillan, 1960), p. 352; James M. Ansara, "Syrian-Lebanese Immigration to the United States," *The National Herald* 3, no. 2 (February 1958).

14. Interview with Philip K. Hitti, Princeton, New Jersey, November 8, 1973; Interview with George M. Barakat, Centerville, Massachusetts, September 21–22, 1973.

15. Hitti interview.

16. Minutes of Meeting of the Advisory Board [of the Institute of Arab American Affairs], December 18, 1947, Papers of Virginia C. Gildersleeve, Butler Library, Columbia University. (Hereafter cited as Gildersleeve Papers.)

17. New York *Herald Tribune*, March 3, 1948.

18. "Memorandum from Virginia C. Gildersleeve to His Excellency Warren Austin," March 8, 1948, Gildersleeve Papers.

19. Kermit Roosevelt to Gildersleeve, May 5, 1948, Gildersleeve Papers.

20. Interview with Benjamin Freedman, New York City, November 15, 1973.

21. Freedman interview.

22. See, for example, Chicago *Daily Tribune*, February 9, 1948.

23. *FACTS* 3, no. 6 (June 1948):25.

24. Ibid.

25. Elmer Berger, as early as 1946, described the American Council for Judaism's view of Freedman as follows: "All of us in the Council are insufficiently satisfied as to his stability for us to establish any working procedure with him." Berger to E. P. Adler, July 1, 1946, Administrative File, ACJF.

26. Arnold Forster and Benjamin Epstein, *The Trouble-Makers*, 2d ed. (Westport, Conn.: Negro University Press, 1970), pp. 202–03.

27. Freedman interview.

28. For comments along these lines by radio station managers, see J. C. Burnell to Berger, September 20, 1944; Hayden R. Evans to Berger, September 7, 1944; John Fitzpatrick to Berger, n.d., Radio File, ACJF. Similar comments by Christian clergymen may be found in The President of Washington and Jefferson College to Morris Lazaron, June 20, 1944; John M. Versteeg to Lazaron, June 9, 1944; Robert W. Searle to Berger, February 7, 1944, Christian Opinion 1944 File, ACJF.

29. Marshall Sklare, ed. *The Jews: Social Patterns of an American Group* (New York: The Free Press, 1958), pp. 448–49.

NOTES TO CHAPTER 5

1. Cordell Hull, *Memoirs*, 2 vols. (New York: Macmillan, 1948), II, p. 1531.

2. *Survey of Palestine*, III, pp. 1216–19.

3. The American Consul at Jerusalem to the Secretary of State, January 8, 1940, 867n.01/1685, N.A., 1940–44.

4. FRUS, 1941, Vol. III, pp. 601–02.

5. Ibid., pp. 596–97.

6. Ibid., pp. 596–97.

7. Ibid.

8. The significance of the APC's prestigious membership should not be underestimated. In early 1944 the Justice Department considered the possibility of investigating Zionist groups in the United States for possible violations of the Foreign Agents Registration Act. Louis Nemzer, of the department's Foreign Agents Registration Section, discussed the department's attitude toward the American Palestine Committee with Evan M. Wilson of the State Department's Near East Division. Nemzer revealed his personal conviction that "there was no doubt in his mind that [the APC] had been inspired by the regular Zionist Organization of America," but added that "it was most unlikely that any evidence of any connection between the Zionists and this Committee would ever come to light." Moreover, concluded Nemzer, even should such evidence be found, his feeling was "it was unlikely that his Department would take any action against the Committee owing to its composition." "Memorandum of Conversation [Telephone] between Mr. Louis Nemzer and Mr. Wilson," February 17, 1944, unnumbered, N.A., 1940–44.

9. See, for example, the following State Department correspondence: Hull to Roosevelt, December 29, 1942, 867n.01/1828, N.A., 1940–44; Hugh Cumming, Assistant Chief of European Division, to Mrs. W. Prince, April 1, 1943, 867n.01/1848, N.A., 1940–44; Sumner Welles to Edward J. Flynn, March 25, 1943, 867n.01/1851, N.A., 1940–44.

10. Weizmann, p. 420.

11. Roosevelt to Brandeis, May 5, 1941, PPF 2335; Roosevelt to Wise, June 9, 1941, OF 700, FDRL.

12. Grace Tulley to Frankfurter, July 15, 1942, PPF 140, FDRL.

13. Morgenthau Presidential Diaries, V, pp. 1200–01, December 31, 1942, FDRL. See also pp. 90–91, Chapter 6.

14. William D. Hasset, *Off the Record with F.D.R.* (New Brunswick, N. J.: Rutgers University Press, 1958), p. 209.

15. Morgenthau Presidential Diaries, V, p. 1061, January 27, 1942, FDRL.

16. Ibid., p. 1135, July 7, 1942. Wingate had become completely devoted to the Zionist cause from the first days of his arrival in Palestine in 1936. For an account of Wingate's life, see Christopher Sykes, *Orde Wingate* (London: Collins, 1959).

17. Morgenthau Presidential Diaries, V, July 7, 1942, FDRL.

18. Ibid.

19. Ibid. Despite the president's apparent efforts on his behalf, however, Wingate never returned to Palestine. After distinguishing himself in the Ethiopian campaign, he was posted to Burma where as a brigadier-general leading irregular

forces behind Japanese lines, he was killed before the end of the war.

20. Yale finally published this article. "Ambassador Henry Morgenthau's Special Mission of 1917," *World Politics*, April 1949.

21. Berle to Yale, March 20, 1942, 867n.01/1800, N.A., 1940-44.

22. Taylor to Welles, January 6, 1943, 867n.01/1837, N.A., 1940-44.

23. Welles to Taylor, January 27, 1943, 867n.01/1837, N.A., 1940-44.

24. FRUS, 1941, Vol. III, pp. 597-98.

25. Ibid., p. 599.

26. Schechtman, pp. 54-55.

27. Ibid.

28. The fate of Palestine's Jews in the event of a serious Allied reversal in Egypt was very much on Berle's mind during this period. Following his meeting with Neumann, Berle apparently asked the Near East division to consider how Ibn Saud might be useful in preventing Arab violence against Jews in Palestine should the British be forced to withdraw from that country. At the same time, Berle apparently suggested that Saud might be asked by Washington to offer physical protection to Palestinian Jews. Although in this instance Berle seems to have been thinking along lines involving the entry of Saudi forces into Palestine, it does not appear unlikely that he may also have considered the possibility of an evacuation of Jews to Saudi Arabia as an emergency measure. In any event, the Near East Division concluded that economic, religious, and political reasons would make it difficult for Ibn Saud to extend physical protection to the Palestinian Jews. However, Wallace Murray suggested that an appeal by Roosevelt to Ibn Saud's chivalry might lead the monarch to exercise moral authority to prevent Arab attacks upon the Jews. Murray also suggested that the United States extend material aid to Saudi Arabia to reinforce such a plea to Ibn Saud. Although no action was taken by the department along these lines, Berle and Murray were sufficiently worried by the military situation to draft a message asking Ibn Saud to protect Palestinian Jews. FRUS, 1941, Vol. III, pp. 603-04.

29. Weizmann, pp. 425, 435-36.

30. Schechtman, pp. 57-58; FRUS, 1941, Vol. III, pp. 618-19.

31. FRUS, 1941, Vol. III, pp. 618-19.

32. Ibid., p. 621.

33. Ibid., pp. 622-23.

34. Ibid.

35. Hull, *Memoirs*, II, p. 1531.

36. Wise to Hull, October 31, 1942, 867n.01/1814, N.A., 1940-44.

37. FRUS, 1942, Vol. IV, p. 538.

38. Ibid.

39. Ibid.

40. Ibid.

41. Ibid., pp. 543-44.

42. *The Present Situation in the Near East: Part II. The United States and the Palestine Problem*, April 20, 1943, 867n.01/1857 1/2, N.A., 1940-44.

43. Hull to Roosevelt, May 7, 1943 (encl.), 867n.01/1857 1/2, N.A. 1940-44.

44. FRUS, 1943, Vol. IV, p. 776.

45. Elliott Roosevelt, *As He Saw It* (New York: Duell, Sloan & Pearce, 1946), p. 193.

46. Hull to Roosevelt, July 19, 1943, 867n.01/1882 1/2, N.A., 1940–44.

47. Hull to Winant, July 24, 1943, 867n.01/1884, N.A., 1940–44.

48. Hull to the American Minister in Egypt (Alexander Kirk), July 26, 1943, 867n.01/1885C, N.A., 1940–44.

49. Patterson to Hull, July 27, 1943, OF 5433, FDRL.

50. Hull to Roosevelt, July 30, 1943, OF 700, FDRL.

51. Ibid., marginal notation by Roosevelt.

52. Wise to Hull, August 3, 1943, 867n.01/1904, N.A., 1940–44.

53. Celler's statement was issued on August 12, 1943. Henry S. Villard, of the Division of Near Eastern Affairs, subsequently prepared an analysis of its contents. Villard to Hull, August 25, 1943, 867n.01/1984, N.A., 1940–44. Celler's charge that American oil companies were heavily involved in efforts to promote anti-Zionist sentiment in the State Department was frequently repeated by others in the years leading up to the creation of Israel. An examination of the department's diplomatic files on Palestine for the years 1939–47 reveals very little contact between oil companies and department officials. There is, however, no doubt that officials of American oil companies operating in the Middle East were apprehensive over the possibility that the Palestine problem might produce an anti-American reaction in the Arab world that would be harmful to their business interests. This was freely admitted on the infrequent occasions when Palestine was the topic of conversation between them and officers of the department. See, for example, Memorandum of Conversation between F. H. Henry, of Socony-Vacuum Oil Company, and J. Rives Childs, April 1, 1939, 867n.01/1551, N.A., 1930–39.

Nonetheless, there is nothing in the State Department files indicating that American oil companies tried to influence the government to adopt specific courses of action on Palestine. Moreover, the scarcity of documentary evidence of contacts between the oil companies and the State Department undermines the contention that oil companies conducted a covert anti-Zionist "campaign" between 1939 and 1948. Henderson recalls that as director of the Office of Near Eastern and African Affairs he had contact with oil company officials on various occasions but that Palestine or Zionism were rarely the subject at hand. He explains that since oil company officials realized that State Department officers were aware of their misgivings over the consequences of a pro-Zionist American policy, "there was no reason for them to seek us out." Henderson interview.

Interestingly, officials of some American oil companies not operating in the Middle East at times explicitly urged the government to pursue a pro-Zionist course. See, for example, Julius C. Livingston, president of Mazda Oil Corporation, to E. H. Moore, senator from Oklahoma, January 26, 1944, 867n.01/2151, N.A., 1940–44; Dan Dancinger, Dancinger Oil and Refining Company, to Lindley Beckwork, congressman from Oklahoma (enclosed in Beckwork to Edward Stettinius, February 14, 1944, 867n.01/2188, N.A., 1940–44).

As discussed below, oil was certainly a factor—and one that assumed increasing importance between 1939 and 1948—in the American approach to Palestine. However, it appears to have gained prominence in the minds of American political and military officials largely independently of promotion by U.S. oil company spokespeople.

54. Celler to Roosevelt, August 18, 1943, 867n.01/1918, N.A., 1940–44.

55. Untitled Memorandum by Wallace Murray, December 12, 1943, 867n.01/ 1902 1/2, N.A., 1940–44.

56. FRUS, 1943, Vol. IV, pp. 803–04.

57. Murray to Stettinius, March 9, 1944, 867n.01/3-944, N.A., 1940–44.

NOTES TO CHAPTER 6

1. It is notable in this connection that Patterson's letter of July 23, 1943, to Hull described the military considerations that motivated the War Department to favor a cessation of Zionist agitation as being offensive rather than defensive.

2. Cited by Shwadran, p. 297.

3. FRUS, 1943, IV, p. 859.

4. Harold Williamson et al., *The American Petroleum Industry*, Vol. II: *The Age of Energy, 1899–1959* (Evanston, Ill.: Northwestern University Press, 1963), pp. 700–52.

5. Ibid., pp. 762–75.

6. Gerald D. Nash, *United States Oil Policy, 1890–1964* (Pittsburgh: University of Pittsburgh Press, 1968), pp. 168–70.

7. De Novo, pp. 172–73.

8. Shwadran, pp. 314–25.

9. FRUS, 1943, IV, pp. 768–71.

10. Ibid., pp. 773–75.

11. Ibid., pp. 786–87.

12. Hurewitz, p. 213.

13. "Extracts from a Statement of Mr. St. John Philby, November 17, 1943" (enclosure) Weizmann to Welles, December 13, 1943, OF 5433, FDRL.

14. Memorandum of Conversation between Weizmann and Welles, January 26, 1943, 867n.01/1-2643, N.A., 1940–44.

15. Memorandum by Chaim Weizmann, June 12, 1943 (enclosure) Weizmann to Klotz, June 15, 1943, Morgenthau Diaries, Book 642, pp. 75–79, FDRL.

16. Ibid.

17. FRUS, 1943, IV, p. 796.

18. Ibid., p. 795.

19. Ibid., p. 807.

20. Ibid.

21. Ibid.

22. Weizmann to Welles, December 13, 1943; Weizmann to Rosenman, January 4, 1944, OF 5433, FDRL.

23. Morgenthau Presidential Diaries, IV, pp. 1340–41.

24. Weizmann to Welles, December 13, 1943, OF 5433, FDRL.

25. See Chapter 2, note 68.

26. Memorandum of Conversation between Moshe Shertok and Michael Hare, July 19, 1941, 867n.01/8-141, N.A., 1940–44.

27. Memorandum of Conversation between Weizmann, Murray, et al., January

19, 1943, 867n.01/1-9-43, N.A., 1940–44.

28. Memorandum Submitted to the Bermuda Refugee Conference by the Jewish Agency for Palestine, April, 1943, Senatorial and Vice-Presidential Files, HSTL.

29. See p. 75, Chapter 5.

30. Morgenthau Presidential Diaries, December 3, 1942, V, p. 1200.

31. Ibid., pp. 1200–01.

32. Selig Adler, "Franklin D. Roosevelt and Zionism," *Judaism* (Summer 1972), p. 270; Willard Range, *Franklin D. Roosevelt's World Order* (Athens: University of Georgia Press, 1959), p. 152.

33. Ladislas Farago, "Refugees: The Solution as FDR Saw It," *United Nations World* (June 1947); Henry Field, *"M" Project for FDR, Studies on Migration and Settlement* (Ann Arbor, Mich.: Edwards Brothers, 1962).

34. Stevens, pp. 71–72; Lilienthal, p. 32. In 1941, for example, Moshe Shertok bluntly stressed to an American diplomat that "*the Jews are not interested in any way in immigration into any other area than Palestine itself. . . .*" Memorandum of Conversation between Moshe Shertok and Michael Hare, July 19, 1941, 867n.01/841, N.A., 1940–44. (Original emphasis.)

35. FRUS, 1943, IV, p. 813.

36. Adler, p. 270.

37. FRUS, 1943, IV, pp. 815–16.

38. Ibid., pp. 816–21.

39. Ibid.

40. Ibid., p. 821.

41. Philip E. Mosely to J. C. Dunn, February 18, 1944, 867n.01/201844, N.A., 1940–44.

42. Murray to Stettinius, February 10, 1944, 867n.01/2-1044, N.A., 1940–44.

43. "Special Report of Myron Taylor to President Truman, 1947," Myron Taylor Papers, FDRL.

44. Mosely to Dunn, February 18, 1944, 867n.01/2-1844, N.A., 1940–44.

It is interesting and instructive to examine this document and review briefly the other options considered by the planners and the calculations that led to their rejection as feasible objectives toward which American policy toward Palestine should be directed. In light of subsequent events, some of the considerations can be described as penetrating. At a minimum it is clear that the members of the Interdivisional Committee devoted serious thought to American options before settling upon the religious trusteeship proposal. The rejected options were:

1. *Maintenance of Status Quo of the Mandate*. This was rejected because of a feeling that "the conflict in Palestine has become more intense and has spread far beyond the frontiers [of Palestine] during the period of the Mandate. . . . There are no indications that continuation of the Mandate would solve the basic problems."

2. *A Bi-National State*. This was rejected because "there is little hope under existing conditions of bringing about Arab-Jewish cooperation in a bi-national state."

3. *The Inclusion of Palestine in a Federation of Arab States*. This was rejected because "unless the causes of Arab-Jewish conflict be removed [from Palestine] . . . the conflict would be shifted from Palestine to the capital of federation."

4. *Partition.* This was rejected because "there are no reasons for thinking that such a settlement would either ameliorate or terminate the Arab-Jewish conflict. On the contrary, there is the serious likelihood that partition of Palestine would transfer the conflict from the level of an intra-state struggle which a strong mandatory government could control to the dangerous political level of international conflict. . . . If the United States assumed a responsibility for such a settlement, the American Government might find itself called upon to maintain and protect a Jewish state against attack by neighboring Arab states or to maintain and protect the Arab states against attack by the Jewish state."

5. *An Arab State.* This was rejected because "it is doubtful whether the Arabs can secure outside capital and possess the technical knowledge to [solve] Palestinian economic problems. It is questionable whether the Arabs . . . possess sufficient political maturity to govern a country with a Jewish minority of 500,000."

6. *A Jewish State.* This was rejected because it "would be opposed by the Arab states and by the Muslim world and almost certainly have to be set up and maintained by external force."

7. *An International Territory with Arab and Jewish Communal Governments under a Trusteeship.* This only differed from the plan that was actually proposed by virtue of lacking religious overtones. It was not rejected, but was deemed inferior to the Religious Trusteeship.

45. Memorandum of Conversation between Sir Maurice Peterson, Wallace Murray et al., April 11, 1944, 740.0011/Stettinius Mission/125, State Department Diplomatic Records, R.G. 59, N.A.

NOTES TO CHAPTER 7

1. Stevens, p. 33.

2. Emanuel Celler to Marvin McIntyre, September 27, 1943, OF 700, FDRL.

3. Long to Murray, November 19, 1943, 867n.00/686, N.A., 1940-44.

4. Murray to Hull, November 26, 1943, 867n.00/686, N.A., 1940-44.

5. Memorandum of Conversation by Hull, December 13, 1943, 867n.01/2056, N.A., 1940-44.

6. FRUS, 1944, Vol. V, pp. 562-63.

7. U.S. Congress, House, *Hearings* on H.R. 418 and H.R. 419, p. 1.

8. Stevens, pp. 11-12; Adler, p. 365; Halperin, pp. 270-74.

9. James T. Patterson, *"Mr. Republican": A Biography of Robert A. Taft* (Boston: Houghton Mifflin, 1972), pp. 280-82.

10. Memorandum of Conversation between Nahum Goldmann, Wallace Murray et al., May 19, 1944, 867n.01/2348, N.A., 1940-44.

11. Ibid.

12. Memorandum of Conversation between Breckinridge Long and Rabbi Silver, February 24, 1944, 867n.01/2248, N.A., 1940-44.

13. Memorandum of Conversation between Nahum Goldmann, Wallace Murray et al., May 19, 1944, 867n.01/2348, N.A., 1940-44.

14. Hull, *Memoirs*, II, pp. 1534–35.

15. FRUS, 1944, Vol. V, pp. 560–61.

16. U.S. Congress, House, *Hearings* on H.R. 418 and H.R. 419, p. 498.

17. Stevens, p. 47.

18. FRUS, 1944, Vol. V, p. 563.

19. Ibid., pp. 563–64.

20. Zionist Organization of America, *47th Annual Report*, (Washington, D.C.: 20A, 1944), p. 61.

21. FRUS, 1944, Vol. V, p. 564.

22. Ibid., pp. 565–67, 571, 578.

23. Ibid., p. 571.

24. See, for example, the American Minister in Egypt (Alexander Kirk) to the Secretary of State, Cable 465, February 26, 1944, 867n.01/2214, N.A., 1940–44. Kirk indicated that the Egyptian government had worked to keep news of the Palestine resolutions out of the local press. Similarly, the Iraqi government reportedly was "taking every possible precaution to prevent the resolution from becoming a subject of discussion in Parliament and the press." FRUS, 1944, Vol. V, p. 568; George Wadsworth reported from Beirut that no mention had been made in the local press of the Palestine resolutions. Ibid., p. 566.

25. FRUS, 1944, Vol. V, p. 568.

26. The Secretary of State to the American Legation at Cairo, Cable 408, February 26, 1944, 867n.01/2185, N.A., 1940–44; Secretary of State to American Legation at Jiddah, March 13, 1944, 867n.01/2185, N.A., 1940–44.

27. FRUS, 1944, Vol. V, p. 571.

28. Ibid.

29. Ibid., pp. 567–68.

30. Ibid., p. 567.

31. Ibid., p. 569.

32. Ibid., pp. 581–82.

33. Ibid., p. 574.

34. McCloy to Stettinius, February 27, 1944, 867n.01/2294, N.A., 1940–44. Bloom's proposed resolution, after listing a series of pro-Zionist sentiments, simply read: "Resolved by the House of Representatives (the Senate Concurring), That it is the sense of the Congress that the terms, conditions, provisions, guarantees and pledges under and pursuant to which consent was given by the United States to the British Mandate over Palestine be strictly adhered to." Confidential Committee Print, 78th Congress, 2d. session.

35. FRUS, 1944, Vol. V, pp. 581–82.

36. Ibid.

37. Stevens, p. 51.

38. Schechtman, p. 75.

39. Stevens, p. 51.

40. Memorandum of Conversation with Rabbi Silver, by Breckinridge Long, February 24, 1944, 867n.01/2248, N.A., 1940–44.

41. Ibid.

42. Cited in Stevens, Appendix II.

43. Silver and Wise to Roosevelt, March 13, 1944, 867n.01/2306, N.A., 1940–44.

44. ZOA, *47th Annual Report*, p. 62.

45. Ibid.

46. Silver and Wise to Roosevelt, March 13, 1944, 867n.01/2306, N.A., 1940–44.

47. Hull to the American Legation, Cairo, March 15, 1944, 867n.01/2255, N.A., 1940–44.

48. Memorandum of Conversation between Nahum Goldmann and Murray et al., May 19, 1944, 867n.01/2348, N.A., 1940–44.

49. Silver to Wagner, April 28, 1944, Wagner Papers.

50. Cited in Stevens, Appendix II.

51. Ibid.

52. New York *Times*, June 28, 1944.

53. William Rosenblatt to Senator Wagner, July 18, 1944, Wagner Papers.

54. Cited in Stevens, p. 83.

55. Celler to Berger, September 13, 1944, Congressmen File, ACJF.

56. Ibid.

57. New York *Times*, July 21, 1944.

58. Memorandum for the President by Samuel Rosenman, September 16, 1944, OF 5433, FDRL.

59. Statement made by Governor Dewey, October 12, 1944, Wagner Papers.

60. Roosevelt to Wagner, October 15, 1944, Wagner Papers.

61. Manuel, p. 312.

62. FRUS, 1944, Vol. V, p. 616.

63. Memorandum of Conversation between Wise, Stettinius et al., November 9, 1944, 867n.01/11-944, N.A., 1940–44.

64. Copy of Stimson to Taft, October 10, 1944, Wagner Papers.

65. Memorandum of Conversation between Wise, Stettinius et al., November 9, 1944, 867n.01/11-944, N.A., 1940–44.

66. Stettinius to Roosevelt, November 17, 1944, 867n.01/11-17-44, N.A., 1940–44.

67. Memorandum for the President (unsigned, from Stettinius), November 15, 1944, 867n.01/11-1544, N.A., 1940–44.

68. Murray to Stettinius, November 16, 1944, 867n.01/11-1644, N.A., 1940–44.

69. Schechtman, pp. 84–89.

70. Wise to Stettinius, November 16, 1944, OF 700, FDRL.

71. Stettinius to Roosevelt, November 17, 1944 and Roosevelt to Stettinius, November 20, 1944, OF 700, FDRL.

72. Stevens, p. 60.

73. Bloom to Stettinius, December 2, 1944, 867n.01/12-244, N.A., 1940–44.

74. Wagner to Roosevelt, December 2, 1944, Wagner Papers.

75. Stettinius to Roosevelt, December 5, 1944, 867n.01/12-544, N.A., 1940–44.

76. Ibid.

77. FRUS, 1944, Vol. V, p. 643.

78. Ibid., pp. 643–44.

79. Stettinius to Roosevelt, December 8, 1944, OF 700, FDRL.

80. Roosevelt to Stettinius, December 9, 1944, OF 700, FDRL.

81. Wise to Roosevelt, December 12, 1944, 867n.01/12-1244, N.A., 1940–44.

82. Cited in Schechtman, p. 86.

83. Wise to Stettinius, December 4, 1944, 867n.01/12-444, N.A., 1940–44.

84. Roosevelt to Wagner, December 3, 1944, Wagner Papers.

85. Sidney Wallach to David Delman (and draft answer thereon), February 2, 1945, Wagner Papers.

86. FRUS, 1944, Vol. V, pp. 648–49; Murray to Stettinius, November 16, 1944, 867n.01/11-1644, N.A., 1940–44.

87. FRUS, 1944, Vol. V, pp. 622–26, 631–32, 646–48. See also pp. 138–40, Chapter 8.

88. Ibid., pp. 646–49.

89. Schechtman, p. 83.

90. Wise to Roosevelt, January 24, 1945, OF 700, FDRL.

91. See Celler to Roosevelt, December 15, 1944, and Roosevelt to Celler, January 16, 1945, PSF Palestine, Box 62, FDRL.

92. Wagner to Roosevelt, January 15, 1945, Wagner Papers.

93. FRUS, 1945, Vol. VIII, p. 680.

94. Ibid., p. 682.

95. "Memorandum of Conversation between His Majesty Abdul Aziz al Saud, King of Saudi Arabia, and President Roosevelt, February 14, 1945, aboard the U.S.S. Quincy," 867n.01/5-145, N.A., 1945–49.

96. Ibid. Roosevelt gave a slightly different version of Ibn Saud's comments on this matter shortly after his return from Yalta during a luncheon with Colonel Harold Hoskins: "The President said," reported Hoskins, "Ibn Saud had not minced words regarding the Jews. The King said that, whereas the Arabs could get along with the Jews who lived in that part of the world, they could not get along with the Jews who came from London, New York, Paris, and Berlin." Hoskins to Paul H. Alling, March 5, 1945, 867n.01/5-545, N.A., 1945–49.

97. Memorandum of Conversation between Ibn Saud and President Roosevelt.

98. Elliott Roosevelt, p. 245.

99. Edward Stettinius, *Roosevelt and the Russians* (Garden City, N.Y.: Doubleday, 1949), p. 289.

100. Ibid.

101. Schechtman, p. 106.

102. New York *Times*, March 2, 1945.

103. Samuel I. Rosenman, *Working With Roosevelt* (New York: Harper and Brothers, 1952), pp. 527–28.

104. Frances Perkins, *The Roosevelt I Knew* (New York: Viking, 1946), p. 395.

105. Hoskins to Paul H. Alling, March 5, 1945, 867n.01/5-545, N.A., 1945–49.

106. Cited in Schechtman, p. 110.

107. Stevens, p. 90.

108. New York *Times*, March 17, 1945.

109. FRUS, 1945, Vol. VIII, p. 692.

110. Ibid., p. 698.

111. Ibid., pp. 704, 763. A similar message was sent by Stettinius to the Government of Lebanon. Ibid., p. 703.

112. Hull, *Memoirs*, II, p. 1536.

113. "Suggested Procedure Regarding the Palestine Question" (Summary), January 8, 1945, 867n.01/1-845, N.A., 1945–49.

NOTES TO CHAPTER 8

1. Esco Foundation, II, pp. 1054–55.

2. Hurewitz, pp. 189–90.

3. Yehuda Bauer, *From Diplomacy to Resistance: A History of Jewish Palestine, 1939–1945* (Philadelphia: Jewish Publication Society of America, 1970), p. 356; Hurewitz, p. 239. Hurewitz estimates the membership of Haganah at the close of the war as 60,000.

4. Bauer, p. 356.

5. Hurewitz, p. 239. Bauer (p. 306) gives the following breakdown of arms possessed by the Haganah at the end of 1944: 10,338 rifles, 437 submachine guns, 132 machine guns, 3,933 pistols.

6. Walter Lehn, "The Jewish National Fund," *Journal of Palestine Studies* 3 (Summer 1974): 90–91.

7. Bauer, p. 337.

8. A. J. Granott, "The Strategy of Land Acquisition," in Khalidi, p. 397.

9. Menachem Begin, *The Revolt* (Los Angeles: Nash, 1952), p. 43.

10. Sykes, *Crossroads*, p. 290.

11. Ibid.

12. Hurewitz, pp. 195–200.

13. Bauer, p. 320.

14. Begin, p. 138.

15. Cited in Hurewitz, p. 200.

16. Bauer, pp. 320–24.

17. New York *Times*, November 18, 1944.

18. Bauer, p. 326.

19. Hurewitz, p. 201.

20. Bauer, pp. 327–29.

21. Ibid., p. 399; Begin, p. 151.

22. Bauer, p. 331.

23. Sykes, *Crossroads*, p. 307.

24. Weizmann, pp. 438–39.

25. Hurewitz, pp. 206–07.

26. Ibid., p. 207.

27. The American Consul General in Jerusalem to the Secretary of State, March 10, 1945, 867n.01/3-1045, N.A., 1945–49.

28. Joseph B. Schechtman, *The Mufti and Fuehrer* (New York: Thomas Yoseloff, 1965), Chapter 4, passim.

29. Hurewitz, p. 116.

30. See, for example, the memorandum submitted to the American Consulate General in Jerusalem in April 1944 by Abdul Latif Bey Salah, formerly a member of the Arab Higher Committee and a leader of the minor Palestinian political party known as the National Bloc. The American Consul General in Jerusalem to the Secretary of State, Despatch 1145, April 21, 1944, 867n.00/672, N.A., 1940–45.

31. Hurewitz, pp. 186–88.

32. Esco Foundation, II, p. 1012.

33. Ibid.; Sykes, *Crossroads*; Geoffrey Furlonge, *Palestine is My Country: The Story of Musa al-Alami* (London: John Murray, 1967).

34. Hurewitz, p. 192.

35. Ibid.

36. Esco Foundation, II, p. 1005.

37. Waines, p. 95.

38. This was seen to be the case by observers in Palestine well before the British government extended the deadline for Jewish immigration. See, for example, American Consul General at Jerusalem to the Secretary of State, December 9, 1943, 867n.01/2-71, N.A., 1940–44.

39. George Kirk, *Survey of International Affairs: The Middle East in the War* (London: Oxford University Press, 1952), p. 205.

40. Saul Friedman, pp. 173–77.

41. Memorandum Submitted to the Bermuda Refugee Conference by the Jewish Agency for Palestine, April 1943, Senatorial and Vice-Presidential Files, HSTL.

42. Ibid.

43. Aide-Memoire on Post-War Emigration Needs of European Jewry and Resettlement Possibilities in Palestine, February 1943, Senatorial and Vice-Presidential Files, HSTL.

44. Ibid.

45. Memorandum of Conversation between Dr. Nahum Goldmann and Col. H. B. Hoskins, April 20, 1944, Unnumbered Document, N.A. 1940–44.

46. Ibid.

47. Hungary's prewar Jewish population numbered somewhat over 400,000. By 1944 it was estimated to have doubled, largely in consequence of an influx of Jews from nearby countries who preferred the lesser evil of life under the relatively moderate anti-Semitism of pre-1944 Hungarian authorities to the extreme policies followed in Germany, Czechoslovakia, and Poland. An interesting discussion of conditions that faced Jews in wartime Hungary can be found in Arthur D. Morse, *While Six Million Died* (New York: Random House, 1967).

48. Ibid., p. 350.

49. Saul Friedman, p. 220.

50. Morse, pp. 362–64. For indications that the Hungarian regime was seeking greater independence from German direction, see FRUS, 1944, II, p. 877.

51. FRUS, 1944, I, pp. 1099–1165.

52. Ibid., pp. 1114–15; 1120.

53. Interesting, though severely limited, accounts of the circumstances surrounding these negotiations are found in Morse, pp. 369–74 and Saul Friedman, pp. 220–21. Both writers fail to delve into the calculations that governed American and

British attitudes in these talks. Much information on this point is contained in FRUS, 1944, I, pp. 981–1191.

54. Morse, pp. 371–74.

55. Ibid., p. 342.

56. U.S. Senate, *Congressional Record*, August 24, 1944, p. 7261.

57. New York *Times*, August 24, 1944.

58. Peter Bergson was the nom de guerre of Hillel Kook, son of the Chief Rabbi of Palestine.

59. Memorandum of Conversation between Wallace Murray and Nahum Goldmann et al., September 13, 1944, 867n.01/9-1344, N.A., 1940–44.

60. Ibid.

61. Yehuda Bauer, *Flight and Rescue: Brichah* (New York: Random House, 1970), p. 321.

62. Great Britain, Parliament, *House of Commons, Parliamentary Debates* Official Report, 1938–39, Vol. 347, Col. 2173.

63. Weizmann, pp. 435–36.

64. Memorandum of Conversation between Nahum Goldmann and Colonel H. B. Hoskins, April 20, 1944, Unnumbered Document, N.A., 1940–44.

65. Weizmann, pp. 435–36.

66. Esco Foundation, II, p. 1108.

67. The American Consul General in Jerusalem to the Secretary of State, February 21, 1945, Despatch No. 1715, 867n.01/2-2145, N.A., 1945–49.

68. Ibid.

69. Hurewitz, p. 227; George Kirk, *Survey of International Affairs: The Middle East, 1945–1950* (London: Oxford University Press, 1954), p. 7.

70. Kirk, *Middle East, 1945–50*, pp. 136–38; 151–52.

71. Ibid., pp. 116–17; Stephen Longrigg, *Iraq: 1900–1950* (London: Oxford University Press, 1953), p. 252.

72. Kirk, *Middle East, 1945–50*, pp. 6, 120.

73. Winston S. Churchill, *The Second World War*, 6 vols. (Boston: Houghton Mifflin, 1948–53), Vol. VI, p. 569.

74. Kirk, *Middle East, 1945–50*, p. 192.

75. Churchill, Vol. VI, p. 764.

76. Ephraim Avigdor Speiser, *The United States and the Near East* (Cambridge, Mass.: Harvard University Press, 1947), p. 164.

77. Kirk, *Middle East, 1945–50*, p. 2.

78. L. Welch Pogue, "The Next Ten Years in Air Transportation," *Academy of Political Science Proceedings* 21 (1944–46).

79. "The Logic of the Air," *Fortune* 27, no. 4 (April 1943):73.

80. George Brownell, "American Aviation in the Middle East," *Middle East Journal* 1 (October 1947).

81. Twitchell, p. 132.

82. Speiser, pp. 134–35; Kirk, *Middle East, 1945–50*, pp. 136, 152.

83. Loy Henderson, "American Political and Strategic Interests in the Middle East and Southwestern Europe," *Proceedings of the Academy of Political Science* 22, no. 4 (1946–48):451.

84. Shwadran, p. 319.

85. Millis and Duffield, pp. 357–58.

86. Hurewitz, pp. 180–81.

87. Enclosure No. 1 to Despatch No. 1419, January 26, 1945, from the American Embassy, Moscow: "Indications of Soviet Activity in Several Near Eastern Countries," 867n.01/1-2645, N.A., 1945–49.

88. Enclosure No. 1 to Despatch No. 1319, December 20, 1944, from the American Embassy, Moscow: "Soviet Attitude Toward the Near and Middle East," 867n.01/12-2044, N.A., 1940–44.

89. FRUS, 1944, V, p. 646.

90. Enclosure No. 1 to Despatch No. 1319, December 20, 1944, from the American Embassy, Moscow: "Soviet Attitude Toward the Near and Middle East," 867n.01/12-2044, N.A., 1940–44.

91. Memorandum of Conversation between Wallace Murray and Nahum Goldmann et al., September 13, 1944, 867n.01/9-1344, N.A., 1940–44.

92. FRUS, 1944, V, p. 633.

93. Enclosure No. 1 to Despatch 1319, December 20, 1944, from the American Embassy, Moscow: "Soviet Attitude Toward the Near and Middle East," 867n.01/12-2044, N.A., 1940–44.

94. Suggested Procedure Regarding the Palestine Question (Summary), January 8, 1945, 867n.01/1-845, N.A., 1945–49.

NOTES TO CHAPTER 9

1. Willard Range (p. 70), although perhaps overstating the case, has related this quality to Roosevelt's general approach to international relations by arguing that "what Roosevelt hoped to achieve was nothing less than the moral reconstruction of humanity."

2. "Oral History Interview with A. J. Granoff, Kansas City, Missouri, April 9, 1969," by J. R. Fuchs, Harry S Truman Library, p. 8.

3. Ibid., p. 23.

4. U.S. Congress, Congressional Record, 76th Cong., 1st Sess., p. 2231.

5. Frank J. Adler, Roots in a Moving Stream: The Centennial History of Congregation B'nai Jehuda of Kansas City (Kansas City: The Temple, Congregation B'nai Yehuda, 1972), p. 202.

6. Truman to Rabbi Silver, December 31, 1941, Senate File, HSTL.

7. Truman to Bergson, May 7, 1943, Senate File, HSTL.

8. Truman to Wise, June 1, 1943, Senate File, HSTL.

9. Ibid.

10. Ibid.

11. Truman to A. M. Levine, February 16, 1944, Senate File, HSTL.

12. Harry S Truman, Memoirs, Vol. II: Years of Trial and Hope (New York: Doubleday, 1956), p. 132.

13. Ibid., p. 133.

14. Stevens, p. 127.

15. Although the new president had little experience in foreign affairs, there is no reason to presume that his expertise in domestic politics blinded him to the political dimensions of Jewish immigration into Palestine. The whole question of postwar immigration into the United States was, after all, very much a "political" issue in the American context.

16. Truman, II, p. 1.

17. See p. 205, Chapter 12.

18. See pp. 217–18, Chapter 13.

19. Chicago *Daily News*, October 18, 1945.

20. New York *Times*, June 13, 1946.

21. Stember, pp. 142–54.

22. Harry S Truman, *Memoirs*, Vol. I: *Year of Decisions* (New York: Doubleday, 1955), p. 69.

23. Truman, *Memoirs*, II, p. 162.

24. Ibid., p. 165.

25. See, for example, Larry Collins and Dominique Lapierre, *O Jerusalem* (New York: Simon and Schuster, 1972), p. 213. Henderson was actually promoted to the post of ambassador to India.

26. See for example pp. 166–67, Chapter 10. See also Samuel Burton Hand, "Samuel I. Rosenman: His Public Career," (Ph.D. dissertation, Syracuse University, 1960), pp. 252–58.

27. David B. Sachar, "David K. Niles and United States Policy: A Case Study in American Foreign Policy," (Honors Thesis, Harvard University, Department of History, 1959), p. 1.

28. Alfred Steinberg, "Mr. Truman's Mystery Man," *Saturday Evening Post*, December 24, 1949.

29. Sachar, p. 20.

30. Confidential source.

31. "The Politics of 1948," Clifford to Truman, Clifford Papers, HSTL.

32. Sykes, *Crossroads*, pp. 321–22.

33. Hurewitz, pp. 224–25.

34. Ibid., p. 225.

35. See pp. 136–37, Chapter 8.

36. Memorandum of Conversation between Loy Henderson et al., and Nahum Goldmann, July 20, 1945, 867n.01/6-2045, N.A., 1945–49.

37. Memorandum of Conversation between David Ben Gurion, Nahum Goldmann, Eliezer Kaplan, and Loy Henderson, et al., June 27, 1945, 867n.01/6-2745, N.A., 1945–49.

38. Ibid.

39. Hurewitz, p. 228.

40. Statement of Present Arab Attitude over the Palestine Question, Enclosure No. 1, Despatch No. 24657 from Raymond Hare, First Secretary of the Embassy (London) to the Secretary of State, 867n.01/3-345, N.A., 1945–49.

41. Ibid.

42. Hurewitz, p. 229.

43. Laski to Stanley Mosk, October 10, 1945, Truman Papers, Box 772, File

204, Misc., HSTL.

44. Hurewitz, p. 231.

45. Truman, *Memoirs*, I, p. 69.

46. Ibid., II, p. 133.

47. Ibid., I, p. 69.

48. FRUS, 1945, Vol. VII, pp. 707–09.

49. Stevens, p. 130.

50. Ibid.; form letter from Robert Wagner and Robert Taft to Senate members, May 18, 1945, Wagner Papers.

51. New York *Times*, July 5, 1943.

52. Truman, *Memoirs*, II, p. 135.

53. Ibid., p. 136.

54. Sykes, *Crossroads*, p. 278.

55. Truman, *Memoirs*, II, p. 136.

56. Text of Harrison Report, New York *Times*, September 30, 1945.

57. Bauer, *Brichah*, p. 77. Dr. Schwartz was the European director of the Jewish relief organization, the Joint Distribution Committee (JDC). At Harrison's insistence, the State Department officially requested Schwartz to assist in Harrison's investigation. Although the JDC was officially nonpolitical and was not itself involved in, or even fully aware of, Zionist activities in Europe, Dr. Schwartz had strong Zionist sympathies and at times used his office to render aid to the Zionists through various means that included providing JDC funds to the Brichah organization. Rabbi Klausner, a former American Army Chaplain, was involved with the Zionist Movement in Europe between 1945–48. He was inclined to support "a radical, even extreme Zionism." Ibid., pp. 53, 87, 89, 188.

58. Ibid., p. 77.

59. FRUS, 1945, Vol. VIII, p. 739.

60. Ibid., p. 740.

61. New York *Times*, September 30, 1945.

62. FRUS, 1945, Vol. VIII, pp. 723, 733.

63. Ibid., p. 733.

64. Ibid.

65. Esco Foundation, II, pp. 1188–89.

66. Silver to Wagner, August 27, 1945, Wagner Papers.

67. Silver to Wagner, September 6, 1945, Wagner Papers.

68. Sykes, *Crossroads*, p. 297.

69. Memorandum of Conversation between Dean Acheson and Emanuel Neumann et al., September 20, 1945, 867n.01/9-2045, N.A., 1945–49.

70. Stevens, pp. 136–37.

71. Sumner Welles, *We Need Not Fail* (Cambridge, Mass.: Riverside Press, 1948), pp. 32–33.

72. FRUS, 1945, Vol. VIII, p. 743.

73. Ibid., p. 750.

74. Memorandum of Conversation between Dean Acheson and the Ministers of Egypt, Iraq, Syria, and Lebanon, October 3, 1945, 867n.01/10-345, N.A., 1945–49.

75. FRUS, 1945, Vol. VIII, p. 698.

76. Truman, *Memoirs*, II, p. 140.

77. FRUS, 1945, Vol. VIII, pp. 727-30.

78. Ibid.

79. Truman, *Memoirs*, II, p. 137.

80. Rosenman to Truman, September 7, 1945, Palestine 1945 File, HSTL.

81. FRUS, 1945, Vol. VIII, pp. 746-47.

82. Memorandum of Conversation between Acheson, Neumann et al., September 20, 1945, 867n.01/9-2045, N.A., 1945-49.

83. Henderson to Acheson, October 1, 1945, 867n.01/10-145, N.A., 1945-49.

84. Ibid.

85. Views of the Department of State concerning American promises regarding Palestine, October 2, 1945, attached to Acheson to Truman, October 2, 1945, 867n.01/10-245, N.A., 1945-49.

86. Ibid.

87. FRUS, 1945, Vol. VIII, pp. 745-48.

NOTES TO CHAPTER 10

1. Howard M. Sachar, *Europe Leaves the Middle East* (New York: Alfred A. Knopf, 1972), pp. 387-406.

2. Kirk, *Middle East, 1945-50*, p. 6; Sykes, *Crossroads*, pp. 318-19, 350.

3. FRUS, 1945, Vol. VIII, pp. 771-72.

4. Truman, *Memoirs*, II, p. 142.

5. Rosenman to Truman, October 23, 1945, Samuel Rosenman Papers, HSTL.

6. Ibid.

7. Rosenman to Truman, October 17, 1945, Samuel Rosenman Papers, HSTL.

8. Memorandum of Conversation between the Secretary of State and the British Ambassador, October 29, 1945, 867n.01/10-2945, N.A., 1945-49.

9. Rosenman to Truman, November 1, 1945, Palestine 1945 File, HSTL.

10. Stevens, pp. 140-41.

11. Text available in Crossman, p. 206.

12. FRUS, 1945, Vol. VIII, pp. 827-28.

13. Ibid.

14. Stevens, pp. 111-16.

15. United States, President, *Public Papers of the Presidents of the United States* (Washington, D.C.: U.S. Government Printing Office, 1961), Harry S Truman, 1945, pp. 572-76.

16. Sykes, *Crossroads*, p. 287.

17. Begin, pp. 185-86, 177-83, 212-31.

18. Ibid., pp. 185-86.

19. Kirk, *Middle East, 1945-50*, pp. 194-95.

20. Hurewitz, p. 235.

21. This first attack was a dramatic demonstration of the capabilities of the co-ordinated Jewish military forces. British naval forces lost three small craft, the railway in Palestine was wrecked in 50 places, railway stations were attacked, and an

assault was mounted on the oil refinery at Haifa. Sykes, *Crossroads*, p. 283.

22. FRUS, 1945, Vol. II, p. 1215. The secretary of war, in a memorandum to the secretary of state, pointed out that the influx into the American zones of occupation was primarily a political question, and one which, because of existing agreements and rules of occupation, faced the Army with a dilemma:

> The problem presented . . . is a new one with respect to which no United States policy has been established. In occupying Germany the United States undertook to administer the United States Zone and to care for displaced persons found therein at the time of the German surrender. In the Berlin Protocol the United States, with the United Kingdom, and the USSR, agreed to accept into Germany Germans formerly resident in Poland, Hungary and Czechoslovakia. No agreement has to date been made or responsibility assumed by this Government to grant asylum in the United States Zone to persons who claim to be victims of the discrimination other than German.
>
> It is my strong feeling . . . that the War Department must look to the Department of State for a firm policy decision with respect to this problem.

23. Bauer, *Brichah*, pp. 87–94.

24. Ibid., pp. 76–77, 82, 89, 96.

25. Ibid., p. 96.

26. Ibid., p. 280.

27. Silver and Wise to Truman, November 15, 1945, Official File, HSTL.

28. American Consul General in Jerusalem, L. C. Pinkerton, to the Secretary of State, Despatch No. 2336, December 15, 1945, 867n.01/12-1545, N.A., 1945–49.

29. The American Minister in Cairo to the Secretary of State, November 26, 1945, 867n.01/11-2645, N.A., 1945–49.

30. Cited in Hurewitz, p. 237.

31. Ibid., pp. 239–40.

32. S. Pinkney Tuck, American Legation, Cairo, to the Secretary of State, Despatch No. 1221, December 15, 1945, 867n.01/12-1545, N.A., 1945–49, enclosure: "The Higher Committee's Reply to Mr. Bevin."

33. Tuck to the Secretary of State, Telegram A-668, December 28, 1945, 867n.01/2-2845, N.A., 1945–49.

34. Pinkerton, American Consul General, Jerusalem, to the Secretary of State, March 16, 1946, 867n.01/3-1646, N.A., 1945–49.

35. Great Britain, Parliament (Commons), *Hansard Official Report*, Fifth Series, Vol. 415 (1945–46), Col. 1927.

36. Esco Foundation, II, pp. 1193–94.

37. New York *Times*, November 14, 1945.

38. Celler to Truman, November 15, 1945, Official File, HSTL.

39. Rosenman to Truman, November 19, 1945, Palestine 1945 File, HSTL.

40. New York *Times*, December 7, 1942.

41. David Horowitz, who at the time headed the Jewish Agency's Department of Economic Planning, recorded the perceptive initial impressions he formed upon meeting McDonald, Buxton, and Crum at the committee's first public hearings:

> Frank W. Buxton . . . broadminded, and inclined to favor our cause; James G. McDonald, a man with a reputation for possessing wide knowledge of affairs and sym-

pathetic to Zionism; Bartley Crum, a skilled politician and lawyer with large ambitions . . . and likely to be an ally of our cause.

David Horowitz, *State in the Making* (New York: Alfred A. Knopf, 1953), p. 51.

McDonald had long been extremely active on behalf of Zionism. His candidacy for the Anglo-American Committee of Inquiry, first suggested by Samuel Rosenman, was strongly supported by Senator Wagner, who promised Zionist leaders to secure positions for pro-Zionists on the committee. As a committee member, McDonald was a consistent champion of the Zionist cause. He subsequently became the first ambassador to Israel. See Henderson to Acheson, December 20, 1945, 867n.01/12-1245, N.A., 1945–49; Wagner to Botein, December 7, 1945, Wagner Papers; James G. McDonald, *My Mission to Israel* (New York: Simon and Schuster, 1951).

42. In a private letter to James Byrnes written several months after the creation of Israel, Buxton revealed something of the romantic perspective he brought to bear on the Palestine question:

> How thrilling the Palestine or Israel news is! I've seen the fall or decline of Germany, Japan, France, Italy, and England. Now I am privileged to watch the birth or re-birth of a nation which has been moribund for 2,000 years. Regardless of the relative merits of the Jewish and Arab claims, here's something portentious and exhilarating—"manifest destiny," "the inevitability of history," a conflict between the traditional East and the progressive West, a token of the possibilities of the United Nations. I have you to thank for a reserved seat as the pageant unfolded.

Buxton to Byrnes, November 30, 1948, Papers of James Byrnes, Robert Muldrow Cooper Library, Clemson University.

43. Bartley Crum was also recommended initially for committee membership by Samuel Rosenman. A pro-Zionist British colleague on the investigative team appraised Crum as "the only American with us who had a political future in front of him which could be made or marred by the attitude he adopted toward the Jewish question." Crossman, p. 31.

44. Ibid., p. 28.

45. Crum, p. 35.

46. Ibid., pp. 35–36.

47. Stevens, p. 145.

48. Great Britain, "Report of the Anglo-American Committee of Enquiry Regarding the Problems of European Jews and Palestine," Cmd. 6808 (London: His Majesty's Stationery Office, 1946), p. 4. (Hereafter cited as "Anglo-American Report.")

49. Ibid.

50. Ibid., p. 3.

51. Ibid., pp. 4–5.

52. Ibid., pp. 7–8.

53. Horowitz, p. 94.

54. McDonald, p. 24.

55. Sykes, *Crossroads*, p. 293.

56. While the text of the relevant recommendation in the report of the Inquiry Committee uses the term "award," the appended "Comment" uses "award" and "is-

sue" interchangeably.

57. The exact wording of the recommendation in question is as follows: "We recommend (a) that 100,000 certificates be authorized immediately for the admission into Palestine of Jews who have been the victims of Nazi and Fascist persecution; (b) that these certificates be awarded as far as possible in 1946 and that actual immigration be pushed forward as rapidly as conditions will permit." "Anglo-American Report," p. 2.

58. Ibid., p. 7.

59. Ibid., p. 2.

60. Ibid., p. 1.

61. Ibid., p. 10.

62. Sykes, *Crossroads*, p. 293.

63. For example, in 1945 Nahum Goldmann warned officials of the Near East Division that grave consequences might result from any British policy that precluded the establishment of a Jewish state. "Anything might happen," cautioned the Zionist leader, "in a community where 60,000 young men were fully trained and ready to take up arms in defense of their rights." Memorandum of Conversation between Goldmann and Henderson et al., June 20, 1945, 867n.01/6-2045, N.A., 1945-49.

Similarly, David Ben Gurion informed State Department officials that the Palestinian Jewish community was prepared to destroy itself in fruitless warfare against Britain: "The Jews had no desire to have any trouble with the British Government and they knew perfectly well that if the worst came to the worst, they would not last long against the combined might of the British Empire. They would, however, fight if necessary in defense of their rights and the consequences would be on Great Britain's head." Memorandum of Conversation between David Ben Gurion and Loy Henderson et al., June 27, 1945, 867n.01/6-2745, N.A., 1945-49.

Among the more responsible Arab spokesmen who at times warned that the Arab world might prefer a hopeless and protracted war against the West rather than the establishment of a Jewish state in any part of Palestine were Azzam Pasha, the Egyptian secretary general of the Arab League, and Fadhil al-Jamali, a leading Iraqi political leader.

In an effort to prevent the United States from supporting a United Nations resolution recommending Palestine's partition, Azzam warned that war might result and that the "entire resources of [the] Moslem world would be thrown into the fray even if [the] reaction were American intervention and [the] occupation of large sections of [the] Near East." The American chargé at Damascus, Robert Memminger, to the Secretary of State, Airgram A-392, October 22, 1947, 867n.01/10-2247, N.A., 1945-49.

More than a year earlier, Fadhil al-Jamali, Iraq's foreign minister, had warned that an Anglo-American effort to establish a Jewish state in Palestine could lead to "warfare during a period of 200 years between East and West." According to Jamali,

with both the United States and Great Britain against the Arabs it was probable that [the Arabs] would lose on the battlefield and a Jewish state might be set up. The seeds of destruction would have been sown, however, and the Jewish people would find themselves in a hostile world. . . . the Crusaders came and were eventually eliminated from the Arab world.

Report on Trip of Philip W. Ireland, First Secretary of American Legation, Cairo, to Arab Countries, June 20, 1946, "Confidential File, 1946," Unnumbered Document, N.A., 1945–49.

64. FRUS, 1946, Vol. VII, p. 587.

65. Truman, *Memoirs*, II, p. 146.

66. Hurewitz, p. 242.

67. Sykes, *Crossroads*, p. 295.

68. FRUS, 1946, Vol. VII, pp. 587–88.

69. Waldemar Gallman, American Embassy, London, to the Acting Secretary of State, April 24, 1946, 867n.01/4-2446, N.A., 1945–49.

70. The British Ambassador in Washington, Lord Halifax, to the Acting Secretary of State, April 29, 1946, 867n.01/2-2946, N.A., 1945–49.

71. Acting Secretary of State Dean Acheson to James Byrnes, April 30, 1946, and Acheson to the American Ambassador in London, April 30, 1946, 867n.01/4-3046, N.A., 1945–49.

72. *Public Papers of the Presidents*, Harry S Truman, 1946, p. 218.

73. Ibid.

74. Great Britain, Parliament (Commons), *Hansard Official Reports*, Fifth Series, Vol. 433, Col. 195–97.

75. The British government did not publish intelligence reports confirming the active cooperation then existing between the Haganah, on the one hand, and the Irgun and Stern gangs on the other, until the summer of 1946.

76. Crum, pp. 278–79.

77. Richard Crossman, *A Nation Reborn* (New York: Atheneum Publishers, 1960), p. 82.

NOTES TO CHAPTER 11

1. Both governments requested responses from the governments of Iraq, Syria, Lebanon, Egypt, Transjordan, Saudi Arabia, and Yemen. The leaders of the Arab community in Palestine were also invited to send their views. The United States, but not Britain, additionally asked for a formal presentation from the Arab League Secretariat.

On the Jewish side, Britain preferred to contact only the Jewish Agency, which was the accredited representative of Jewry in matters pertaining to the national home. The United States extended its consultations to include most interested Jewish organizations in America, among which Washington numbered the anti-Zionist American Council for Judaism. However, Washington recognized the Jewish Agency views were of central importance as a barometer of organized Jewish opinion. See Truman, *Memoirs*, II, p. 146; *State Department Bulletin*, June 2, 1946, p. 956.

2. Hurewitz, p. 250.

3. Tuck to the Secretary of State, May 3, 1946, Telegram 770, 867n.01/5-346, N.A., 1945–49.

4. FRUS, 1946, Vol. VII, pp. 604–04.

5. Stevens, p. 150.

6. Hurewitz, p. 251.

7. Horowitz, p. 94.

8. Ibid.

9. Ibid., pp. 94–95.

10. Stevens, pp. 149–50.

11. Hurewitz, p. 253.

12. Stevens, p. 149.

13. Ibid., pp. 116–18.

14. Hurewitz, p. 255.

15. Marlowe, p. 210.

16. FRUS, 1946, Vol. VII, pp. 591–92.

17. Hilldring's pro-Zionism is well-documented. See, for example, McDonald, p. 170.

18. George P. Merriam to Acheson, May 8, 1946, 867n.01/5-346, N.A., 1945–49.

19. Acheson to Hilldring and Henderson, May 14, 1946, 867n.01/5-346, N.A., 1945–49.

20. FRUS, 1946, Vol. VII, pp. 591–92. Loy Henderson recalls that Hilldring never specified what he considered the "military and strategic" American interests in Europe that were being undermined by the large number of displaced persons. Henderson interview.

21. Taylor to Truman, May 15, 1946, Official File, HSTL.

22. Memorandum for the President, by David Niles, May 27, 1946, Official File, HSTL.

23. Ibid.

24. FRUS, 1946, Vol. VII, pp. 595–96.

25. Truman, *Memoirs*, II, p. 146.

26. FRUS, 1946, Vol. VII, p. 606.

27. Truman, *Memoirs*, II, p. 149.

28. Ibid.

29. *Public Papers of the Presidents*, Harry S Truman, 1946, pp. 287, 302.

30. Ibid.; "White House Statement on the President's Meeting with Leaders of the Jewish Agency for Palestine," July 2, 1946, p. 335.

31. On July 8, 1946, for example, Niles wrote to Herbert Lehman, a former governor of New York, on behalf of the president:

> The President added . . . that it was his determination that recent events should mean no delay in pushing forward with the policy of transferring 100,000 Jewish immigrants to Palestine. . . . The President indicated that the Government of the United States was prepared to assume technical and financial responsibility for the transportation of these immigrants to Palestine.

Niles to Lehman, July 8, 1946, File 204 Misc., Box 772, Truman Papers, HSTL.

32. New York *Times*, June 13, 1946.

33. Washington *Post*, July 13, 1946.

34. Memorandum for the President, by David Niles, May 27, 1946, Official File, HSTL.

35. *Public Papers of the Presidents*, Harry S Truman, 1946, p. 302.

36. Kirk, *Middle East, 1945-50*, pp. 219-20; Hurewitz, p. 254.

37. Begin, p. 215. Evidence linking Eliezer Kaplan, Moshe Shertok, Bernard Joseph, and David Ben Gurion to terrorist activities in Palestine was quickly published by the British government in "Palestine Statement of Information Relating to Acts of Violence" (Colonial Office), Cmd. 6873, July 1946 (London: His Majesty's Stationery Office).

Loss of the agency's files proved extremely embarrassing to the Zionist Movement. For example, among the captured material were found copies of several confidential and top-secret U.S. government communications. Among others, these included a photostat of a letter written by Truman to the Egyptian leader Nokrashi Pasha in June 1945; a copy of a top-secret report, dated January 31, 1946, on "Oil in the Middle East" prepared by the American Chief of Military Intelligence; and top-secret "notices" issued by the American and British governments on December 6, 1945, regarding a joint statement concerning a settlement of Lend Lease and Reciprocal Aid debts. See The Consul General at Jerusalem, L. C. Pinkerton, to the Secretary of State, Cable 272, August 6, 1946, 867n.01/8-646, N.A., Confidential Files, 1945-49; see also Dean Acheson to the Consul General at Jerusalem, Cable 326, July 31, 1946, 867n.01/7-2346, N.A., Confidential Files, 1945-49.

38. Hurewitz, p. 254.

39. Ibid., p. 255.

40. Begin, p. 204.

41. Horowitz, pp. 101-21.

42. Ibid., p. 115.

43. Truman, *Memoirs*, II, p. 150.

44. Roberta Barrows (White House Secretary) to Mrs. Klar, June 20, 1946, Truman Papers, File 204, Miscellaneous, HSTL.

45. Celler to Connelly, June 25, 1946, Truman Papers, File 204, Miscellaneous, HSTL.

46. Celler to Truman, July 31, 1946, Truman Papers, File 204, Miscellaneous, HSTL.

47. Wise to Truman, July 8, 1946, Official File, HSTL.

48. Eddy to the Secretary of State, Telegram 165, May 28, 1946, 867n.01/5-2846, N.A., 1945-49. A few days after this report, Eddy was in the United States. He had a meeting with Truman to discuss American relations with Saudi Arabia on June 6, 1946. See J. Rives Childs to the Secretary of State, July 5, 1946, 867n.01/7-546, N.A., 1945-49.

49. Eddy to the Secretary of State, May 28, 1946, 867n.01/5-2846, N.A., 1945-49.

50. Gordon H. Mattison to the Secretary of State, May 22, 1946, 867n.01/5-1046, N.A., 1945-49.

51. Wadsworth to the Secretary of State, Telegram 263, June 5, 1946, 867n.01/6-546, N.A., 1945-49.

52. J. Rives Childs, Minister to Saudi Arabia, to the Secretary of State, October 19, 1946, Telegram 304, 867n.01/10-1946, Confidential File, N.A., 1945-49.

53. Pinkerton to the Secretary of State, Telegram 226, July 10, 1946, 867n.01/7-1046, N.A., 1945-49.

54. "Report on Trip of Philip W. Ireland, First Secretary of Legation, to Arab Countries of Palestine, Lebanon, Syria, Transjordan, May 15-30, 1946," June 10, 1946, Enclosure No. 1 to Despatch No. 1667 dated July 1, 1946, from the American Legation, Cairo, Unnumbered Document, N.A., 1945-49.

55. Ibid.

56. Memorandum of the Board of Alternates to the Cabinet Committee on Palestine as to Certain Matters to be Discussed with the British in London, n.d., 867n.01/7-946, N.A., 1945-49.

57. Matters Re Palestine to be Considered before London Conference, n.d., 867n.01/7-946, N.A., 1945-49. A marginal notation on this document indicates that Truman gave his approval on July 9, 1946.

58. Ibid.

59. "Jewish Population in Europe" (4th rev. ed.), Research Department, the American Jewish Joint Distribution Committee, May 2, 1946, Official File, HSTL; Bauer, *Brichah*, pp. 319-20, 261, 289-98.

60. Matters Re Palestine.

61. FRUS, 1946, Vol. VII, p. 647.

62. Ibid., pp. 652-67.

63. Ibid., p. 659.

64. Ibid.

65. Ibid., p. 663.

66. Ibid.

67. Ibid., p. 667.

68. Ibid.

69. Ibid., p. 652.

NOTES TO CHAPTER 12

1. Begin, pp. 215-16.

2. The Haganah command authorized the attack on the King David at the end of June. Ibid., pp. 213-14.

3. Horowitz, p. 197.

4. Moshe Smolensky, "The Anglo-American Report Points the Way," *Commentary* 2, no. 1 (July 1946):1-6.

5. Cited in Stevens, p. 152.

6. FRUS, 1946, Vol. VII, pp. 667-68.

7. Millis and Duffield, pp. 188-89.

8. FRUS, 1946, Vol. VII, p. 669, n. 18.

9. Ibid., pp. 669-70.

10. Ibid.

11. Ibid., p. 671, n. 20.

12. Ibid., pp. 671-73.

13. Ibid.

14. Ibid.

15. Ibid.

16. Ibid., pp. 673–74.

17. Ibid., p. 677.

18. *Public Papers of the Presidents*, Harry S Truman, 1946, p. 367.

19. FRUS, 1946, Vol. VII, p. 675.

20. Great Britain, Parliament (Commons), *Hansard Official Report*, Fifth Series, Vol. 426, Cols. 962–71.

21. FRUS, 1946, Vol. VII, pp. 677–78.

22. Evan M. Wilson, *Decision on Palestine: How the U.S. Came to Recognize Israel* (Stanford, Calif.: Hoover Institution Press, 1979), p. 94.

23. Truman, *Memoirs*, II, p. 152.

24. Judge Robert G. Simmons to Truman, June 9, 1947, OF Misc., HSTL.

25. Truman to Simmons, June 16, 1946, OF Misc., HSTL.

26. Further evidence of Truman's basic approval of the Morrison-Grady Plan is found in unpublished memoirs by Henry F. Grady. Discussing the aftermath of his negotiations in London in the summer of 1946, Grady recalls that "privately, the President . . . several times said to me that he thought the plan for provincial autonomy was the best of all the solutions proposed for Palestine." Unpublished manuscript, Henry F. Grady Papers, HSTL.

27. Wilson to the Secretary of State, Telegram 324, March 18, 1946, 867n.01/ 1846, N.A., 1945–49. During this same period several highly placed Egyptian political figures were also privately voicing moderate views. Ali Maher Pasha, former prime minister and Egyptian representative at the 1939 London Conference, told a representative of the Jewish Agency in 1946 that he favored a "compromise solution" in Palestine. Egypt's Prime Minister Sidki Pasha went even further, telling the Agency's representative and the American Minister in Cairo that he believed the "only suitable compromise" in Palestine would be some sort of partition plan. Azzam Pasha, secretary general of the Arab League, privately stated his willingness to assist in bringing about a Zionist-Arab compromise, including one "which might take the form of partition." Lutfi Pasha, former Egyptian foreign minister, was also privately inclined to stress the need for a compromise in Palestine. See Nahum Goldmann to Dean Acheson, November 18, 1946, and enclosure, 867n.01/1846, N.A. and the American minister in Cairo to the Secretary of State, Telegram no. 1986, December 20, 1946, 867n.01/12-2046, Top Secret File.

28. Gallman to the Secretary of State, August 2, 1946, 867n.01/9-246, N.A., 1945–49.

29. FRUS, 1946, Vol. VII, p. 675.

30. Ibid., p. 684, n. 48.

31. *Public Papers of the Presidents*, Harry S Truman, 1946, p. 424.

32. Memorandum of Conversation between Nahum Goldmann and Dean Acheson, Doc. 9–16, August 7, 1946, 867n.01/8-746, N.A., 1945–49.

33. Begin, p. 210.

34. Sykes, *Crossroads*, p. 303; Horowitz, p. 117.

35. Dr. Nahum Goldmann in a private letter to the writer, March 31, 1973.

36. Ibid.

37. FRUS, 1946, Vol. VII, p. 681.

38. Ibid.

39. Ibid., pp. 679–82.

40. Ibid.

41. Memorandum of Conversation between Nahum Goldmann and Acheson, August 7, 1946, 867n.01/8-746, Confidential Files, N.A., 1945–49.

42. *Public Papers of the Presidents*, Harry S Truman, 1946, p. 424.

43. Sykes, *Crossroads*, p. 360.

44. Hurewitz, p. 262.

45. FRUS, 1946, Vol. VII, pp. 685–86.

46. Memorandum of Conversation between Eliahu Epstein and Loy Henderson et al. "Refusal of Jewish Agency to Participate in London Conference," by Evan Wilson, September 5, 1946, 867n.01/9-546, N.A., 1945–49.

47. Cited by David Sachar, p. 41.

48. Hurewitz, pp. 263–64.

49. FRUS, 1946, Vol. VII, pp. 697–98.

50. Ibid.

51. Sykes, *Crossroads*, p. 303.

52. FRUS, 1946, Vol. VII, pp. 700–01.

53. Bevin later explained this incident to the House of Commons:

> I advanced the idea of an interim arrangement, leading ultimately to self-government. I indicated that I did not mind whether this interim arrangement was for five years, or ten years, or three years, or whatever it was. I said to them "if you will work together [with the Arabs] for three, five or ten years, it might well be that you will not want to separate. Let us try to make up the difference." At that stage things looked more hopeful. There was a feeling—I do not think I overestimated it—when they left me in the Foreign Office that day, that I had the right approach at last.

Great Britain, Parliament (Commons), *Hansard Official Record*, Fifth Series, Vol. 433, Cols, 1907–08.

54. Memorandum of Conversation between Eliahu Epstein and Henderson et al. October 3, 1946, 867n.01/10-346, N.A., 1945–49.

55. FRUS, 1946, Vol. VII, pp. 700–01.

56. Clayton to Truman, September 12, 1946, cited in David Sachar, pp. 42–46.

57. Ibid.

58. Ibid.

59. New York *Times*, September 30, 1946.

60. Millis and Duffield, p. 347.

61. FRUS, 1946, Vol. VII, pp. 701–03.

62. Ibid., p. 704.

63. Ibid.

64. Great Britain, Parliament (Commons) *Hansard Official Record*, Fifth Series, Vol. 433, Col. 1908.

65. FRUS, 1946, Vol. VII, pp. 704–05.

66. Ibid., pp. 701–03.

67. New York *Times*, October 7, 1946.

68. In late October, Truman again defended his position on the 100,000 in a strong letter to Ibn Saud, written in answer to criticisms the monarch had made of the Yom Kippur statement. Truman informed Ibn Saud that he considered neither his

position on behalf of the admission of "considerable numbers of displaced Jews into Palestine" nor his statements "with regard to the solution of the problem of Palestine" as constituting in any sense actions "hostile to the Arab people."

Frank E. Manuel considers Truman's letter to Saud as "the first diplomatic document . . . in which the United States, in however circumscribed a manner, stated its historic obligations toward the Jewish homeland." Manuel, p. 328.

The fact that Truman's letter, dated October 26, 1946, was made public soon after it was sent indicates that the president was once again to some extent motivated by his concern over the outcome of the upcoming congressional elections. For the text of Truman's letter, see New York *Times*, October 29, 1946.

69. Epstein to Goldmann, October 9, 1946, Weizmann Archives, HSTL.

70. Gelber to Epstein, October 15, 1946, cited in David Sachar, p. 47.

71. Hurewitz, p. 267.

72. Ibid.; Sykes, *Crossroads*, p. 363.

73. Stevens, p. 122.

74. Ibid.

75. Weizmann, pp. 442–43.

76. Stevens, p. 122; Hurewitz, p. 269.

77. During the interval, the British government had extended amnesty to several leading followers of Haj Amin al-Husseini who had been excluded from Palestine since the Arab revolt of 1936–39. This gesture, undoubtedly reinforced by pleas from Arab governments, appears to have induced the Higher Executive to participate formally in the second stage of the conference. Hurewitz, pp. 269–72.

78. Ibid.

79. FRUS, 1946, Vol. VII, pp. 732–33.

NOTES TO CHAPTER 13

1. For a contemporary assessment of the importance of global U.S. strategy to Washington's approach to Palestine see Sidney Hertzberg, "This Month in History," *Commentary* 3, no. 4 (April 1947):357–58.

2. FRUS, 1947, Vol. V, pp. 1048–49.

3. Ibid.

4. Ibid., p. 1051.

5. Bauer, *Brichah*, p. 211. Bauer estimates that as many as 95,000 Polish Jews eventually fled to Western Europe after anti-Semitic violence broke out in Kielce. Bauer argues that lower figures given by the American Joint Distribution Committee are inaccurate.

6. Ibid., p. 299.

7. Ibid.

8. Ibid., p. 302.

9. Wolfson to Slawson, June 28, 1948, Papers of Joel Wolfson, HSTL; Report of Chaplain Abraham Klausner to the American Jewish Conference, May 2, 1948, Administrative Files: Refugees, ACJF.

10. Bauer, *Brichah*, p. 300.

11. Lilienthal, pp. 193–94.

12. New York *Times*, May 5, 1948.

13. Klausner Report, May 2, 1948, Administrative File: Refugees, ACJF.

14. Haber to Grossman, May 26, 1948, Administrative Files: Refugees, ACJF.

15. *Public Papers of the Presidents*, Harry S Truman, 1947, p. 10.

16. U.S. Congress, *Congressional Record*, 80th Cong., 1st Sess., House of Representatives, H.R. 2910, p. 2999.

17. New York *Times*, May 19, 1947.

18. New York *Times*, June 5, 7, and 8, 1947.

19. Lilienthal, p. 35.

20. *Public Papers of the Presidents*, Harry S Truman, 1947, p. 248.

21. Ibid., pp. 324–29.

22. New York *Times*, June 8, 1948.

23. New York *Times*, May 3, 1948.

24. Hurewitz, pp. 259–60.

25. "Income-Tax Status of Certain Zionist Organizations," May 21, 1947, 867n.01/5-2147; Marshall to Snyder, June 17, 1947, 867n.01/5-2147; Memorandum of Conversation between the Secretary of State and the British Ambassador, January 4, 1947, 867n.01/1-447, N.A., 1945–49.

26. Marshall to Snyder, June 17, 1947, 867n.01/5-2147; Memorandum of Conversation between Mr. Vallance and Mr. Leming, October 3, 1947, 867n.01/9–1747, N.A., 1945–49.

27. *Public Papers of the Presidents*, Harry S Truman, 1947, p. 267.

28. Stevens, p. 168.

29. FRUS, 1947, Vol. V, pp. 1068–85.

30. Stevens, p. 166.

31. Jacob Robinson, *Palestine and the United Nations: Prelude to Solution* (Westport, Conn.: Greenwood Press, 1971), pp. 100–40.

32. New York *Times*, May 8, 13, 1947.

33. Hurewitz, p. 287.

34. Sykes, *Crossroads*, p. 317.

35. Jon Kimche and David Kimche, *Both Sides of the Hill* (London: Secker and Warburg, 1960), p. 31.

36. By 1947 the Labour government was maintaining more than 80,000 troops (almost 10 percent of Britain's military strength) in Palestine. In addition, the British government was bearing the burden of over 16,000 British and local police in the country. Security requirements had cost London some $200 million since Labour's assumption of power. It should also not be forgotten that the British government bore the responsibility for providing for nearly 12,000 illegal immigrants interned on Cyprus. Rising casualties among Britons in Palestine added to domestic pressure upon the Attlee cabinet to abandon the mandate. All of this, of course, underlay London's consistent efforts to make clear its determination to avoid responsibility for implementing a settlement not supported by both major communities in Palestine. A penetrating discussion of these points is available in Hurewitz, pp. 274–83.

37. Sidney Hertzberg, "This Month in History," *Commentary* 3, no. 4 (April 1947):356.

38. Sidney Hertzberg, "This Month in History," *Commentary* 3, no. 5 (May 1947):469.

39. Ibid.

40. For Ghuri's speech, see the New York *Times*, May 13, 1947.

41. The American Chargé in Cairo to the Secretary of State, June 10, 1947, 867n.01/6-1047, N.A., 1945–49.

42. Sidney Hertzberg, "This Month in History," *Commentary* 3, no. 6 (June 1947):559.

43. FRUS, 1947, Vol. V, p. 1084.

44. Hertzberg, *Commentary*, June 1947.

45. FRUS, 1947, Vol. V, p. 1089.

46. Stevens, p. 166.

47. Millis and Duffield, p. 304.

48. Great Britain, *Report to the General Assembly by the United Nations Special Committee on Palestine, Geneva, Switzerland, 31 August, 1947* (London: His Majesty's Stationery Office, 1947).

49. Ibid., pp. 70, 78–81.

50. Ibid., pp. 89–91.

51. Ibid., p. 68.

52. Ibid., p. 75.

53. Ibid., p. 97.

54. If one accounts for Bedouin cultivators and stock owners who would seek seasonal grazing lands in other areas of Palestine, the Jewish state would have contained 498,000 Jews and 497,000 Arabs. This point is discussed cogently in Wilson's *Decision on Palestine*, pp. 112–13. On the other hand, Maurice Goldbloom, writing in October 1947, suggested that the actual balance would have been 506,000 Arabs to 500,000 Jews. See "This Month in History," *Commentary* 4, no. 4 (October 1947):359.

55. It could be expected that the Bedouin would not immediately participate in the political process; the percentage of adults was lower in the Arab community; and the Jewish population of the internationalized city of Jerusalem (estimated at 100,000) would exercise full political rights in the Jewish state. Institute for Palestine Studies, *The Partition of Palestine* (Beirut: Institute for Palestine Studies, 1975), Appendix I; Goldbloom, p. 359.

56. Hurewitz, p. 299.

57. Stevens, pp. 171–72.

58. Begin, pp. 332–34; Goldbloom, p. 362.

59. Sami Hadawi, ed., *United Nations Resolutions on Palestine, 1947–1966* (Beirut: Institute for Palestine Studies, 1967), p. xii.

60. New York *Times*, July 19 and 27, August 6 and 21, September 7, 27, and 30, 1947.

61. New York *Times*, August 31 and September 11, 1947.

62. Sykes, *Crossroads*, pp. 382–83; Begin, pp. 275–90.

63. New York *Times*, August 1, 1947.

64. The American Consul General at Jerusalem to the Secretary of State, Despatch No. 174, October 4, 1947, 867n.00/10-447, N.A., 1945–49.

65. The Consul General at Jerusalem to the Secretary of State, Airgram 3543, August 15, 1947, 867n.00/8-1547, N.A., 1945–49.

66. The Consul General at Jerusalem to the Secretary of State, August 15, 1947, Airgram 3544, 867n.00/8-1547, N.A., 1945–49.

67. The Consul General at Jerusalem to the Chief of the Division of Near Eastern Affairs, August 4, 1947, 867n.01/8-447, N.A., 1945–49. Dr. Judah Magnus, president of the Hebrew University of Jerusalem, was acknowledged leader of a loosely knit group within the Yishuv that favored a binational Arab-Jewish state in Palestine. The best work on Jewish binationalists in mandated Palestine is Susan Lee Hattis, *The Bi-National Idea in Palestine During Mandatory Times* (Haifa: Shikmona, 1970).

68. The Consul General at Jerusalem to the Chief of the Division of Near Eastern Affairs, August 4, 1947, 867n.01/8-447, N.A., 1945–49.

69. The Consul General at Jerusalem to the Secretary of State, September 13, 1947, 867n.01/9-1347, N.A., 1945–49.

70. Ibid.

71. The Chargé in Damascus to the Secretary of State, Airgram A-356, September 23, 1947, 867n.01/9-2347, N.A., 1945–49.

72. The Consul General at Jerusalem to the Secretary of State, Airgram A-225, October 22, 1947, 867n.01/2247, N.A., 1945–49.

73. An example of this is found in remarks made by the secretary-general of the Arab League, Azzam Pasha, to an officer of the American Legation in Damascus near the end of October 1947. While Azzam Pasha spoke with certainty of a war between Palestinian Arabs and individual recruits gathered from the Arab world on the one hand, and the Jewish community of Palestine on the other, should a Jewish state be created, he indicated that the Arab states would become involved "if necessary." The activities of Arab delegations at the United Nations during October and November 1947 also establish the Arab governments' hope to avoid fighting a war in Palestine. Meminger to the Secretary of State, Airgram A-329, October 22, 1947, N.A., 1945–49.

74. The Consul General at Jerusalem to the Secretary of State, October 11, 1947, 867n.01/1147, N.A., 1945–49.

75. New York *Times*, September 24, 1947.

76. New York *Times*, September 28, 1947; October 17, 1947.

77. FRUS, 1947, Vol. V, p. 1151.

78. Ibid., p. 1132.

79. Ibid., p. 1133.

80. Ibid., p. 1134.

81. Ibid., p. 1149.

82. Ibid., pp. 1153–58.

83. Ibid.

84. Ibid.

85. Henderson interview.

86. Hilldring became an advisor to the American delegation on September 19. David Niles obtained the general's appointment by persuading Truman that such a step would win approval from American Zionists. David Sachar, p. 60; New York *Times*, September 19, 1947.

87. FRUS, 1947, Vol. V, pp. 1173–74.

88. Ibid.

89. Ibid.

90. U.S. Department of State, "Statement by U.S. Deputy Representative to the United Nations, *The Department of State Bulletin* 18, no. 4 (October 19, 1947):761–62.

91. FRUS, 1947, Vol. V, pp. 1183–84.

92. Ibid., pp. 1177–78.

93. Ibid., p. 1178, n. 2.

94. Ibid., pp. 1181–82.

95. Henderson interview.

96. FRUS, 1947, Vol. V, pp. 1188–92.

97. Ibid.

98. Ibid., pp. 1195–96.

99. Ibid., p. 1196, n. 3.

100. Ibid., p. 1199.

101. Ibid., pp. 1186–87.

102. Ibid., pp. 1200–01.

103. Hurewitz, p. 302.

104. FRUS, 1947, Vol. V, pp. 1200–01.

105. Ibid., pp. 1219–22. The quoted remarks were made by the ambassador at a press conference on October 31, 1947. Writing to the chief of the Division of Near Eastern Affairs on the same day, an advisor to the U.S. delegation, Fraser Wilkins, explained the actual reasoning behind the idea of a U.N. Commission:

> It was the Delegation's belief that the UN Commission would represent the great moral authority of the UN in Palestine behind which and through which the UK could actually transfer the powers of government to the new states. It was our hope that London would recognize this facade which, in our view, would have the effect of removing the onus of actual partition to which the British have very reasonably objected.

Ibid., p. 1225.

106. Ibid., pp. 1209–12.

107. Ibid., pp. 1207–09.

108. Ibid., pp. 1215–16.

109. Ibid., p. 1222.

110. Ibid., pp. 1231–34.

111. Ibid., n. 1.

112. Ibid., pp. 1234–36.

113. Hurewitz, pp. 305–06.

114. FRUS, 1947, Vol. V, pp. 1259–61.

115. The roll-call vote in the General Assembly was as follows: *For*: Australia, Belgium, Bolivia, Brazil, Canada, Costa Rica, Czechoslovakia, Denmark, the Dominican Republic, Ecuador, France, Guatemala, Haiti, Iceland, Liberia, Luxembourg, the Netherlands, New Zealand, Nicaragua, Norway, Panama, Paraguay, Peru, the Philippines, Poland, Sweden, the Ukraine, South Africa, Uruguay, the So-

viet Union, the United States, Venezuela, White Russia. *Against*: Afghanistan, Cuba, Egypt, Greece, India, Iran, Iraq, Lebanon, Pakistan, Saudi Arabia, Syria, Turkey, Yemen. *Abstentions*: Argentina, Chile, China, Colombia, El Salvador, Ethiopia, Honduras, Mexico, the United Kingdom, Yugoslavia. *Absent*: Thailand.

116. FRUS, 1947, Vol. V, pp. 1281–82.

117. Wagner to Truman, September 29, 1947; Truman to Wagner, October 1, 1947, Wagner Papers.

118. Weizmann, p. 459.

119. Bohlen to Lovett, "U.S. Position on the Negeb," November 19, 1947, 867n.01/11-1947, N.A., 1945–49.

120. On the evening of November 19, Truman spoke with Dean Acheson about his earlier call to Hilldring. The president denied that his intention had been to alter any instructions already given by the Department of State to the American delegation. Truman stated that "he only intended to recommend our ultimate acceptance of the majority view." However, it appears that the effect of the president's intervention was to reduce the incentive of the American delegation to work for the inclusion of the Negev in the Arab state. Notation by Dean Acheson on Bohlen to Lovett, November 19, 1947, 867n.01/11-1947, N.A., 1945–49.

121. FRUS, 1947, Vol. V, pp. 1283–84.

122. Henderson interview.

123. Welles, p. 63.

124. James Byrnes to Bernard Baruch, May 24, 1948, Byrnes Papers.

125. Thomas J. Hamilton, "Partition of Palestine," *Foreign Policy Reports* 23 (February 15, 1948):291.

126. Jorge Garcia Granados, *The Birth of Israel: The Drama as I Saw It* (New York: Alfred A. Knopf, 1948), pp. 268–69.

127. Horowitz, p. 301.

128. *United Nations Bulletin* (December 9, 1947):775–76.

129. FRUS, 1947, Vol. V, pp. 1192–94. On Arab willingness to compromise, see also note 27, p. 203, Chapter 12.

130. Ibid.

131. Ibid., pp. 1253–54.

NOTES TO CHAPTER 14

1. FRUS, 1947, Vol. V, p. 1336.

2. Ibid., pp. 1319–20.

3. The Consul General at Jerusalem, Robert B. Macatee, to the Secretary of State, December 12, 1947, 867n.01/12-1247, N.A., 1945–49.

4. Marlowe, p. 243.

5. Ibid.

6. Ibid.

7. Fauzi al-Qawuqji, "Memoirs, 1948: Part I," *Journal of Palestine Studies 1*, no. 4, pp. 27–29.

8. Ibid.

9. Khalidi, Appendix VIII.

10. See, for example, al-Qawuqji, *passim*; Begin, p. 362.

11. Wilson, p. 131.

12. David Ben Gurion, *Rebirth and Destiny of Israel* (New York: Philosophical Library, 1954), p. 530.

13. Arnold Krammer, "Arms for Independence: When the Soviet Bloc Supported Israel," in Khalidi, pp. 745–53.

14. Nadev Safran, *From War to War* (New York: Pegasus, 1969).

15. Khalidi, Appendix VII, pp. 856–57.

16. Ibid.

17. Lorch, "Plan Dalet," in Khalidi, p. 757; Khalidi, Appendix IX-A.

18. Pablo Azcarate y Flores, *Mission in Palestine: 1948-1952* (Washington, D.C.: The Middle East Institute, 1966), p. 33.

19. Jon Kimche, "Deir Yassin and Jaffa," in Khalidi; Jacques de Renier, "Deir Yassin," in ibid., pp. 761–66.

20. New York *Times*, April 15, 1948.

21. Erskine B. Childers, "The Other Exodus," in Khalidi, pp. 795–803; Nafez Abdullah Nazzal, "The Zionist Occupation of Western Gallilee, 1948," *Journal of Palestine Studies*, 3, no. 3 (Spring 1974): 58–76.

22. Waines, pp. 123–24.

23. Weizmann to Truman, December 9, 1947, Official File, HSTL.

24. Morgenthau to Truman, November 29, 1947, OF 204, Misc., HSTL.

25. Emanuel Celler to Truman, December 3, 1947, OF 204, Misc., HSTL.

26. Neumann to Matthew Connelly, December 5, 1947, OF 204, Misc., HSTL.

27. New York *Times*, December 6, 1947. The actual decision to impose the embargo was taken on November 10, 1947.

28. See, for example, Mrs. D. L. Isaacs, Chairman, Palestine Committee, Women's League of Palestine, to Truman, December 12, 1947, OF, 204, Misc., HSTL.

29. Nonetheless, available evidence indicates that the State Department's Near East specialists loyally upheld the administration's policy on partition. In early December, for example, Henderson was asked by Dr. Fadhil Jamali, Iraq's foreign minister, whether any hope existed that Washington might be persuaded to abandon its support of partition in favor of a cantonal settlement. Henderson stated "that it would be misleading to hold out any such hope: the U.S. had determined its policy of supporting partition after long and careful consideration, with full realization of the seriousness of the decision, and that the decision was final and would undoubtedly be adhered to." FRUS, 1947, Vol. V, p. 1311.

30. Millis and Duffield, p. 360.

31. The Position of the United States with Respect to Palestine, February 17, 1948, Clark Clifford Papers, HSTL.

32. Ibid.

33. Ibid.

34. Millis and Duffield, pp. 347, 349, 357, 359–63.

35. Ibid., p. 347.

36. Memorandum for the President by Clark Clifford, November 19, 1947, Clifford Papers, HSTL.

37. Ibid.

38. Examples abound in the Truman Library. See, for example, Moss to Truman, February 23, 1948; Moor to Connelly, February 9, 1948; Doyle to Truman, February 14, 1948; Green to Truman, February 19, 1948, all in OF 204, Misc., HSTL.

39. John Snetsinger, *Truman, the Jewish Vote, and the Creation of Israel* (Stanford, Calif.: Hoover Institution Press, 1974), p. 80.

40. Allen Yarnell, *Democrats and Progressives: The 1948 Presidential Election as a Test for Postwar Liberalism* (Berkeley: University of California Press, 1974), pp. 553–54.

41. Ibid., pp. 552–54.

42. On November 29, 1947, the General Assembly elected the following members to the UN Committee on Palestine: Bolivia, Czechoslovakia, Denmark, Panama, and the Philippines.

43. Hurewitz, p. 311.

44. Azcarate y Flores, pp. 5–15.

45. Stevens, p. 190.

46. Millis and Duffield, pp. 376–77.

47. Dean Rusk was preoccupied with this possibility. Ibid., p. 410.

48. Ibid.

49. Truman to M. J. Slonim, March 6, 1948, OF 204, Misc., HSTL.

50. Truman, *Memoirs*, II, p. 160.

51. United States, Department of State, *Department of State Bulletin* 18 (March 7, 1948), p. 295.

52. Stevens, pp. 191–93.

53. Jack Redding, *Inside the Democratic Party* (New York: Bobbs-Merrill, 1958), p. 149.

54. New York *Times*, March 20, 1948.

55. *State Department Bulletin* 18, p. 407.

56. Ibid.

57. See, for example, Manuel, pp. 345–50; Sykes, *Crossroads*, pp. 413–14; Herbert Feis, *The Birth of Israel* (New York: W. W. Norton, 1969), pp. 53–59; Weizmann, p. 472; Zvi Ganin, *Truman, American Jewry, and Israel, 1945–1948* (New York: Holmes & Meier Publishers, 1979), pp. 161–63; Clark Clifford, "Recognizing Israel," *American Heritage* 28, no. 3 (April 1977): 4–11.

Clifford's *American Heritage* article (first delivered as a paper to a joint session of the American Jewish Historical Society and the American Historical Association in 1976) is particularly interesting in that it offers an analysis considerably different from that apparently presented to Truman shortly after Austin's statement. This is, perhaps, explained to some extent by Evan Wilson's contention that Harold P. Luks (a George Washington University graduate student thanked by Clifford for research assistance) actually wrote the article. See Wilson, pp. 219–20.

58. Notes by Charles G. Ross, March 29, 1948, Charles G. Ross Papers, HSTL. (Hereafter cited as Ross Papers.)

59. Undated notes. Clifford Papers, HSTL. The information contained in Clifford's notes is corroborated by Loy Henderson. Henderson's recollections add the following details to the story of Austin's March 19 statement: The original draft of the statement was prepared by Henderson and refined by members of the Near East

Division. Lovett and Marshall may have refined it still further before passing it on to Truman. Lovett originally showed the draft to Truman. Henderson interview. See for further elaboration FRUS, 1948, Vol. V, pp. 744–46.

60. That is, unless one argues that Lovett and Marshall deliberately conspired to betray the president's policy on Palestine. Truman, whose initial private reaction upon hearing that Austin had issued the statement was to conclude that he had been victimized by the State Department, never suggested that Marshall or Lovett might be involved. Instead, the president blamed persons on the "third or fourth" levels of the department for his difficulties (see below). Nor did the president ever subsequently suggest that Marshall or Lovett might have acted improperly or unwisely in any respect in the matter of Austin's statement.

61. This possibility is strengthened by the account of the reversal presented in Charles Ross' notes:

> What caused all the trouble? The cause lay in the fact that no final check had been made with the President before Austin spoke. He [Truman] had assumed that the alternative plan would not be urged till after *a vote in the Security Council* had demonstrated the impossibility of putting over the partition plan (original emphasis).

If the president had indeed "assumed" that Austin's statement would be triggered by the failure of partition in a Security Council vote, he evidently failed to make this clear to his secretary of state.

Additional evidence that Truman was disturbed by the timing, rather than the substance, of Austin's statement is provided by Secretary of State Marshall's account of a conversation with the president three days after Austin spoke to the Security Council. Truman, Marshall recorded,

> said the reason he was so much exercised in the matter was the fact that Austin made his statement without the President having been advised that he was going to make it at that particular time. He had agreed to the statement but said that if he had known when it was going to be made he could have taken certain measures to have avoided the political blast of the press.

See Wilson, p. 135.

62. Jacobson to Dr. Joseph Cohen, April 1, 1952, Weizmann Archives, HSTL.

63. Ibid.; Sykes, *Crossroads*, pp. 411–12

64. Truman, *Memoirs*, II, p. 161.

65. Jonathan Daniels, *The Man of Independence* (Philadelphia: Lippincott, 1950), p. 318.

66. Margaret Truman, *Harry S Truman* (New York: William Morris, 1973), p. 388.

67. Ibid. At the same time, the president seems to have acknowledged his responsibility for Austin's statement by writing: "I approved the speech and statement of policy by Senator Austin to [the] U.N. meeting." Truman's diary entry does not reveal why he felt betrayed by the State Department despite this admission. Margaret Truman does not take up the question.

68. Ross Papers, Notes, March 29, 1948, HSTL.

69. Each of these men attended the meeting because of an interest in the implica-

tions of Palestine for the November elections. J. Howard McGrath was chairman of the Democratic National Committee. Oscar Ewing was federal security director. He subsequently was heavily involved in Truman's presidential campaign, holding the key post of "anchor man" in Washington while the president was absent on his famous "Whistlestop" tour.

70. Ross Papers, Notes, HSTL.

71. Ibid.

72. Statement by the President, March 25, 1948, Official File, HSTL.

73. Ibid.

74. Stevens, p. 199.

75. New York *Times*, March 24, 1948.

76. Current Popular Opinion on U.S. Palestine Policy, by Andie Knutson, Clifford Papers, HSTL.

77. Stevens, p. 203.

78. Sir John Fletcher-Cooke, "The United Nations and the Birth of Israel 1948," *International Journal* 28, no. 4 (1973):623.

79. Ibid.

80. Hurewitz, pp. 312–13.

81. Fletcher-Cooke, pp. 623–25.

82. Ibid.

83. *U.N. World*, July 1948, p. 32.

84. Fletcher-Cooke, pp. 623–25.

85. The administration's proposal that the United States, France, and Belgium participate in a round-table conference stemmed from the fact that the consuls representing these states in Jerusalem had been called upon by the UN Security Council on April 23, 1948, to act as a truce commission in Palestine.

86. Ibid.

87. Redding, p. 166.

88. New York *Times*, April 17, 1948.

89. Stevens, p. 204.

90. Weizmann to Truman, April 9, 1948, Official File, HSTL.

91. Undated, unsigned memorandum, Clifford Papers, HSTL. This memorandum was almost certainly prepared by Lowenthal since it appears among others he sent to Clifford and shares with them a distinctive format. Its content establishes that it was written in late April or early May 1948.

92. Ibid.

93. Weizmann to Truman, May 13, 1948, OF 204, Misc., HSTL. Zionists had announced this publicly some time before Weizmann wrote to Truman. Fletcher-Cooke, p. 624.

94. Snetsinger, pp. 104–05.

95. Arthur G. Klein to Truman, May 3, 1948; Truman to Klein, May 5, 1948, OF 205, Misc., HSTL.

96. Snetsinger, p. 108.

97. OF 204-D, Misc., HSTL.

98. Jon Kimche, *Seven Fallen Pillars* (London: Secker and Warburg, 1950), pp. 225–26.

99. The president's decision was strongly opposed by Secretary of State Marshall. See Wilson, pp. 142–43.

NOTE TO CHAPTER 15

1. The "Johnston Plan" envisaged functional cooperation among Israel, Lebanon, Jordan, and Syria in a program for more effective distribution and use of the waters of the Jordan, Yarmuk, and Litani rivers. As President Eisenhower's special representative, Eric Johnston conducted discussions with Arab and Israeli representatives for nearly two years before the plan was finally abandoned in 1955. Robert Anderson, a representative of the American government charged with facilitating a meeting between David Ben Gurion and Egyptian President Gamal Abdul Nasser, found that neither Israel nor Egypt rejected the notion of such an encounter out of hand. Anderson traveled from the United States to the Middle East several times between December 1955 and March 1956 before his mission was deemed a failure.

BIBLIOGRAPHY

BOOKS

Acheson, Dean. *Present at the Creation*. New York: Norton, 1969.

Adler, Frank J. *Roots in a Moving Stream: The Centennial History of Congregation B'nai Jehuda of Kansas City*. Kansas City: The Temple Congregation, Congregation B'nai Jehuda, 1972.

Anderson, Patrick. *The President's Men: The White House Assistants of Franklin D. Roosevelt, Harry S Truman, Dwight D. Eisenhower, John F. Kennedy and Lyndon B. Johnson*. New York: Doubleday and Co., 1968.

Andrews, Fannie Fern. *The Holy Land under the Mandate*. 2 Vols. Boston: Houghton Mifflin, 1931.

Antonius, George. *The Arab Awakening*. London: Hamish Hamilton, 1938.

Azcarate y Flores, Pablo. *Mission in Palestine: 1948-1952*. Washington, D.C.: The Middle East Institute, 1966.

Bain, Kenneth Ray. *The March to Zion: United States Policy and the Creation of Israel*. College Station: Texas A & M University Press, 1979.

Baker, Liva. *Felix Frankfurter*. New York: Coward-McCann, 1969.

Baram, Philip. *The Department of State in the Middle East, 1919-1945*. Philadelphia: University of Pennsylvania Press, 1978.

Barbour, Nevill. *Nisi Dominus*. London: George G. Harrap, 1946.

Bauer, Yehuda. *Flight and Rescue: Brichah*. New York: Random House, 1970.

———. *From Diplomacy to Resistance: A History of Jewish Palestine, 1939-1945*. Philadelphia: Jewish Publication Society of America, 1970.

Begin, Menachem. *The Revolt*. Los Angeles: Nash, 1972.

Ben Gurion, David. *Ben Gurion Looks Back in Talks with Moshe Pearlman*. New York: Simon and Schuster, 1965.

———. *Rebirth and Destiny of Israel*. New York: Philosophical Library, 1954.

———. *Recollections*. London: MacDonald Unit 75, 1970.

Berger, Elmer. *The Jewish Dilemma*. New York: Devin-Adair, 1946.

Blum, John Morton. *Roosevelt and Morgenthau*. Boston: Houghton Mifflin, 1970.

Bullitt, Orville H., ed. *For the President Personal and Secret: Correspondence Between Franklin D. Roosevelt and William C. Bullitt*. Boston: Houghton Mifflin, 1972.

Burns, MacGregor J. *Roosevelt: The Soldier of Freedom*. New York: Harcourt Brace Jovanovich, 1970.

Churchill, Winston S. *The Second World War*. 6 Vols. Boston: Houghton Mifflin, 1948-53.

Claude, Inis Jr. *National Minorities: An International Problem*. Cambridge, Mass.: Harvard University Press, 1955.

Cohen, Aharon. *Israel and the Arab World*. London: W. H. Allen, 1970.

Cohen, Israel. *A Short History of Zionism*. London: Frederick Muller, 1951.

Collins, Larry and Dominique Lapierre. *O Jerusalem*. New York: Simon and Schuster, 1972.

319

Crossman, Richard. *A Nation Reborn*. New York: Atheneum, 1960.

_____. *Palestine Mission: A Personal Record*. New York: Harper and Brothers, 1947.

Crum, Bartley. *Behind the Silken Curtain*. New York: Simon and Schuster, 1947.

Daniels, Jonathan. *The Man of Independence*. Philadelphia: Lippincott, 1950.

Daniels, Robert L. *American Philanthropy in the Near East*. Athens: Ohio University Press, 1970.

The Dearborn Independent. *The International Jew: The World's Foremost Problem*. 4 vols. Dearborn, Mich.: Dearborn Publishing Co., 1920-22.

De Novo, John. *American Interests and Politics in the Middle East*. Minneapolis: University of Minnesota Press, 1963.

Edidin, Ben. *Jewish Community Life in America*. New York: Hebrew Publishing Company, 1954.

Esco Foundation for Palestine. *Palestine: A Study of Jewish, Arab and British Policies*. 2 vols. New Haven, Conn.: Yale University Press, 1947.

Feis, Herbert. *The Birth of Israel*. New York: Norton, 1969.

_____. *Churchill, Roosevelt and Stalin*. Princeton, N.J.: Princeton University Press, 1957.

Field, Henry. *"M" Project for F.D.R., Studies on Migration and Settlement*. Ann Arbor, Michigan: Edwards Brothers, 1962.

Fink, Reuben, ed. *America and Palestine*. New York: American Zionist Emergency Council, 1944.

Forster, Arnold and Benjamin Epstein, eds. *The Trouble Makers*. 2d ed. Westport, Conn.: Negro University Press, 1970.

Freedman, Max, annotator. *Roosevelt and Frankfurter: Their Correspondence, 1928-1945*. Boston: Little, Brown, 1967.

Friedman, Isaiah. *The Question of Palestine, 1914-1918*. London: Routledge & Kegan Paul, 1973.

Friedman, Saul. *No Haven for the Oppressed*. Detroit: Wayne State University Press, 1973.

Friedrich, Carl Joachim. *American Policy Toward Palestine*. Washington, D.C.: Public Affairs Press, 1944.

Furlonge, Goeffrey. *Palestine Is My Country: The Story of Musa al-Alami*. London: John Murray, 1967.

Ganin, Zvi. *Truman, American Jewry, and Israel, 1945-1948*. New York: Holmes & Meier, 1979.

Garcia Granados, Jorge. *The Birth of Israel: The Drama as I Saw It*. New York: Alfred A. Knopf, 1948.

Gervasi, Frank. *To Whom Palestine*. New York: D. Appleton Century, 1946. 1946.

Gildersleeve, Virginia. *Many a Good Crusade*. New York: Macmillan, 1954.

Glubb, John Bagot. *Britain and the Arabs*. London: Hodder and Stoughton, 1959.

Goldmann, Nahum. *The Autobiography of Nahum Goldmann*. New York: Holt, Rinehart and Winston, 1969.

Hadawi, Sami, ed. *United Nations Resolutions on Palestine, 1947-1966*. Beirut: Institute for Palestine Studies, 1967.

Halperin, Samuel. *The Political World of American Zionism*. Detroit: Wayne State University Press, 1961.

Halpern, Ben. *The Idea of the Jewish State*. Cambridge, Mass.: Harvard University Press, 1961.

Hanna, Paul L. *British Policy in Palestine*. Washington, D.C.: American Council on Public Affairs, 1942.

Hasset, William D. *Off the Record with F.D.R.* New Brunswick, N.J.: Rutgers University Press, 1958.

Hattis, Susan Lee. *The Bi-National Idea in Palestine During Mandatory Times*. Haifa: Shikmona, 1970.

Hitti, Philip K. *History of the Arabs*. 2d. ed. London: Macmillan, 1944.

Horowitz, David. *State in the Making*. New York: Alfred A. Knopf, 1953.

Hourani, Albert. *Arabic Thought in the Liberal Age, 1798-1939*. London: Oxford University Press, 1962.

Howard, Harry N. *The King-Crane Commission*: Beirut: Khayats, 1963.

Hull, Cordell. *Memoirs*. 2 vols. New York: Macmillan, 1948.

Hurewitz, J. C. *The Struggle for Palestine*. New York: Norton, 1950.

Hutchison, E. H. *Violent Truce*. New York: Devin-Adair, 1956.

Israel, Fred L., ed. *The War Diary of Breckinridge Long*. Lincoln: University of Nebraska Press, 1966.

Jeffries, J. M. N. *Palestine: The Reality*. London: Longmanns, Green, 1939.

Johnsen, Julia E., ed. *Palestine: Jewish Homeland?* New York: T. H. Wilson, 1946.

Joseph, Bernard. *British Rule in Palestine*. Washington, D.C.: Public Affairs Press, 1948.

Khadduri, Majid. *Independent Iraq: 1932-1958*. London: Oxford University Press, 1960.

_____. *Political Trends in the Arab World*. Baltimore: Johns Hopkins University Press, 1970.

Khalidi, Walid, ed. *From Haven to Conquest*. Beirut: The Institute for Palestine Studies, 1971.

Kimche, Jon. *Seven Fallen Pillars*. London: Secker and Warburg, 1950.

Kimche, Jon and David Kimche. *Both Sides of the Hill*. London: Secker and Warburg, 1960.

Kirk, George. *Survey of International Affairs: The Middle East in the War*. London: Oxford University Press, 1952.

_____. *Survey of International Affairs: The Middle East, 1945-1950*. London: Oxford University Press, 1954.

Kritzeck, James and R. Bayly Winder, eds. *The World of Islam: Studies in Honor of Philip K. Hitti*. London: Macmillan, 1960.

Leahy, William D. *I Was There*. New York: McGraw-Hill, 1950.

Lenczowski, George. *The Middle East in World Affairs*. Ithaca, N.Y.: Cornell University Press, 1956.

Lilienthal, Alfred. *What Price Israel*. Chicago: Henry Regnery, 1953.

Liptzin, Sol. *Generation of Decision: Jewish Rejuvenation in America*. New York: Block, 1958.

Litvinoff, Barnet. *To the House of Their Fathers: A History of Zionism*. New York: Frederick A. Praeger, 1965.

Longrigg, Stephen. *Iraq: 1900–1950*. London: Oxford University Press, 1953.

_____. *Oil in the Middle East*. 3rd. ed. London: Oxford University Press, 1968.

Madison, Charles A. *Prominent American Jews*. New York: Frederick Unger, 1970.

Magnes, Judah, ed. *Toward Union in Palestine*. Westport, Conn.: Greenwood Press, 1972.

Manuel, Frank E. *The Realities of American-Palestine Relations*. Washington, D.C.: Public Affairs Press, 1949.

Marlowe, John. *The Seat of Pilate*. London: The Cresset Press, 1959.

McDonald, James G. *My Mission to Israel*. New York: Simon and Schuster, 1951.

McInnis, Edgar. *The War*. 6 vols. London: Oxford University Press, 1940–46.

Millis, Walter and E. S. Duffield, eds. *The Forrestal Diaries*. New York: Viking Press, 1951.

Morse, Arthur D. *While Six Million Died*. New York: Random House, 1967.

Motter, T. H. Vail. *The United States Army in World War II, the Middle East Theater: The Persian Corridor and Aid to Russia*. Washington, D.C.: U.S. Department of the Army, Office of Military History, 1952.

Nash, Gerald D. *United States Oil Policy, 1890–1964*. Pittsburgh: University of Pittsburgh Press, 1968.

Nutting, Anthony. *The Arabs*. New York: Mentor Books, 1964.

Patterson, James T. *"Mr. Republican": A Biography of Robert A. Taft*. Boston: Houghton Mifflin, 1972.

Peare, Catherine Owens. *The Louis D. Brandeis Story*. New York: Thomas Y. Crowell, 1970.

Perkins, Frances. *The Roosevelt I Knew*. New York: Viking Press, 1946.

Porath, Yehoshua. *The Emergence of the Palestinian-Arab National Movement*. London: Frank Cass, 1974.

_____. *The Palestinian Arab National Movement 1929–1939: From Riots to Rebellion*. London: Frank Cass, 1977.

Range, Willard. *Franklin D. Roosevelt's World Order*. Athens: University of Georgia Press, 1959.

Redding, Jack. *Inside the Democratic Party*. New York: Bobbs-Merrill, 1958.

Robinson, Jacob. *Palestine and the United Nations: Prelude to Solution*. Westport, Conn.: Greenwood Press, 1971.

Roosevelt, Elliott. *As He Saw It*. New York: Duell, Sloan & Pearce, 1946.

Rosenman, Samuel I. *Working with Roosevelt*. New York: Harper and Brothers, 1952.

The Royal Institute of International Affairs. *Information Papers No. 20. Great Britain and Palestine*. 3rd ed. London: Oxford University Press, 1946.

Sachar, Howard M. *Europe Leaves the Middle East*. New York: Alfred A. Knopf, 1972.

_____. *A History of Israel, From the Rise of Zionism to Our Time*. New York: Alfred A. Knopf, 1976.

Safran, Nadev. *From War to War*. New York: Pegasus, 1969.

Schechtman, Joseph B. *The Mufti and Fuehrer*. New York: Thomas Yoseloff, 1965.

_____. *The United States and the Jewish State Movement*. New York: Herzl Press, 1966.

Schor, Samuel. *Palestine and the Bible*. London: The Book Society, 1934.

Selzer, Michael, ed. *Zionism Reconsidered*. New York: Macmillan, 1970.

Shwadran, Benjamin. *The Middle East, Oil and the Great Powers*. New York: Council for Middle Eastern Affairs Press, 1959.

Silverberg, Robert. *If I Forget Thee O Jerusalem: American Jews and the State of Israel*. New York: William Morrow, 1970.

Sklare, Marshall, ed. *The Jews: Social Patterns of an American Group*. New York: The Free Press, 1958.

Snetsinger, John. *Truman, The Jewish Vote, and the Creation of Israel*. Stanford, Calif.: Hoover Institution Press, 1974.

Speiser, Ephraim Avigdor. *The United States and the Near East*. Cambridge, Mass.: Harvard University Press, 1947.

Stein, Leonard. *The Balfour Declaration*. London: Vallentine Mitchell, 1961.

Stember, Charles H. et al. *Jews in the Mind of America*. New York: Basic Books, 1966.

Stettinius, Edward R. *Roosevelt and the Russians*. Garden City, N.Y.: Doubleday, 1949.

Stevens, Richard P. *American Zionism and U.S. Foreign Policy, 1942-1947*. Beirut: Institute for Palestine Studies, 1970.

St. John, Robert. *Ben Gurion*. New York: Doubleday, 1971.

Sykes, Christopher. *Crossroads to Israel*. London: Collins, 1965.

———. *Orde Wingate*. London: Collins, 1959.

Taylor, Alan R. *Prelude to Israel*. New York: Philosophical Library, 1959.

Thomas, Helen Shirley. *Felix Frankfurter*. Baltimore: Johns Hopkins University Press, 1960.

Truman, Harry S. *Memoirs*. 2 vols. New York: Doubleday, 1955-56.

Truman, Margaret. *Harry S Truman*. New York: William Morris, 1973.

Twitchell, Karl S. *Saudi Arabia*. Princeton, N.J.: Princeton University Press, 1947.

Waines, David. *The Unholy War: Israel and Palestine, 1897-1971*. Montreal: Chateau Books, 1971.

Waldman, Morris D. *Nor by Power*. New York: International Universities Press, 1953.

Weizmann, Chaim. *Trial and Error*. New York: Harper and Brothers, 1949.

Welles, Sumner. *We Need Not Fail*. Cambridge, Mass.: Riverside Press, 1948.

Williamson, Harold F. et al. *The American Petroleum Industry*. Vol. II: *The Age of Energy 1899-1959*. Evanston, Ill.: Northwestern University Press, 1963.

Wilson, Evan M. *Decision on Palestine: How the U.S. Came to Recognize Israel*. Stanford, Calif.: Hoover Institution Press, 1979.

Wise, Stephen S. *Challenging Years*. New York: G. P. Putnam's Sons, 1949.

Wyman, David. *Paper Walls*. Amherst, Mass.: University of Massachusetts Press, 1968.

Yaffe, James. *The American Jews*. New York: Random House, 1968.

Yarnell, Allen. *Democrats and Progressives: The 1948 Presidential Election as a Test of Postwar Liberalism*. Berkeley: University of California Press, 1974.

Ziff, William B. *The Rape of Palestine*. New York: Longmans, Green, 1938.

Zurayk, Constantine K. *Palestine: The Meaning of Disaster*. Beirut: Khayats, 1956.

ARTICLES AND PUBLISHED PAPERS

Adler, Selig. "Franklin D. Roosevelt and Zionism." *Judaism*, Summer 1972.

Al-Qawuqji, Fauzi. "Memoirs, 1948: Part I." *Journal of Palestine Studies* 1, no. 4 (1972).

Ansara, Cosmo M. "A Program for the National Federation." *National Herald* (official publication of the Federation of Arab-Americans) 3, no. 11 (1958).

Ansara, James M. "Syrian-Lebanese Immigration to the United States." *National Herald* (official publication of the Federation of Arab-Americans) 3, no. 2 (1958).

Ben Gurion, David. "What Roosevelt Told Us." *Jewish Observer and Middle East Journal* 1 (October 1947).

Clifford, Clark M. "Recognizing Israel." *American Heritage* 28, no. 3 (April 1977).

Crossman, Richard. "Framework for a Jewish State." *Commentary* 4, no. 5 (1947).

Farago, Ladislas. "Refugees: The Solution as FDR Saw It." *United Nations World*, June 1947.

Fletcher-Cooke, Sir John. "The United Nations and the Birth of Israel, 1948." *International Journal* 28, no. 4 (1973).

Frechtling, Louis E. "War in the Eastern Mediterranean." *Foreign Policy Reports* 16, no. 22 (1941).

Goldbloom, Maurice J. "This Month in History." *Commentary* 4, no. 4 (1947).

Hamilton, Thomas J. "Partition of Palestine." *Foreign Policy Reports* 23 (1948).

Henderson, Loy. "American Political and Strategic Interests in the Middle East and Southwestern Europe." *Proceedings of the American Academy of Political Science* 22, no. 4 (1948).

Hertzberg, Sidney. "This Month in History." *Commentary* 3, no. 4, 5, 6 (1947).

Howard, Harry N. "The United States and the Middle East." In *The Middle East in World Politics*. Syracuse, N.Y.: Syracuse University Press, 1974.

Lazaron, Morris S. "Compromise on Palestine." *Annals of the American Academy of Political and Social Science* 240 (July 1945).

Lehn, Walter. "The Jewish National Fund." *Journal of Palestine Studies* 3, no. 4 (1974).

Lewin, Kurt. "Self Hatred Among Jews." In *Resolving Social Conflicts: Selected Papers on Group Dynamics*, ed. Gertrude W. Lewin. New York: Harper and Brothers, 1948.

"The Logic of the Air." *Fortune*, April 1943.

Malouf, Faris S. "History of the Federations: (1) The Eastern States Federation." *National Herald* (official publication of the Federation of Arab-Americans) 3, no. 8 (1958).

_____. "History of the Federations: (2) The Southern Federation." *National Herald* 3, no. 9 (1958).

Nazzal, Nafez Abdullah. "The Zionist Occupation of Western Gallilee, 1948." *Journal of Palestine Studies* 3, no. 3 (1974).

Parkes, James. "The Jewish World Since 1939." *International Affairs* 21, no. 1 (1945).

Pogue, L. Welch. "The Next Ten Years in Air Transportation." *Academy of Political Science Proceedings* 21 (1944–46).

Quigly, Carrol. "Lord Balfour's Personal Position on the Balfour Declaration." *Middle East Journal* 22, no. 3 (1968).

Roosevelt, Kermit. "The Partition of Palestine: A Lesson in Pressure Politics." *Middle East Journal* 2 (January 1948).

———. "Fallacies of Palestine." *Colliers*, March 23, 1948.

Rosenwald, Lessing J. "Reply to Zionism." *Life*, June 28, 1943.

Smolensky, Moshe. "The Anglo-American Report Points the Way." *Commentary* 2, no. 1 (1946).

Steinberg, Alfred. "Mr. Truman's Mystery Man." *Saturday Evening Post*, December 24, 1949.

Sulzberger, C. E. "German Preparations in the Middle East." *Foreign Affairs* 20, no. 4 (1942).

Wilson, Evan M. "The Palestine Papers, 1943–1947." *Journal of Palestine Studies*, Summer 1973.

Yale, William. "Ambassador Henry Morgenthau's Special Mission of 1917." *World Politics*, April 1949.

DISSERTATIONS, THESES, AND UNPUBLISHED MANUSCRIPTS

Dohse, Michael. "American Periodicals and the Palestine Triangle, April 1936 to February 1947." Ph.D. dissertation, Mississippi State University, 1966.

Grady, Henry F. "Memoirs." Unpublished manuscript, Henry F. Grady Papers, Harry S Truman Library.

Hand, Samuel Burton. "Samuel I. Rosenman: His Public Career." Ph.D. dissertation, Syracuse University, 1960.

Sachar, David B. "David A. Niles and United States Policy. A Case Study in American Foreign Policy." Honors B. A. thesis, Harvard University, Department of History, 1959.

GOVERNMENT PUBLICATIONS AND PUBLISHED GOVERNMENT DOCUMENTS

Government of Palestine. *A Survey of Palestine*. 3 vols. Palestine: Government Printer, 1946.

———. Cmd. 1700. Correspondence with the Palestinian Arab Delegation and the Zionist Organization, June 1922. London: His Majesty's Stationery Office, 1922.

Great Britain. Cmd. 1540, 1921. Palestine. "Disturbances in May 1921. Report of the Commission of Inquiry with Correspondence Relating Thereto." London: His Majesty's Stationery Office, 1930.

———. Cmd. 3530. "Report of the Commission on the Palestine Disturbances of August 1929." London: His Majesty's Stationery Office, 1930.

———. Cmd. 3686. Palestine. "Report on Immigration, Land Settlement and Development." Sir John Hope Simpson, 1930. London: His Majesty's Stationery Office, 1930.

———. Cmd. 6808. "Report of the Anglo-American Committee of Inquiry Regarding the Problems of European Jewry and Palestine." London: His Majesty's Stationery Office, 1946.

———. Cmd. 6873. "Palestine Statement of Information Relating to Acts of Violence." London: His Majesty's Stationery Office, 1946.

Great Britain. Parliament. *Parliamentary Debates* (House of Commons), 5th Series, Vols. 347, 415, 426, 433.

United States. Congress. *Congressional Record.* Proceedings and Debates, 67th–80th Congresses. Washington, D.C.: U.S. Government Printer, 1922–47.

United States. Department of State. *Foreign Relations of the United States, 1939–1948.* Washington, D.C.: U.S. Government Printing Office, 1955–76.

United States. President. *Public Papers of the Presidents of the United States, Harry S Truman, 1945–1947.* Washington, D.C.: U.S. Government Printing Office, 1961–63.

MISCELLANEOUS BULLETINS, PAMPHLETS, AND NONGOVERNMENTAL REPORTS

American Council for Judaism. *Information Bulletin of the American Council for Judaism.* 1945–48.

———. *Statement of Principles.* 1943.

Arab National League. *An Appeal to American Justice and Fair Play on Behalf of Palestine Arabs.* New York: Arab National League, 1938.

———. *Whither Palestine: A Statement of Facts and of the Causes of the Arab-Jewish Conflict in the Holy Land.* New York: Arab National League, 1936.

Institute of Arab American Affairs. *Bulletin of the Institute of Arab American Affairs.* 1945–48.

Institute for Palestine Studies. *The Partition of Palestine.* Beirut: Institute for Palestine Studies, 1967.

International Conference for Palestine. *Plan for Cooperation of World Pro-Palestine Committees.* Washington, D.C.: International Conference for Palestine, 1945.

Zionist Organization of America. *47th Annual Report.* Washington, D.C.: Zionist Organization of America, 1944.

———. *48th Annual Report.* Washington, D.C.: Zionist Organization of America, 1945.

ARCHIVES AND PRIVATE PAPERS

Files of the American Council for Judaism, Madison State Historical Library, Madison, Wisconsin.

Private Papers of George M. Barakat, Centerville, Massachusetts.

James Byrnes Papers, Robert Muldrow Cooper Library, Clemson University, Clemson, South Carolina.

Clark Clifford Papers, Harry S Truman Library, Independence, Missouri.

Papers of Virginia Gildersleeve, Butler Library, Columbia University, New York City.

Oral History Interview of A. J. Granoff, Harry S Truman Library, Independence, Missouri.

Papers of Howard McGrath, Harry S Truman Library, Independence, Missouri.

Presidential Diaries of Henry A. Morgenthau, Jr., Franklin D. Roosevelt Library, Hyde Park, New York.

Palestine, Diplomatic and Consular Files of the Department of State, Record Group 59, 1939–1948. National Archives of the United States, Washington, D.C.

Papers of Franklin D. Roosevelt, Franklin D. Roosevelt Library, Hyde Park, New York.

Papers of Samuel Rosenman, Harry S Truman Library, Independence, Missouri.

Papers of Charles G. Ross, Harry S Truman Library, Independence, Missouri.

Papers of Myron Taylor, Franklin D. Roosevelt Library, Hyde Park, New York.

Papers of Harry S Truman, Harry S Truman Library, Independence, Missouri.

Papers of Robert F. Wagner, Georgetown University Library, Georgetown University, Washington, D.C.

Chaim Weizmann Archives, Harry S Truman Library, Independence, Missouri.

Papers of Joel Wolfson, Harry S Truman Library, Independence, Missouri.

INTERVIEWS AND CORRESPONDENCE

Mr. George M. Barakat, Centerville, Massachusetts, September 1973.

Dr. Elmer Berger, New York City, October 1973.

Mr. Benjamin Freedman, New York City, November 1973.

Dr. Nahum Goldmann, Paris, March 1972; April 1975.

The Hon. Loy W. Henderson, Washington, D.C., October 1973.

Dr. Philip K. Hitti, Princeton, N.J., November 1973.

Dr. Alfred Lilienthal, New York City, November 1973; March 1975.

Mrs. Faris S. Malouf, Boston, September 1973.

INDEX

About The Author

ROBERT DANIEL TSCHIRGI specializes in U.S. relations with the Middle East and in Middle East politics. He is currently an Associate Professor of International Relations at the University of the Americas in Puebla, Mexico. From 1979 to 1981 he was a Research Fellow at the Center for International and Strategic Affairs at the University of California, Los Angeles.

Dr. Tschirgi's recent publications appear in *ACIS Working Paper Series*, *CISA Research Notes*, and *The Christian Science Monitor.*

Dr. Tschirgi holds a B.A. and an M.A. from the American University of Beirut and a Ph.D. from the University of Toronto. His first-hand knowledge of the Middle East is rooted in extensive traveling and over ten years' residency in the region.

Other Titles in the Studies in International and Strategic Affairs Series of the Center for International and Strategic Affairs, University of California, Los Angeles:

William Potter (ed.), *Verification and SALT: The Challenge of Strategic Deception* (Westview, 1980).

Bennett Ramberg, *Destruction of Nuclear Energy Facilities in War: The Problem and Implications* (Lexington Books, 1980).

Paul Jabber, *Not by War Alone: The Politics of Arms Control in the Middle East* (University of California Press, 1981).

Roman Kolkowicz and Andrzej Korbonski (eds.), *Soldiers, Peasants, and Bureaucrats: Civil-Military Relations in Communist and Modernizing Societies* (George Allen & Unwin, 1982).

William Potter, *Nuclear Power and Nonproliferation: An Interdisciplinary Perspective* (Oelgeschlager, Gunn & Hain, 1982).

Stephen Spiegel (ed.), *The Middle East and the Western Alliance* (George Allen & Unwin, forthcoming).

Jiri Valenta and William Potter (eds.), *Soviet Decisionmaking for National Security* (George Allen & Unwin, forthcoming).